Created and Directed by Hans Höfer

INSIGHT GUIDES

NewEngland

Edited by Brian Bell and Jay Itzkowitz

Update Editor: Sandy MacDonald

Editorial Director: Brian Bell

APA PUBLICATIONS

ABOUT THIS BOOK

Itzkovitz

Bell

Muppet Studios, home of Kermit the Frog and Miss Piggy, may not seem the most likely place for the hatching of a book, but it was there that Apa Publications' publisher **Hans Höfer** and project editor **Jay Itzkowitz**, then a recent Harvard graduate and now a lawyer in California's entertainment industy, first conceived *New England* as an Insight Guide title.

The book became one of the most popular titles in Apa Publications' acclaimed series, and it has now been thoroughly re-edited and updated under the supervision of **Brian Bell**, Apa's editorial director. Bell is an Irishman (which makes him an honorary Bostonian) and, though based in old London rather than New London, spends as much time as he can in New England with his Connecticut-born wife.

A region with such a rich history and culture as New England lends itself especially well to the approach taken by the 188-title *Insight Guides* series. Each book encourages readers to celebrate the essence of a place rather than try to reshape it to their expectations and is edited in the belief that, without insight into a people's character and culture, travel can narrow the mind rather than broaden it.

The book is carefully structured: the first section covers New England's history and culture in a series of lively essays. The main Places section provides a comprehensive run-down on the places worth seeing. Finally, a fact-packed listings section contains all the information you'll need on travel, hotels, shops, restaurants and opening times. Complementing the text, remarkable photography sets out to communicate directly and provocatively life as it is lived by the locals.

Despite its image of unchanging tradition, New England has been undergoing many transformations in the 1990s. The task of bringing this edition bang up-to-date fell to **Sandy MacDonald** who, from her base in Cambridge, Massachusetts, sifted through every syllable of the previous edition as well as producing a major rewrite of the Travel Tips listings section.

In the *Insight Guides* tradition, most of the writers are either natives of the destination or have a close connection with it. **Peter Spiro**, a prolific contributor, worked for the US Department of State and may be the only Apa writer to have held a "Top Secret Clearance" from the United States government. **Adam Nossiter** claims knowledge of and affection for New England from his days as a student at Harvard, where he studied history and literature. He has traveled extensively throughout the region.

Mark Muro's ties to Boston go back to the warm fall day he showed up at Harvard fresh from the vastness of the Pacific Northwest. A native of Seattle, he improved his knowledge of his adopted New England home as a staff writer for the region's preeminent daily newspaper, the *Boston Globe*.

Inez Sherman Keller is a graduate of Classical High School in Providence, Rhode Island, and Boston University. **Jonathan Keller**, a lifelong Cambridgeite, hosts the popular "Jon Keller Show" on Boston's WRKO Radio, heard in all six New England states, and has written frequently for *People* magazine. He scored a major scoop by being the first reporter to tour the Martha's

Spiro

Vineyard home of Jacqueline Kennedy Onassis.

Tom Brosnahan has freelanced for many magazine and book publishers. Among his publications is a book entitled *How to Beat the High Cost of Travel.*

Molly Kuntz has worked as a researcher-writer for Washington-based interest groups concentrating on architecture, energy policy and public transportation issues.

Julie Michaels, author of "The Berkshires" and "Connecticut," put her knowledge of New England to good use as associate editor of *New England Monthly* magazine. Formerly a reporter for *The Berkshire Eagle* in Pittsfield, Mass., she claims Berkshire County is the single most beautiful piece of real estate east of the Mississippi River.

Kay Cassill, an identical twin, won critical acclaim for her book *Twins: Nature's Amazing Mystery.* A former national synchronized swimming champion, Cassill is also an accomplished artist whose works hang in many museums including the Metropolitan Museum of Art in New York.

Mark Bastian has written travel articles for *Yankee* and other publications. He spends his weekends in Brattleboro, Vermont, gathering material for a book on New Age living.

Norman Sibley, who together with his wife founded *Korea Quarterly* magazine and Dragon's Eye Graphics, was also involved in the production of *Insight Guide: Korea.*

Mark Silber has been a reporter for, among others, the *Middlesex Daily News* in Marlboro, Massachusetts; the *Harvard Lampoon* at Cambridge; and the *Columbia Journalism Review* in New York.

Bryan Simmons wrote the chapter on the Puritans' Intellectual Legacy.

While the text was being updated, Brian Bell set about updating the visual content. He relied heavily on the work of **Marcus Brooke**, editor of the companion *Insight Guide: Boston*, and on the archives of **New England Stock Photo** to produce more than 60 new images. But the existing photographs were already well up to Apa's high standards. In particular, the work of **Carole Allen** added an intimacy and magic to *New England*. A registered nurse-turned-professional image magician, Allen spent some years in Columbia where her husband served with the Peace Corps. Her work has appeared in *Audubon*, *Sports Illustrated* and *Yankee*, New England's leading regional magazine. The work of New York-based **Joseph Viesti** continues to play an important role in the book.

Viesti

T he book's other two principal photographers, **Ping Amranand** and **Hisham Youssef**, natives of Thailand and Egypt respectively, add a unique vision of the region through the lenses of late-comers from abroad. Amranand, who holds a degree in Oriental history from London University, is currently based in Washington, DC. His work has appeared in many *Insight Guides* and in such publications as *Architectural Digest*, *Asia* and *Sawasdee*, the Thai International inflight magazine.

Youssef is a graduate of Harvard, where he was principal photographer and photo editor for several campus publications. He was also a teaching assistant in graphic design in Harvard's Visual and Environmental Studies Department. Youssef spent some years working in Egypt.

The book was proofread and indexed by **Mary Morton**.

Youssef

nranand

Brooke

CONTENTS

CONTENTS

TRAVEL TIPS

A FINISHED PLACE

"New England is a finished place," wrote Bernard DeVoto in 1936. "Its destiny is that of Florence or Venice, not Milan, while the American empire careens onward towards its unpredicted end... It is the first American section to be finished, to achieve stability in its conditions of life. It is the first old civilization, the first permanent civilization in America."

Not everyone has been so enamoured with New England's virtues. The acerbic commentator H. L. Mencken saw Connecticut as "made up, in almost equal parts, of golf links and squalid factory towns" and he dismissed Maine as being "as dead, intellectually, as Abyssinia." Mark Twain joked that "in the spring I have counted one hundred and thirty-six different kinds of weather inside of four-and-twenty hours."

The region's variety extends far beyond the climate, however. New England's rich endowment includes many of America's most cherished memories: Paul Revere's midnight ride, the Battle of Bunker Hill, the charisma of the Kennedys. It was here that the first cries of independence were heard, here that the movement to abolish slavery found fertile ground, here that education achieved its fullest flowering, here that American art and literature attained their greatest refinement.

This is America's attic, crammed with marvelous antiques of every description. Here are the homes of Hawthorne, Emerson, Dickinson, and Melville; souvenirs of clippers and whaling ships from centuries past; houses and churches in whose gables and steeples can be read a national architectural history. The countryside abounds in inspiring vistas, enchanted with the bright golds and reds of autumn, slumbering beneath winter's heavy snows, bursting with the worshipful energy of spring's ritual rebirth, and joyful in summer's ceaseless flowering.

The alluring variety embraces Maine's coast, its rocky promontories pointing to adventure; New Hampshire's lakes, deep with silent wonder; Vermont's mountains, shimmering in spring's verdant cloak and majestic in winter's whiteness.; the Berkshires' charmed forests; Connecticut's celebrated colonial heritage; Newport's well-preserved luxury, Cape Cod's quaint villages and rolling dunes, Boston's vibrant cityscape.

If Boston is a state of mind – a remark variously attributed by the city's contentious academics to Mark Twain, Ralph Waldo Emerson and Thomas G. Appleton – so is New England to an even greater degree. And it is a state of mind well worth embracing.

Preceding pages: corn on door; fall colors; fishing on Maine's Allagash Waterway; sailboats racing on Penobscot Bay, Maine; Queechee Balloon Festival, Vermont; sleigh ride on Come Spring Farm, Union, Maine.<u>Left</u>, history re-enacted on Hampton Beach, New Hampshire.

NEW ENG

The moſt remarqueable parts thus
by the high and mighty Prince C
nowe King of great Britaine

THE PORTRAICTVER OF CAPTAYNE IOHN SMITH ADMIRALL OF NEW ENGLAND

Ætatis 37
A.º 1616

Schooters hill

Sandwich

Dartmouth

Ipſwich

Snadoun hill

P. Kent

P. Reeves

Boſton

Poynt Dauies

Hull

Smith Iles

These are the Lines that ſhew thy Face; but thoſe
That ſhew thy Grace and Glory, brighter bee
Thy Faire-Diſcoueries and Fowle-Overthrowes
Of Salvages, much Civillizd by thee
Beſt ſhew thy Spirit; and to it Glory Wyn
So, thou art Braſſe without, but Golde within

If ſo; in Braſſe too ſoft Smiths Acts to beare
I fix thy Fame, to make Braſſe Steele out weare

Thine as thou art Virtues
Iohn Dauies Heref.

SouthHampton

P. Wynthrop

Cape ANNA

COGN

GENS IN

Briſtow

Salem

Talbotts Bay

Fawmouth
Charles Towne

Franncis Ile

The River CHARLES
Medford

Boſton
Roxbury
winniſine
Dorcheſter

Charlton

Claiborns Ils

P. Saltonſtale

London

Poynt

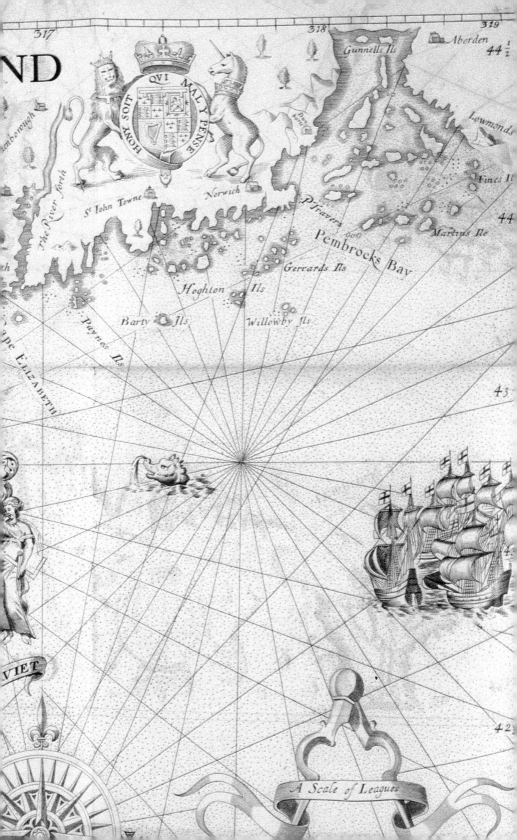

ND

HONY SOIT QVI MALY PENSE

Aberden

44 ½

Gunnells Ils

Lowmonds

Fines It

enborough

the River forth

Norwich

St John Towne

P.Travers

Martins Ile

44

Pembrocks Bay

Gerrards Ils

Hoghton Ils

43

Barty Ils

Willowby Ils

Paynes Ils

ape Elizabeth

VIET

42

A Scale of Leagues

A crumbling stone wall in the middle of a forest: this is New England. Separating trees from other trees, this wall stands as a reminder of what man can and cannot do, of what the pioneers accomplished and what nature has reclaimed, of what New England was and what it is. The frontier no longer faces the rolling hills and woodlands; the Indians no longer hunt and fish undisturbed; the white man no longer clears the forest to eke out a precarious life. Now, spruces and firs tower over this crumbling stone wall, dwarfing the

centuries of American lineage – embody the strength of diversity. Its history – a long trail of advance and retreat – provides an enduring inspiration. And its landscape – the elegance of time-worn peaks, the tranquility of forests that will never be conquered, the lulling crash of ocean waves against sand and rock – draws countless visitors.

Lay of the land: As defined today, New England encompasses 66,672 sq. miles (172,680 sq. km) including the states of Massachusetts, Connecticut, Rhode Island,

achievements of those pioneers who toiled so hard in the excitement and uncertainty of a new land.

New England's work, for good or bad, has been done; its limits have been met. But its spirit lives on to grapple with the intricacies of a different age. The same urge that impelled the explorer to chart an unknown land, the freeman to stake his claim and the immigrant to make his fortune now lead the politician to guide the nation, the engineer to create new technology and the scholar to study the past and plan for the future.

And so the stone wall stands proud. Its people – the newly arrived and those with

Vermont, New Hampshire and Maine. It is bounded by Canada to the north, the Atlantic Ocean to the east, Long Island Sound to the south, and New York to the west. Moving inland from the coastal lowlands in the south and east, the terrain gradually rises to forested hills and culminates in the weather-beaten peaks of the Appalachian system, represented by the White Mountains to the north and the Green and Taconic Mountains and Berkshire Hills to the west.

Perhaps 2 billion years ago, a vast ocean trough, under the pressure of more than 500,000 cubic miles (2 million cubic km) of silt and sediment, was convulsed upward by an upheaval of the earth's crust. The mountains thus created were ancestors of the Appalachians. Its foundation a great buckling fold, the chain continued to shift and shudder. The intense heat generated by the formation of these mountains metamorphosed sandstone and limestone deposits into the schists and marble now found in the southeastern lowlands and Berkshire Hills of Massachusetts and in Vermont's Green Mountains. Later, streaks of intrusive rocks formed, represented by the granite of Rhode Island, New Hampshire and Maine, and the reddish rocks found in the Connecticut River Valley.

About 200 million years ago, the thrusts from below the earth's crust stopped. The geologic revolution complete, the Appalachians towered about 30,000 ft (some 9,000 meters), the Himalayas of another time.

The elements, unopposed by new surges from below, went to work on the jagged landscape, until much of southern and central New England was no more than a featureless plain. Some outcroppings fared better against the wind and rain than others, accounting for the few scattered mounts that stand unescorted out of the lowlands – now called monadnocks after New Hampshire's Mount Monadnock. (Other examples are Mount Kearsage in New Hampshire and Mount Ascutney in Vermont.) About 8 million years ago, meanwhile, the rest of the flats were gently folded one final time into the hills we see today.

The great swamplands that surrounded the Appalachian core and the hot, muggy climate created the perfect habitat for dinosaurs, the rulers of the day. Although nature mysteriously decided not to allow these impressive creatures to grace man with their presence, it thoughtfully left traces of their extended stay in New England. Between 200 and 300 million years ago, dinosaurs roamed the Triassic mud of the Newark Bed, which runs approximately along what is now the Connecticut River Valley. Such primitive dinosaurs as *coelophysia* (an early two-leg-

ged herbivore), *rhychosaurus* (a tusked four-legger with an eery rodent look) and more than 150 other species of reptiles and amphibians left tracks by the thousands in Smith's Ferry and South Hadley in central Massachusetts and, of course, at Dinosaur State Park in Rocky Hill, Connecticut.

Legacy of the Ice Age: The marauding glaciers of the Ice Age added the finishing touches to the landscape. About 1 million years ago, a sudden drop in the world's average summer temperature thickened al-

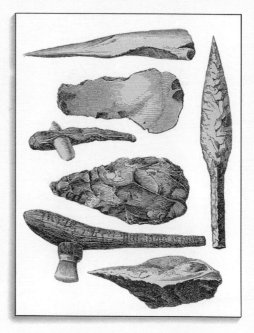

ready existing ice masses to 200 ft (61 meters). Under this pressure, their foundations spread outward, grasping for new ground, until the glaciers eventually claimed more than one-third of the globe's total area. Ice swallowed up northeastern America on four different occasions during the Pleistocene Era, retreating and readvancing over the millennia, finally leaving New England about 10,000 to 12,000 years ago.

This last flooding etched the New England landscape we admire today. Although the glaciers left unchanged the land's basic geologic make-up, they did leave reminders of their former supremacy. Working like steel

Preceding pages: early English map of the region. **Left,** a prehistoric inhabitant. **Right,** primitive tools unearthed in forests.

wool, the glaciers – often more than 2 miles (3 km) deep – rounded out slopes and valleys from the underlying rock.

Carving scratches (glacial striations) on exposed rock, the glaciers left behind evidence of the path they traveled. Glacial till, the chaff that the ice scraped off the ground, was carried south. As the glaciers receded, this material was left behind; much of New England's bedrock is blanketed with a thin layer of this till, composed of clay, sand and broken rock. Rounded hills of glacial till, called drumlins, are found scattered throughout New England, with Bunker Hill in Boston the most famous.

A similar process gave birth to Cape Cod, Charlotte, Vermont, more than 150 miles (240 km) from the Atlantic Ocean, unearthed the skeleton of an improbable resident, a whale. How could this sea beast have strayed so far from home? When the glaciers melted in force, they released a vast amount of water, perhaps as much as 8 million cubic miles (33 million cubic km) worldwide. The floods were great, and the oceans claimed many areas that are landlocked today.

In parts of Maine, Atlantic waves crashed against shores up to 75 miles (120 km) inland from the present coastline; Lake Champlain was a sea which transformed northern New England into an Atlantic peninsula. Evidence of marine activity has been found at

Martha's Vineyard and Nantucket Island. Other dramatic legacies of the Ice Age include glacial cirques (large bowl-shaped depressions), glacial erratics (boulders, weighing as much as 5,000 tons, dragged for miles by the moving ice) and kettle lakes (crater-like indentations, of which Walden Pond is a good example). Like the towering Appalachians millions of years ago, many of these features are slowly wearing away. The erosion can only be measured in thousands of years, however, and the distinctiveness these features lend to New England's landscape will survive far into the future.

In 1848, workers laying railroad tracks in more than 500 ft (150 meters) above today's sea level. Hundreds of lakes and ponds once thrived where there are none now.

The waters gradually evaporated, and New England assumed its present configuration. Tundra plants and (later) trees took hold as the ice and sea receded. A flourishing fauna could live once again on the land but, this time, with a new creature in its midst: man.

Frustrated explorers: History remembers success more kindly than it does failure. Although, as the name suggests, it was the English who sowed the seeds of New England's fortune, they were by no means the first to gaze on these northern shores and forests. Anthropologists generally agree that the first pilgrims to North America were a people of mixed Mongolian descent. Having trekked an overland route across Asia and over the then-frozen Bering Straits, these early pioneers arrived on the continent between 12,000 and 25,000 years ago.

The oldest fossil finds of human activity in New England, uncovered in Shawville, Vermont, and Wapunucket, Massachusetts, date respectively to 9000 and 4000 BC and include a variety of spear points, knives, pendants and ancient house floors. These early settlers were to witness the landing of the Vikings, first documented European visitors to North America. In 1000 AD, King Olaf of

with several families and a few cattle, intending to establish a permanent settlement in Vinland. At first, the new frontier treated these Vikings well. They were impressed by the fertile land, the fish-filled streams and the game-packed forests.

The Skrellings: But the natives proved too strong for the small band of Norse homesteaders. Initial relations between the two groups were good; a cordial exchange system was established where Viking cloth was traded for local furs. All was well, says one saga, until the *skrellings* (Norse for dwarfs) were startled to martial frenzy by a bellowing Viking bull. A fierce battle ensued in which several Vikings fell (including Leif's

Norway commissioned young Leif Ericson to bring Christianity to the new Viking settlement in Greenland, founded only 15 years earlier by Eric the Red, Leif's father. Despite the winds that blew his *knarr* (Viking longboat) south of his appointed mission, Leif the Lucky lived up to his name and discovered for his sovereign a new land where grapes and wheat grew wild, Vinland the Good.

A few years later Thorfin Karlsefni set sail

Left, Vikings, according to legend, reached Cape Cod around AD 1000 in longboats such as this one. **Above**, *A Noble Savage*, the native New Englander, from an 1876 painting.

brother Thorwald). Concluding that "although the country thereabouts was attractive, their life would be one of constant dread and turmoil" because of the natives, Karlsefni and his followers headed home to Greenland. The aborted expedition cured the Vikings of their wanderlust; they did not return.

The Vikings' visit to North America is clearly documented, but exactly where Vinland the Good lies on a contemporary map of North America is a matter of much debate. Some claim that the stump of a round stone tower found in Newport, Rhode Island, marks the southernmost extent of their explorations. Other evidence pointing to an 11th-century Norse visit to New England includes a Viking axe discovered at Rocky Nook, Massachusetts (only a few miles from Plymouth Rock); early English accounts of blue-eyed natives; and reports that Karlsefni and his band wintered in a place without much snow. Dismissing such material as either circumstantial or forged, other historians refuse to believe that the Norse ventured anywhere south of Nova Scotia. No historical continuity has been established between Leif's *skrellings* and the tribes of the Algonquin language group.

The Algonquins: The Algonquins were the Indians of the real Age of Discovery and the Indians who were first befriended and then

destroyed by European fortune hunters and refugees. Represented as far west as the Rockies and as far south as the Carolinas, the Algonquin tribes were related to one another approximately as the French are to the Spanish. Although intertribal communication often demanded an interpreter, the two languages shared basic grammatical and phonetic constructions.

The Algonquins seeped into the New England forests probably sometime during the 14th or 15th centuries. They did not come in droves; by 1600, no more than 25,000 Indians populated New England, fewer than one for every 2 sq. miles (5 sq. km). Nor did this population comprise a unified culture: the Algonquins broke down into at least 10 tribal divisions. Tribes included the Narragansetts of present-day Rhode Island, the Abnaki of Maine, the Pennacooks of New Hampshire and the Massachusetts of their namesake, as well as lesser groups such as the Nipmucs, Nausets, Pocumtucks and Niantics. Some tribes could boast no more than 200 or 300 members.

Far from being the crazed nomads of later characterizations, the Algonquins were agricultural and semi-sedentary, wandering little more than the fashionable Bostonians who summer on Cape Cod. Tribal communities moved with the seasons, following established routes restricted to particular tribal domains. In the winter they occupied the sheltered valleys of the interior, in the warmer months the fertile coastal areas.

But the Indians had to toil year-round to feed and clothe themselves. With an excellent understanding of agricultural techniques, they grew crops such as beans, pumpkins and tobacco, but relied most heavily on maize, the Indian corn. Meat and fish sufficiently balanced the vegetable fare. Plentiful moose and beaver, turkey and goose, lobsters and clams, salmon and bass, along with other delectables, made for an enviably varied menu.

Everyone contributed to the efficient workings of the typical Algonquin community. While the men took care of the chase, the women sowed and harvested the fields, tended the children, and maintained the portable family wigwams. The Algonquins were, in fact, dumbfounded by the inequity of European sex roles. As one Englishman reported the Indians' reaction to the white female's social function: "They say *Englishman* much foole, for spoiling good working creature meaning women. And when they see any of our English women sewing with their needles, or working coifes, or such things, they will cry out Lazie *Squaes!*"

Politics and state affairs were left in the charge of the *sachem*, a hereditary chief who commanded each tribe in much the same way that monarchs ruled medieval Europe. Although men usually controlled the sachemships, there were many cases of women filling the top posts. Sub-*sachems* and war captains, the Indian equivalents of lords and knights, paid material tribute to these rulers and were nominally subject to their will. The *powwows*, or medicine men, gained considerable political might as the vicars of Indian religion. They combined healing with religion and enjoined their parishioners in intense mystical rites.

In no sense did the Algonquins comprise a nation in the modern European style. Unlike their Iroquois neighbors to the west, no council, senate or chief-of-chief disciplined the Algonquin tribes toward unified action. Divided into sachemships, New England's Indians were not simply disunited; they were constantly at each other's throats, "The savages… for the most part," reported the merchant-adventurer George Peckham, "are at

the advancing white settler, a formidable common enemy.

The early European explorers of North America were not mere adventurers, but determined fortune hunters seeking an easier passage to the Orient and its treasures. When the Genoese sailor Cristoforo Colombo (better known by the latinized Christopher Columbus) was trying to persuade a monarch to finance his expedition, he spoke of riches and trade and a new path to the wonders of India. So when he returned with a new continent, but with no gold or spices, he was ridiculed and disgraced.

Columbus' countryman Giovanni Caboto (John Cabot), searching for the Northwest

continuall warres with their next adjoyning neighbor." These conflicts could be extremely vicious, typified by the grotesque torture of prisoners and the parading of a slaughtered adversary's head and hands.

Path to settlement: Tribal animosities so hardened by generations of battle would later contribute to the Algonquins' downfall by preventing the tribes from unifying against

Left, contact is established with the natives **Above**, French explorer Jacques Cartier, on left, who discovered the St Lawrence River in 1534, and Giovanni da Verrazano, an Italian who charted the New England coast in 1524.

Passage to the East, received slightly better treatment from his patron, Henry VII of England. The first European to visit America's northern shores (at Labrador, historians believe) since the Norse, Cabot was blessed with a whopping royal pension of £20 a year after his 1497 expedition. It was a good bargain for the Crown, considering that England based its claim to all America east of the Rockies and north of Florida on the extent of Cabot's exploration.

For the greater part of the 16th century, Spanish *conquistadores* dominated the New World, where they profitably exploited resource-rich Central and South America. After Cabot's venture, the less inviting and accessible north was largely neglected and the Northwest Passage remained no more than a merchant's dream.

Sailing for the French King François I, Giovanni da Verrazano traveled the Atlantic seaboard in his *Dolphin* as far north as Narragansett Bay. Jacques Cartier laid the foundation for what would later become New France by navigating the important St Lawrence River. The Portuguese joined the French in fishing the teeming waters of the Grand Banks. But, as yet, there was very little talk of settling the then-unchristened land of New England.

The English take over: In the closing decades

of the 16th century, Elizabeth I's England eclipsed Spain as master of the seas. Recognizing conquest and colonization as a path to power, the late-starting English were to take over from the *conquistadores* as pioneers of the New World.

In 1583, equipped with a royal charter to discover "remote heathen and barbarious land not actually possessed by any Christian prince or people... and to have, hold, occupy and enjoy" such territories, Sir Humphrey Gilbert was the first Englishman to attempt the settlement of North America. Sailing from Plymouth with his flagship *Delight* and three other vessels, Gilbert intended to es-

tablish a trading post at the mouth of the Penobscot River. But after reasserting English control of Newfoundland, he sailed south to disaster. The expedition never reached its goal: three out of the four ships sank and Gilbert himself lost his life.

The misfortune of Gilbert proved only a temporary inhibition to other pathmakers. The first years of the 17th century saw a renewed interest in exploration. Between 1602 and 1606, expeditions led by Bartholomew Gosnold, Martin Pring and George Weymouth went smoothly and, although not ambitious enough to plant settlements, these voyages did discover a commercial lure to New England – plentiful sassafras bark, then considered a powerful cure-all. Weymouth also had another interesting cargo – five Indians abducted from the coast of Maine.

In 1606, James I granted charters for two new ventures, the Virginia Companies of London and Plymouth, giving the latter rights to found a colony somewhere between North Carolina and Nova Scotia. Directed by luminaries such as Sir Ferdinando Gorges, Raleigh Gilbert (son of Sir Humphrey) and the veteran Pring, 100 adventurers set out from Plymouth in early 1607. Loaded with the usual arms and foodstuffs, some livestock and trinkets to trade with the natives, the crew built Fort St George on Parker's Island in Maine. There they wintered, but, finding no evidence of precious metals, and the weather "extreme unseasonable and frosty," the group abandoned its foothold the following spring.

Recognizing the need to plan more carefully, the Plymouth Company next commissioned the experienced surveyor John Smith to take a critical look at the region's potential for settlement and profit. Smith is credited as the first to give the region its name of "New England." Although the early English pioneers had come no closer to establishing a permanent settlement in New England than had their Viking predecessors, their eyewitness descriptions – the guidebooks of other times – painted an attractive picture for those who would soon be seeking refuge from their mother country. John Smith, for example, wrote in his widely circulated *Description of New England:* "And surely by reason of those sandy cliffes and cliffes of rocks, both which we saw so planted with Gardens and Corne fields, and so well inhabited with a goodly, strong and well proportioned people, besides the greatnesse of the Timber growing on Them, the greatnesse of the fish and moderate temper of the ayre… who can but approve this a most excellent place, both for health & fertility? And of all the four parts of the world that I have seen not inhabited, could I have but means to transport a Colonie, I would rather live here than anywhere… "

Smith's dreams would soon come true. Determination would triumph, the new land would be settled.

Answering a higher call: "What the Puritans gave the world was not thought, but action," said Horace Greeley. Certainly, the explorers of the 16th century were driven by the heretics mounted the same scaffolds as did traitors. To the Puritans, devotees of more extreme Protestant beliefs, the symbols of papal domination – jeweled miters, elaborate rituals and power-hungry bishops – were the Devil's work. Satan himself was said to be a representative of the Apostolic See.

Perhaps even more disturbing to the Puritans was the persecution they suffered under Catholic sympathizer James I. The Puritans had enjoyed years of respectability during Elizabeth I's reign. Their followers included highly placed academics and public officials, many merchants and local clergymen. The shock of disgrace under James I, therefore, was all the more frightful. The new king

profit motive. Since they discovered neither the coveted Northwest Passage nor gold and diamonds, they couldn't discern the promise of the New World. Decades of work produced no more than a few crude maps and travelogues. The Cabots and Gosnolds and Weymouths were not interested in settling New England; only a higher call would people the new land.

Renaissance Europe could not imagine religious tolerance. Dissent was treason, and

Left, eight-year-old Anne Pollard, the first white woman to set foot in Boston (1630). **Above**, Pilgrims at Plimouth Plantation.

wasn't lopping off any heads, but harassment went beyond mere inconvenience. "Some were taken, & clapt up in prison, others had their houses besett & watcht night and day, & hardly escaped their lands," related Puritan leader William Bradford in his oft-quoted *History of Plimouth Plantation*, "and ye most were faine too flie & leave their houses & habitations; and the means of their livelihood."

Where to? In 1602, a group of several hundred Puritans from the county of Lincolnshire migrated to the quaint college town of Leyden, Holland, but they did not prosper. The exacting Puritans found their travel along the True Path hindered by the fact that "the morals of the people in the Low Countries were loose." And so, the Puritans struck a deal with the Plymouth Company to finance a settlement in the unpopulated north of America. In the early summer of 1620, 66 of the Leyden community sailed with the *Speedwill* from Delftshaven to Southampton to prepare for the trials that lay ahead. "They knew they were pilgrims," Bradford wrote, and so they are remembered by history.

Leaving from Plymouth on the 180-ton *Mayflower*, the Pilgrims packed everything they needed to start and maintain a self-sufficient community. The trip itself was no luxury cruise, and after more than two months

at sea the travelers "were not a little joyful" to sight Cape Cod on November 11. Deciding that the sandy cape was not the best place to till the land, the group dispatched Captain Miles Standish (who was nicknamed "Captain Shrimp" because of his height) to find a more fertile site. In mid-December, the Pilgrims disembarked at Plymouth Rock.

The first winter was a miserable ordeal, testing fully the hardened Puritan will. Scurvy, pneumonia and other infections killed more than half of the settlers, including Governor John Carver and the wives of Bradford and Standish. At any one time, no more than six or seven remained in good health. But

with warmer weather came better times and the critical cooperation of the local Indians. As luck would have it, Squanto, one of those brought back to England by George Weymouth, had returned to his homeland and was there to greet the Pilgrims. Squanto persuaded Massasoit, the local *sachem*, to help the beleaguered English pioneers. A treaty of friendship was signed.

Heavenly aspirations: Acknowledging the native contribution, the Pilgrims hosted a feast of celebration nearing the first anniversary of their arrival. In this first Thanksgiving, natives and newcomers enjoyed a meal of roasted game (including turkey), eel, fruits, vegetables and cornbread. A few weeks later, 35 freedom-seekers, well stocked with provisions, joined the *Mayflower* survivors, and by the spring of 1624, Plymouth was a thriving village of more than 30 cottages.

With tracts such as Edward Winslow's *Good Newes From New England* making their way back to the mother country, more settlers overcame an understandable timidity to join the religious migration.

In 1628 another group of Puritans, led by Thomas Dudley, Thomas Leverett and John Winthrop, obtained a royal charter as the "Company of the Massachusetts Bay in New England." The next summer, 350 hopefuls arrived at Salem, followed by another 1,500 in 1630. Like the Pilgrims before them, these later settlers suffered many casualties during the early days. But they, too, were determined not only to establish themselves permanently in the New World but also to live fully their religious ideals, in order to become an example for the chosen.

"For wee must consider that wee shall be as a Citty upon a hill," Governor Winthrop declared. "The eies of all people are upon us; so that if we shall deale falsely with our god in this worke… wee shall shame the faces of many of God's worthy servants, and cause their prayers to be turned into Cursses upon us till wee be consumed out of the good land." Driven by such heavenly aspirations, these religious refugees fared well with their worldly pursuits. The founding of New England was a Puritan achievement.

As Charles I and his Archbishop William Laud tightened the screws of persecution back home, the Massachusetts Bay Colony grew quickly despite primitive conditions. An estimated 2,000 immigrants joined the settlement every year between 1630 and 1637, and, to accommodate these arrivals, new communities such as Ipswich, Dorchester, Concord (the first inland village), Dedham and Watertown sprang up.

In 1636, the Puritan clergy established Harvard College to train future ministers. A General Court was formed to manage administrative and judicial affairs, a governor and deputy governor being indirectly chosen by the colony's freeholders (those who owned Bay Company stock). At lower levels of government, the founders of each town ordinarily convened to confront problems of general interest; this was an entirely practical mechanism of administration given that,

ing post on Maine's Kennebec River since 1627, and New World magnates John Mason and Sir Ferdinando Gorges tried to develop vast property grants in New Hampshire and Maine, but these ventures were humbled by the region's inhospitability.

Elsewhere, groups of New Englanders helped pave the frontiers outside the region. Puritan communities transplanted to New York, North Carolina and Georgia maintained ties with their old homes. One such group, originally from Westmorland, Connecticut, continued to send representatives to the Connecticut Assembly long after moving to Pennsylvania.

The social satirist and Revolutionary War

even as late as 1700, the average town included no more than 200 or 300 families.

Growth was not limited to the area of the first landings on the Massachusetts shore. The reverends Thomas Hooker and Samuel Stone, along with former Bay governor John Haynes, left Cambridge for Connecticut, where they settled the towns of Hartford, Wethersfield and Windsor. Londoners Theophilus Eaton and John Davenport soon after established themselves at New Haven. The Plymouth Colony had been operating a trad-

Left, the seal of the Plymouth Colony. **Above**, barricading a house against Indian attack.

general Artemus Ward once observed: "The Puritans nobly fled from a land of despotism to a land of freedom, where they could not only enjoy their own religion, but could prevent everybody else from enjoying his." Dictating rules of conduct not just for the church but for all worldly pursuits (theater, for example, was banned until the late 1700s as ungodly), the rigorous Calvinistic standards made the Puritans far less tolerant of social or theological deviation than their oppressors back in England had been. Indeed, in 1661, the king himself intervened to protect Quakers in the Bay Colony after several were hanged publicly on Boston

Common. As has often been the case in American history, tragic deeds of injustice belied the ringing slogans of liberty.

Such intolerances did, however, bear an unwanted but ultimately productive child in the new colony of Rhode Island. In the early years of Massachusetts Bay, the Reverend Roger Williams, a graduate of Cambridge University, took it upon himself to condemn the shackles of imposed religion, preaching from his pulpit in Salem that "forced worship stinks in God's nostrils." Williams' compatriots in the General Court banished him from the colony in 1636.

But Williams did not return to England. He turned instead to Canonicus and Miantono-

plantations proved an unholy thorn in Massachusetts' underbelly. No kind words here: Hutchinson, with her "very voluble tongue," lambasted her former parish with "Call it whore and strumpet not a Church of Christ"; while back in Massachusetts, the ordinarily restrained Cotton Mather continually insulted the colony as the "fag end of creation," "the sewer of New England" and, ever so cleverly, "Rogue's Island." But Rhode Island lived up to its intent, and religious freedom was guaranteed by a 1663 royal charter. Aside from outcast Puritans, the new community welcomed New England's first Jewish émigrés in 1662, along with scores of Quakers and French Huguenots.

mi, the two Narragansett *sachems* whom he had befriended in the course of studying the native population. The chieftains saw fit to grant him, *gratis*, a large tract on the Pawtuxet River. Here, Williams founded the town of Providence. Fellow exiles joined him over the next few years – Anne Hutchinson (mother of 15 children) and William Coddington on nearby Rhode Island (so named after a fancied resemblance to the Greek island of Rhodes), and Samuel Gorton in Warwick.

Though the new settlement grew slowly – from fewer than 20 families in 1638 to no more than 1,000 individuals three decades later – the Providence and Rhode Island

A much worse oppression than Williams had suffered was imposed upon the indigenous population. Although the Puritans owed much to the Algonquins for their cooperation in the early days of settlement, and although they professed no racial prejudice against the Indians (one contemporary theory held that they were descended from a lost tribe of Israel), the Puritans soon assumed the task of converting their new-found neighbors from their heathen ways.

Missionary efforts did show some initial promise. The Bible was translated into the Algonquian language. The Reverend John Eliot set up a string of "Praying Towns," along the Connecticut River and near Cape Cod, in which Christian Algonquins had their own preachers, teachers and magistrates. During the 1660s and early 1670s, these communities may have accounted for as many as one-fifth of all New England Indians. But the Puritans were looking for more than religious fellow-travelers; they sought to create nothing less than a breed of neo-Englishmen. As the historian Alden T. Vaughan concluded, the natives would have had to "forsake their theology, their language, their political and economic structures, their habitations and clothing, their social mores, their customs of work and play" – in short, commit cultural suicide – to

ary zeal and led to bloodshed. At first, there was plenty of room for the natives and settlers to coexist peacefully. About a third of the Algonquin inhabitants had fallen victim to a great plague in the early 1600s, leaving their lands underpopulated when the *Mayflower* landed. And as the English pushed south, the Indians realized that the white settlers intended to expand their holdings.

In 1636 war erupted with the Pequots (a fearsome tribe whose name means "destroyer" in Algonquian), and battles at Fort Mystic and Fairfield, Connecticut, saw several hundred lives lost on both sides. It was King Philip's War (1675–76), however, that marked the demise of Indian society in most

please the Puritans sufficiently.

Several Algonquins were sent to Harvard for ministerial training, but only Caleb Cheeshahteaumuck graduated. Many natives took to drinking the "strong water" introduced by the English, and were chastised for their supposed indolence, a cardinal Puritan sin. A few might have made the crossing to "civilization," but to expect all to do so was unreasonable and typical of a profound disrespect for a proud society.

Soon empire-building replaced mission-

Left, Roger Williams, founder of Providence.
Above, King Philip's War broke the Indians' will.

of New England. The Nipmuc, Narragansett and Wampanoag forces, nominally led by Philip (whose real name was Metacom), suffered from chronic tribal disunity and were outnumbered by at least five to one. At the "Great Swamp Fight" near present-day South Kingston, Rhode Island, 2,000 Narragansetts were slain (many of them women and children trapped in burning wigwams) in one of the fiercest battles ever fought on New England soil. The Indian will was broken; for them, the war had been a holocaust.

For the settlers, whose initial ascetic zeal had been diluted, politics, not religion, would be the rallying call of a new era.

Painted by Chappel.   Engraved by Phillibrown.

BATTLE OF BUNKER'S HILL.

From the original painting in the possession of the Publishers.

Johnson, Fry & Co. Publishers, New York.

Q: Were you not oppressed by the Stamp Act?

A: I never saw one of those stamps. I certainly never paid a penny for one of them.

Q: Well, then, what was the matter? And what did you mean in going in the fight?

A: Young man, what we meant in going for those Redcoats was this: we always had governed ourselves, and we always meant to. They didn't mean we should.

– Captain Preston, a veteran of the Revolutionary War, interviewed by Mallen Chamberlain in 1842

Politics were not new to New England. But the northern colonies had, for the most part, been left to their own devices from the first landing at Plymouth until the dramatic Stamp Act crisis of 1765. When the mother country attempted to rein in her distant child, the reaction had been quick and biting, a portent of the more drastic rebellion that lay ahead.

Suffering serious political turmoil in the early 17th century, highlighted by the beheading of Charles I and the subsequent ascendancy of the Great Protector Oliver Cromwell, England had little time to attend to the governing of dissident settlers 3,000 miles from London. The Puritans gladly filled the vacuum and took on the responsibilities of de facto autonomy. Even before reaching their destination, the Pilgrims signed the famous Mayflower Compact, creating a government "to enact, constitute, and frame such just and equal Laws, Ordinances, Acts, Constitutions, and offices, from time to time, as shall be thought most meet and convenient for the general good." John Winthrop and his followers carried with them their royal charter when they sailed to Massachusetts, and in 1631 the freemen of the new colony gave an oath of fidelity not to the King but to the Bay Company and its officers. The settlers agreed that if England tried to impose its own governor on them, "we ought not to accept him, but defend our lawful possessions."

Dominion days: Fifty-five years later, they

were given the chance. In 1686, James II unilaterally revoked the northern colonies' sacred charters and consolidated English holdings from Maine to New Jersey into a vast Dominion of New England in America. The monarch justified his decision as a security measure, a benevolent protection from the French and Indians. The colonists knew better: who could presume that the Puritans would kowtow to a royally appointed governor? The king's first envoy, Joseph Dudley, an avid Anglican, was scorned as having "as many virtues as can consist with so great a thirst for honor and power." His successor, Edmund Andros, was ridiculed as "the greatest tyrant who ever ruled in this country." When the new administration extorted taxes, "ill Methods of Raising money without a General Assembly," the disenfranchised populace grew more incensed.

A strong cue from England itself moved New England to action and revolt. At the "Glorious Revolution" of early 1689, William and Mary, in cahoots with Parliament, seized the throne from James II. New England spontaneously erupted; Andros and his cronies were dragged from state house to jail cell. The old powers of self-government were largely restored, along with a certain mutual respect between Crown and colonies. Though only three years long, the Dominion days had nonetheless decisively molded the New Englanders' political instincts.

But Hanoverian monarch George III would have a prostrate America or none at all. Britain's first *faux pas* on the road to losing its New World empire was the Revenue Act of 1764, which imposed duties on sugar, silk and certain wines. The tax was duly denounced and boycotts proclaimed.

The infamous Stamp Act followed a year later, requiring that all commercial and legal documents, newspapers and playing cards

the Commons, "I dare tax America," Parliament passed the Townsend Acts, imposing harsh duties on such imports as paper, glass and tea. Two regiments of British troops landed at Boston to put some muscle behind Governor Hutchinson's waning control.

A tea party: The Redcoats were not pleasantly received. On the night of March 5, 1770, a crowd of several hundred rowdy Bostonians gathered to taunt a lone "lobsterback" standing guard outside the customs house on King Street (present-day State Street). When shouts turned to stones and snowballs, seven Redcoats came to aid the sentry. One fired into the melee without orders, others followed and, after the smoke

be taxed. The measure was fiercely assailed. Stamp distributors were hanged in effigy and ridiculed at mock trials. Liberty was buried in symbolic funerals. Citizens of all stripes throughout New England, both of city and country, gathered to decry the new tax. Many of the demonstrations were peaceful, but in Boston, mobs ransacked the houses of stamp-man Andrew Oliver and Governor Thomas Hutchinson. Parliament, led by commoner William Pitt, took the hint and repealed the Stamp Act in March 1766.

But Britain had not learned a proper lesson. In the summer of 1767, with Prime Minister Charles Townsend boasting before

had cleared, three colonists lay dead (including a black man named Crispus Attucks) and two were mortally wounded. The American revolt had its first martyrs, and the growing anti-British element in New England had a field day with the nocturnal showdown.

Tempers cooled after the Boston Massacre. In the early 1770s, economic prosperity returned to the colonies. A once-again pragmatic Parliament struck down the Townsend Acts – all except one, that is. Just to make sure nobody questioned who was still boss – or king – Britain maintained the tax on East Indian tea, a not insignificant gesture given that tea was about as important as bread to the 18th-century diet. American addicts turned to smuggled Dutch blends or to "Liberty Tea," a nasty brew made from sage, currant or plantain leaves. The British responded by subsidizing their brand and, in September 1773, flooded the market with about half a million pounds of the "pestilential herb," with shipments to points all along the Eastern seaboard. It didn't work.

Boston emerged once again as the focus of resistance. The Massachusetts Committee of Correspondence, an unofficial legislature, and the local chapter of the Sons of Liberty, a fast-growing secret society at the forefront of revolutionary activism, barred the piers and demanded that Governor Hutchinson

called, was a display of profound disrespect to the Londoners. Parliament responded with the so-called Coercive Acts. Most infamously, the Boston Port Act sealed off the city by naval blockade. This time, the colonies had had enough. The First Continental Congress convened in Philadelphia on September 5, 1774. Revolution was at hand.

A shot heard round the world: An uneasy stalemate prevailed from the fall of 1774 to the spring of 1775. British garrisons controlled only the major towns. The countryside became virtually unpoliceable. New Englanders stockpiled arms and ammunition to prepare for the inevitable conflict.

The rebels didn't have to wait long for war.

send home the tea-laden *Dartmouth*. When he refused, the protesters' reaction was swift and theatrical. On December 16, 60 men (among them Sam Adams and John Hancock) disguised as Mohawk Indians and blacks descended on the *Dartmouth* and two sister ships. Boston Harbor was turned into a giant teapot as 342 crates were dumped over the railings.

The Boston Tea Party, as it came to be

Left, *Retreat of the British from Concord.* As the Redcoats fled from the colonies, enthusiastic citizens raised their "Liberty" flag over the land. **Above**, *The Battle of Lexington.*

In early April 1775, London instructed Boston commander General Thomas Gage to quash seditious activities in rural Massachusetts, where a Provincial Congress had assumed *de facto* governmental control. Late on the night of April 18, Gage accordingly dispatched a contingent of 700 soldiers to destroy a makeshift arms depot in Concord, located 20 miles (32 km) west of Boston. At Lexington 70 ragtag colonial soldiers, the original Minutemen, lay in wait for the British by dawn's light, having been forewarned by the daring early-morning rides of patriots Paul Revere and William Dawes.

The two forces met on the town common.

A musket was fired. Minutes later, eight Americans lay dead. The unscathed Brits continued on to Concord, where the colonial militia triggered, in Ralph Waldo Emerson's words, "the shot heard round the world." The Minutemen made up for what they lacked in numbers by employing unconventional guerrilla tactics, harrassing their enemies with crack sniper fire. By nightfall they had knocked off 273 British soldiers.

Sensational accounts of these skirmishes sent settlers from Maine to Georgia reaching for their rifles. "The devastation committed by the British troops on their retreat," reported one, "is almost beyond description, such as plundering and burning of dwelling hous-

hope of holding Boston. On June 17, Redcoats scaled Breed's slopes twice but were rebuffed. In a desperate third attempt they succeeded, but only because the colonial force had exhausted its supply of ammunition. It was for this reason, and not out of bravery, that Colonel William Prescott issued his famous command: "Don't fire until you see the whites of their eyes, men."

Bunker Hill was an expensive triumph for the Crown, which suffered more than 1,000 casualties. Optimism, seen in remarks like General John Burgoyne's "We'll soon find elbow room," was reduced to the doubting reflections of another British officer: "This victory has cost us very dear indeed... Nor

es and other buildings, driving into the street women in child bed, killing old men in their houses unarmed." Among the dead bodies, the card of compromise lay discarded.

The first major engagement of the war, the Battle of Bunker Hill, broke out in June on the Charlestown peninsula, across the Charles River from Boston. To consolidate control of overland access to the port city, Continental Army General Artemus Ward ordered the fortification of Bunker's Hill (as it was then known), although it was actually on adjoining Breed's Hill that the Americans dug in.

The British could not allow such a buildup if they were to entertain even the faintest

do I see that we enjoy one solid benefit in return, or likely to reap from it any one advantage whatever." Less than a year later, Gage evacuated his troops to Halifax.

A few months later, on July 4, 1776, the Declaration of Independence was adopted by the Continental Congress. Of the proud signatories, 14 came from the charter states of Massachusetts, Connecticut, New Hampshire and Rhode Island. Except for Newport, Rhode Island, which was not taken from the British until October 1779, the rest of New England had achieved its independence.

Once the Revolutionary War was over in 1781, the magnates of New England's prosperous cities turned to protect their newly established interests as the 13 independent colonies hammered out an integrated union. Concerned that a centralized federal government would prove as insensitive to local sentiment as had the Crown, revolutionary heroes Sam Adams and John Hancock gave only grudging support to the Constitution. Rhode Island, in more than a dozen votes between 1787 and 1789, voted down the Constitution and only ratified it after the Bill of Rights was added.

The Industrial Age: New England's leaders became increasingly reactionary as they went about guarding their economic interests. In Massachusetts, poor hill farmers rose against

seas that New England's money was made. Codfish and whale products provided a lucrative export to Catholic Europe. New England was at the pivot of the profitable triangular trade: in harbors like Newport, a fleet of 350 ships unloaded West Indian molasses and reloaded with rum. From there, the rum was transported to Africa, where it was traded for slaves who were shipped to the West Indies and, in turn, traded for molasses. New England shipyards gained world fame for crafting swift, easily managed ocean-going vessels, a tradition launched even before Pilgrim settlement with the construction of the *Virginia* in the short-lived Popham, Maine, colony in 1607.

the state government in Shays' Rebellion of 1786, demonstrating that genuine equality remained a dream. In 1812, fearing the loss of a thriving maritime trade, New England firmly opposed renewed and greater conflict with Great Britain.

When not calling comrades to religious or political barricades, the colonial New Englander attended to the more practical pursuit of commerce: it was out of the seas and on the

Left, whaling was an early source of New England's wealth. **Above**, the 19th century saw many improvements in transportation, including the Fall River paddle steamer.

Disrupted by the Revolution, maritime trade bounced back quickly, mining the riches of China and India so coveted by the early American explorers. In 1792, Boston's *Columbia* threaded the Straits of Magellan en route to Canton to trade for tea, spices, silk and opium. The magnates of rival Salem – Elias Haskett Derby, Joseph Peabody and Billy Gray – preferred to sail east, skirting the southern tip of Africa on frequent and successful ventures to the Orient.

But, alas, the first two decades of the 19th century demonstrated how vulnerable maritime trade was to the whims of international politics. The Napoleonic Wars, President

Thomas Jefferson's Embargo Acts and the War of 1812 ("Mr Madison's War") severely hampered New England's chase after an honest, apolitical dollar. Recognizing that it is best not to put all one's commercial eggs in one flimsy basket, its merchants turned to the herald of a new industrial age.

In the fall of 1789, a teenaged Samuel Slater sailed from England to New York disguised as a common laborer. Slater departed in defiance of British laws forbidding the emigration of skilled mechanics. For seven years Slater had apprenticed to Jedediah Strutt, a partner of famed industrial innovator Richard Arkwright, and had memorized the specifications of Arkwright's fac-

With underpaid workers kept at the grind for 70 hours a week, Pawtucket became the site of the nation's first strike in 1800. It was left to Bostonian Francis Cabot Lowell (from the family that would later produce a Harvard president, a celebrated astronomer and a cigar-smoking poetess) to take a more enlightened approach.

During a two-year visit to England, Lowell became an avid industrial tourist and, on his return to Massachusetts, he was determined to duplicate British weaving feats. Putting up $10,000 of his own money, he collected another $90,000 from the so-called "Boston Associates" – the families of Lawrence, Cabot, Eliot, Higginson and others –

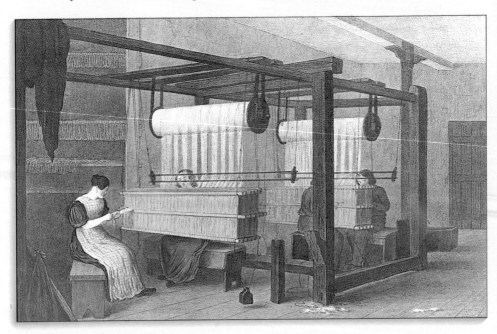

tory-sized, cotton-spinning machine.

In America, the reduction of raw cotton was still being done by the notoriously inefficient "put-out" system, where laborers worked in their own homes on individual looms. An early attempt at consolidating the process, a mill at Beverly, Massachusetts, had been a miserable failure owing to the crudeness of its machinery. Arkwright's device, already proven across the Atlantic, was the answer, so Quaker financier Moses Brown engaged Slater to come to Providence and put his knowledge to use. Together, they built America's first successful cotton mill on the Blackstone River at Pawtucket.

to establish a small mill (with a power loom and 1,700 spindles) at Waltham.

A "commercial utopia": Lowell died in 1817, but his plans were realized by his associates under the aegis of the Merrimack Manufacturing Company. In 1820, the mill was moved to a tract on the Merrimack River, just above the village of Chelmsford.

Paying dividends as high as 28 percent, the operation was wildly profitable. Sales went from a respectable $3,000 in 1815 to an unprecedented $345,000 in 1822; 100,000 spindles wove more than 30 miles (48 km) of cloth daily. In 1826, the growing community was named after its founder.

The Merrimack Company took care of its people. Though grievously overworked by modern standards, "mill girls" enjoyed clean, safe dormitory housing and opportunities for cultural enrichment. New England's first company town was, in the words of English novelist Anthony Trollope, "the realization of commercial utopia."

As had been the case with politics during the revolution, New England was the acknowledged center of industrial America. The region boasted two-thirds of the nation's cotton mills, half of them in Massachusetts; tiny Rhode Island alone processed more than 20 percent of America's wool.

In Connecticut, Sam Colt (of six-shooter ton's Frederick Tudor made a fortune exporting thousands of tons of ice to places as far away as Calcutta.

Life on the frontier: Not everybody shared in the boom. During the last half of the 18th century, the northern areas of New England had enjoyed a dramatic infusion of people, as land began to grow scarce in the densely populated coastal areas. More than 100 new towns were established in New Hampshire in the 15 years preceding the Revolution; between 1790 and 1800, the populations of Vermont and Maine nearly doubled.

On the craggy hillsides, the pioneers set up small farms, built their own houses and barns, and raised wheat, corn, pigs and cattle to fill

fame) and Eli Whitney, better known for his invention of the cotton gin, manufactured the first firearms with interchangeable parts. Edward Howard applied the same concept with his Roxbury wristwatch business, using screws so minute that 2,000 of them weighed not a pound. In the paper, shoe and metalworking industries, New England also stood unchallenged. The Connecticut firm of Edward and William Pattison minted coins for South American governments, while Bos-

Left, new textile machinery made it possible to produce cheap cloth using low-skilled labor. **Above**, State House, Boston, *circa* 1801.

the dinner table. These rugged families prided themselves on being almost completely self-sufficient. This was a new frontier, New England's frontier.

But this frontier's potential was limited by nature. The climate was inhospitable: in 1816, for instance, a June snowfall resulted in total crop failure. Agricultural machinery could not plough the irregular farmland. Property consolidation was difficult, as families jealously guarded original claims; small-scale production could not compete with more efficient new suppliers elsewhere in the United States and around the world. Save for a few scattered industrial concentrations like

Manchester, New Hampshire, northern New England had seen its zenith by 1850.

After that, a slow, sapping decline attacked upland vitality. By the turn of the century, population growth had leveled and agricultural production dived. More than half of New Hampshire's farmland lay abandoned. Cheese production in Maine, New Hampshire and Vermont fell by some 95 percent between 1849 and 1919. Young men went off on the more promising Western trails, girls to the Massachusetts mills.

Cultural laurels: Long before the wheels of industry started to turn, New England minds had been establishing a cultural life unparalleled in the New World. In education, the media, the arts and letters, America looked to New England for guidance and inspiration. Boston led the way in the first flowering of American culture.

As one might expect, New England boasted the laurels of many cultural firsts. Ever mindful of the intellectual responsibilities of being God's chosen, the Puritans had hardly built their churches before they set about looking after the proper education of their future clergymen. The nation's first secondary school, Boston Latin, opened its doors in 1635, and Harvard College, destined to join Oxford and Cambridge among the world's finest academic institutions, was founded the next year. New Haven's rigorous Yale, established by a cabal of young Harvard graduates, followed in 1701.

During the 18th century, New Englanders continued to establish colleges that today number among the finest in the country: Rhode Island College, founded in 1764 and later renamed Brown University; Dartmouth College, established in 1769; and Bowdoin College in Maine, which counts among its alumni Nathaniel Hawthorne, Henry Wadsworth Longfellow, Admiral Robert Peary and President Franklin Pierce.

In 1639 a printing press was assembled in Cambridge. Its early releases included the *Bay Psalm Book*, the *New England Primer* and the freeman's oath of loyalty to Massachusetts. In 1690, the colonies' first newspaper, *Publick Occurrences Both Foreign and Domestick*, appeared in Boston but was succeeded by the more popular *Boston News-Letter* in 1704.

Other memorable tabloids, including *The Rehearsal*, the *Massachusetts Spy* and the *Independent Advertiser*, kept New England informed, if not always accurately, as the country roared to revolution. By the 1850s, the region hosted no less than 424 periodical publications.

Libraries, meanwhile, gave the ordinary citizens the chance to investigate the issues of their day, and of other days, in greater depth. The Wadsworth Atheneum in Hartford, founded in 1842, and the Providence Atheneum, a haunt of Edgar Allen Poe, provided members with access to impressive collections and cultural events. And in 1854 the Boston Public Library became the world's first free municipal library.

Sophisticated tastes: "High culture," traditionally a preserve of the privileged classes, was similarly opened up to broader audiences during the late 19th century. In 1871 came the Museum of Fine Arts. The Boston Symphony Orchestra, established a decade later by Henry Lee Higginson, took its place among the globe's foremost ensembles and soon gave rise to a less strictly classical offshoot, the Boston Pops, which debuted in 1885; the BSO's summer festival at Tanglewood in the Berkshires, inaugurated in 1936, flourishes as a mecca for music lovers everywhere.

As a favored tryout spot, New Haven significantly influenced the development of Broadway theater; an experimental counterpart was spawned in a Cape Cod fishing shack by Eugene O'Neill and the Provincetown Players.

Such institutional achievements are impressive. But behind them lay great individual minds, the region's many intellectual and artistic giants. Among these were transcendentalist philosopher and essayist Henry David Thoreau (1817–62), famed for his celebration of nature in *Walden*; poet Emily Dickinson (1830–86); and painter Winslow Homer (1836–1910).

The cultural roster does not end here. The painting of John Singleton Copley, and the prose and poetry of Ralph Waldo Emerson, Henry Wadsworth Longfellow, John Greenleaf Whittier, Nathaniel Hawthorne, Herman Melville, Robert Lowell and Robert Frost are known the world over. Their lives testify to the spirit of New England.

Right, the faces that built New England: a composite of portraits of the leaders of 19th-century manufacturing and industry.

The prosperity of my native land, New England, which is sterile and unproductive, must depend hereafter on the moral qualities, and secondly, on the intelligence and information of the inhabitants.

– John Lowell, Jr.

By the beginning of this century, New England had done all that it could. It had been America's leader in politics, in economics, in culture. In many ways, New England was America, epitomizing its ideals, drive, deter-

set. The White House was no longer the domain of Harvard and the Adamses.

New England turned to the task of managing itself after two last gasps of political preeminence: the abolitionist crusade led by William Lloyd Garrison and his *Liberator* in the years before the Civil War; and the social-reform movements of the late 1800s, which focused on correcting shocking conditions in the nation's prisons, mental institutions and public hospitals.

Difficulties on the homefront were formi-

mination and success. Considering the heights attained, however, New England could not help but falter, as other regions competed for political and economic ascendancy.

The symptoms of political decay emerged both at the national level, where New England's influence diminished, and locally, where corruption and social divisions humbled once proud democracy. If only by virtue of America's physical expansion – the great westward surge of the 19th century – New England suffered in Washington. The region no longer represented a physical or psychological frontier; it was not here that battles had to be fought, decisions made, examples

dable indeed. Most important, ethnic and religious homogeneity, which had contributed to the political consensus, was diffused as migrating flocks of non-Anglo, non-Protestants hit the northern shores. Uprooted by the Great Potato Famine of 1840, the Irish sailed with high hopes to the land of opportunity. Two centuries after the *Mayflower*, they arrived in Boston at a rate of more than 1,000 people a month. Others, primarily Catholic, followed from Italy, French Canada, Portugal and Eastern Europe.

In Massachusetts, immigration accounted for two-thirds of the total population growth during the 19th century. By 1907, almost 70 percent of that state was of foreign stock (with at least one parent born outside the United States), a majority of them Catholic. The influx touched every corner of New England; even in backwater New Hampshire, one out of every five residents had adopted, not inherited, the American flag.

Electoral corruption: In the wake of this unprecedented human shock wave, a predictable, if deplorable anti-immigrant backlash erupted among the established citizenry, whose forebears had fought so hard to achieve democracy and equal rights.

memberships in their efforts to contain the electoral power of their upstart neighbors.

Their efforts failed. No matter how unfamiliar the immigrants were with the workings of democracy, they soon learned the power of votes well orchestrated – particulary the Irish. In 1881, John Breen of Tipperary became the first Irish-born politician to take high office as mayor of Lawrence, Massachusetts. His triumph launched fellow Irishmen not only to political influence but political domination. Hugh O'Brien won the

The doors of society were shut to even the most successful of new arrivals, and their children and grandchildren. Politically, anti-immigration groups campaigned for tightened entry requirements. In the 1850s, the openly racist Know-Nothing party controlled governorships in Massachusetts, Rhode Island, Connecticut and New Hampshire. Later organizations such as the American Protective Association and the Immigrant Restriction League gathered substantial

Left and **above**, Boston wharves at the end of the 19th century.

mayoral election in Boston three years later, and Patrick Andrew Collin represented Suffolk County with a congressional seat in Washington. By the turn of the century, all levels of government, from the state house to city hall to milltown council, were being run by what was, after all, the majority.

But with newfound responsibility also came vast and insidious corruption. Rhode Island, once again, was the object of biting criticism as "Boss" Charles Brayton and the *Providence Journal* ring bought their way to office. "The political condition of Rhode Island is notorious, acknowledged and it is shameful," deplored journalist Lincoln Steffens; "Rhode Island is a State for sale and cheap." Individual votes cost the machine between $2 and $5 in normal elections, as much as $30 in hotly contested ones. Sam Adams would have cringed at such perversions of the democratic process.

Many leaders, vividly embodied in the figure of James Michael Curley, abused the privileges of solid ethnic support. Curley displayed enormous political staying-power: he was elected mayor of Boston five times in the first four decades of this century; and governor of the state for one term, 1934–38. The "Irish Mussolini," as his detractors tagged him, undoubtedly improved the economic welfare of his less privileged constit-

uents. His imperious methods, however, left much to be desired. Inspired by New York's Tammany Hall, perhaps the most corrupt political machine of all American history, Curley doled out jobs and money to community leaders who in turn carefully steered their neighborhoods in the appropriate direction when election day rolled around. There was some justice to the critics' call, "This is a Republic and not a Kingdom." When the mayor went to a ball game at Fenway Park, howitzers trumpeted his arrival.

Cultural suppression: In Boston, cultural freedoms came under increasingly harsh attack. Led by Catholic leader William Cardi-

nal O'Connell and the associated Watch and Ward Society, moralists lobbied successfully for prohibitions on such classics as Theodore Dreiser's *An American Tragedy* and Ernest Hemingway's *The Sun Also Rises*.

"Banned in Boston!" sang the crusaders, and the phrase survives in the American idiom today. The Puritans, of course, might have burned the authors themselves at the stake, but one would have expected a little more progress in the course of 300 years.

Days of industrial glory passed. In much the same way that international competition now threatens America's economic might, other regions of the country challenged and overcame New England and its once-proud manufacturers. It was a question of costs, specifically labor costs, and the South underbid New England. Hourly wages in New England averaged 16 to 60 percent higher than those below the Mason-Dixon line. Owners gravitated to the cheaper work force, in an industrial exodus dramatically illustrated by statistical indices. Up from a mere 6 percent in 1880, the South wove almost half the nation's cotton goods by 1923. Industrial production in Massachusetts alone fell by $1 billion during the 1920s. Unemployment in factory towns left idle a quarter of the total labor pool. Gone too were the heady days of Lowell's 28 percent dividends: expenditures in New England mills now surpassed the factories' earnings.

New England felt the brunt of the Great Depression. In Boston, the Depression cramped even the upper-class lifestyle; as one magazine noted, the old guard now dined only "annually upon champagne and terrapin in the memory of a crushed world." Hardships were, of course, far more shocking in already squalid working-class quarters. In 1930, only 81 out of 5,030 apartments in the North End had refrigerators, and only one in two had toilets. Here, wages plunged by half, and unemployment jumped to almost 40 percent in the months after the stock-market crash on Wall Street.

It took New England a long time to recover from this economic displacement. Employment in textiles bottomed out at 75,000 in the early 1970s, a far cry from the hundreds of thousands who had once operated the power looms. Virtually bereft of natural resources, including oils, the region was hostage to Louisiana, Texas and the Middle East during the energy crisis of the early 1970s. But New England survived, and has bounced back as a nexus of the high-tech revolution.

Political revival: Despite the decline of New England's political and economic fortunes during much of the 20th century, the region looks forward to a new and useful role within the American colossus.

Political scandals still erupt from time to time, but the "new" New Englanders have more than mastered the mechanisms of democracy; they have long since adopted its spirit, its essence. Irish leaders forged a partnership with the old establishment on equal terms; indeed, it was the "Green Brahmins" (Irish successors to Boston's self-appointed

an undeclared war – an outright condemnation of the tragic conflict in Vietnam. Today, New England plays a prominent role in a number of grass-roots campaigns, from violence prevention to nature preservation.

The 1980s saw a resurgence in its industrial base. Precision products – computers, electronic and biomedical machinery, special papers and plastics, and photographic hardware – made Route 128, skirting Boston, a center of technological innovation equaled only by California's famed Silicon Valley. Boston maintained a prominence as the nation's mutual-fund capital. Hartford's insurance companies, capitalized at billions of dollars, continued to protect much of

aristocracy) who produced one of the nation's mostly highly regarded chief executives, John Fitzgerald Kennedy.

Having cleaned up its own political house, New England returned its attention to national politics with a thoughtful, progressive voice. New England leads efforts to strengthen anti-pollution laws, consumer rights, handgun control and civil rights. In 1970, the Massachusetts Supreme Court, heir to the country's oldest democratic tradition, ruled that its citizens could not be forced to fight in

Left, Boston's legendary mayor James Curley. **Above**, school busing was an issue in the 1970s.

American business against damage and risk.

But the recession of the early 1990s deeply wounded the long-standing economic complacency that had sustained New England for so many years. For the first time in living memory, white-collar jobs came under threat as corporations ruthlessly trimmed their workforces. It was deeply unsettling.

As elsewhere in America and in Europe, service industries assumed a new importance as manufacturing industries retreated. In this respect, New England was fortunate. Graced with a unique scenic beauty, it turned to tourism, already its second largest industry, as a major growth area.

The product of centuries of "plain living and high thinking," New Englanders have long considered themselves the conscience of the nation. New England has contributed more distinguished legislators, writers, teachers and thinkers to the United States than has any other region. It's true that it got a head start on the rest of America. But even after the other states had caught up in terms of population, the flow of outstanding people produced by this unpromising land never let up.

The Puritan heritage, and the region's harsh landscape and weather, have led New Englanders to view life a bit more seriously than do the residents of more forgiving cultures and climes. Although New Englanders have, as a rule, eschewed frivolity, they're quite in favor of individualism, provided that it enhances self-reliance and does not impinge on others' rights to pursue their own individual vision. This mindset pervades both the opulent enclaves of the ultra-rich (from the Berkshires to Newport and Bar Harbor) and the plainest of rural villages; it even informs the day-to-day dealings of city life.

Most would consider this fierce independence to be a carryover from colonial days. However, the genius of the New England style is that it is an amalgam of all the disparate groups that have settled here and forged common bonds and goals: Native American, English, African-American, Irish, Italian, French Canadian, Latin American, Asian... The list continues to grow.

The Algonquins: New England's oldest inhabitants have been in the area since about 12,000–10,000 BC. When the first English settlers arrived in the early 17th century, most of the native population was concentrated in Rhode Island, Connecticut and Massachusetts. They were divided into tribes with well-established rivalries and territorial boundaries. All of Algonquin blood, they had two distinct but grammatically similiar languages, within which 13 different dialects have been identified.

Preceding pages: former Boston Red Sox stars gone fishing. **Left**, William Garrett poses with the picture of his Brahmin great-great grandfather Ira Garrett. **Right**, a Micmac from Connecticut.

These Algonquins were friendly to the first English settlers, who seemed far too few in numbers to represent any threat. The Mohegans and Pequots of Connecticut, the Wampanoags of Massachusetts and the Narragansetts of Rhode Island imparted their age-old hunting, fishing, farming and canoe-making skills to the newcomers.

But this honeymoon was to last only about 15 years. In 1636, the English waged war against the Pequots in revenge for some real or imagined Indian outrage. The Narra-

gansetts took the fatal step of allying themselves with the English, destroying the possibility of a united native front. When the war was over, the Pequots had been obliterated as a people. By 1670, there were 75,000 English settlers in New England and only about 10,000 Indians. The natives had sold much of their land, their settlements having been penetrated everywhere. Many had been converted to Christianity and lived in what were called "praying towns."

The wars of 1675–76 marked the last desperate gasp of native resistance. In 1675, an alliance to fight the English – formed by the Wampanoag sachem Philip with several smaller tribes – was crushed. Philip was beheaded, his body quartered, and the parts displayed in Plymouth for 24 years.

The English weren't content until the last threat of a native uprising had been eliminated. After the Pequots and the Wampanoags, it was the Narragansetts' turn. By the time the English were through with them at the end of 1676, fewer than 70 were left out of the original 4,000 to 5,000.

Beginning of the end: The Algonquin's cultural integrity was shattered. Many fled west. Some native groups, like the Narragansetts on Rhode Island, were granted reservations. Those who stayed on the reservations never adopted European farming methods (the notion of private property was entirely foreign to their way of life); instead, they rented out their land, while eking out a meager existence from the manufacture of craft items.

These native-held territories steadily dwindled over the following two centuries; great tracts of land were sold off by the tribes or simply appropriated. Although the reservations were allowed some degree of self-government (they had, for example, their own magistrates or justices of the peace), they were also appointed nontribal overseers, who often administered to the natives' detriment. In 1869 the Massachusetts legislature voted to end reservation status for those Indians still on reservations, and 11 years later the Rhode Island legislature abolished the Narragansett tribe as a legal entity. Their disenfranchised descendants became ordinary US citizens with no special rights – until recently, when activists began mobilizing for the restoration of tribal lands.

Most Indians did not live on reservations, however; they simply merged into the surrounding population at the lowest level of colonial society, assuming menial jobs as indentured servants or day laborers. Some signed on board whaling ships – a grueling and perilous, if colorful, livelihood. In Rhode Island, Indians gained renown for their skill in building stone walls.

For the most part, the 18th and 19th centuries saw a sad, slow decline of the old tribal associations. The colonists' diseases finished what their guns had begun, causing a continual attrition in population. (In 1763, for instance, during one six-month period, 222 of the 358 natives living in Nantucket succumbed to an epidemic.) The Algonquin

dialects died out almost completely, and Indians in New England became so marginal that they faded out of public consciousness.

Although Indians fought bravely in both the Revolutionary and Civil wars, few outstanding figures emerged from their own ranks to guide and lead them. An exception was Samson Occom, a Mohegan born in Connecticut in 1723. Occom was a brilliant student at Eleazer Wheelock's school for the "Youth of Indian Tribes" (which later became Dartmouth College); he learned Latin, Greek, some Hebrew and English. He became a vigorous Christian missionary among the natives and was probably the single most important factor in the large-scale conver-

sion of the Mohegans and other tribes.

Occom met with great success when he traveled to England to raise money for the movement to Christianize the tribes. He was bitterly disappointed when his mentor Wheelock decided to move his school from Connecticut to its present location in rural New Hampshire, where, as Occom pointed out, there were few indigenous residents left.

Native Americans today: Today, there are only about 21,000 American Indians in New England; about a third live on the nine existing reservations. Many are not the descendants of the natives encountered by the Puritans in the 17th century. Except in Maine, a great many of New England's current Indian residents have relocated from other parts of the country. For most of this century, Indians in New England lived an unobtrusive, unnoticed life. In recent years, however, there has been something of a renaissance.

A new consciousness of tribal identity has taken hold. It has found expression in cultural events and in attempts to right some of the wrongs perpetrated by the colonists. Throughout the 1960s, the annual Powwow of the Wampanoag Indians of Massachusetts, which had been a modest affair, grew to include more dances, rituals, performances of music and meetings with other tribes. In 1972, the Wampanoag communities in Mashpee and

in perpetuity in 1660. The Gay Head Wampanoags fared a bit better: in 1987 the federal government granted them $4.5 million for the repurchase of 475 acres (192 hectares).

The Narragansetts – 4,000 to 5,000 people of mixed American Indian, European and African ancestry in southern Rhode Island – filed a similar suit in 1976; in an out-of-court settlement, they were awarded 1,900 acres (780 hectares). The 700 Penobscots of Maine, the only New England natives who still speak their original tongue, sued the state in 1975 for recovery of 10 million acres (4 million hectares), and reached a compromise settlement three years later. The legal battles are far from done, but for the first time in 300

Gay Head, Martha's Vineyard, elected tribal councils. Four years later the councils moved into action. They brought suits against their respective New England towns contesting the 1869 law which, in effect, deprived Indians of their reservations. Denied their tribal status in two trials (in 1977 and 1982), the Mashpee Wampanoags, who now number about 600, have as yet had no success reclaiming any part of the 10,500 acres which the Plymouth General Court accorded them

Left, a park ranger, Ferry Beach State Park, Maine. **Above**, graduation ceremony at Brookfield High School, Connecticut.

years, New England's Native Americans have begun to recoup some small portion of the losses they suffered at the hands of high-minded colonists.

The proud Puritans: The world has rarely seen a group of immigrants quite like the New England Puritans of the 17th century. Fleeing religious persecution in England, they were fired by an extraordinary sense of mission. As the first immigrants to America, they would create a civilized society in the harsh, inhospitable New England wilderness, and they would set an example of purpose and industry for the rest of the world.

Because their motive for coming to New

England was primarily religious and not economic, the Puritans were a socially diverse lot. Although most of these early comers were peasants and artisans, an unusually large number of educated men – ministers, theologians and teachers – were among them. These learned men set a tone for the Puritan community of strict disciplined piety, with religion pervading every aspect of life.

The religious organization of the Puritan church was congregational: that is, members of the community elected the governors of the church. Leaders of church, community and state were usually the same. From the earliest days of colonization, the Puritan leaders felt compelled to settle the rest of

tionary democratic ideas, this community was thought of as a distinctive nation-within-a-nation by other Americans at the end of the 18th century. According to Dwight, New Englanders were distinguished by their "love of science and learning," their "love of liberty," their "morality," "piety" and "unusual spirit of enquiry." Dwight, of course, was a New Englander himself and he naturally idealized his origins. For him the typical New Englander was a combination of Ethan Allen, the Connecticut boy who led a daring guerrilla fight against the English in the hills of Vermont; fire-breathing Massachusetts preacher Cotton Mather; and learned statesman and patriot John Adams.

New England. There were two reasons: a high birth rate called for the rapid expansion of the Puritan community beyond the boundaries of Massachusetts; and the churchmen were eager to Christianize the Indians.

For 200 years, New England's settlers consisted of this tightly knit, homogeneous group. What Yale president Timothy Dwight said of Bostonians in 1796 could have been applied to *all* New Englanders: "They are all descendants of Englishmen and, of course, are united by all the great bonds of society – language, religion, government, manners and interest." Having grown from a strictly controlled religious state to a cradle of revolu-

The rest of the country was more likely to characterize Yankees, as they became known, as speculators, entrepreneurs, inventors or investors. They were men like early 19th-century Boston textile baron Francis Cabot Lowell, whose factory at Waltham was one of the first modern factories in America; or members of a great Boston family that made its fortune in the China and East India trade.

The "exalted" Brahmins: New Englanders considered themselves the national elite. The self-proclaimed heads of this elite were the Boston Brahmins – rich Boston families like the Lowells, Cabots, Welds, Lodges and Saltonstalls, who secured their fortunes in the first half of the 20th century in the railroad, banking, shipping and textile industries. The Welds, for example, forebears of Massachusetts governor William Weld, had been in 17th-century Governor John Winthrop's entourage and had fallen into obscurity for six generations before they prospered in shipping and railroads in the 19th century. This elite group carefully nurtured itself at a group of socially select schools and colleges like Harvard. Boston Brahmin Edmund Quincy once said of the Harvard Triennial Catalogue, which contained a list of all Harvard University graduates: "If a man's in there, that's who he is. If he isn't, who is he?"

Despite this and the fact that many of

today's Brahmins hold exalted notions of the extent of their lineage, few descend from the *Mayflower* pilgrims, from prominent Puritans of the 17th century, or even from rich merchants of the 18th century. For the Boston social system was not an aristocratic one; when Brahmins lost their money, as happened to a good many of them in the 18th century, they ceased to be Brahmins. The

Left, a Russian Orthodox priest in Richmond, Maine; a Puritan lives again at Old Sturbridge Village, Massachusetts. **Above**. Nobel prizewinning geneticist and cancer researcher Dr George Snell in Bar Harbor, Maine.

Brahmins may think of themselves as European-style aristocrats (some have even adopted family coats-of-arms), but James Michael Curley, the notorious Irish mayor of Boston, was not far wrong when he remarked acidly that Boston's prominent Yankee families "got rich selling opium to the Chinese, rum to the Indians, or trading in slaves."

Indomitable Yankees: Other Yankees might contest this characterization. President Calvin Coolidge, a famous Vermonter, once declared at Vermont's Bennington College: "I love Vermont… most of all because of her indomitable people. They are a race of pioneers who have almost beggared themselves to serve others. If the spirit of liberty should vanish in other parts of the Union and support for our institutions should languish, it could all be replenished from the generous store held by the people of this brave little state of Vermont."

The first inhabitants of the state were hardy trappers, not farmers; and this has contributed to the independent and self-reliant characteristics of the modern Vermonter. Freedom is a personal issue for the Vermonter, not just an abstract historical one, although Vermont has a long tradition of idealism. When neighboring states were laying claim to its territory during the Revolution, Vermont declared itself an independent republic. It maintained this status for 14 years, during which time it declared universal suffrage (excepting women, of course) and prohibited slavery. It was the first state to do so.

New Hampshire Yankees are much like their cousins to the west, but have the reputation of being somewhat less tolerant than Vermonters, and more frugal and stubborn. The Maine Yankee was historically the most isolated inhabitant of the three northern New England states. In fact, until recently, a form of Elizabethan English was spoken in Washington County's Beals Islands (as well as parts of Appalachia and the Ozarks). Roads connecting Maine to the outside were traditionally poor. "Downeasters," as they have come to be called, had to put up with bad weather and unyielding terrain. This may explain why they're commonly characterized as crusty and quirky; they have a reputation for being down to earth and for saying little beyond what counts.

Rhode Island and Connecticut Yankees are perhaps less distinctive than other old

New Englanders. The original populations of these states were the products of the first emigrations from Massachusetts, and today these states tend to be conservative. Unlike those in Massachusetts, the original Yankees here retained political control long after the waves of 19th- and 20th-century European immigration greatly reduced their proportion of the areas' total populations.

After the Civil War, New Englanders knew their region was in decline and their numbers were fast dwindling. Nevertheless, they continue to think of themselves as the essential representatives of the nation's most cherished values and to this day remain convinced that they symbolize all that is best

Hill. Though poor, it was organized and ambitious. About 2 percent of the population were doctors, ministers, teachers or lawyers. Several fraternal organizations were founded to serve as a safety net for the indigent. The most famous, the African Society, founded in 1796 as a mutual-aid and charity organization, stressed temperance and mirrored Puritan morality. Black-owned shops served as informal community centers, and black churches helped bring the community together. Ministers were looked up to as leaders, and towering above them were figures like anti-slavery activist Jehial C. Bemon.

Although blacks in 19th-century Boston rarely lived outside their own quarter, they

about their country.

African Americans: The first African Americans in New England came to Boston from the West Indies in 1638 as "perpetual servants." Within a century, slavery was well implanted in the region: by 1752, Boston's 5,000 African Americans constituted 10 percent of the population. That percentage declined dramatically during the Revolution, when Tory masters fled the region, removing their entire households. By the end of the 18th century, Massachusetts abolished slavery. Connecticut and Vermont soon followed.

In Boston, a thriving black community congregated on the northern slope of Beacon

did mingle freely. Black and white laborers drank together in North End taverns, and after 1855, when schools were desegregated, children of both races studied together. Black students attended Harvard before the Civil War. Freemen laborers could be found in every New England industry, especially along the coast. Often half of the crews of whaling vessels were African American, and black labor contributed largely to the construction of Providence and New Haven.

As the vanguard of the Abolitionist movement, Massachusetts was unique in allowing blacks to stand for a political party (the Abolitionist Free-Soil Party in 1850) in elections to the state legislature. Their ability to excel was never in question, partly because of the accomplishments of such prominent figures as John Swett Rock, an abolitionist, doctor and lawyer, and Charles Remond, the first black to argue a case before the Supreme Court. Over the past century, Massachusetts has produced an extraordinary number of Civil Rights activists.

Despite such efforts, the decline suffered by the region after the Civil War was particularly devastating to those struggling to subsist as porters, laborers, janitors and household domestics. Even well into the 1950s, few gains were made in improving the lot of this underclass. Although the number of

blacks holding white-collar jobs in Boston nearly doubled between 1950 and 1970, the vast majority remained poor and resolutely working-class. In recent decades, Boston's black community – now representing roughly a quarter of the population – has made considerable strides, but inequities persist.

To this day, Boston retains vivid memories of ugly race riots touched off by a Federal judge's order in 1974 to desegregate schools through busing. Although the situa-

Left, student in a Boston high school lab; a professor at Brandeis University, Boston. **Above**, father and son at a Connecticut apple festival.

tion has calmed down considerably since then, inter-racial strife is still rampant in Boston's more clannish neighborhoods, such as "Southie" (the Irish stronghold of South Boston) and Charlestown. Adding to the tension is fierce competition for jobs in a local economy hit hard by the recession of the early 1990s. However, the era of equal opportunity, a long time in coming, is quickly becoming a reality, as evidenced by such African American role models as newscaster Liz Walker and numerous politicians, including Cambridge mayor Kenneth Reeves.

Connecticut is the only other New England state with a large and long-standing black population. A small number arrived in the Colonial days, and a great many relocated from the South in the 1870s to work on the Connecticut Valley tobacco farms. Like Boston, Connecticut cities have had their share of racial tensions. Busing met with opposition in New Haven and Hartford, and in the summer of 1967 these towns and many others were shaken by riots. Despite enduring obstacles, blacks are at last making inroads in politics and other areas of influence.

Irish power: The potato famine of 1845 killed 1 million people in Ireland in five years, and drove another million to seek better conditions elsewhere. Many came to Massachusetts. No precise figures are available, but one statistic claims that by 1860, 61 percent of Boston's population was foreign-born. Virtually all of these people would have been Irish, the only immigrant group to come in large numbers at that time.

The Irish did not receive a warm welcome either from the entrenched aristocracy or the ordinary citizenry. Not unlike the British oppressors back home, Yankees showed great contempt for Catholicism, and in turn, the Irish had little sympathy for the idealism of the reform-minded Yankees. During the Civil War, Irish in Boston rioted when faced with a draft for the freeing of slaves, a cause in which they had no specific interest.

The Irish community in Massachusetts grew at an extremely rapid rate. Before long, the Irish went into politics, with great success. The first Irish-born mayor of Boston was elected in 1884, and the first Irish governor took office in 1918. Between the world wars, the Irish controlled both Boston and state politics. Economic as well as political clout was assured once Joe Kennedy, the father of the late President John F. Kennedy, penetrated the Yankee stronghold of finance and banking on Boston's State Street.

Middle-class Irish have long been assimilated into the mainstream of Boston and Massachusetts life. Blue-collar Irish are a different story. Especially in South Boston and Charlestown, the Irish have fiercely maintained the separateness both of their communities and of their ethnic identity. To this day, many residents tend to identify more with their neighborhoods than they do with the city as a whole.

In South Boston pubs, Irish Americans sing a song called "Southie Is My Home Town." This "tribalism," as it has been called, erupted in 1974 when "Southie" rioted over busing. The Irish felt that their neighborhoods were gravely threatened, and busing had been forced on them by upper-class Yankees, their traditional enemies.

Eighteen months after busing began, public schools had lost one-third of their white pupils. In 1980, Melvin King, a black who was then state representative, ascribed racial hatred in Boston to the historical relationship between Irish Catholics and "WASPs" (White Anglo-Saxon Protestants): "The Irish still view themselves as a persecuted minority and therefore don't play the positive role in race relations that one would expect from people who experienced bigotry."

French Canadians: French Canadians have been emigrating to New England since the middle of the last century. Although there are more French Canadians in Massachusetts than in any other New England state, their influence is most evident in New Hampshire, where they make up as much as a quarter of the population; and in Maine, where 15 percent of the people are only one or two generations from Canadian birth.

The Canadians came to work in the textile mills, and (in Maine) as lumberjacks. More than any other group in New England, they have clung to their ethnic identity and maintained a remarkable degree of distinctiveness. They are strongly loyal to the Catholic church, and they still consider French their first language, although most children attend English-speaking schools.

French Canadians in Maine live together in close-knit communities, have their own radio station, and frequently visit Quebec. Although French Canadians have been slower than some other groups to move up the social and economic scale, they have a reputation for being hard-working and thrifty, and for keeping to their own.

The Italian and Jewish influx: Italians came to the United States in the first decades of the 20th century, most of them as poor peasants from southern Italy and Sicily. Many of them settled in Massachusetts and Rhode Island. Italians and Irish have traditionally been rivals in Massachusetts, the Italians tending to vote with the Yankee Republicans, the Irish with the Democratic party. Despite the incursions of gentrification, Italians – representing a tenth of the city's population – have managed to preserve a distinctive village

subculture in certain neighborhoods, such as Boston's North End and East Boston.

The Italians are among the wealthiest ethnic groups in the state, having made their money in law, real estate, construction and a variety of other businesses. The success of the Italian community in Rhode Island is reflected in the career of John O. Pastore, the first Italian-American governor, who later went on to the US Senate.

Jewish settlers were among the earliest colonists: a community was established in Newport, Rhode Island, in 1658, with the help of Puritan dissident Roger Williams. The first families, from Holland, were

Sephardics, descendants of exiles expelled from Spain at the end of the 15th century. Nineteen years after arriving in Newport, they organized North America's second congregation (the first was in New York). Free of the restrictions imposed on them in the Old World, they prospered in Newport.

The Newport community began to dissolve around the beginning of the 19th century as members emigrated to other parts of the country. For 100 years, there was little Jewish presence in New England, mainly because of the intolerance and rigidity of the Protestant Yankee establishment. But by the end of the century, Boston had become a much more ethnically and religiously di-

Louis Brandeis, was the first non-sectarian university sponsored by Jews in the West.

Other late arrivals: New England boasts pockets of small ethnic groups which contribute greatly to the region's diversity. Among the more unusual are the Arabic-speaking Syrian-Lebanese of Rhode Island, Christians who fled the religious persecution by the Turks at the beginning of the 20th century. Portuguese communities exist along the coast, in such fishing ports as New Bedford and Provincetown. These Portuguese arrived in the middle of the 19th century from the Azores, as whaling hands picked up by American ships which stopped at their islands. When whaling foundered, they shift-

verse place, and so Jews from Eastern Europe began to settle there in large numbers.

By 1910, 42,000 East Europeans, mostly Jewish, lived in the Boston area. Ten years later 10 percent of Boston's population was Jewish. Jews have made their mark in Boston, notably in education. In 1948, Brandeis University was established in Waltham, near Boston, thanks largely to the efforts of the Jewish business community. Brandeis, named for former Supreme Court Justice

Left, demolishing a watermelon. **Above**, on board the coastguard *Eagle* at New London, Connecticut; the crafts tradition – caning a chair.

ed to fishing and into the textile mills.

The 1988 presidential campaign of second-generation Greek Michael Dukakis, though unsuccessful, is just one example of New England's growing acceptance of "outsiders." In the 1990s, among the newcomers making appreciable inroads in New England are large numbers of Hispanic and Asian immigrants; in Boston, these groups represent 11 and 5 percent of the population.

The transition may not always be easy, but the presence of these groups signals how a region once widely regarded as inflexible and stodgy has been enriched by an ever-expanding ethnic diversity.

THE PURITAN TRADITION

The Puritans did more than settle New England; they created it. Out of the Calvinistic doctrines regarding humanity's inherent evil and the predestination of the soul grew a society that was stern and uncompromising. At its best, the Puritans' was a hard creed, an ultimate faith that required everyone – from the most prominent minister to the humblest child – to strain toward an ineffable God. Puritans argued that humans, in their fallen state, could never know God and could thus never truly know the state of their own souls. Salvation came not through human action, but through God's mysterious grace. Abject though we human creatures may be, we must always examine our conscience, always repent our inevitable sin, always attempt to lead a just life.

Spiritual values: The Puritans' difficult faith stood them in good stead: regarding discipline and hard work as spiritual values, these early settlers labored long for the greater glory of God – and incidentally accumulated wealth and built prosperous communities. At their worst, the Puritans came to identify worldly success with godliness, nonconformity with devil-worship. Their faith found little room for gentleness or pleasure.

The many world-class schools and colleges found in New England stand as tangible reminders of that legacy. Education was essential to the Puritans' vision of what their new society in America was to be. Most of the settlers were well educated; four officers of the Massachusetts Bay Colony – John Winthrop, Sir Richard Saltonstall, Isaac Johnson and John Humphrey – had attended Cambridge University. For them, the journey to the New World was more than an adventure to a new frontier; it was a chance to transport their old society in purified form to a new land. Discontented in a country where they were persecuted for their religious practices, they came to America to build an ideal society, their "city on a hill." These men knew that unless they provided for the education and training of clergymen,

they might quickly lose sight of the New (and perfect) England.

In America, as in England, class distinctions were important. But the Puritans, eschewing such worldly signs of status as expensive clothes and fancy carriages, had to devise other more subtle ways of indicating social class. Thus, the title "Master" was reserved exclusively for educated men.

A society in which education established one's credentials before God and the world was destined to develop an impressive school

system. As early as 1635, Boston voted a declaration that "our brother, Mr Philemon Pormont shall be intreated to become scholemaster for teaching and noutering of children with us." He established Boston Latin School, the country's first secondary school and still one of Boston's finest high schools. In 1642, the General Court of the Bay Colony required every town to see to the education of its youth. By 1671, all colonies but Rhode Island, ever the renegade, had instituted compulsory education.

Higher education: Still, the settlers had yet to provide their colony with an institution of higher learning. In 1636, the Bay Colony's

Left, guns and God – early settlers on their way to worship. **Right**, John Winthrop, the Cambridge-educated Puritan leader.

General Court voted £40 toward a public "school or college." What was then the village of Newtowne, across the Charles River from Boston, was chosen as the site for the institution, which opened that same year as Newtowne College. In 1638, a newly arrived young Charlestown minister named John Harvard, a graduate of Emmanuel College at Cambridge, died and left his 400-volume library and half of his estate to the college. In 1638 it was renamed Harvard in his honor, and Newtowne was renamed Cambridge to signify the community's new role.

For the rest of the 17th century, the college served primarily as a training ground for the Puritan clergy. At the outset of the 18th

1804, upon its relocation from Warren to Providence. Reverend Eleazar Wheelock founded Dartmouth College in 1769 "for the education of Youth of the Indian Tribes" as well as for "English Youth and Others."

In 1778, Samuel Phillips and his uncle, Dr John Phillips, complaining of "a growing neglect of youth in our time," founded the Phillips Academy at Andover, Massachusetts. Several years later, Dr Phillips established a similar school, the Phillips Exeter Academy in Exeter, New Hampshire. Exeter's charter illuminates the Puritan mind: the school's purpose was "to promote piety and virtue" in its students and "to learn them the great and real business of living."

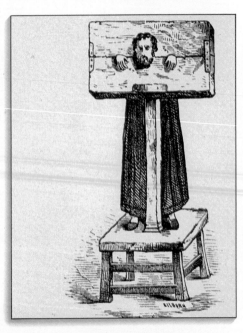

century, however, Harvard, feeling the effects of Enlightenment, liberalized its curriculum and added the teachings of Locke and Newton. Decrying the change in their alma mater's educational philosophy, James Pierpont and several other Harvard graduates – all Congregational ministers – founded the Collegiate School in Saybrook, Connecticut, in 1701. The school was renamed Yale College in honor of its benefactor, Elihu Yale, when it moved to New Haven in 1716.

Nicholas Brown, who made his fortune in the molasses, rum and slave trade, founded Rhode Island College as a Baptist school in 1764; it was renamed Brown University in

Proselytizing through persecution: A far less benign expression of Puritan didacticism emerged in the Salem witch trials of 1692. Since its founding in 1626, the town (whose name derives, ironically, from *shalom*, the Hebrew word for peace) had never been a bastion of tolerance and goodwill: it was from Salem that Roger Williams, the founder of Rhode Island, had been exiled for preaching religious freedom.

The townspeople's rigid ways took a destructive turn when Tituba, a Barbados slave serving the household of Salem's minister, Samuel Parris, began regaling his daughter, Elizabeth, and niece, Abigail Williams, with vivid accounts of voodoo. Fascinated, Elizabeth and Abigail invited a handful of their friends to listen to Tituba's tales. Meetings of such a nature, being strictly forbidden in Puritan Salem, held an illicit appeal that the girls must have found difficult to resist, but no doubt they also found their guilty pleasure difficult to live with, for all soon began to exhibit bizarre behavior: they would crawl on the floor, making choking sounds, and cry out that needles were piercing their flesh. The town doctor was called in to examine the girls and, after medicine failed to cure them, he diagnosed them as victims of witchcraft.

The Rev. Mr Parris suggested that Tituba might be their tormentor, and the slave was with everything from bewitching cattle to using voodoo dolls. Enflamed by the oratory of such self-promoting preachers as Cotton Mather, subsequent accusations spread like wildfire. Ultimately, 400 people ended up accused – many of them marginal members of society, whose lack of prosperity the Puritans took to mean a lack of godliness.

Imprisoned in cold, damp cells, several of the accused women died while awaiting trial. Of those found guilty in Salem, 19 were hanged between June and September, and many more might have been sacrificed had Governor General Sir William Phips not returned from the north woods, where he had been fighting an alliance of French and Na-

charged with witchcraft. In confessing, under pain of torture, she gave a lurid account of how a tall man from Boston, accompanied by witches, had molested the girls. Satan himself, she claimed, had ordered her to murder the girls, and other witches had beaten her for her refusal to comply; she merely tormented them, trying to abate her own pain. In her stories, she pointed a finger at two women unpopular in the village, Sarah Osborne and Sarah Good, who were charged

Far left, a pillory. **Left**, the trial of Mrs Hutchinson in Salem's era of Puritan hysteria. **Above**, the trial of George Jacobs, accused of witchcraft.

tive Americans, and put a stop to the madness. In December 1692, he ordered all the suspects released – including his own wife.

Always ready to discover depravity in someone else, the Puritans sat in eager judgment on the accused. Unrelenting in their desire to purge their world of evil and in their arrogant belief in their own righteousness, they sent innocents to their death. Too late, the Salemites repented of their actions: in 1693, the Salem jurors wrote that they humbly begged the forgiveness of everyone who had been harmed by their actions.

A transcendentalist manqué: The gradual liberalization of New England's colleges in the 18th century gave way to a true intellectual flowering in the 19th. Flushed with the success of the Revolutionary War and the founding of the nation, growing prosperous from the lucrative China trade, the Puritan temperament was ready for a transformation. Casting off the dour, joyless outlook of their Puritan forebears, New England's intelligentsia readily embraced the sweet optimism of transcendentalism, a mystical philosophy which argued the existence of an Oversoul unifying all creation, and which preached the primacy of insight over reason and the inherent goodness of humankind.

The movement spawned several experiments in living, the best known being Henry witchcraft trials, was cursed by a woman he convicted. Hawthorne would later use this story in *The House of the Seven Gables*. In fact, much of Hawthorne's work was drawn from real life. In the 1836 tale, *The Minister's Black Veil*, the protagonist explains: "If I hide my face for sorrow, there is cause enough, and if I cover it for secret sin, what mortal might not do the same." Hawthorne was no doubt familiar with the story of the Rev. Joseph Moody of York, Maine, who, after accidentally shooting and killing a friend while on a hunting trip, became morbidly frightened of having his friend's family and fiancée look upon him, and therefore covered his face with a black handkerchief.

David Thoreau's solitary retreat on Walden Pond and short-lived communal farms at Brook Farm in Concord and Fruitlands in Harvard. Led by Ralph Waldo Emerson, the transcendentalist movement attracted some of the brightest minds of the day – including, for a short while, Nathaniel Hawthorne, one of the founding members of Brook Farm. His disillusionment with this experiment reinforced his essentially somber cast of mind, however. Far from being sweetly optimistic, his writing broods on human sin.

The descendant of Salem Puritans, Hawthorne grew up with a family legend of a Judge Hawthorne who, as a magistrate at the *Young Goodman Brown*, one of Hawthorne's greatest tales, also draws on his Salem heritage. In what may be a dream, Brown, wandering in the dark forest, comes upon the devil, who leads him to a clearing where villagers are engaged in devil-worship; among the congregation is Faith, Goodman's wife. In this tale, Hawthorne depicts a world sunk in evil: if Goodman Brown's vision is true, the devil rules; if not and if Goodman has imagined innocent people in Satan's service, he reveals, like the Salem Puritans, the depth of his own corruption.

Cradle of reformation: As if to live down the small-mindedness of their predecessors, the

New England philosophers and legislators of the 19th century stood in the very vanguard of political reform. Having abolished slavery themselves by the end of the 18th century, high-minded New Englanders dedicated themselves to nationwide abolition. William Lloyd Garrison founded his weekly newspaper *The Liberator* in Boston in 1831 (not all shared his views at that time: he was nearly killed by a Boston mob in 1835) and persisted until 1865, when the 13th amendment was finally passed. Joining him in the struggle were writers like Harriet Beecher Stowe, who delivered one of the Abolitionist movement's most effective tracts in the form of her best-selling 1852 novel, *Uncle Tom's*

tain change – reinforced by decades of stability and prosperity – remnants of the Puritan strain persisted. For the most part, New England remained a deeply moral, and occasionally moralistic, society. At their worst, New Englanders banned books they deemed offensive to public taste (a practice their descendants now deplore among less enlightened, Fundamentalist backwaters). They considered theater – and worse yet, actors – a pernicious influence on impressionable minds. Blue laws, first introduced in Connecticut in 1781 to control public and private conduct, especially on the Sabbath, enjoyed regular revivals in the 19th and 20th centuries and linger to this day in very watered-

Cabin. After the Civil War, New England's reformists turned their attention to the labor abuses brought on by the Industrial Revolution and to the role of women in society. The first women's college to open in the US was Vassar Female College, founded in Poughkeepsie, New York, in 1861. By 1879, four outstanding colleges for women had been established in Massachusetts: Smith, Wellesley, Holyoke, and Radcliffe.

Despite this growing willingness to enter-

down form; in Massachusetts, for instance, on Sundays liquor stores are closed and would-be imbibers must wait till noon to be served at a bar.

It seems a small inconvenience to pay homage to the settlers who, with admirable fortitude if little sense of fun, established so firm a foundation for the New World. And just as the Puritans struggled mightily to maintain a spiritual purity, New Englanders today are in the forefront of the drive to preserve some degree of ecological integrity. The Puritans' conservative zeal lives on – in what has become, ironically enough, one of the country's most progressive regions.

Left, Ralph Waldo Emerson and Nathaniel Hawthorne. **Above**, a typical re-enactment at Plymouth today of a Pilgrim Thanksgiving.

The Pilgrims would not have known what to make of our modern mania for lobster. The colonists considered the crustaceans fit only for pig food, or bait; well into the late 19th century, boatloads sold for pennies, and prisoners rioted at the prospect of yet another lobster dinner. New England's lobster harvest is now a $150 million-a-year enterprise.

The settlers weren't quite so blind to the appeal of oysters. As early as 1601, Samuel de Champlain had singled out the area now known as Wellfleet, on Cape Cod, for its

a somewhat messy proposition, they're dipped first in brine (to wash off the grit), then melted butter.

Clambakes were once a New England tradition, especially on Cape Cod. The customary procedure was to lay out a stone pit on the beach, build a driftwood fire, cover the hot stones with seaweed and then the clams and their accompaniments (typically, lobsters, potatoes, corn on the cob), and top it all off with more seaweed, a sailcloth tarp, and plenty of sand, leaving the whole to bake

exceptional beds; he named the harbor "*Porte aux huitres.*" To this day, tiny Wellfleet, as well as the Cape town of Cotuit, is world-renowned for its home-grown delicacies.

New England's fabled clam chowder got its name from the French settlers of Breton in Canada, who simmered their soups in a *chaudière* (cauldron). Such long, slow cooking is needed to render large hard-shell quahogs (pronounced "*co*-hogs") palatable. The small and medium-size versions – cherrystones and littlenecks – are delectable served raw, on the half-shell. Soft-shell, longneck clams – commonly known as "steamers" – are also a favored repast all along the coast:

for about an hour. Most restaurants these days dispense with the clambake *per se*, and just serve what's called a "shore dinner" – all of the above, steamed.

But it was the abundant cod that initially lured English fishermen, and eventually settlers, to this land, and filet of young cod, called scrod (from the Dutch *schrood*, for "a piece cut off"), still graces traditional menus.

Exposure to European traditions has introduced two relatively "new" seafood treats. Mussels, long ignored by New England restaurants, are now very nearly ubiquitous, usually served marinière or poached in white wine. Seasonal bay scallops have always enjoyed greater gourmet cachet than the larger, tougher sea scallop, but until recently, restaurants invariably threw away the tastiest part, serving only the adductor muscle. Thanks to the efforts of scallop cultivator Rod Taylor of Fairhaven, Massachusetts, bay scallops are now available year-round, and the more adventurous fine restaurants have begun serving them whole, whether on the half-shell or cooked.

Another specialty is available only a few weeks out of the year, and enthusiasts await late spring to feast on shad roe, harvested in the Connecticut River. As comic poet Ogden Nash once wrote, "I'm sure Europe never had / A fish as tasty as the shad."

Unlikely elixirs: Cranberries – so named by Dutch settlers who thought the bushes' flowers resembled cranes – are one of the few fruits native to North America (among the others are Concord grapes and blueberries, a major cash crop in Maine). Native Americans used the sassamanesh – "bitter berries" – as a dye, a poultice, and as food, pounded with venison to make "pemmican" (preserved meat cakes) or sweetened with maple sap. Long before the need for Vitamin C was recognized, whalers would set off to sea with a barrel of cranberries to prevent scurvy.

New Englanders have also continued the Indian practice of boiling maple sap into syrup, and Vermont is America's leading producer of maple syrup. The trees of the "sugarbush" are tapped in early spring, when just the right combination of cold nights and warm days sets the thin sap rising. However modern the equipment, it still takes 40 gallons of sap to boil down to just one of syrup, and during the process, visitors are welcome at dozens of commercial sugarhouses throughout the state. Some may even be treated to "sugar on snow" – on contact, the boiling syrup cools into a sweet, chewy mass.

With no access to safe drinking water, the Pilgrims – adults and children alike – had no choice but to drink beer (the alcohol content kept the microbes in check). Today they could travel around New England and never

wander far from a micro-brewery. It's even possible to find good locally produced wine: New England's notoriously rocky soil is at long last proving good for something. Many vineyards are still in the fledgling stage, but at least three have a proven track record: Stonington Vineyards in Stonington, Connecticut; Sakonnet Vineyards in Little Compton, Rhode Island; and Chicama Vineyards on Martha's Vineyard in Massachusetts.

Sundry delights: Where once the settlers scratched at the soil for subsistence, a new

wave of "back-to-landers" has created a trendy land of plenty, raising deer for venison, goats for farmstead chevre, trout and salmon for smoking. In Connecticut, actor Paul Newman has claimed a third of the $3.3 billion salad dressing market with Newman's Own, profits from which go to charity. In Vermont, some 300 specialty food producers whip up everything from "Putney pasta" to salsa from Stowe; the entrepreneurs behind Ben & Jerry's ice cream empire, based in Waterbury, parlayed a $5 correspondence school diploma into a business grossing $500 million a year. Clearly, the region's potential has yet to be exhausted.

Left, what the Pilgrims ate at Plimouth Plantation. **Right**, fine dining in 19th-century Boston.

The little ship had been at sea for two months. It was November, 1620, in the North Atlantic, not a kind season for a vessel barely bigger than a pleasure yacht. The passengers and crew, more than 100 people, had squeezed into this one ship after its sister ship had proven unseaworthy. They were headed for the tiny English colonies in America.

At last, the call came: "Land ho!" The weary passengers who crowded the railings could barely make out the tops of several small islands on the horizon. As the ship drew closer, they discovered that the "islands" were actually hills arising above a long bar of sand. Weary from the months at sea and eager to set foot in the New World, the Pilgrims disembarked at the tip of Cape Cod to rest and reconnoiter. After five weeks on land, they set sail again for Virginia. But, battered by storms that seemed endless, the tiny but sturdy barque *Mayflower* was driven across Cape Cod Bay and into the mainland at a place the Pilgrims named Plymouth.

A path to the New World: The sea had allowed these early New Englanders to escape the spiritual confines of the old country. It had brought them to the New World. But it had not given them any choice about their landing place. Down through the centuries, the sea has written the history of New England and determined its people's destiny.

The sea could move people speedily between continents – or condemn them to a watery grave. It has toppled granite buildings, even torn away the land itself, and it has made men fabulously wealthy overnight. A rich merchant, pillar of his community, might come into his warehouse on Boston's Long Wharf one morning only to find that his entire fleet and all its cargo had been swept away and lost forever, and that he was no better than a beggar. Or a lonesome beachcomber slowly tracing the sinuous miles of Cape Cod's sandy shores might come upon 100 gold doubloons washed up only minutes before by a whim of the sea.

New Englanders have had no choice but to learn the sea's strict laws and abide by them. The sea brought them here, the sea nourished them and, if it did not destroy them, the sea even made them rich. Only one of the six

New England states (Vermont) has no maritime coast. For the rest, the outlet to the sea is a source of continuing prosperity.

The first generation of Europeans in America all had the same "baptism by sea:" a two-month voyage across the stormy North Atlantic. Most of the settlers who came were landlubbers; many had never seen the ocean before. Shipbuilding was one of the first enterprises the early colonists undertook. Ships maintained the connection to the homeland and provided an income from trade. The

vast virgin forests of the New World supplied ready-at-hand materials for their construction. One hundred years after the Pilgrims stepped on Plymouth Rock, New England's coastal shipyards were launching a ship a day. With labor and lumber costs so cheap compared to those in England, American-made ships dominated the market.

For the early colonists, the sea brought news from home, fresh legions of colonists to do battle with the wilderness and ships involved in the Triangular Trade (the transport of slaves, molasses and rum between ports in Africa, the Caribbean, and New England). The vast virgin forests of colonial

Maine seemed an inexhaustible storehouse of straight, lofty white pines for the masts of the Royal Navy. The fishing grounds along the coasts teemed with marine wealth.

One of the first important acts of the Great and General Court of Massachusetts was to set standards for the regulation and encouragement of the fishing industry. Early on, fishing was seen as a prime source of the region's prosperity. In fact, many settlers came not so much to enjoy religious freedom as to catch fish. Codfish, high in protein,

The whaling boom: The lamps of colonial New England were fired by vegetable and animal oils; candles were made from animal tallow. The light was dim and the lamps were smoky until someone made a fortuitous discovery: the blubber from a beached whale could be rendered, and the oil thus extracted would provide a clearer, brighter light.

Whales beached themselves frequently on the New England shores during the early colonial days, and whaling got its start as a shore activity. Teams of townsfolk gathered

iodine and Vitamin A, nourished and strengthened not just the New England colonists, but those in Mid-Atlantic and Southern towns and even in many ports of Europe. As the basis of New England's livelihood, the "Sacred Cod" – a wooden effigy presented to the legislature by a Boston merchant in 1784 – was enshrined in the Massachusetts Colony House, and now hangs in the House of Representatives' gallery at the State House on Beacon Hill.

Preceding pages: tall ships off Newport, Rhode Island. **Left**, the Port of Boston in 1768. **Above**, a 19th-century lobsterman.

whenever they saw a whale, tethering the creature to a stake to prevent the tide from taking it out to sea. The blubber was cut away, rendered in the kettles of a "tryworks" set up on the beach and transformed into a high-quality oil which could be burned in the town's lamps or traded for other goods.

The demand for this excellent oil became so great that fishermen, hoping to get rich from the sale of oil, began actively to pursue whales along the shore, thus initiating New England's famous whaling industry. The trade took a great leap forward in 1712, when Captain Chrisopher Hussey of Nantucket was blown off course into deep water and accidentally bagged the first sperm whale. Although it had teeth in lieu of coveted baleen – bony upper jaw slats useful as stays for collars and corsets – the spermaceti oil proved far superior to that of the already endangered "right" whale (so called because it was the right one to pursue). Nantucket whalers came to specialize in the pursuit of this purer, lighter and more profitable oil.

Whalers out of Nantucket and New Bedford pursued their mammoth quarry for months, even years, as far as the Pacific, until their holds were completely filled with barrels of the oil that would fire the nation's lamps and illumine the capitals of Europe. The whaling ships served as complete whaler, the *Charles W. Morgan*, tied up at Mystic Seaport in Connecticut, or take a turn through the whaling museums in Nantucket or New Bedford.

Watery highways and coastal connections: The sea formed the path from England to America, and served as the road system from one point in America to the next. In colonial times, roads were expensive to build and maintain, and the colonies did not have the resources to establish a good system of roads. Nor did they have the need. Coastal freighters and passenger boats carried colonists and their wares from Boston to New York and Philadelphia. Every young American knows the story of Master Benjamin Franklin, a loaf

processing plants. Once a whale was sighted, men pursued it in small dories, harpooned it and then braced themselves for the "Nantucket sleighride" which followed. The hapless whale would drag the men in the dory many miles before exhausting itself. Tied up alongside the whaling ship, the whale carcass was stripped of blubber. Rendered in a tryworks right on deck, the oil was then stored in casks in the hold.

Until 1859, when petroleum-derived kerosene was discovered in Pennsylvania, the sea was the world's great proven oil reserve. For a closer look at this fascinating chapter in maritime history, visit the last surviving of bread under each arm, arriving from Boston on the docks in Philadelphia, where he would make his fortune.

Dozens of boats out of Salem harbor headed for home with decks full of salt cod. But the enterprising captains headed south, where they unloaded their cod at Philadelphia or Annapolis and took on corn and flour, beans and barrels of pork, which could be sold at a greater profit in the home port than could codfish. New England never produced such

<u>Above</u>, New England's twin traditions of sea and land are captured by a mural painter at an ice cream shop in Mystic, Connecticut.

goods in sufficient quantities. Cod it had in great abundance.

Though a boon to New England's maritime economy, the coastal trade, like fishing and whaling, was not an easy way to make a living. Every trip between Boston and ports to the south involved a voyage around Cape Cod, and the weather which had so discouraged the Pilgrims was a constant threat. Ships and men were regularly lost to the ravages of the sea.

Though fishing and the coastal trade helped New England employ its people and pay its bills, the region was not a rich one. Because New England always imported more goods than it exported, ways had to be found to balance the trade deficit. New endeavors were always welcomed, and Yankee ingenuity was always coming up with new ideas.

Merchants and sea captains from New England towns saw themselves as the world's transport agents: if they couldn't produce the goods from their rocky soil and primitive industries, they reasoned, at least they could carry across the oceans the goods produced by others. Like the whalers that roamed the world for years in search of their fortune, New England merchant vessels undertook long and arduous voyages to Europe, Africa and the Orient. And not just the cargoes were put up for sale: the ships themselves were frequently on the auctioning block, bringing added revenue to their builders back home in New England.

Trade was good to New England. While the pioneer towns of inland America were primitive and rough, New England seaports took on the polish of wealth and culture. Fortunes made at sea were translated into fine mansions and patronage of the arts. From the profits of their voyages, captains brought home art treasures, luxury goods and curiosities from China, Zanzibar, Indonesia and the Turkish empire. The Peabody Museum of Salem is filled with the incredible wealth that came to New England on returning merchant ships.

Clocks, shoes and ice: As time went by, the new republic developed industries that produced goods for trade. Connecticut's household utensils, machines, clocks, pistols and rifles, plus shoes and cloth from Rhode Island and Massachusetts, ultimately made their way around the world.

Perhaps the most ingenious export of all was ice. Cut from freshwater ponds, rivers and lakes, ice was packed in sawdust, loaded into fast clipper ships and sent off to Cuba, South America and beyond. The rulers of the British Raj in India sipped drinks cooled by ice from New England ponds. In exchange for a commodity that was free for the cutting, New Englanders brought back spices, fine porcelain, silks and other items.

The volume of New England's trade soon fell behind that of the Southern ports on the coasts of the Atlantic and the Gulf of Mexico. But trade continued to be important in maintaining the region's economy and its cosmopolitan outlook.

The taming of the sea: The end of the 19th century saw profound changes in the way New Englanders put to sea. The speedy sloops, or clipper ships, with small holds, were economical only for high-profit items (such as ice). For a while, the profits shifted to larger, heavier craft such as the great schooners with four, five and even six masts. But the magnificent six-masted schooners that could carry huge payloads of coal went nowhere when the wind died, and the newfangled steamships went anywhere on schedule. Steamships could sail around Cape Cod, ignoring the winds that had caused so much trouble since the time of the Pilgrims.

With the coming of steam came the railroads, and maritime trade went through another great change when the Atlantic and Pacific coasts were finally connected by steel rails. Where once the ships had sailed all the way around South America to reach California, rail transport steamed West in a straight line, undaunted by storms.

Yet transport by sea, for both goods and passengers, hung on in New England well into the 20th century. What finally laid it to rest was not the railroad but the highway – the truck and the automobile.

Safer waves: Today, the sea is still a major source of income for the people of New England – and at a much lower price in lives lost to storms. Although yachts, motorboats and fishing fleets fill the harbors, disasters at sea are a relative rarity. A century ago whole families, even most of a town, might be lost to a single ferocious storm. There are still tragedies at sea – oil tankers breached, pleasure craft wrecked, swimmers drowned – but the sea has been tamed as much as one can reasonably expect. Radio beacons and radar pierce the fog, and stricter safety precautions help prevent many accidents.

The taming of the sea has allowed New Englanders to put it to other uses. Dependable passenger service by steamship opened up the coasts to vacation travelers in the early part of this century. Newport, Block Island and Bar Harbor turned into flourishing resorts as soon as they became accessible swiftly, comfortably and safely by sea.

These newer settlements are not the only ones to have benefited from the taming of the sea. The whalers and clipper ships may be gone, but for a few rare survivors. However, the beautiful port towns built by the wealth of maritime commerce survive. Tourists

In fact, New England's seacoast has become a major playground, and the variety of maritime sports seems limitless. As in so many other realms, the world of work has become the world of play, and occupations once perilous or tedious are now pursued just for fun. One hundred years ago "wreckers" used to trudge the beaches of New England with a keen eye for the remains of lost ships.

Today, the beaches serve a distinctly different purpose. Forty miles (64 km) of Cape Cod's sandy beaches have been set aside as the Cape Cod National Seashore, one of the great tourist attractions of New England. The beaches of Connecticut, Rhode Island, New Hampshire and Maine continue to at-

come in droves to stroll among the handsome sea captains' houses of Nantucket, Edgartown, Salem and Newport. Having seen the houses, they explore in museums the world of the seafaring men who built them.

A salty playground: In other times, a New Englander either went to sea or remained a landlubber. Now every New Englander is part mariner, taking a motorboat or yacht out for a Sunday cruise or climbing aboard a launch for a tour of Boston Harbor. There is a direct service by sea between Boston and Provincetown each summer, and Nantucket, Martha's Vineyard, Block Island and other islands are all served by ship.

tract visitors from near and far.

The whalers that sailed out of New Bedford and Nantucket are long gone. Or are they? Boats from a dozen New England ports still head out each day in search of whales, but now it's the camera lens and not the harpoon which "captures" the whale for good. Whale-watching cruises are among the most popular summer activities at sea. It's ironic, and heartening, that the leviathans that once made New England "oil-rich" should still be helping its economy.

Seafood feasts: Fishing, both commercial and amateur, is booming. Conservation and regulation maintain New England's fishing grounds and guarantee supplies for the table. The gathering of clams, mussels, oysters, scallops and lobsters is closely monitored by each town and state so that future generations may enjoy the bounty of New England's waters. Many a full-time lawyer, tailor, teacher or administrator is a part-time lobsterman or clamdigger. A heap of clamshells outside a restaurant is an echo, over the centuries, of similar heaps stacked outside Indian dwellings.

Perhaps the clearest indication of the taming of the sea is this: the perilous voyage undertaken by the Pilgrims in 1620 is now done for sport. Transatlantic yacht racing began over a century ago when the *Henrietta*

raced the *Vesta* to England in 1866. In 1851, the schooner *America* won the Royal Yacht Squadron Cup, and the America's Cup became the great event of yachting with the first race held in Newport in 1870. The beauty and science of yacht design and racing is pursued passionately in Newport and in dozens of other ports along the coast.

New England's waters are particularly suited to the sport: Long Island, off the coast of Connecticut, protects spacious Long Is-

Left, contenders in the "Whatever Race" on the Kennebec River, Maine. <u>Above</u>, a more seaworthy vessel is launched from Maine's Bath Iron Works.

land Sound; and Cape Cod Bay has provided calm sailing ever since the days of the Pilgrims. With the cutting of the Cape Cod Canal and the establishment of the Intracoastal Waterway, coastal cruising has been made safer and more enjoyable than ever before. No more is it necessary to brave the storms off Cape Cod to travel between New York and Boston.

The highpoint of coastal cruising in New England is undoubtedly the rocky shore of Maine. The jagged coast, cut with bays, inlets, coves, peninsulas and islands, is some 3,500 miles (5,600 km) long, and blessed with exceptional beauty. One of the most thrilling ways to see it is aboard a windjammer out of Rockport or Camden. Since 1935, these sturdy sailing ships have taken amateur crews out into the cold waters to experience New England's maritime heritage firsthand.

New England's relationship with the sea is changing. The codfish has yielded to the computer as the most important element in New England's economic life; the schooner and whaler have yielded to the yacht and, more recently, sailboard. Over the years ahead New Englanders will no doubt discover new ways to enjoy and profit from the sea.

Facing the future: Scientists say we have barely begun to tap the wealth of the sea, and that the potential is enormous. To explore that potential, New England has its own world-class research facilities at Woods Hole, Massachusetts, just south of the old town of Falmouth. Woods Hole attracts tens of thousands of tourists each summer, most of them merely passing through to board the ferryboats to Martha's Vineyard. However, a knowledgeable few come specifically to see what's new at the National Marine Fisheries Service, established here in 1871; at the Marine Biological Laboratory, founded in 1888; or the Woods Hole Oceanographic Institute, begun with a $2.5 million Rockefeller grant in 1930.

Whatever shape the future may take, New England will observe it against a backdrop of water. News may now arrive by satellite, not by barque, and whale-oil lamps are rarer than the whales themselves. Still, New England depends upon the sea as much as ever. For native New Englanders, what began as a stormy love affair is now a marriage. Like all good marriages, this one is based on closeness, dependence, affection and respect.

Shingles and clapboards, gables and steeples – an array of traditional architectural images forms in the mind's eye at the mention of New England. Buildings capture the essence of New England's character; they sum up what was at once noble and humble about the ambitions of the region's settlers. And the charm of the old houses and churches is not lost on today's New Englanders, whose tireless efforts have succeeded in preserving much of the architectural traditions of the previous centuries.

A visitor might stand in wonder at the palatial splendor of The Breakers at Newport, but nowhere in that building can the true character of the region be found. That mansion symbolizes a departure from the honesty and utility that inspired the first 200 years of New England building. The work of those years, from the mid-17th to mid-19th centuries, holds the secret to New England's appeal and charm. Styles changed over that period, but these changes refined rather than departed from existing tradition.

To learn New England, read its buildings, for they tell tales rich in wisdom about the lives of their builders and inhabitants. Always aware of its heroic past, New England has wisely held on to enough of its architectural heritage to sketch a vivid picture of a distinguished history. Studying its buildings will not only stimulate the mind and seize the imagination; it will delight the eye as well.

Purity and practicality: Beauty is not the strong point of New England homes of the 17th century, although their simplicity can be attractive. The heavy, medieval feel of early Yankee houses caused one writer to note as early as 1848 that "happily… they will not much longer remain to annoy travelers" in New England. Fortunately, her prediction did not come to pass, for enough 17th-century structures have been preserved throughout to tell much – in however basic a vocabulary – about their beginnings.

The stark simplicity of the earliest houses,

those built by the first several generations of settlers, is a testament to the unaffected motivations of the people. Stylistic vestiges of English country homes governed housing design and construction, but none of these was applied solely for decorative effect. On the contrary, there is virtually no indulgence whatsoever in ornament in Massachusetts houses such as the 1640 Whipple House in Ipswich or the ca. 1641 Wing Fort House in East Sandwich. After all, when one was living for the glory of God and laboring for

the good of the community, there was little room for excess.

The Whipple and Wing Fort houses and the handful like them were in fact nothing more than offspring of the homes the Pilgrims left behind in southeastern England. Simple oblong boxes, they were framed painstakingly and filled with the wattle-and-daub left visible on the half-timbered country homes of England. Clapboards, which provided an extra blanket of protection against the New England winters, created a stern, dark appearance that was relieved only by small, randomly placed windows. The steep roof and the massive central chimney, shared by the two lower and two upper rooms, crowned the house with an air of authority.

In the very early homes, the second floor extended slightly beyond the first, creating an overhang that served no purpose but to make construction more difficult. The 1683 Capen House in Topsfield, Massachusetts, offers a marvelous example of this device. The overhang, recalling English townhouses where the first floor stepped back in deference to the street, was among those features which were dropped as housing designs began to accommodate expansion and reflect the colonists' growing sense of security. Those peering, diamond-paned windows were replaced by a double-hung variety that

their message, depending on the place and time. Along the coast, where maritime trading and fishing were making their mark on the landscape, money and the exposure to new styles from abroad combined to produce splendid mansions. Inland, where farmers and craftsmen produced almost anything that the increasingly far-flung marketplace would absorb, the changes in building style were more subtle and slower to peak.

The inspiration for the new Georgian style of architecture, as the pre-Revolutionary period of 18th-century design is known, stemmed from misfortune back in England. London burned in 1666, and out of the ashes rose buildings in a new style, tributes to the

substantially brightened the facade as well as the interior. Roofs were extended, which provided more room on the first floor, and the resulting style was dubbed "salt box."

Coming of age: With a growing sense of confidence, the colonists began adding some flourishes to their humble homes. At the turn of the century, commerce was growing beyond the borders of the towns, and with expanding horizons came a more excited, adventurous spirit among the people and a weakening of the strict principles of religion that had dampened individual expression.

Economic change was gradual, and the architectural symbols of this change vary in

ideas of the 16th-century Italian architect Andrea Palladio. Palladio's work recalled the classical architecture of antiquity and restated it in a refreshing, heroic way.

Inigo Jones and, later, Christopher Wren championed this Renaissance spirit in London, and their works inspired generations of English architects. In the United States, Palladian ideas spread through the publication of Palladio's *Four Books of Architecture* as well as scores of other imported design handbooks. With these guides in hand, the first tentative but unmistakable steps were taken toward the establishment of a conscious aesthetic in this country. Not insignificantly, a style was born that is as often termed Colonial as it is Georgian, and the modern American landscape certainly attests to its staying power.

Symmetry, a sense of strength and a quality of ease characterize the Georgian style. The Georgian house was a simple two-story rectangle, but classical elements gave it definition: scrolled, often broken pediments capped doorways and windows; fluted attached columns marked the entrances of houses; and, in the grander examples, bulging cornerstones bracketed the corners of the structures from the eaves to the foundations. Many of these same Georgian touches were built out of granite or sandstone in Europe,

and richness outside and leaving room for a hallway in the place where the chimney had formerly stood.

Georgian charm: Examples of Georgian buildings abound in New England. In Deerfield, Massachusetts, stand several charming examples of early renderings of Georgian ideas. At the north end of a marvelous mile of 18th-century historical structures stand the 1733 Ashley House and the 1743 Hawks House. There is something about the precision of the barest Georgian proportion and detail exhibited in these buildings that exudes calm and assurance. At the same time, their dark, unpainted clapboards suggest a ruggedness absent in later painted facades.

and the simulation in wood was carried off with precision by the skilled carpenters of New England.

The plan of the Georgian home expanded to allow greater room and privacy. One of the most notable changes was the use of two separate chimneys servicing the two, now larger, halves of the house. Four full rooms both upstairs and down were the norm. The massive central chimney was replaced by two leaner towers, adding to the elegance

Left, the gristmill at Longfellow's Wayside Inn, Massachusetts, uses materials in a classically simple form. **Above**, the Federal style.

Indians were regularly raiding Deerfield, and several bloody massacres had occurred, but when one's eyes rest upon these buildings, one feels no sense of trepidation, and the marvelous doorways welcome visitors warmly.

Equally gracious is the Dwight-Barnard House of 1754. This rambling residence is a lovely example not only of Georgian architecture but also of the common New England practice of interconnecting the house, the barn and any other outbuilding that had to be reached during the bitter days of winter.

By mid-century, activity at the coastal ports was in full swing, and the houses of the captains and merchants suggest that business was decidedly profitable. Many of the houses built in this era were later remodeled to keep up with architectural styles, making it sometimes difficult to find the purely Georgian. Portsmouth, New Hampshire, is blessed with unsullied originals in its 1763 Moffatt-Ladd House – as handsome as any to be found – and the delightfully understated 1760 Wentworth-Gardner House, where it is hard to resist touching the facade to verify that it is, indeed, wood and not stone.

Aspects of Georgian architecture, particularly Palladian motifs, remained in the language of New England design beyond the 18th century, but for the most part the style

had run its course by the Revolutionary War. One lovely exception is the handsome town of Litchfield, Connecticut, where pristine homes lining the roads north and south of the village green compose the perfect picture of the idyllic New England town.

Some of the finest homes were built or remodeled after 1780, when the Litchfield China Trading Company brought wealth and increased notoriety to the town. The residence of one of the company's founders, a Mr Deming, and the remodeled Sheldon's Tavern are impeccably Georgian, down to the three-part Palladian window not commonly used before 1780. All other buildings

in the borough of Litchfield are meticulously preserved, although not necessarily in their original state. The predominantly white exteriors date from a later 19th-century taste that has stuck not only in Litchfield but throughout New England and conveys a considerably different feel than would the yellow, blue or red hues that comprised the Georgian palette.

No style since the Georgian has lingered for so long a time in New England. Deriving as it did from familiar forms, with simply more space and embellishments added, it was adapted with ease by New England builders. If the Georgian style took a long time to mature into its successor, the Federal, the lag was surely a result of the many preoccupations of a nation in adolescence, rather than an absence of active architectural acumen. The century that followed was to prove that.

The Federal style: Despite the debilitating physical and economic effects of the war, the remarkable victories of the Revolution gave birth to a vigorous self-confidence across the new nation. Litchfield's homes of the 1790s were a last provincial gasp of Georgian charm, for, as the 19th century approached, a new sophistication was exhibited in buildings that, for the first time, were the work of native American architects.

Elsewhere in the colonies at the turn of the 19th century, visiting architects from abroad, as well as native sons like Thomas Jefferson, drew from their academic knowledge of European architecture to design daring buildings of Roman inspiration. In New England, where few foreign architects traveled, a less radical transformation took place, fueled by the accumulation of wealth and the booming economy along the coast.

Optimism must indeed have been palpable in the harbors of Salem and Boston. Even inland, whaling, shipbuilding and the expansion of trade brought the sea into the lives of many New Englanders as the coastal merchants commanded the goods and natural resources of the whole region. But no country carpenter could rival the skills of Salem's Samuel McIntire or Boston's Charles Bulfinch, whose combined work represents the finest of the period.

The Salem of Samuel McIntire's time was a far cry from the city that had been home to hysterical witch-hunters 100 years earlier.

Success in the pepper trade and other undertakings made wealthy men of captains and cabin boys alike. It is fortuitous that McIntire and Salem grew together, for the local carpenter may otherwise have had no outlet for his self-taught architectural proficiency.

In McIntire's work are the clearest notations of the Federal style. While New England's roofs had lost some of their cant in the Georgian period, their Federal counterparts virtually disappeared behind delicately carved balustrades. The effect was urbane, as evidenced by the 1804 Gardner-Pingree house, a rather neat summation of Federal motifs. Although boxy, its facade is relieved by the semicircular portico, its refined col-

The full impact of McIntire's work on the rest of Salem is best grasped on Chestnut Street, which in its entirety has been designated a National Historic Landmark. Up and down both sides of this majestic street are stunning Federal-style mansions, built in the early 1800s when the sea captains decided to move a short distance away from the noise and clutter of the port.

Elsewhere in Salem, a 1970s facelift not only turned around a declining city but, in doing so, reversed plans to topple many Federal-era buildings, which have been renovated and put to new use. A similar turnabout occurred in nearby Newburyport, where life and charm have been reintroduced to the

umns and the arching fanlight over the door – a signature of the Federal era.

McIntire performed his own carpentry with a skill that left him in constant demand up until his death in 1811. His inspiration was Robert Adam, the English architect who raised the art of interior decoration to exquisite heights with his dainty stucco reliefs. McIntire introduced these same embellishments to Salem, as can be seen inside the Gardner-Pingree house.

Left, early American carpenters copied styles they'd seen in English books. **Above**, Victorian houses marked a departure from austerity.

dilapidated, deserted commercial buildings.

The brilliance of Bulfinch: The Federal era peaked with the work of Charles Bulfinch. Bulfinch pursued architecture first as a leisure activity and then as a profession. Building – or his speculations in it – bankrupted him twice. One can only surmise, however, that misfortune fired rather than smothered his talents. Unfortunately, many of his more daring buildings have been destroyed, but the jewel among those standing, his State House, rests atop Beacon Hill. Here is as grand a composition as any Bulfinch realized, and to picture it surrounded by open land is to begin to appreciate what a dazzling paean to the promise of government it must have appeared to the Bostonian of 1798.

The classical State House, again very Palladian in inspiration, has been extended twice in two contradictory styles. The 1890 addition to the back of the building is a lumpish but highly mannered baroque echo of its opposing side. The second addition of 1914 totally neutralized the first by blotting it out, at least from the front, behind two thoroughly impassive marble wings – dull perhaps, but a mute backdrop to the golden-domed Bulfinch original.

Bulfinch was in on the beginning of Beacon Hill speculation, and the three homes he built for the investor Harrison Gray Otis

con Hill and, indeed, set the tone for the rest of the neighborhood.

The uniqueness of Beacon Hill and Bulfinch's contributions to it was recognized long ago by its residents, who in 1955 established the Beacon Hill Historic District. This organization has overseen the preservation of a beautiful cluster of buildings and also protected a rare haven of tranquility in the heart of busy, modern Boston.

Greek grandeur: Tranquility is what so much of New England is about, and among the emblems of this serenity are the scores of white steeples, visible on every horizon as landmarks for travelers. The source for this ubiquitous New England image is traced

summarize not only his growth but the maturation of the Federal residential style. The 1796 house, now the headquarters for the Society for the Preservation of New England Antiquities, is the least developed, a harmonious but basic expression of Federal-style concepts. In the 1802 house, Bulfinch took a few cautious steps to animate the street facade – the first-floor windows are recessed inside well-defined brick arches. By the third house, completed around 1805, Bulfinch's confidence had been established. This Beacon Street residence, of noble proportions and refined detail, projects a sophistication that was repeated in his other work on Bea-

back to one of the most influential forces in turn-of-the century New England architecture, Asher Benjamin. It was in the first of Benjamin's seven widely read architectural handbooks that he rendered a steepled church that became the basis for decades of church design. The simple classicism of the facade changed little over time, but the detailing, particularly of the steeple, incorporated changing architectural fashions, giving a clue to the era in which a church was built.

It was Benjamin who, in his final 1830 volume, judged New England ready for the Greek Revival style that elsewhere in America was already vying with the Gothic.

The same sense of self-importance that had characterized the Federal era, along with the influence of learning and intellectualism, gave the imposing Greek style a certain snob appeal. New England allowed the style in without totally letting go of the integrity of its architectural traditions. Particularly in non-residential examples, the Greek Revival style produced buildings that were a logical extension of the refinements made during the Federal era. Greek Revival houses proved less successful.

The economy of Greek architecture gives it a superior air, and scale is the key to its grandeur. Civic buildings, institutions and halls of commerce lent themselves to the

been beautifully restored, its cast-iron balconies once again offering an elegant setting for shops.

Certainly the most celebrated New England project of its kind, Faneuil Hall Marketplace, as restored by Ben Thompson & Associates, is now a consumer's cornucopia, with food and every kind of specialty store galore. The renovation was carried out with care and charisma; although the sober Greek references of Alexander Parris' 1826 domed building are generally overwhelmed by their surroundings, it seems somehow fitting that this hive of activity be housed in such splendor.

The addition of heavy columns and crush-

heroic Greek scale; houses were dwarfed by it. Although New England is not particularly rich in examples of the style, two of its more exemplary Greek Revival buildings, both of them marketplaces, happen to be among the most clever and renowned examples of recently restored 19th-century buildings.

Providence's 1828 Arcade has been described as "something worthy of London or Paris," an apt compliment to its crisply colonnaded and handsomely detailed facade. Inside, the two-story, sky-lit interior has

Left, Boston's Old State House and New State House. **Above**, Faneuil Hall Market, Boston.

ing pediments did little, however, for otherwise well-proportioned Federal and Georgian homes. Neither remodeled nor new Greek Revival houses carry themselves with particular ease, but one of their fundamental features was assimilated into the vocabulary of vernacular New England design quite effortlessly – the passion for white paint, stemming from the association of white with Greek temples.

Some unusually fine examples of this style can be found in Grafton, Vermont, a quiet town remarkable less for the quality of its architecture than for the story of its rescue by the Windham Foundation, which since 1963 has restored the entire core of this idyllic New England village.

Enlightened industry: Harrisville, New Hampshire, survives as an unchanged emblem of how pervasive the textile industry was in New England after 1830. The town, comprising handsome granite and brick mills, boarding-houses and storehouses which now house a weaving school, offers an abridged version of the story of the rapid rise and fall of New England's mill towns, a story that began with windmills and small-town enterprise and climaxed with the building of entire towns designed to support the textile industry. The effects on the social fabric were profound and lasting.

It is appropriate that in Lowell, Massachusetts, named after one of the fathers of the power loom, aggressive efforts are underway to preserve an extensive architectural legacy of the industrial past. Decades of intense activity has resulted in the creation of the Lowell National Historic Park and the Lowell Historic Preservation District. Dozens of factory buildings, designed in the boxy, brick, frugal industrial version of the Federal style, line the city's intricate canal system, with rows of boardinghouses nearby. These and many once-abandoned commercial buildings are being renovated and reused at a rapid pace.

As a result of foresight and dedication on the part of many people, Lowell is once again a healthy and active city, a rich visual lesson in the architecture of a tumultuous chapter of our history. Fortunately, the Lowell Mills are among many that are being saved from the wrecking ball and reused for housing, commercial and retail purposes. Towns like Fall River, Manchester and Pawtucket are the richer for these efforts.

The loss of innocence: The opening of the industrial age marked the closing of an era of architectural innocence in New England. For its first 200 comparatively stable years, New England architecture had been governed by conservative principles that emphasized function first; form existed to serve the central purpose of shelter. While European ideas had clearly dictated design, they had been tempered by restraint. But by 1850, something had changed. Perhaps for no other reason than boredom with symmetry, scale and four-square plans, architecture took off in all directions, most in opposition to the language of the past.

Gothic and Italianate, Renaissance and Romanesque – even Egyptian – are among the labels attached to the late 19th-century architectural revivals. In the hands of architects like Henry Hobson Richardson and McKim, Mead and White, or many lesser known but dexterous carpenters, these styles could be expressed with uncommon panache. But the spiritual link to New England grew remote, and these buildings have only distant kinship with the carefully proportioned, cautiously decorated creations of New England's early centuries.

Further European grafts have been attempted, with varying degrees of success: Harvard University, for instance, boasts the only LeCorbusier building in the United States (Carpenter Center), and Gropius built a model Bauhaus house in the Boston suburb of Lincoln. The future of New England architecture, however, clearly lies in the hands of native architects, such as Graham Gund of Cambridge, who acknowledge the contributions of their forebears even as they strive to break new ground.

Contrasting styles in Boston: a Federal-style brick house on Chestnut Street (left), and the contemporary John Hancock Building which dwarfs the old Trinity Church (right).

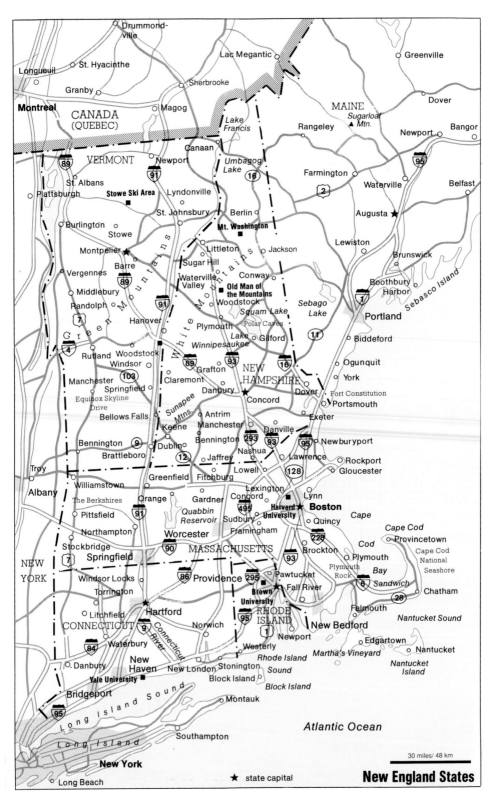

New England States

30 miles/ 48 km

★ state capital

PLACES

Meanwhile it occurs to me that by a remote New England fireside an unsophisticated young person of either sex is reading in an old volume of travels... The young person gazes in the firelight at the flickering chiaroscuro of the future, discerns at last the glowing phantasm of opportunity, and determines with a wild heartbeat to go and see it all – twenty years hence!

—Henry James

There's no need to wait 20 years to see New England – no need to delay at all, for New England is a polished place, ready to reward the visitor with riches rarely equaled in America. New England is six politically defined states and a thousand states of mind – Maine and solitude and contemplation, Massachusetts and bustle and culture, Vermont and beauty and peace.

New England can mean running across a priceless antique in an out-of-the-way backwoods store, or dining out in a sophisticated Boston restaurant. It can mean rafting down a Maine river or skiing down a New Hampshire mountain, scrounging through a Connecticut flea market or lounging on a Nantucket beach.

State delineations serve as convenient although somewhat artificial labels for New England's varied regions. In the following pages, each state is explored in depth and treated as a self-contained unit; but Massachusetts, the most populous, has been divided into subsections on Boston, the North and South Shores, Cape Cod, Martha's Vineyard and Nantucket, Central Massachusetts and the Berkshires. Marginal maps will help orient armchair travelers to specific locations.

States of mind – calm, contentment, excitement, pride, surprise, intrigue, enjoyment, pleasure – are to be found in all parts of New England. From the scrub pines of East Chop on Martha's Vineyard to the granite outcroppings of Vermont's Green Mountains, from the cobbled streets of restored Newburyport to the sleek modernity of Boston's skyline, from Rhode Island's natural wonderland, Block Island, to the man-made history that persists in Lexington and Concord, this is New England, home of American dreams.

Preceding pages: winter in the White Mountains, New Hampshire; summer in the White Mountains; Back Cove, Maine.

BOSTON

To visit Boston is to visit a city that Americans have looked at with mingled admiration, horror, love and annoyance for more than 350 years. Three and a half centuries is a long time in America, time enough to build a fine city, to join bricks and mortar, to raise townhouses and office towers, to construct docks and statues and bridges. And it's plenty of time to lay twisting cobblestone streets and concrete freeways, to decorate avenues and churches with lawns and trees, ponds, spires and fences. New York may be grander, Seattle more beautiful, but no city in America so nobly mingles its past with its present, tradition with innovation.

Hub of the Universe: Not that everyone favors such a staunch attachment to the past. In large measure because of it, few cities have evoked so varied a response in their visitors. There has been, for instance, revulsion: "I hate Boston," said the journalist Lincoln Steffens. "I don't know why... The general spirit is so far, far, far back that it gets on my nerves." The fervid Reverend Cotton Mather was less uncertain in one of his 17th-century jeremiads: "Boston is almost a hell upon earth, a city full of Lies and Murders and Blasphemies; a dismal Picture and an emblem of Hell."

There have been other expressions of displeasure. The thriller writer Raymond Chandler decided that "God made Boston on a wet Sunday," and Edgar Allan Poe remarked: "The Bostonians are very well bred – as very dull people generally are." Oliver Wendell Holmes, author, philosopher, and professor of anatomy at Harvard, even surmised that the citizens of Boston, through the blueness of their blood, had remained unpleasantly English into the late 19th century. "As the Englishman is the physical bully of the world," he wrote, "so the Bostonian is the aesthetic and intellectual bully of America."

But then again, there has been veneration. "This town of Boston has a history," wrote the poet and essayist Ralph Waldo Emerson. "It is not an accident, not a windmill, or a railroad station, or a crossroads town, but a seat of humanity, of men of principle, obeying sentiment and marching to it…"

Holmes, in a better mood, was even more extravagant: "All I claim for Boston is that it is the thinking center of the Continent, and therefore of the Planet." He went on to christen his city "The Hub of the Universe," a nickname taken with surprising seriousness in these parts.

Short story of a long history: Founded in 1630 when a band of Puritans who had landed in Salem (north of Boston) went searching for drinking water, Boston early on felt that "the eies of all people are upon us," as their first leader, John Winthrop, said. Driven by this relentless self-consciousness and the certainty that God, too, was watching, the little "Bible Commonwealth" quickly made something of itself.

Prosperity came from the sea. By 1700, thanks to cod fishing and the maritime trade made possible by Boston's natural harbor, the colony was

booming: its fleet was the third largest in the English-speaking world, its population the largest in North America.

Success, however, brought attention from home, and in the mid-18th century, the English Crown began to tighten its hold on its precocious offspring, imposing a series of tough new revenue measures which cooled relations between the colonies and the motherland. Tensions escalated until, on the night of March 5, 1770, British troops fired into a rioting crowd and killed three people, including an African American named Crispus Attucks. The funeral for the victims of the Boston Massacre was the first occasion for a great patriotic demonstration.

Relations deteriorated further in 1773 when a heavily taxed shipment of British tea arrived in Boston Harbor. Not only did the town refuse to unload the crates of "East India Bohea," but on the evening of December 16, some 60 patriots disguised as Mohawk Indians hurled 342 of the crates from the ship into the Harbor, thus celebrating the Boston Tea Party. The port was closed immediately and a sort of martial law was declared. It soon flared into a brief but famous war – the American Revolution. Boston's great moments in those events shine in the mind of every schoolchild from Maine to Alaska. Paul Revere's Midnight Ride, "The Shot Heard Round the World" and the Battle of Bunker Hill are the exploits of American myth.

The Athens of America: Despite such vivid colonial and Revolutionary doings, it was during the high noon of the 19th century that Boston took its present-day form. During that period, the merchant princes created a great city that would eventually become known not only as "The Hub," but also as "The Athens of America."

Slowed by the Revolution, Boston's maritime industries surged again with the coming of peace. Piloting swift clipper ships, indefatigable sea captains traded in ports farther abroad – Java, the West Coast and newly opened China. The Boston fishing fleet increased tenfold between 1789 and 1810, and creat-

The landing of the Pilgrims.

ed a "codfish aristocracy" of fortunes netted from the sea. A seemingly unending flow of gold made Boston – or at least those Bostonians with names like Cabot, Lowell, Otis and Hancock – incredibly rich. These wealthy mercantilists, adopting the name of the priestly class of the Hindus who performed sacred rituals and set moral standards, emerged as the self-styled "Brahmins" of a modern caste system.

Growth accelerated through the century as Yankee ingenuity triumphed again and again, and helped Boston lead America into a prosperous Industrial Age. A Boston traveling salesman named Gillette dreamed up the safety razor, while Alexander Graham Bell invented the telegraph in his attic at 109 Court Street. Even more important, the Boston-designed sewing machine and the power loom, imported from England, inaugurated an era of heavy textile and shoe manufacturing.

To accommodate itself, Boston began to manipulate its land. The city's humble hills were shoveled into the surrounding marshes and coves to make new land for homes and industry. By century's end, in one of the great testimonies to the American knack for making something from nothing, Boston had tripled its size with landfill.

Growth was more than physical; Boston was also expanding its mind. With its legacy of Puritan high-mindedness, its publishing houses and its fashionable literary salons run by earnest first citizens, Boston suddenly found itself at the radiant center of intellectual America. Longfellow, Lowell, Whittier, Emerson, Thoreau, Holmes, Parkman, Alcott, Hawthorne: all were at one time or another citizens of the New England Parnassus; all could be found browsing at the Old Corner Book Store or dictating standards for civilization over seven-course meals at the Parker House, where Emerson convened his luminous Saturday Club.

Magazines like the *North American Review* and the *Atlantic Monthly* were founded to spread the word, while a whole slew of cultural institutions celebrated and embodied it. Among these were the Boston Public Library, the Boston Symphony Orchestra, the Massachusetts Institute of Technology (MIT) and Boston University, the first American university to admit women on an equal basis with men. Harvard, of course, had already ascended from its status as "that country college in Cambridge" to its place among the world's great universities.

The great immigration: But while the Boston of privileged thought and power was progressing so mightily, a catastrophe occurred in Europe that was to affect the city more seriously than any other single event. The Irish potato famine would change the city decisively and permanently. When it began in 1845, Boston was at the apogee of its gleaming social and cultural pre-eminence. Suddenly, thousands of impoverished Irish immigrants arrived, promptly constituting a new underclass.

As the population exploded – swelled further by additional waves of Italians, Poles and Russians in the 1880s – census figures multiplied thirtyfold during

the 19th century to about 560,000 people in 1900. Newcomers and incumbents clashed, and Boston was divided into two distinct cultures with no more intercourse than if 3,000 miles of ocean still separated them. While the ethnics became a clannish foreign element, established Bostonians withdrew into their own carefully defended elite of genealogy and crypto-Puritanism.

Yet if the new citizens became virtual slaves as they sweated in factories and did handwork, they remade Boston in their own image. Once dominated by English names, the Puritan "City upon a Hill" became a predominantly Catholic megalopolis of Irish and Italian names: numbers prevailed, most dramatically in the arena of city politics.

Having groped steadily upward through the 1870s and 1880s, the Irish finally elected Hugh O'Brien, the city's first foreign-born mayor, in 1884. Successes were quickly consolidated as men like Martin Lomasney, the greatest of Boston's bosses, built political fiefdoms by allocating "favors" in exchange for instructions to vote Democrat.

For much of the 20th century, Irish politicians dominated the mayor's office and the civil service while also giving the nation such leaders as John W. McCormack, a former Speaker of the House of Representatives; Thomas P. ("Tip") O'Neill, another Speaker; and, of course, the ever-present Kennedy clan. If the Brahmins owned Boston, the Irish ran it.

Yet for all Boston's glory and growth during the 1800s, the century's end brought decline, a decline that would continue until the 1960s. While the skyscrapers of frenzied Manhattan and industrious Chicago shot up with rude confidence, Boston kept a low profile, as much out of economic inertia as a matter of aesthetic preference.

New York superseded Boston as a port; the textile mills and shoe factories headed south for cheaper labor and lower taxes. Lacking vitality, conscience hardened into prudery, and culture softened into effeteness. By the 1940s and 1950s, Boston was shrinking, the only large city to lose substantial numbers of

Greater Boston Area

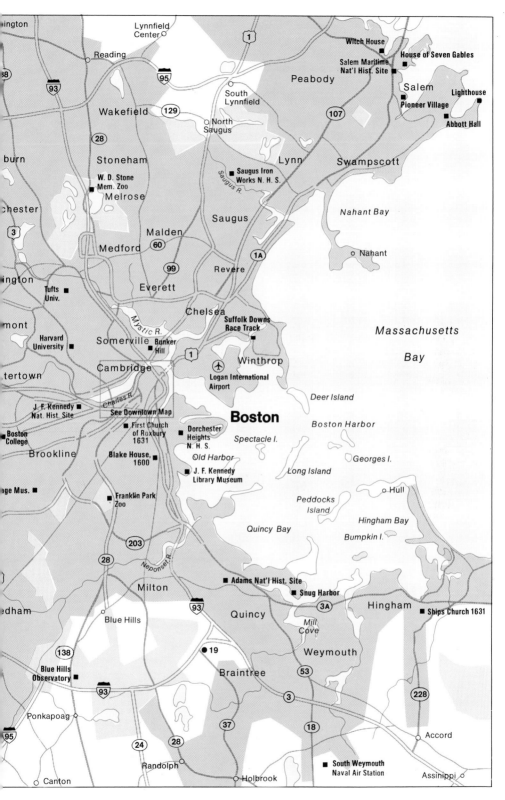

ington

Lynnfield
Center

Reading

Witch House

Salem Maritime
Nat'l Hist. Site

House of Seven Gables

95

93

38

Peabody

South
Lynnfield

Salem

Lighthouse

107

Pioneer Village

Wakefield

129

North
Saugus

Abbott Hall

28

Stoneham

W. D. Stone
Mem. Zoo

Melrose

Saugus Iron
Works N. H. S.

Lynn

Swampscott

Nahant Bay

chester

Malden

Saugus

burn

3

Medford

60

99

1A

Nahant

ington

Tufts
Univ.

Everett

Revere

Harvard
University

Somerville

Bunker
Hill

Mystic R.

Chelsea

Suffolk Downs
Race Track

Massachusetts

Bay

mont

1

tertown

Cambridge

Winthrop

Logan International
Airport

Charles R.

See Downtown Map

Deer Island

J. F. Kennedy
Nat. Hist. Site

Boston

Boston Harbor

Boston
College

First Church
of Roxbury
1631

Dorchester
Heights
N. H. S.

Spectacle I.

Brookline

Blake House,
1600

Old Harbor

Georges I.

Long Island

age Mus.

J. F. Kennedy
Library Museum

Hull

Franklin Park
Zoo

Peddocks
Island

203

Hingham Bay

28

Neponset R.

Quincy Bay

Bumpkin I.

Adams Nat'l Hist. Site

Milton

Snug Harbor

93

Quincy

3A

Hingham

Ships Church 1631

edham

Blue Hills

Mill
Cove

138

19

Weymouth

Blue Hills
Observatory

93

Braintree

53

Ponkapoag

3

228

95

37

18

Accord

24

28

Randolph

South Weymouth
Naval Air Station

Assinippi

Canton

Holbrook

people during the post-war Baby Boom.

But then, just as suddenly as the city had lapsed into torpor, it woke up. For the first time, Boston's Protestant elite, representing wealth, and its Irish Catholics, representing political power, co-operated in the management of city affairs and began a success story of rejuvenation that has been nothing less than astounding. Prudential Center, including what was then the tallest skyscraper outside New York, materialized. Government Center supplanted Scollay Square. The silk purse of the Faneuil Hall Marketplace was created from the sow's ear of some wholesale meat warehouses – an example followed throughout the US. The waterfront was revived. Suddenly, Boston was a different and altogether exciting place.

The city further benefited as the Baby Boom grew up, went to college, then looked for jobs and apartments. Millions of young people have attended one of the three score colleges in Boston. Many, having graduated from schools like MIT, have set up shop and trans-formed the Boston area into one of the centers of the Technology Revolution. With the transfusion of new blood, the Boston of today is young in demographics as well as spirits, with a sizable portion of its population under the age of 25, and a large percentage unmarried. It's also well educated and energetic.

Despite urban development, one of Boston's primary charms remains unchanged: its tangled streets and the art of walking them, exploring their beguiling turns and primitive angles, getting lost in them. Boston is charmingly, perversely bereft of a main drag, and its streets practice the old European vices of waywardness and digression. The visitor should, too. There's no telling what you'll find.

The hub of history: Ask most Bostonians which is the city's oldest neighborhood and they're likely to reply, "Back Bay." Wrong: the answer is the **North End**, a busy little neighborhood north of the waterfront and northeast of the downtown business core. This picturesque old jumble is Boston's true heart, and to

Paul Revere's House.

walk these streets is to walk among legends. Indeed, many of the attractions along Boston's official **Freedom Trail**, a tour of the historical sites of the Revolution, are found here.

But the North End does more than serve as a sort of Early America theme park. This neighborhood is the ethnic heart of Boston: once Irish, then Jewish, now Italian, the North End is a place where laundry hangs from lines stretched from building to building and where freshly ground sausages are invitingly displayed in storefront windows.

A stroll through the North End should start at **Paul Revere's House** in North Square. Built around 1680, it is the oldest building standing in the city, and the period furnishings on display include some items owned by the Reveres. From here, head toward Hanover Street and the Old North Church, but walk at a leisurely pace and take in the sights – and smells – of Old World Italy.

Here is a paradise of fresh-baked bread, dried squid, pastries, provolone and braided garlic. In summer, a fortunate visitor may witness one of several saint's festivals, when the streets are spanned by arcs of colored lights and jammed with people surrounding Madonnas bedecked with dollar bills. But at any time, strolling the narrow streets is a delight – particularly around dinnertime. Within a few blocks of Hanover Street are dozens of first-class Italian restaurants.

At the end of Hanover Street stands the **Paul Revere Mall** with its rather comic equestrian statue of Revere looking a tad drunk. At the end of the tranquil, tree-shaded mall, also occupied by a fountain and old Italian men playing checkers, stands Boston's oldest church, Christ Church or the **Old North Church** of Paul Revere's lanterns and Longfellow's poem. The graceful spire of Old North stands as a beacon to hundreds of tourists. Inside, the stately pulpit presides, and the soft glow of light that filters through the surrounding treetops gives the lofty sanctuary a gentle aura of serenity. The beauty of this space finds lovely accompaniment in the "royal peal" of its eight bells, con-

sidered the best and sweetest in America. The largest weighs 1,545 pounds (695 kg) and the smallest 620 pounds (270 kg). One is inscribed, "We are the first ring of bells cast for the British Empire in North America, Anno 1774."

Behind Old North, between Hull and Charter streets, stand the weathered headstones of **Copp's Hill Burying Ground**, where the bones of many early Bostonians, including Cotton Mather, are buried.

Military memorabilia: Across Charlestown Bridge from the North End a famous bit of history lies at anchor: the *USS Constitution*, the venerable frigate built in 1797 but still commissioned in the United States Navy (it makes one voyage a year, a ceremonial "turnabout" at the 4th of July). The majestic masts make an inspiring beacon as they soar above the **Boston Naval Shipyard**. For the record, the *Constitution* fought over 40 battles in the War of 1812 and never lost one.

It's not far from here to the **Bunker Hill Pavilion**, where a multimedia ex-

The USS Constitution.

travaganza depicts the Patriots' heroic loss to the Redcoats in the second battle of the Revolution. Nearby rises the outsized obelisk of the **Bunker Hill Monument** itself, a granite needle 221 ft (67 meters) high.

Climb this – there are 294 steps, for those who want to know – and contemplate the bewildering, immense complexity of the Harbor, in which float dozens of islands ranging in size from a few square feet at low tide to many acres with stands of trees. Many of these islands have odd histories, some having to do with Native American legends, others – as in the case of Nix's Mate Island – with the visits of pirates like Captain Kidd. Two islands have supported hospitals, another a prison, and several others have been fortified. During the Civil War, hundreds of soldiers trained for the Union Army at Fort Warren on **Georges Island**, and more than 1,000 Confederates were imprisoned there.

Since the mid-1970s, a handful of these islands, maintained by the Metropolitan District Commission and the Department of Environmental Management have, have been open to the public. Visitors can ferry to Georges Island, the terminus of several commercial ferry lines, and from there take a free water ferry to several others. **Bumpkin Island** offers trimmed, grassy trails walled with raspberry bushes in which pheasants hide, while **Peddocks Island**, once known for its harvest of turkeys, presents giant buildings, brick ghosts that look more like Southern mansions than the Army barracks of **Fort Andrews**; these were last used to house Italian prisoners during World War II. If the prospect of a breezy day spent exploring the Harbor sounds beguiling, contact one of the harbor cruise companies located on Long Wharf near the Aquarium. They'll take visitors out among the islands and the sailboats scudding on the water.

The Waterfront District: Back on the mainland, on the eastern boundary of the North End is the Waterfront District, a fine place of leisure for citizens, suburbanites and tourists alike. If the tall

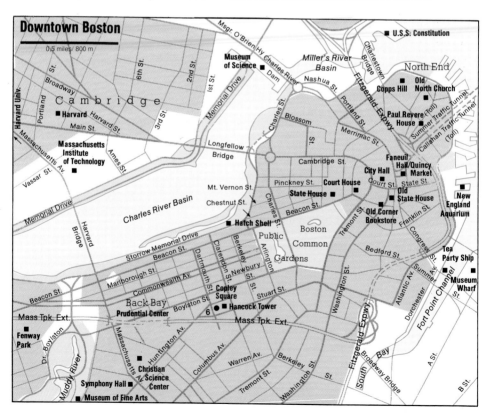

ships – or rather, their modern copies – now appear only sporadically, the great wharves remain, many now recycled as apartments, shopping arcades and up-scale restaurants. At the center of it all is the **Christopher Columbus Water-front Park**, a pleasant stretch of lawns, trees and trellises.

And there are museums. For example, the fine **New England Aquarium**, on Central Wharf at the harbor end of Milk Street, boasts what is reputed to be the largest seawater fish tank in the world, a gargantuan three-story, 180,000-gallon (819,000-liter) ocean in which sharks, four-eye butterfly fish and noble salmon cruise, dart and glide.

Farther south, along Fort Point Channel, is the **Boston Tea Party Ship and Museum**, which offers an instructive lesson in American mythology for schoolchildren of all ages. For added fun, the museum dispenses tea chests for visitors to hurl defiantly into the Harbor from the deck of the *Beaver II*, a full-size replica of one of the three tea ships whose cargo, on that chilly night

in 1773, helped make the Harbor into a rather large pitcher of iced tea.

Next door is the Museum Wharf, home of the **Computer Museum** and the **Children's Museum**, both housed in renovated warehouses. The former is a hacker's paradise for all ages, the latter a hands-on adventure, where children can improvise TV shows on-camera, and take their shoes off to enter an authentic Japanese house transplanted piece by piece from Boston's sister city, Kyoto. Children accustomed to constant warnings of "Don't touch!" and "Be careful!" will find a paradise of things to squeeze, crank, push, pull and explore. In summer, the wharf in front becomes a lovely place to waste any number of hours. The scene is made pleasantly surreal by the presence of an immense milk bottle (a vestige of 1930s advertising kitsch) which dispenses ice cream and more substantial snacks, such as sandwiches and salads.

Returning north to Christopher Columbus Park, turn a few hundred yards inland to **Faneuil Hall Marketplace**,

lodestone of the tourist trade and a famed experiment in urban redesign. Everyone goes here, and almost everyone has a great time.

Faneuil Hall, the fulcrum of the place, was donated to Boston by Peter Faneuil, a French Huguenot merchant who traded in slaves. This future "Cradle of Liberty," where Patriot orators would soon stir the embers of Revolution, was built in 1742 on a site that was at the time, remarkably enough, Boston's Town Dock. In 1976, after 250 sometimes glorious, sometimes scruffy years of service, **Quincy Market** and Faneuil Hall opened again, this time rising phoenix-like from a massive renovation that converted their boisterous, rugged markets into a chic, cleverly remodeled and wildly successful array of fern bars, jewelry emporia and designer-clothing outfits. In addition, several score food stands line the long hall of the central building, tempting strollers with an endless array of classic American and international snacks, from freshly shucked oysters to Italian sausage subs and exquisite French pastry. Faneuil Hall/Quincy Market is elegant, clean and wholesome – as well as mobbed – yet it is also polished, sanitized and cellophane-wrapped.

Some miss the exuberant grunginess of bygone days (still evident around the corner on **Blackstone Street**, when the Haymarket puts on its weekend produce market). But why carp? This thriving center of the knick-knack trade remains one of the principal ornaments of Boston, and perhaps the finest architectural example of its period in America.

For those who may wonder why all the shopping bags and restaurant menus bear an image of a cricket: when Faneuil gave Boston the hall, he had a large cricket weathervane placed atop its cupola. During the War of 1812, "cricket" became a password and patriot rallying cry of the Boston port. Strangers who could not identify the cricket as the image of the city of Boston met uncertain fates as spies.

Government Center: Looming just inland from the Hall, across Congress

Faneuil Hall, reborn as Quincy Market.

Street, is **Government Center**. Here, in the 1960s, Boston Redevelopment Authority director Edward Logue, Mayor Collins and architect I.M. Pei leveled the colorful tenements of the West End and constructed a city of their own, a radical "New Boston." This was urban renewal on a grand scale – either inspiring or forbidding, depending on the viewpoint of the beholder.

At any rate, it is big. Starting with **Scollay Square**, a sleazy jumble of shooting galleries, tattoo parlors and burlesque houses, the designers razed buildings and removed streets until they had cleared a huge open space – some 56 acres (23 hectares). On this new plaza, they arranged several buildings of imposing scale and abstract design. A massive new **City Hall** designed by Kallmann, McKinnell and Knowles dominates. Described as an "Aztec temple on a brick desert," this huge affair of poured concrete provides a fitting, though rather inhospitable, monument to the nearly religious role politics plays in Boston. Arranged neatly around City

Hall are additional government buildings, all in the modernist style.

For a little comic relief, the quirky little **Sears Crescent**, built in 1816, has been allowed to remain from pre-Pei days. A 227-gallon (1,033-liter) teapot, steaming happily, hangs from a corner of the adjoining 1848 Sears Block building; a late 19th-century advertising gimmick, it lives on as a charming totem for a key government institution, the bureaucrat's breakfast.

To the southeast rises the tall confusion of pin-striped Boston, the banks and office towers along **Franklin**, **Congress**, **Federal**, **State** and **Broad** streets. Rising confidently from a primitive warren of jumbled byways, these well-tailored behemoths constitute the Hub of Business. They are evidence that in one way, at least, Boston has not changed much since the 17th century. Even today, it regards money as sacred, a sign of election.

Historic downtown: To the southwest beats the throbbing heart of downtown, as well as some buildings illuminated

ft, Faneuil all. Right, s yesterday ce more.

brightly in history. At Washington Street's intersection with Court and State streets stands the **Old State House**, a glorious center of 18th-century public life that today exhibits its heritage of survival by the stubbornness with which it holds the city's predatory skyscrapers at bay. It was here, in 1761, that James Otis first fulminated against the British Writs of Assistance in a spellbinding speech that prompted John Adams to write that "then and there the child Independence was born." In 1770, the infamous Boston Massacre took place just outside the State House. Some years later, after the Revolution, the building served as the meeting place for the Commonwealth Government until the present State House was built.

Now, having survived use as a commercial building and evaded the demolition plans that were halted only when the city of Chicago offered to buy and relocate it in 1882, the Old State House, gloriously renovated, still stands, with a lively little museum inside and a subway stop directly below.

The **Old Corner Bookstore**, at the corner of Washington and School streets, was once a sort of clubhouse for the likes of Hawthorne, Emerson and Thoreau. Later the home of the *Atlantic Monthly* when it was launched in 1857, and of the *Boston Globe*, Boston's journal of record, it is now a prettified bookstore specializing in regional titles.

Turning right at School Street, wander past the **Old City Hall**, a grand affair that out-Second Empires the French Second Empire, and then **King's Chapel** (1750), one of this Puritan town's first attempts at real architectural class.

Turn left at Tremont Street and stroll through the **Granary Burial Ground**, a pleasant glade where generations of tourists have contemplated their mortality among the graves of Peter Faneuil, John Hancock, Samuel Adams, Paul Revere, six Massachusetts governors and the victims of the Boston Massacre.

A few more paces down Tremont lead to Peter Banner's elegant **Park Street Church** (1809), which Henry James

Ranger gives directions on Boston Common.

decided was "perfectly felicitous" and "the most interesting mass of brick and mortar in America." On July 4, 1829, William Lloyd Garrison made his first anti-slavery speech here, launching his far-reaching emancipation campaign.

An alternate route, continuing down Washington Street from The Old Corner Bookstore, leads to the **Old South Meeting House**, from which 60 whooping "Mohawk Indians" set off for Griffin's Wharf and a Tea Party.

After the Meeting House comes **Downtown Crossing**, where hordes of wild suburban shoppers stampede the city's major department stores. Probably the busiest intersection in Boston, it is the location of the phenomenal **Filene's Basement**, the world's most celebrated bargain store. Every day, thousands of sharp-eyed professionals, discerning matrons, and blown-dry teen angels can be seen shoving and elbowing each other as they rummage frantically through this cut-rate El Dorado in search of designer seconds, three-piece suits, and household essentials.

An uncommon place: Every metropolis has a great park somewhere in its outline, but only Boston can claim the oldest, the venerable **Boston Common**, a magical swath of lawn and trees and benches bounded by Tremont, Park, Beacon, Charles and Boylston streets. Sitting in the sun-mottled shade, watching pigeons strut and children frolic around Frog Pond, the out-of-towner can understand how Bostonians might mistake this spot for the very center of the world.

The land that was to become the Common originally belonged to Boston's first English settler, one Reverend William Blaxton. Having fled first England and then an aborted colonial attempt farther south, Blaxton settled in 1625 on the western slope of what is now known as Beacon Hill. There, he tended his orchard and read in peaceful solitude until his serenity was somewhat rudely interrupted in 1631 by the arrival of a band of new settlers led by Governor John Winthrop of the Massachusetts Bay Company. The new Bostonians

evivalist
eeting on
e Common.

were nobly determined, as Winthrop had written on the ship, to "be a Citty upon a hill," and their presence did not please Blaxton. In 1634, he sold his land to the town for around $150 and fled farther into the wilderness.

The 45 acres (18 hectares) he left behind quickly became a versatile community utility. During the next 150 years, it was used as a cattle and sheep pasture and as a drilling ground. And although, as an account written in 1663 says, "the Common was the beauty and pride of the Town, ever suggesting the lighter side of life," it also proved useful as a place to hang people – for stealing, for piracy, for being a Quaker, or a Native American, or a woman who snatched a bonnet worth 75 cents.

The whipping post and the pillory stood there, and many a duel took place at dawn. As a military post, the Common put up the Redcoats all through the Revolution, and during the Civil War it provided a backdrop for the tears of recruiting and departures.

Now the Common is an urban oasis, a park and nothing else. Climb the little knolls and walk the meandering paths past bronze statues and dignified fountains. Near the Park Street "T" stop, which as the main crossing of the country's oldest subway has disgorged passengers since 1897, there may be a street musician playing saxophone or mellow guitar. The Common is at its best throughout the year, when the magnolias bloom or when falling snow at sunset evokes the impressionist paintings of Childe Hassam.

West from the Common and across Charles Street, the elegant **Public Garden** beckons, and, though it continues the pleasant green of the Common, it has quite a different past. Indeed, these variegated trees, meandering paths, and ornate beds of flowers were mere marsh when the Common was well into its second century of tempestuous history. First deeded at the end of the 18th century as a riverside ropewalk – the Charles had not yet been filled here – these 24 acres (10 hectares) at the Common's foot were bought back by the city in **The Public Garden.**

1825 for $55,000. In a series of disputes during the first half of the 19th century, some argued that the valuable land would be best sold. But the park soon began to be laid out, though the destruction by fire of an early conservatory for birds and camellias slowed development. By 1867, the Garden had taken its present graceful shape, complete with weeping willows, a bridge for daydreamers, and a shallow 4-acre (2-hectare) pond. In summer, one can't overlook the swan boats, those fabled gondolas that carry happy tourists across the placid waters. At the Commonwealth Avenue entrance, an equestrian **George Washington bronze** by Thomas Ball presides.

Beacon Hill: Back up at the east end of the Common rises the gold dome of the **State House**, gleaming atop Beacon Hill (*see photograph on page 88*). Completed in 1798 when the Old State House became too small, this design by Charles Bulfinch, with additions by several others, symbolizes the eminence of politics in Boston. It is less intrusive than City Hall at Government Center, and more

serenely elegant. A visit to the grand legislative chambers is a must. The walk to the chambers passes through a series of splendid halls, beginning with the Doric Hall of the Bulfinch era and leading to the Senate Staircase Hall and the Hall of Flags, both symphonies of *fin de siècle* marble opulence supplied plentifully with statues, busts, flags and patriotic mottos.

But none of this dulls the eye to the House Chamber in the Brigham extension, a paneled hall under a two-stage dome. The decorations are inspirational to the point of absurdity: great moments of Massachusetts' freedom decorate the walls in a series of Albert Herter paintings, while above circles a frieze carved with a roll-call of the state's superachievers. The portentous codfish, a sleek, stiff carving in pine that commemorates Boston's great Federal-era fishing industry, was first hung in the Old State House. Without this odd mascot, the House refuses to meet.

The State House, now hemmed in by Beacon Hill residences, seems about as

Swan boats in the Public Garden.

centrally located as a building can be, but it wasn't always that way. In 1797, residents of Boston thought that the Wild West itself began on the far side of the Common, hardly a quarter-mile from the State House. Cows still grazed there, and much of the surrounding land had the bucolic air of pastures trailing off into forest. Even Beacon Hill rose, not as a polite demi-hill, but as a rugged mass of wilderness, then called the Trimount because of its triple-peaked summit. The westernmos peak was isolated enough from the Puritan stronghold that it could be put to the purposes suggested by the name Mount Whoredom.

Predictably enough, moving the State House into this setting focused the city's attention on this area and changed things for good. While the Common became a true park, the Trimount became the subject of land speculation. It was quite ingeniously leveled and quickly became the compressed but still idyllic neighborhood of bow-fronted townhouses now known as "The Hill." At first, everyone expected that the new residences of Beacon Hill would be urban estates along the lines of Bulfinch's **No. 85 Mount Vernon Street**, which is to this day one of Boston's most majestic houses. But the mansion plans were quickly scaled down to the smaller blocks one sees today. At No. 55 Mount Vernon, the **Nichols House** offers a more typical example of Beacon Hill building. Also a Charles Bulfinch project, the house is now a small museum.

To get a sense of The Hill, walk west down Beacon Street from the State House. At numbers 39 and 40 Beacon stand **twin 1818 Greek Revival mansions**, one built for Daniel Parker, owner of the Parker House, Boston's oldest hotel. At numbers 42 and 43, the **Somerset Club**, built in 1819 as a mansion for David Sears, was acquired by the most exclusive of Boston social clubs in 1872. At number 45 Beacon stands the third of Harrison Gray Otis's houses, built in 1805.

Charming Charles Street: At the foot of the hill, a right turn leads to **Charles Street**, which is among the city's most charming and most sophisticated places to stroll, shop and snack. Here is Boston's leading concentration of antique stores – **George Gravert Antiques** and **Marika's** are especially worth investigating, as are a diverse collection of coffeehouses, bakeries, florists, cafes and boutiques. **DeLuca's Market** brims with the smells of ripe melons, fresh sausage and coffee beans, while nearby, Romano's Bakery serves exquisite homemade pastries and delicious soups and sandwiches.

The street's principal landmark is the **Charles Street Meeting House** at the corner of Charles and Mount Vernon streets. Built first for the Third Baptist Church in 1804, it served as the home of the African Methodist Episcopal Church and later the Unitarian-Universalist Church. At street level, this unpretentious building houses shops and a cafe-scale outpost of the popular New American restaurant Rebecca's, also on Charles Street, closer to the Common.

Wander off Charles onto the shady, peaceful streets that parallel it and lead back up the hill. Many of the houses

Greengrocer in the Haymarket.

118

here are noteworthy either for the talent of their architects or the luminous names of their former occupants. Polar explorer Admiral Richard E. Byrd lived in No. 7–9 Brimmer Street, and No. 44 Brimmer was the lifelong home of the great historian Samuel Eliot Morison. The Victorian clergyman and philosopher William Ellery Channing lived at No. 83 Mount Vernon Street, next door to the Otis mansion.

Louisburg Square, developed between Pinckney and Mount Vernon streets around 1840, epitomizes the Beacon Hill style and its urban delicacy. The Square has long stood at the summit of Boston society. William Dean Howells, the novelist and *Atlantic Monthly* editor; Louisa May Alcott, author of *Little Women*; and Jenny Lind, the "Swedish Nightingale," all lived at one time or another in the houses surrounding the Square's elegant green. Lind married her accompanist Otto Goldschmidt at No. 20 during an American tour in 1852.

Another charming example of Bea-con Hill's spirit can be found at numbers 13, 15 and 17 Chestnut Street, where Bulfinch built for the daughters of his client Hepzibah Swan three exquisite townhouses in a prim little row. Chestnut Street vies for the title of prettiest street on the hill, so fetching is the gently animated conversation of its porches and windows, flower-box geraniums and romantic gaslights.

Elegance made from mud: From Beacon Hill, it's an easy transition both in distance and architectural feeling to the handsome streets of **Back Bay**, the area that has come in recent years to epitomize "Old Boston." Don't be fooled by its old-money airs, though. Back Bay literally crawled from the mud into prominence. The massive program of filling by which the Back Bay came into being epitomizes the practical stubbornness that is altogether Bostonian. In defying topography, in ignoring what previously existed, Back Bay proclaims the triumph of Puritan doggedness over adversity, in this case a festering swampland that, in 1849, was declared "offen-

sive and injurious" by the Board of Health.

The heroic story begins in 1857 when the legislature adopted a grand plan for the Back Bay: there would be long vistas down dignified blocks, and a wide boulevard with a French-style park down the middle. In 1858 the first load of fill, which had been collected with an innovative new tool called the steam shovel, arrived by train from Needham, about 10 miles (16 km) to the southwest. During the next 20 years, some 600 acres (242 hectares) of dry land emerged from the muck that was Back Bay.

And sure enough, as houses began to appear, they were dignified. Despite the vagaries of individual taste and the piecemeal selling of lots, the new blocks went up with a harmoniousness that from the beginning gave Back Bay the stately unity it still possesses. One young man who planned to build his bride a house in Back Bay was icily informed by his prospective father-in-law that he would never allow a daughter of his to live on "made ground." But such qualms

were rare, and the new streets quickly became fashionable.

Today, the area is as elegant as ever, and its streets offer a truly civilized display of urban living. Indeed, Back Bay presents as great a showing of the Boston domestic architecture of the second half of the 19th century as Beacon Hill does of the first. The verdant mall of **Commonwealth Avenue** centers things, and the houses that line it, as well as the residential streets of Marlborough and Beacon, reveal their beauty in the subtle detailing of their architecture.

Starting at the Arlington Street entrance to the Public Gardens, the visitor may want to cross over to the **Ritz-Carlton Hotel**, on the corner of Newbury Street. The Ritz-Carlton is the perfect place to fortify oneself with a cocktail or a cup of tea and to observe Brahmin society in its element. From here, head north to No. 137 Beacon Street, between Arlington and Berkeley (the cross-streets ascend in alphabetical order). Built in 1860 at the start of Back Bay construction, the **Gibson House**

Copley Square with the Public Library and "new" Old South Church

120

has been left substantially as it was; it now houses a museum that recreates the feel of Back Bay living in its heyday. Continue to the corner of Commonwealth and Clarendon for a look at the **First Baptist Church**, a handsome design by H.H. Richardson. Its tower is graced with figures modeled after celebrities of the day – Emerson, Hawthorne and Longfellow.

In the block between Clarendon and Dartmouth, Commonwealth Avenue (known as "Comm Ave" to most of the locals) displays its most memorable structures. The romantic houses that march down this stretch perfectly justify the avenue's reputation as America's Champs-Elysées.

Paralleling Commonwealth on the south are Newbury and Boylston streets, the Back Bay that has been taken over by commerce and the rarefied air of uptown chic. On Newbury Street, the hairstyles are elaborate and the clothes are designer. Pricey restaurants, sidewalk cafes and seductive storefronts abound, and a number of fine galleries

operate in sleekly converted townhouses. The best of the contemporary galleries – **Alpha** and **Barbara Krakow** – are located at No. 14 and No. 10, respectively. **Vose's Gallery**, at No. 238, specializes in American painting, 1669 to 1940. A fixture since 1897, Vose's is the oldest private gallery in the United States. Five generations of the same family have faithfully maintained the tradition.

Classical Copley Square: Follow Dartmouth Street to Boylston for one of the most stimulating displays of architecture in the city: **Copley Square**. First, H.H. Richardson's wonderful **Trinity Church** (1877), a *tour de force* in Romanesque inventiveness, somehow fuses almost brutal power with an endless array of delicate details. Inside, the first-time visitor will be amazed by the sheer size of the place and the fabulous wealth of murals, mosaics, carvings and stained glass.

Across the square stands Charles McKim's **Boston Public Library** (1895), a classical contrast to Trinity's

The Public Library.

medievalism. This simple, serene and high-minded Parnassus might well be the center of the Boston that claims to be the "Athens of America." What better monument to a literary legacy populated by the likes of Emerson, Hawthorne, Thoreau and Alcott? (Bret Hart once observed that in these parts it was impossible to fire a pistol without bringing down the author of a two-volume work.)

With more than 5 million volumes, this is one of the great libraries in the world. But it's more than a building of books. There's art everywhere – murals by Sargent, statues by Saint-Gaudens and Daniel Chester French – and, at the center of a maze of stairs and passages, a peaceful inner courtyard. Philip Johnson's massive but compatible 1972 addition completes the complex.

Above everything looms I.M. Pei's magnificent blue-green mirror, the **John Hancock Mutual Life Insurance Tower**, built in 1976. Proud to be a building, proud to be in Boston, it has the look of a shimmering prism breaking free of the city's prim humility; it sings of strat-

ospheric freedom. At an excellent observatory on the 60th floor, visitors can speculate madly on everything below as well as attend to informative multimedia exhibits about Boston, including a diorama of Paul Revere's ride.

The only flaw in this gargantuan prism was its propensity to lose the huge sheets of glass covering it; that problem was brought under control soon after it was completed, when all 10,344 panes – some 13 acres (5 hectares) worth – were replaced at a cost of $8.5 million. Miraculously, no one was hurt, so Bostonians can laugh at the Tower's fickle ways and dangerous beauty.

This corner of Back Bay has seen the most ambitious building sprees in the past few decades. A controversial project, **Copley Place**, a megaplex occupying over 9 acres (4 hectares) atop the Massachusetts Turnpike, has proved – despite a considerable degree of initial skepticism – an enjoyable addition to city life, with its 11-screen cinema and dozens of inviting restaurants and shops. Although many of the latter are clones of those found in other upscale malls, a few are unique, such as the **Artful Hand Gallery** (exceptional crafts) and **Treasured Legacy** (African American literature and art).

Connected to this complex by a "skyway," is Boston's original skyscraper, the early 1960s **Prudential Center**. Envisioned as a bold new look for the city, "The Pru" turned out to be, in fact, a rather graceless development of the sort favored by the builders of the former Soviet Utopia. Developed out of an old railroad yard, the complex encompasses the **John B. Hynes Veterans Memorial Convention Center** (a striking 1988 design by Kallmann, McKinnell & Wood), a hotel, two department stores, and a lively mix of shops and restaurants spruced up in 1994.

Above these rises the 52-story **Prudential Insurance Tower**. It's not beautiful, but there is a bar and restaurant (undistinguished) at the top which offers a view of sparkling lights and sunsets. Every April, on Patriots' Day, the Prudential becomes the destination of the thousands who enter the famous

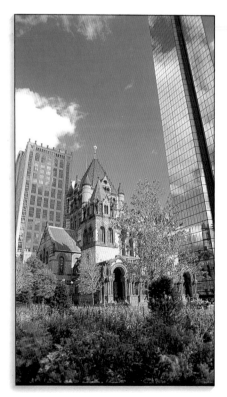

Trinity Church and the John Hancock Tower.

Boston Marathon, perhaps the most celebrated running event on the planet.

The story of Christian Science: The **Christian Science Church Center** occupies the 22 acres (9 hectares) immediately south of the Prudential Center. The complex includes three older buildings – the Romanesque **Mother Church** (1894), the Italianate **Mother Church Extension** (1904) and the **Publishing Society** (1933) – as well as I.M. Pei's recent additions. The expanded center, a happy marriage of old and new architectural styles, makes an impressive Vatican for a religious denomination scarcely a century old.

The founding of Christian Science dates to 1866 when a frail, impoverished 45-year-old woman named Mary Baker Patterson took a severe tumble on the ice as she was walking home from a temperance meeting in Lynn, north of Boston. Several days later, after turning to the New Testament for strength and inspiration, Mrs Patterson was suddenly healed, not only of the injuries she'd suffered in the fall, but of the chronic illness that had plagued much of her younger womanhood.

After several years of Bible study, she set out to heal others. In 1875, she posted a notice on her Lynn house designating it as a "Christian Science Home." She was on her way to establishing a major American religious movement at an age when she might have been expected, in her own ironic words, to be a little old lady in a lace cap.

After marrying a follower named Asa Eddy, she moved to Boston, where she continued teaching, writing and guiding the establishment of her church. In 1908, at the age of 87, she founded the *Christian Science Monitor*, a respected daily newspaper which today boasts hundreds of thousands of readers worldwide. More than 3,000 Christian Science societies have been established in some 50 countries.

To the south and east of the Christian Science Center sprawls the **South End**, a semi-gentrified expanse of Victorian bowfront townhouses – in fact, the largest such concentration in the US. The

The Christian Science Mother Church.

safety of this neighborhood – Boston's most ethnically diverse – can vary from block to block, so those wanting to take in such architecturally pleasing sites as the residential areas around **Worcester Square**, **Rutland** and leafy **Union Park Square** should stay on the alert.

The **Boston Center for the Arts**, at Clarendon and Tremont streets, is almost always hopping: this lively complex encompasses artists' studios and galleries, several small experimental theatres, the **Cyclorama** (an 1884 dome now used for antique markets and special exhibits and events), and one of the city's favorite bistros, Hamersley's.

The hub of the arts: From the South End, **Huntington Avenue** leads southwest past several of Boston's greatest institutions. At the northwest corner of Massachusetts Avenue ("Mass Ave") stands the majestic gable-roofed **Symphony Hall**, the acoustically impeccable 1900 building that is home to the renowned Boston Symphony Orchestra and, in summer, its less formal offshoot, the Boston Pops Orchestra. Tickets can

be hard to come by, but any amount of exertion toward admission will be well rewarded.

Continuing down Huntington Avenue, one arrives at the spectacular **Museum of Fine Arts**. Built in 1909 to house holdings that were bursting the joints of an earlier building situated in Copley Square, Guy Lowell's imposing design affords space for plenty of Impressionists – including the largest number of Monets outside France. This incredible museum boasts the most complete assemblage of Asian art under one roof anywhere; the world's best collection of 19th-century American art; and the finest collection of Egyptian Old Kingdom objects outside Cairo. The latter includes what some consider one of the greatest portraits ever executed by the human hand – a limestone bust of Prince Ankh-haf (2520 BC) that is wholly unearthly in its magnificence.

In 1981 I.M. Pei added a stone-clad, glass-topped new wing that perfectly complements that original building and creates an inspiring, expansive space

The chorus at a Greater Boston Youth Symphony Orchestra concert.

ideal for a changing array of exhibits.

Within sight of the Museum of Fine Arts stands the **Isabella Stewart Gardner Museum**, an exquisite 1903 neo-Venetian palazzo assembled by Boston's most flamboyant grand dame. The unstoppable "Mrs Jack" may have scandalized Brahmin Boston (she was known to parade two pet lions down Beacon Street), but she proved a generous and astute patron of the arts. During the 1890s, she set her sights on such masterpieces as Titian's *Rape of Europa*, Rembrandt's *Storm on the Sea of Galilee*, and Vermeer's *The Concert*. In 1896, when her collection was bursting the seams of two adjoining Beacon Hill brownstones, she commissioned her fantasy palace at the very edge of town, alongside the marshes of the Fens.

The galleries that frame the four-story glass-roofed courtyard remained, by her posthumous order, unchanged until March, 1990, when thieves, disguised as policemen, made off with works of art worth $300 million, including the Vermeer, three Rembrandts, five works by Degas and a Manet. To date, none have been recovered. There is still much to see, however, and this eclectic collection, displayed in a charmingly hodge-podge fashion, constitutes one of the great small museums in the world

North of the museums broods another of Boston's great shrines, **Fenway Park**, on whose brightly-lit green baseball diamond the Boston Red Sox do heroic, if usually tragic, battle for the pennant. Here, as the world turns slowly during a muggy twilight doubleheader, the out-of-towner can experience first-hand how Boston turns sport into religion. Indeed, such past stars as Ted Williams and Carl Yastrzemski have been almost deified.

The Charles River: Great cities embrace great rivers from which they are inseparable. This is true of Boston. Here, before the townhouses of Back Bay, the Charles River, having meandered 40 miles (64 km) from its source, widens into a large basin, like a giant mirror held up to the city's profile. It was designed to do just that, by the civic-minded citizens who created the Charles

River Dam in 1908 and in ensuing decades landscaped the lovely **Esplanade**, a winding park of lagoons, trees and walks. Once a festering, polluted eyesore, the river's edge has become one of the city's favorite places to stretch its legs. Roller skaters wired for sound, joggers, bike riders and sunbathers all migrate here. So do the great crowds that turn out to hear the Pops play under open summer skies at the **Hatch Shell**.

The dam itself is home to Boston's **Museum of Science**. Here, visitors can watch simulated lightning, climb into a model of the Apollo lunar module, cower under a plastic Tyrannosaurus Rex, and enjoy a wide variety of ever-changing hands-on exhibits.

Hallowed halls: Elizabeth Hardwick once described Boston and **Cambridge** as two ends of the same mustache. Indeed, across the Charles lies a separate city that is absolutely inseparable from its companion metropolis. Neither suburb nor next town down the pike, Cambridge is the brains of the act, the nerve center of the body.

Crossing **Harvard Bridge**, one first comes to the **Massachusetts Institute of Technology** (MIT). Housed in solid, geometrical buildings, as impersonal and mysterious as natural laws, MIT produces Nobel laureates, new scientific advances and White House science advisors with absolute reliability.

Yet the true *raison d'être* of Cambridge lies another mile or so to the north, up Massachusetts Avenue. Here, standing proudly above the red brick and green ivy, are the spires of **Harvard University**, America's oldest institution of higher learning. Self-confident and backed by enormous wealth, Harvard has been a world index of intellectual accomplishment almost since that day in 1638 when the first 12 freshmen convened in a single frame house bordered by cow pastures. The alma mater of six American presidents to date, Harvard remains a formidable force.

The heart of the place is the fabulous, ancient **Harvard Yard**, withdrawn tranquilly behind the walls that separate it from the maniacal whirl of human and **Harvard Square**.

126

automotive madness in Harvard Square outside. Passing through the gate which proclaims "Enter to Grow in Wisdom," the visitor finds a half-believable fairyland of grass and trees, ghosts and venerable brick. These buildings, and those in surrounding blocks, provide a living, eminently walkable museum of American architecture from colonial times to the present.

Massachusetts Hall (1720), Harvard's oldest standing building, shows the beautiful simplicity of its period, but its history is complex. While it has always provided students with rooms, the Hall has also quartered American Revolutionary troops, as well as housed a lecture hall, a famous drama workshop and, since 1939, the offices of the University president. Nearby stands little **Holden Chapel** (1744), once described as "a solitary English daisy in a field of Yankee dandelions."

At the Yard's center stands Charles Bulfinch's **University Hall**, built of white granite in 1815. In front of it is Daniel Chester French's 1814 statue of John Harvard, the young Puritan minister for whom the college was named after he left it half his estate and all his books. Since no likeness of Harvard existed, French fashioned an idealized figure for his statue, using a student as his model.

East of University Hall, three massive buildings set off the central green on which commencement is celebrated each June. These are H.H. Richardson's 1880 masterwork **Sever Hall**, with its subtle brick decorations; **Memorial Church** (1932), with its Doric columns; and the monumental **Widener Library**, fronted by a broad flight of steps and 12 stone columns. Given by the mother of one Harry Elkins Widener, who died on the *Titanic*, the library is the center of Harvard's network of 92 libraries, which together house over 12 million volumes, America's third largest book collection.

Around this historic core, the university sprawls throughout central Cambridge. The **Harvard Houses** (1930), between the Yard and the Charles, represent a return to the Georgian traditions of the 19th century. These are the residences of sophomores, juniors and seniors. To the east of the Yard stands the **Carpenter Center for the Visual Arts** (1963), a cubist, machine-like design that represents the only American work of the great French architect Le Corbusier. Adjacent to the Harvard campus, to the west, is **Radcliffe**, the sister school which merged with Harvard in 1975. And Harvard extends even beyond the banks of the Charles; the Business School is located across the river, and the Medical School is in Boston, near the Museum of Fine Arts.

Of special interest to visitors are the university's museums. Just outside the Yard to the east is the **Fogg Art Museum**. The Fogg's massive holdings include such masterpieces as Van Gogh's *Self Portrait*, Renoir's *Seated Bather*, Fra Angelico's *Crucifixion* and several early Picassos. It also owns a world-class collection of Chinese cave paintings and archaic Chinese jade.

Adjoining the Fogg, **Werner Otto Hall** houses central and northern European art. The **Arthur Sackler Muse-**

um, across the street, accommodates Harvard's Ancient, Islamic and Oriental collections.

A few blocks north on Oxford Street stands a huge complex housing four oustanding science museums. At the **Botanical Museum**, visitors may behold one of the more unusual achievements of human artisanry – the "Glass Flowers," a collection of true-to-life models of more than 700 plant species executed by Leopold Blaschka and his son Rudolph in 19th-century Dresden.

In the same building, the **Museum of Comparative Zoology** houses, among other things, a whale skeleton, the largest turtle shell ever found, the Harvard mastodon, the lobe-finned coelacanth "living fossil," the giant sea serpent Kronosaurus, George Washington's pheasants (stuffed), the world's oldest reptile eggs and an insect collection containing more than 4 million specimens. If these aren't enough, gems, minerals and meteorites are on display at the **Mineralogical and Geological Museum**, and ancient baskets and masks, as well as other fascinating artifacts, are at the **Peabody Museum of Archaeology and Ethnology**.

A fine, exuberant end to the tour lies in lively **Harvard Square**, the frenetic playground of bookstores, coffeehouses, and shops to the west and north of the Yard. At its center, as a matrix for all wanderings, is the international Out of Town newsstand, housed in a historic kiosk, and beside it, Dmitri Hadzi's gently humorous stone sculpture, *Omphalos*, suggesting that Harvard is indeed, as its supporters have long held, the center (or navel) of the universe.

Opposite Out of Town News is the venerable **Harvard Cooperative Society** ("Coop" for short), a Harvard institution founded in 1882 as an alternative to overpriced local shops; today the prices are pretty much at a par (except for affiliated students and faculty, who enjoy a discount), but the full-scale department store is a favorite with tourists stocking up on Harvard-seal mementos.

But again, wander the streets. Every block presents some window or door to investigate. Browse the fine bookstores like WordsWorth and the Harvard Book Store, check the movie schedules at the area's local collegiate-oriented theaters. There's even a great old tobacco store, a dark cave called Leavitt and Peirce, that carries an interesting collection of ruminative games. In fair weather, chess-masters invariable hold court – and court challengers – at the Au Bon Pain cafe within **Holyoke Center**, a Harvard administrative building that now hosts a corridor of inviting restaurants and shops.

Nearby, on **Dunster Street**, is a mecca for ice cream fans, Herrell's, and John Harvard's Brew House, an atmospheric brew-pub based on the conceit that Harvard's pious benefactor was descended from brewmasters.

But enough said. Just disappear into Harvard Square's incredible menagerie of horn-rimmed professors, head-shaved punks, remnants of the 1960s, "B School" overachievers, fresh-looking undergraduates, tourists from every corner of the universe, and assorted good souls. This is Boston of the 1990s.

Left, memorial to immigrants who came to East Cambridge from all over the world. **Right**, student with founding father John Harvard.

GREATER BOSTON

Even Boston's most committed cosmopolitans would concede that a lot of the city's charm lies outside its boundaries – amid the quiet splendor of hidden beaches and historically rich countryside. Despite a proliferation of unsightly development, the periphery to the north, west, and south still abounds in cultural sites, from Puritan homesteads to Revolutionary battlesites and Transcendental communes. It's here that you'll find the most astonishing little restaurants, and bucolic retreats.

While world-renowned spots like Plymouth Rock attract a million or more visitors a year, lesser-known attractions – for example, a Gropius house tucked away in suburban Lincoln – remain almost private pleasures. Those with time to explore such offbeat delights will be well rewarded by the detour.

The North Shore: A thorough tour should begin in **Newburyport**, 35 miles (56 km) north of Boston, where careful preservation and loving restoration have retained the period flavor of a port that once was home to a magnificent merchant fleet and a thriving shipbuilding industry.

Drivers approaching the old port via US Highway 1 will pass through miles of sleepy farmland in **Topsfield** (the site, every October, of the oldest country fair), Rowley, and Newbury. In fact, it was farming interests that settled the banks of the Merrimack River in 1635.

The visitor who registers culture shock upon emerging from the hinterlands into the European-like sophistication of town might be interested to know that a tussle between rural and citified forces – that is, the incumbent farmers and the emerging mercantile class who drew their living from the sea – erupted over two centuries ago, resulting in the incorporation of the harbor as an independent city in 1764. A decade later, the colonists did manage to cease internal bickering to unite, at least temporarily, in opposition to the British.

Preceding pages: old Coast Guard Station at Eastham. Below, Newburyport

The harbor continued to prosper, enough to survive a devastating fire in 1811 – it's then that the handsome brick buildings of Market Square were constructed – and to finance elaborate dwellings. High Street is where the more successful sea captains built their Greek Revival and late Georgian palaces, some with the symbolic "widows' walks" atop the roofs, where anxious wives strained for a glimpse of their husbands' return to port. The **Cushing House**, a three-story brick mansion at No. 98 High Street, belonged to Caleb Cushing, a 19th-century lawyer (and Newburyport's first mayor) who was appointed the first US Ambassador to China; visitors to the house, now home to the Historical Society of Old Newbury, can view the exotic booty he brought back.

Farther up the street is the **Court House**, where Daniel Webster once practiced law; this handsome brick building was designed by Boston's renowned architect Charles Bulfinch; unfortunately, an overzealous 1853 renovation stripped the building's facade of its columns and arches, but it's still a handsome structure.

The undisputed apogee of self-aggrandizing architecture is the **Lord Timothy Dexter House** at No. 201 High Street. Dexter, an eccentric speculator, bought this plain, boxy 1722 house in 1798 and immediately set about gussying it up. His major contribution was a set of 40 columns topped by carvings of his heroes (Napoleon, Washington, *et al*), in whose august company he decided to include himself. His own likeness bore the inscription: "I am the first in the East, the first in the West, and the greatest philosopher in the known world." The statues are long gone, and the house is in private hands, but it's still an imposing sight, topped with a cupola and curious minarets.

By the early 20th century, the arrival of freighters had reduced the "Clipper City" to an aging relic. However, a model renewal program begun in the 1960s has restored Newburyport's beauty and popularity. The renovated Market Square district is a symphony of

brick and bustle, with dozens of fine shops and restaurants, plus live outdoor entertainment in good weather.

While natives of the North Shore's historic cities are proud of their reconstructed heritage, they especially savor the easy proximity to the immutable pleasures of sea and sand. Newburyport is blessed with the **Parker River National Wildlife Refug**e, just 3 miles (5 km) away via Water Street and known to all simply as **Plum Island**. Depending on the season, the 6 miles (10 km) of sand dunes and ocean beach yields a riot of false heather, dune grass, scrub pine and delicious wild beach plums and cranberries that are harvested by visitors in the fall (three quarts per person, no rakes allowed). Geese, pheasants, rabbits, deer, woodchucks, turtles and toads roam freely over the preserve. Fishing, hiking and bird-watching are encouraged, but in typical New England fashion appreciation of nature goes only so far – nudism is prohibited, much to the dismay of the assorted flying insects that feast on tender exposed flesh during midsummer. Only a limited number of visitors (350 cars) are allowed into the refuge at one time.

City and country meet about 4 miles (7 km) out of town in the **Spencer-Pierce-Little Farm**, a manor house built around 1675–1700 and now owned by the Society for the Preservation of New England Antiquities. A uniquely sturdy building for its day (it was built of stone and brick, instead of the wood customary to the time), it survived three and a half centuries of continual cultivation, under the care of prosperous merchants. Today, with its layers of structural alteration, it's a prime site for architectural archaeology.

The road to Ipswich: State Highway 1A leads out of Newburyport toward Ipswich along a lazy, tree-lined road, where hand-built stone walls (too low to keep people out but high enough to keep sheep in) give way to quaint roadside stands proffering eggs, apples, ice cream, fresh fish and lobsters-to-go. The durables are worth looking into, too: there are some fine antique bargains to be

The Clam Bo in Ipswich, home of the classic fried clam.

found along these roads. This rural entrepreneurship has both roots and a rationale: a look at the treacherous currents off the rocky coastline and the thin topsoil that yielded the pickings for these endless stone walls will explain why neither fishing nor farming alone has ever provided adequate sustenance for the people who live here.

The old streets of the town of **Ipswich** are lined with restored 17th- and 18th-century houses. On Main Street, the 1640 Whipple House is furnished in period style. Worlds apart, and 6 miles (10 km) outside of town, Castle Hill, a mansion built in 1927 by plumbing heir and industrialist Richard T. Crane, presents a wild contrast to the gracious old houses in town. Money was no object when it came to this summer house modeled on 17th-century English manors in the Stuart style: it was lavished on the marble fireplaces, crystal chandeliers, and yes, sterling-silver bathroom fixtures. The house is only opened for tours a few times a year, but concerts are often held within, and on the grounds,

graced with an Italian garden and a scenic Grand Allée leading to the sea. Adjoining the estate and administered by the Trustees of the Reservations (the world's first land trust, founded in 1891 by landscape architect Charles Eliot) is the Crane Memorial Reservation, with 4 miles (7 km) of sandy beach, open to the public and understandably popular.

Despite local claims to grandeur, Ipswich is perhaps best known for its humble clams, an obsession it shares with the neighboring town of **Essex**, 5 miles (8 km) southeast on State 133, where, folk legend has it, the fried clam was born. Raw clams had been a staple of the New England diet since pre-Colonial days, and they're still a regional delicacy. There are those who would argue, however, that the clam had not met its golden ideal until it was dipped in batter and fried in oil, and that's where Woodman's restaurant comes in.

The story goes that on a hot July day in 1915, local restaurateur Lawrence Woodman was frying potato chips and complaining to a fisherman friend that

The rocky
North Shore.

business was slow. "Why not toss some clams in with those chips?" suggested the unsympathetic friend. "That ought to bring in some traffic." Woodman did, thus creating not only the first fried clam but the first fried-clam platter, which hordes of hungry visitors now wait in line to devour. Happy diners in Woodman's wooden booths regularly toast the day that the creative clam juices flowed in Lawrence Woodman's veins.

Proud Cape Ann: From Essex, follow State 1A to State 128, and at Riverdale, take State 127, the scenic drive along the coast of Cape Ann. Visitors to **Cape Ann** (named for the mother of England's King Charles I) should take special care not to compare it with Cape Cod, lest they infuriate the locals, who consider the better known and more commercialized cape to be an elongated slum compared with their regal turf. Partisans are quick to point out that it was Cape Ann fishermen who kept other Massachusetts Bay colonists alive with the catch they shipped down to Boston.

From **Annisquam**, at the mouth of Ipswich Bay, to **Pigeon Cove**, the landscape along this drive looks like old New England – quaint fishing villages and rockbound coast. Despite the benign appearance of the towns and harbors here, they have witnessed some violent behavior. A gang of pirates headed by one John Phillips terrorized Gloucester during the 1720s, until one day a captive fishing crew gained the upper hand and sailed into Lobster Cove, near Annisquam, with Phillips' head hanging from the mast. Today, the populace lead somewhat more sedate lives, and visitors can enjoy the vistas of sea, shanty and rugged landscape that have lured artists like the great American painter Winslow Homer to this lovely peninsula.

Bustling **Rockport**, a former fishing village-turned-artists' colony and tourist attraction, may come as a surprise after this succession of quiet villages. In the early 18th century, the Cape Ann fleet roamed as far south as Havana and as far east as London. The seagoers' cottages crowded onto **Bearskin Neck** have found a new use as tourist-oriented

Fishing boats in Gloucester Harbor.

shops – some kitschy, some charming.

In the 19th century, a new twist was added to Rockport's maritime trade. Granite, quarried nearby, was shipped to ports around the world. Today, an alluring nature preserve can be enjoyed at **Halibut Point State Park** in the quarries which once provided granite for Boston's buildings.

The sea and fishing together dominate **Gloucester**, one of the the oldest seaports in the United States. Here, Leonard Craske's famous statue of the Gloucester Fisherman grips the wheel and peers oceanward, a moving tribute with the legend "they that go down to the sea in ships." The city still boasts an active fishing fleet that scours Georges Bank, and the catch is processed in plants near the waterfront. Every year, the fishermen, who are predominantly of Portuguese and Italian ancestry, participate in the Blessing of the Fleet.

Landlubbers get into the act as well: visitors can take one of the whale-watching cruises that leave daily from the **Cape Ann Marina**. To learn more about the heyday of whaling, and the lifestyle that went with it, visit the Cape Ann Historical Association, for its small but select collection of furnishings and artwork, ranging from 19th-century painter Fitz Hugh Lane's rather sentimental seascapes to semi-abstractions by modernist Milton Avery.

An inspiring view: Facing off across Gloucester Harbor are two intriguing examples of monomaniacal nesting instincts. On Eastern Point Boulevard, the early 1900s **Sleeper-McCann House**, also known as "Beauport," serves as a repository for interior designer Henry Davis Sleeper's extraordinary haul of 18th- and 19th-century furnishings (an advisor to Isabella Stewart Gardner, he was something of a society packrat but an astute collector nonetheless).

Just south of Gloucester, off State 127 on Hesperus Avenue, stands **Hammond Castle**, the 1920s fantasy abode of inventor John Hays Hammond, Jr. With unabashed acquisitiveness, Hammond plundered Europe for authentic elements to work into his dreamhouse, including

a medieval village facade to overlook the indoor pool. His monumental 8,600-pipe organ, the largest such instrument in the US in a private home, is in use.

Strung along the shoreline south of Gloucester are a series of affluent communities, once summer-only but now year-round. Named for the locally abundant swamp flower, **Magnolia** was once the site of luxury hotels drawing summer visitors from as far away as New York and St Louis, then later the scene of extravagant summer living by an elite that built palatial mansions and moored their yachts in the harbor. Outsiders then referred to Main Street's expensive shops as "Robbers' Alley."

A bit farther along State 127 is **Manchester**, a lovely resort town that some still call Manchester-by-the-Sea. The town features stately mansions and **Singing Beach**, where a bare foot scraped across the hard-packed white sand produces a sweetly musical tone.

Bewitching Salem: Though the scandalous witch trials earned **Salem** enduring fame, the area has much else to recommend it. Salem (on State 1A south of State 128) owes its grandeur, now carefully restored, to its former prominence as a seaport. At the **Salem Maritime National Historic Site**, visitors may tour the Derby Wharf and a replica of a 19th-century brigantine, the *Republic*; the Custom House, where Nathaniel Hawthorne once worked; and Derby House, a merchant's mansion built in 1761. Nearby on Turner Street is the House of the Seven Gables, which inspired Hawthorne's novel of that name; interpretive tours are offered.

On Essex Street, the **Essex Institute** preserves six houses that span two centuries of New England architecture, from the Colonial through the Georgian and Federal styles. On the institute's grounds is a museum displaying exhibits of period furniture and local memorabilia.

No visit to Salem should omit the **Peabody Museum**, which features excellent displays related to the maritime trade and a superb collection of artifacts brought back from the Far East.

Salem's maritime glory notwithstand-

Left, bewitching artwork. Right, Salem's Witch Museum.

ing, most visitors will want to tour the scenes of the infamous witchcraft trials of 1692, no mere instance of "hysteria," as it has so often been described, but essentially an act of political repression. The accusations and trials capped off an intense battle for power and property between the conservative, established gentry and an individualist faction. The gentry, personified by the convicting judges, fell back on the time-honored method of attacking political and social upstarts as moral deviants.

Reminders of the witch hunts still exist. The **Salem Witch Museum** reenacts, in a rather sensationalist fashion, key scenes. Far more moving, for all its silent subtlety, is the **Salem Witch Trials Tercentenary Memorial**, a stark granite court adjoining Charter Street Burying Point, the final resting place of Witch Trials Court magistrate John Hawthorne. Incised along the paving stones and walls are passages from the accuseds' pleas of innocence.

A short side trip from Salem, **Marblehead** makes a refreshing day-trip destination. A former port, it abounds in Federal captains' houses; the pre-Revolutionary Old Town section invites strolling. While in town, pay a visit to Hood Sailmakers, a living monument to Yankee ingenuity. Frederick E. (Ted) Hood, who came from a yachting family, had a boyhood hobby of tinkering with sails in the family living room. In 1951, his father helped him buy two looms to make his own sailcloth. With his custom-made sails as his trademark, Ted Hood went on to become a world-famous yachtsman, a successful defender of the America's Cup for 19 years and a highly regarded sail manufacturer.

Echoes of the work ethic: Northwest of the North Shore, via Routes 128 and 93, the one-time model mill town of Lowell, long an industrial dinosaur (and eyesore), is now, improbably enough, enjoying a belated renaissance as a tourist attraction, drawing hundreds of thousands of visitors. Sightseeing ferries ply the old canals, trolleys clang through the streets, and looms pound again at the **Boott Cotton Mills Museum**, operated

ioing fishing.

in conjunction with the Lowell National Historical Park Visitor Center. The many ethnic restaurants in the vicinity, from Greek to Thai, provide reason enough to go. Added incentive is offered by the **New England Quilt Museum**, showcasing outstanding piecework, antique to contemporary.

Home of the Minutemen: From Lowell, Route 3 leads southward to the historic sites at Lexington and Concord. Americans tend to forget that the colonists' uprising was a truly conservative revolution, fought largely by well-to-do landowners concerned with a growing British bite out of their profit margins as well as with theories of liberty and participatory democracy. A visit to **Lexington Green** reveals spacious 18th-century homes, and the largely overpriced shops and restaurants that lie a musket shot away from Henry Kitson's **Minuteman Statue** reflect the town's well-heeled past and present. A further sense of that not-so-distant time and place is provided by a tour of the 1690 **Buckman Tavern**, now restored to its original appearance. Here, on April 19, 1775, Captain John Parker and his 77 Minutemen sipped beer while awaiting Paul Revere's warning.

After the brief skirmish at Lexington, where the greatly outnumbered Minutemen lost eight men, the colonial forces fled to their arms cache at Concord. Modern-day visitors should do the same, for **Concord** offers unmatched New England beauty and atmosphere.

For true historical contrast, travel Route 128 ("America's Technology Highway") past the familiar names of the contemporary high-tech revolution such as Raytheon and Digital, and enter Concord via State 2. Stop at any of the farm stands that border the road and buy a picnic lunch of fresh local fruit and apple cider in season. Then proceed to the Lowell Road bridge over the Concord River and rent a canoe for an approach to the **Old North Bridge** that few tourists experience. Paddling slowly along the winding river, with the branches of stately trees providing shade as they have for more than two centu-

Left, Minuteman statue at Lexington. Right, on parade.

ries, one can understand why the colonists were willing to spill blood to defend this land and preserve its contemplative wonders as their own. At the bridge (a replica), dock and walk the road and bridge where General Gage's British troops, crowded into the narrow pathway, were easily routed by the ragtag Americans. Here, too, nature has shaped history: the annual spring floods had left much of the hill under water and rendered the road unusually narrow, the better to ambush British soldiers.

Although the Minutemen probably had other motives, it's nice to think they fought in part to preserve the freedom of thought and lifestyle that later Concordians explored so fruitfully. Spend a half-day visiting the **Ralph Waldo Emerson House** off State 2A; the Wayside, on Lexington Road, where Hawthorne lived; the Orchard House next door, where Louisa May Alcott wrote *Little Women*; and Henry David Thoreau's famous cabin site in the peaceful woods at **Walden Pond**.

Continuing on Route 128, which cir-

cles Boston en route to the South Shore, there are several worthwhile side trips. In **Lincoln**, the **DeCordova Museum and Sculpture Park** shows intriguing contemporary work in a turreted 1880 mansion; the 35-acre grounds house oversize sculpture (often playful in mood) and an outdoor amphitheater ideal for a summertime series of jazz concerts. Also in Lincoln, off Route 126, is the **Gropius House**, built in 1938 by the seminal Bauhaus architect; it's now the most modern of the historic homes preserved by the Society for the Preservation of New England Antiquities.

In nearby **Weston**, the **Cardinal Spellman Philatelic Museum** on the campus of Regis College contains one of the world's largest stamp inventories. The campus of **Brandeis University** in **Waltham** has some impressive examples of modern institutional architecture as well as the **Rose Art Museum**, which houses an ever-evolving array of outstanding contemporary art.

On State 16, off Route 28 farther South, **Wellesley** is the home of Welles-

On a lazy river at Concord.

ley College, a bucolic campus with notable art holdings, now housed in the dazzling Davis Museum and Cultural Center, a modernist brick cube completed in 1993. The college's holdings, some 5,000 pieces, span medieval, Renaissance, classical and contemporary.

The South Shore: The stretch of picturesque coastal towns and hard-working inland communities loosely known as the South Shore may not exhibit its riches as readily as the North Shore, but they're there for the gleaning. The otherwise undistinguished town of **North Easton**, for instance, has a bevy of public buildings designed by Boston's premier 19th-century architect, Henry Hobson Richardson, as a favor to client Oliver Ames, who manufactured shovels here; Richardson's equally famous collaborator, landscape architect Frederick Law Olmsted (whose credits include New York City's Central Park, as well as Boston's Emerald Necklace), laid out the modest Common.

Few tourists venture this far inland, however, preferring to cleave closer to the shoreline, where centuries of history have left their mark. Within 8 miles (13 km) of Boston, **Quincy's "Old House,"** built in 1731 and repeatedly enlarged, housed four generations of the illustrious Adams family, including a unique father-and-son presidential pair, John Adams (second President of the US), and his son, John Quincy Adams (the sixth). Today their homestead, as well as their birthplaces nearby, constitute the Adams National Historic Site, where guided tours are offered mid-April to mid-November; the high points of the tour are the stone library, packed with 14,000 volumes, and the formal garden, especially appealing when the daffodils are in bloom.

Further down the coast is **Hingham**, beautified, like North Easton, by Frederick Law Olmsted; his handiwork here is the World's End Reservation, a 250-acre harborside estate that is a protectorate of the Trustees of the Reservations. Also noteworthy in Hingham, at the center of town, is the **Old Ship Meetinghouse**, the oldest wooden church in America in continuous use.

Built by ship's carpenters in 1681, the interior resembles a giant hull turned upside down.

Enclosing **Hingham Bay** and curving toward Boston like a beckoning finger is the sandy spit of **Nantasket**, a long-time summer playground (note the 1928 Carousel under the Clock) grown tacky over the years but still offering, from the tiny town of Hull at the tip, an optimal view of Boston Light, said to be the oldest operating lighthouse in America. The **Hull Lifesaving Museum** gives a good idea of the heroic measures required when the lighthouse warnings didn't succeed in staving off disaster.

Every schoolchild in America knows the (probably apocryphal) tale of John Alden, who approached a Pilgrim maiden on behalf of his friend Myles Standish, only to be advised, "Speak for yourself, John." He and Priscilla set up house in the coastal town of **Duxbury**, and their last home there, built in 1653, survives as the **John Alden House**.

Quite close by is the very modern, idiosyncratic, and appealing **Art Com-**

Country fair photographer.

plex Museum, showcasing the collections of lumber heir Carl Weyerhaeuser, whose passions spanned Asian art and Shaker crafts. Contemporary shows are mounted regularly, and on the grounds is an authentic Japanese teahouse where occasional formal tea ceremonies are held. Also worth a visit is the **King Caesar House**, a Federal-style captain's mansion which is packed with China Trade treasures.

From here, King Caesar Road leads – via the longest wooden bridge on the East Coast – to spacious **Duxbury Beach**, one of the few South Shore beaches open to the public.

Plymouth and its rock: Directly southward is Plymouth, which proudly claims the distinction of being "America's Home Town." Earlier attempts at colonization had been assayed, but, thanks to the Pilgrims' grit and determination, this was the first to make a go of it. The very rock they landed on (or so the story goes, passed down to the next generation) enjoys a place of honor under an elaborate portico overlooking the harbor.

The **Pilgrim Hall**, the first custom-built museum in the US, designed in 1824 by Alexander Parris, gathered the more outstanding relics of Pilgrim life early on (though they're rather unimaginatively displayed), and several houses from the period still survive in town, tucked in haphazardly among younger contenders. Actually, it's two fairly recent replicas that give the best sense of what early colonial life was really like.

Docked in the harbor, the *Mayflower II* is a full-scale replica that was built in England and sailed to Plymouth in 1957; skilled actors on board portray the original passengers, and field visitors' questions with accuracy and wit.

About 3 miles (5 km) south of town, on State 3, **Plimoth Plantation** is a painstaking reconstruction of the 17th-century Pilgrim village, also inhabited by actor/interpreters who so convincingly enact the quotidian rituals of the original village, visitors can easily lose themselves in the fantasy of those heady days full of hardship and dreams.

eft,
limouth
Plantation.
Right,
Mayflower II
n Plymouth.

CAPE COD

Shaped like a bodybuilder's flexed arm, Cape Cod extends 31 miles (50 km) eastward into the Atlantic Ocean, then another 31 miles to the north. Well-forested up to about the "elbow," then increasingly reduced to scrub oak and pitch pine, this sandy peninsula is lined with more than 310 miles (500 km) of beaches. The crook of the arm forms Cape Cod Bay, where the waters are placid and free of often treacherous ocean surf. Lighthouses along the ocean side guide mariners plying the cold Atlantic waters.

Though Bostonians consider it their own private playground, Cape Cod's fame has spread so far that it attracts international travelers. In high season (July and August), lodgings are filled to capacity, traffic on the Cape's few highways is heavy, and local merchants work hard to make the profits that will carry them through the all-but-dormant winters. (The pleasures of the Cape off-season, however, are a well-guarded secret not likely to remain a secret much longer.) Even at the height of its summertime popularity, when the roads, restaurants, and beaches tend to be jammed, Cape Cod manages to preserve its wild charm and dramatic beauty.

Much of this beauty is protected within the boundaries of the Cape Cod National Seashore, a vast 27,000-acre (11,000-hectare) nature reserve established by foresighted legislators in 1961. Precisely because it has not been commercially exploited, this huge expanse of untouched dunes – a natural phenomenon created by geological forces about 1 million years ago – survives as one of the Cape's most alluring features.

Formed during the Ice Age, Cape Cod is relatively "young" as geological features go. An enormous ice sheet several miles thick moved southward out of Hudson Bay, covering the northeastern United States all the way to Long Island, Nantucket and Martha's Vineyard. There, the slow-moving river of ice, laden with glacial debris, met warmer air and water, which melted the leading edge of the ice and freed the soil and rock to sink in the ocean. For hundreds of thousands of years, this leading edge was poised where Nantucket and Martha's Vineyard are today, and the soil and rock dumped during that long period of treadmill activity formed glacial moraine. The air and water grew even warmer, and the glacier retreated 25 or 30 miles (40 or 50 km) to the area known now as Cape Cod. The wall of ice melted here, laying down another moraine, the foundation of the Cape.

When the glacier retreated to the polar ice cap, the ice turned to water, filling the oceans. But the earth, long compressed under the weight of ice, rebounded and thrust the moraines above the surface of the sea. Wind and water erosion, over tens of thousands of years, finished sculpting Cape Cod.

Simple pleasures: A stroll through subdued and elegant Chatham or an evening out in bustling Provincetown might lead one to think of Cape Cod as the eternal summer resort. Not so. The first hordes

eceding ges: all the ar for ostering. t, Douse's ach. Right, iting for waves.

of tourists arrived late in the 19th century, brought by steamship, railroad and – eventually – automobile. Escaping the heat of the cities (Boston, Providence and New York) for the cool sea breezes along the shore, early visitors found low prices, inexpensive real estate and simple pleasures in abundance.

Before the advent of modern transport, Cape Cod was a hardscrabble area peopled by the Wampanoag tribes, hardy Yankees and industrious immigrants from the coasts and islands of Portugal. Since the land was too poor to farm for more than local consumption, most people earned their living from the sea. Fishing, saltmaking, whaling, shipbuilding and "wrecking" – scavenging the beaches for the flotsam and jetsam of ships lost at sea – provided the local people with a livelihood, however uncertain. One year might bring a small fortune in whale oil, or a windfall of English cloth washed ashore from an unfortunate wreck or a hoard of doubloons dumped on the sand at whim by the sea; the next might bring little income, more death at sea and much destruction from drought and storm.

In 1602, British mariner Bartholomew Gosnold, sailing by this long arm of sand, noted a great many codfish in the waters and added the name "Cape Cod" to his map. In 1620, the *Mayflower* pulled into the harbor of what is now Provincetown and, before debarking to explore, drew up the Mayflower Compact, whereby they constituted themselves as a "civil Body Politick" and vowed to work together under just laws for the good of all. This early "constitution" grew into the government of the Commonwealth of Massachusetts.

Across the canal: Purists could actually call Cape Cod an island, for in 1914, after five years of work, the Cape was effectively severed from the mainland by the **Cape Cod Canal**. Improved and widened in 1927, the canal is a boon to north-south ships, which no longer have to venture out into the stormy Atlantic to circumvent the Cape.

Visitors come to Cape Cod by air, sea and road. The Cape towns of Hyannis

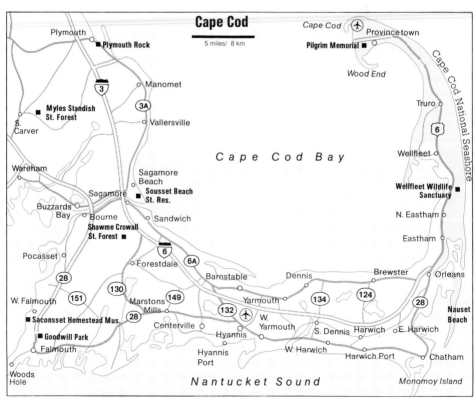

and Provincetown have scheduled air services to and from Boston; there are New York-Hyannis flights as well. Small planes shuttle passengers from Hyannis across the water to the islands of Nantucket and Martha's Vineyard. In summer, excursion boats leave Boston Harbor each morning for Provincetown, three hours away. The return trip can bring day-trippers back to Boston the same afternoon. There is also a regular bus service and charter tours. Barring impenetrable traffic jams – common on summer weekends – the trip from Boston to Provincetown takes two hours.

In the early heyday of the Cape, summer visitors arrived by train – an option still available in summer from New York. The **Cape Cod Scenic Railroad** runs sightseeing and dinner excursions along a pastoral stretch of track between Hyannis and the Canal. Otherwise, with a singular lack of foresight, most of the trail network has been dismantled. However, at least one long section of roadbed has been put to an energy-saving, pleasure-making use: running from

Dennis through Nickerson State Park to Eastham, the **Cape Cod Rail Trail** is a 20-mile (32–km) paved recreational path ideal for bicycling, skating, hiking and jogging. Another popular network of paved paths is the **Cape Cod National Seashore Trail**, found at the northern tip of the Cape. It's a spectacularly sculpted landscape of sweeping dunes descending into green hollows of scrub brush and stunted forest, with the sea all around to provide invigorating breezes.

Today, by far the most popular way of getting to Cape Cod is by bus or car. Expressways funnel traffic to the two access bridges over the Canal. To the north is the **Sagamore Bridge**, a graceful arched structure with one foot in the Cape town of Sagamore. State 3 comes south from Boston and crosses the Sagamore Bridge to join US Highway 6, the Mid-Cape Highway. Near the southwestern end of the Canal is the **Bourne Bridge**, leading to State 28 headed for Falmouth and Woods Hole. Information booths at the mainland foot of each bridge offer directions and help in find-

Cape Cod
escarpment.

ing accommodation. For the packed summer months, though, it's best to reserve well ahead.

Before venturing too far "down-cape," the visitor must learn the nomenclature. "Upper Cape" refers to the portion nearest the mainland; "Mid-Cape" is roughly from Barnstable County eastward to Chatham and Orleans, where the "arm" bends; "Lower Cape" is the "forearm" jutting northward to Eastham, Truro and Provincetown.

Itineraries on the Upper and Mid-Cape offer a choice of speedy, featureless highways or scenic, meandering roads. Those intent on reaching the Outer Cape in a hurry generally opt for US 6, the four-lane, limited-access Mid-Cape Highway; those headed for Falmouth and Woods Hole can take the equally speedy State 28. Anyone wishing to get a true sense of the Cape, however, will be well rewarded by taking the somewhat pokier, but much prettier non-highway counterparts. Roughly parallel to the Mid-Cape Highway, two-lane State 6A starts in **Sagamore** and runs eastward through charming old towns full of graceful historic houses, crafts and antique shops, and charming restaurants. The same can be said of State 28A, hugging the shore en route to Falmouth. As 28 veers northeastward from Falmouth to **Chatham** it's marred by recurrent stretches of overdevelopment, but again, one has only to venture off the main road a bit to discover such lovely towns as **Osterville** and **Centerville**, **Harwich Port** and Chatham itself. Once 28 and 6 merge in Orleans, Route 6 north is pleasant all the way to Provincetown, if traffic-clogged.

The placid bayside: From the motels, gas stations and businesses at the southern end of the Sagamore Bridge, Route 6A loops around under the Sagamore Bridge. Just past it, keep an eye out on the left side of the road for the **Pairpoint Glass Works**, where glassblowers give demonstrations daily. This region gained world renown for its glass after Boston merchant Deming Jarvis founded a glass factory in the neighboring town of Sandwich in 1825. By taking advantage of **Clamming.**

local resources (sand shipped in from the Outer Cape, local timber to stoke the furnaces, and salt marsh to pack the delicate product,) and using mass-production techniques, Jarvis put glassware – formerly a rare and precious commodity – within the reach of ordinary people. His Boston and Sandwich Glass Company factory thrived until threatened by coal-powered plants in the Midwest; that, and a strike by exploited workers, shut the enterprise down in 1888. However, examples of their output, in an astounding range of styles, can still be found in the **Sandwich Glass Museum**, and in the many antique shops that line this historic old route.

Sandwich was the first town to be founded on the Cape, in 1637, and today – with the factories long since razed, the groves of trees regrown – it's one of the prettiest, and best preserved, towns on the Cape. At its center stands the restored **Dexter Mill** and the **Hoxie House**, dating from colonial times. For more glimpses into the American past, follow the signs – past a lovely historic

cemetery overlooking **Shawme Pond** – to **Heritage Plantation**, a spacious museum complex whose grounds, in spring, are awash in the vivid pinks and purples of flowering rhododendrons. Several buildings display extraordinary collections, from children's toys (including a working carousel) to military artifacts and artwork. A round stone barn (copied from the Shaker original in Hancock, Massachusetts) houses an outstanding array of early cars, including a beauty, Gary Cooper's 1931 Deusenberg.

Motoring east, into the county of Barnstable, you'll pass a 6-mile barrier beach, **Sandy Neck**, which is a favored habitat of the endangered piping plover. Hikers and swimmers are welcome to explore this sandy spit, provided they don't disturb nesting sites. Whalewatching cruises depart from **Barnstable Harbor** (it's a shorter trip to Stellwagen Bank from Provincetown, but for those who don't mind some extra time out on the water, this departure point is just as good).

Just up the hill from the harbor is the

Windsurfing ff Truro.

Trayser Museum, the former Custom House that now houses fascinating exhibits on local history.

Some miles east of Barnstable, **Yarmouth Port** is a delightful village with fine old houses to tour, including the **Captain Bangs Hallett House**, an 1840 Greek Revival showcase house now owned by The Historical Society of Old Yarmouth, and the **Winslow Crocker House**, a Georgian manse from around 1780 now maintained by the Society for the Preservation of New England Antiquities. For a pleasurable glimpse of more recent history, stop for an ice cream soda at **Hallett's**, a well-preserved 1889 drugstore.

In the town of **Dennis**, follow signs for the **Scargo Hill Tower**, a stone turret from which it's possible to see, on a clear day, Cape Cod laid out like a map, with Provincetown easily visible at the northern tip. Dennis is home to America's oldest, and most outstanding, professional summer theatre: aspiring thespians such as Bette Davis (an ambitious usher) and Henry Fonda be-

gan their careers at the Cape Playhouse, founded in 1927 by Raymond Moore, a renegade from Provincetown's "little theatre" movement. Productions here are skilled and lavish, and movies at the adjoining Cape Cinema are a sensory treat: it features leather armchairs with antimacassars and Art Deco frescoes by Rockwell Kent.

Besides its fine old houses and inns, **Brewster** has a variety of attractions. The **Cape Cod Museum of Natural History** explores the local habitat with hands-on exhibits and a small network of nature trails. The **New England Fire and History Museum** has large collections of vintage fire-fighting equipment and memorabilia. One of the most picturesque sights, the **Stony Brook Mill** (on Stony Brook Road southwest off State 6A) grinds cornmeal several days a week; there's a small museum upstairs. Each spring, from mid-April to early May, the mill hosts an eye-catching event: here, in a timeless ceremony similar to a salmon run, schools of alewives (a fish resembling herring) leap up a **Wellfleet**.

series of ladders to spawn in the freshwater pond behind the mill.

Railroad magnate Roland Nickerson once owned 2,000 acres (800 hectares) of open land in Brewster and held them as his personal hunting and fishing preserve. In 1934 his widow donated most of this tract to the state; today **Nickerson State Park** is a popular spot for camping, swimming, picnicking, and walks.

The National Seashore: A popular base for touring the Cape, Orleans also offers the first sight of **Cape Cod National Seashore** (which extends along the Atlantic coast all the way to Provincetown) in the form of **Nauset Beach**, one of the Cape's finest. The settlement was called by its Indian name of Nauset until it was incorporated in 1797 and renamed for the Duke of Orleans (the future king of France), a recent visitor. Orleans has another "French connection" – it was the stateside terminus for a transatlantic telegraph cable to Brest in France. Hooked up in 1879, the cable performed well for decades before it become obsolete, and is now commemorated in the French Cable Museum on State 28.

Eastham's town green contains a 1793 windmill. For a deeper side trip into Cape Cod's history, head west to **First Encounter Beach**. It's here that a Pilgrim scouting party out of Provincetown first encountered a band of Indians, who, wary after earlier encounters with kidnappers, attacked the Pilgrims and were rebuffed by gunfire. This uneasy meeting is among the reasons the Pilgrims pressed on to Plymouth. Today the historic site is a peaceful town beach which, like most, charges a parking fee in summer.

Further up State 6A, still in Eastham, is the **Salt Pond Visitor Center** of the Cape Cod National Seashore. Interpretive films and exhibits explain the ecology of the Cape, and a bicycle trail (bikes can be rented nearby) winds through pine forests and marshes to end at **Coast Guard Beach**, where, in the 1920s, Henry Beston wrote his classic *Outermost House*, and, further north, **Nauset Light Beach**, graced with a picturesque lighthouse. Just across from the Salt Pond Visitors' Center, behind a

gateway fashioned from the jawbones of a whale, is the 1869 **Schoolhouse Museum**, housing the collections of the Eastham Historical Society.

Famous for its oysters, **Wellfleet** is one of Cape Cod's most appealing towns, full of fine galleries and fun restaurants, and surrounded by inviting wildlife areas. Just south of town, off US 6, the Audubon Society maintains the 700-acre (283-hectare) **Wellfleet Bay Wildlife Sanctuary**; to the west of town is Great Island (part of the Cape Cod National Seashore), which re-attached itself to the mainland and became a barrier beach. To the east is **Marconi Beach**, where Guglielmo Marconi set up the first wireless station in the United States and transmitted the first trans-Atlantic wireless message to Europe in 1903. The **Atlantic White Cedar Swamp Trail**, starting from the Marconi site, is especially beautiful.

Farther north, the landscape becomes ever more wild and barren. Scrubby vegetation gives way to desert-like sand dunes. East of **Truro**, the **Cranberry**

Where cycles really score.

Bog Trail (within the Cape Cod National Seashore) offers a look at the natural habitat of the tiny red fruit which proved such a boon to Cape Cod agriculture. Another road east leads to **Highland Light**, towering over Head of the Meadow Beach.

Portrait of Provincetown: The very tip of Cape Cod – which is almost entirely within National Seashore boundaries – is unusual and fascinating. Two vast beaches, **Race Point** and **Herring Cove**, invite exploration: by bike, on horseback, on foot, and off-road vehicle tours. For an overview and information, drop in at the Province Lands Visitors' Center.

Contrast the subtle beauties and serenity of the National Seashore lands with the raucous and sometimes tawdry atmosphere along Commercial Street in **Provincetown**. Sidewalk artists will do a pastel portrait, or perhaps a cartoon caricature, in a flash. Shops emblazoned with advertisements sell fine works of art, bad works of art, kitsch souvenirs, and an infinite variety of snacks. There are good restaurants and bad ones, beau-tiful old inns and inexpensive guest houses, tacky shacks and beautiful landscaped captains' mansions.

With its well-protected harbor, Provincetown started out as a natural fishing port – long before the Pilgrims came along. So it remains to this day. Portuguese fishermen, many from the Azores, came here in the heyday of the whaling trade and stayed on for the good fishing. Their descendants still make up a sizable proportion of the town's year-round residents. Led by painter Charles Hawthorne, who in 1899 founded the Cape Cod School of Art, hordes of artists and writers from New York's Greenwich Village flocked to Provincetown in the early decades of the 20th century, drawn partly by the area's stark beauty and largely by the cheap rents and food to be found here (thanks to the tourist boom they inspired, the latter are of course history).

Among the innumerable notables who passed through here, if only briefly, are dramatists Eugene O'Neill and Tennessee Williams, and writers Sinclair Lewis

and John Dos Passos. Perhaps the best-known recent writer-in-summer-residence is Norman Mailer. A dozen or more illustrious painters, such as Robert Motherwell, have left their mark, with new contenders cropping up year after year, in such cutting-edge galleries as the Long Point and Bertha Walker. A number of galleries, including Walker and the Julie Heller gallery, now specialize in Provincetown art going back to the beginning of the century.

Other places to catch outstanding early work are the **Provincetown Art Association and Museum**, founded in 1914; the relatively new **Provincetown Heritage Museum**, which also harbors a half-scale model of a fishing schooner; and the poorly-lit corridors of the 1878 **Town Hall**, where concerts and performances are held throughout the year.

The lofty Italianate tower looming above the town is the **Pilgrim Memorial**, built early in the century to ensure that Provincetown's place in colonial history not be overlooked. The determined climber (there's also an elevator) will be rewarded with a panoramic view of the town and the entire Cape. At the monument's foot is the **Provincetown Museum**, with intriguing local history exhibits and an open lab where the spoils from the *Whydah*, a pirate ship discovered off Wellfleet in 1984, are being cleaned and catalogued.

The Southern Shore: Cape Cod's southern shore, from Chatham to Falmouth, is a zone where the battle for – and against – commercialization has raged for the past few decades. Some pockets of subdued gentility still reign just off the honky-tonk stretches.

Chatham numbers among the aristocratic enclaves. The handsome **Chatham Bars Inn** was built as a private hunting lodge early in the century. The nearby Fish Pier is a perfect spot to watch the fishing fleet bring in the daily catch. The **Chatham Railroad Museum** is housed in the town's ornate Victorian railroad station, out of commission for several decades. **Chatham Light**, yet another picturesque Coast Guard lighthouse, overlooks South

Beach. Bird fanciers will want to visit **Monomoy Island**, a stopping point for hundreds of species of birds traveling the Atlantic Flyway. Protected as the **Monomoy National Wildlife Refuge**, it is accessible only by boat; both the Audubon Society and the Cape Cod Museum of Natural History offer cruises.

Picturesque **Harwich** and **Harwich Port** are the last peaceful settlements before the Cape's commercial belt. From West Harwich to Hyannis, State 28 is lined with motels, restaurants, businesses and amusements. It's a long, tawdry stretch, where traffic usually crawls all summer.

Hyannis, the Cape's year-round commercial center, boasts more than a score of worthwhile restaurants and nightclubs, the **Cape Cod Melody Tent** (for intimate concerts featuring top-name talent), and, in the old Town Hall, the **John F. Kennedy Museum**, featuring photos and mementos of the President who summered in adjoining Hyannis Port. (Although the **Kennedy Compound** is the object of many a pilgrim-

age, it is not open to the public and very little of it can be seen from the road). A small park dedicated to Kennedy's memory adjoins **Veterans Beach**, on Hyannis's harbor.

West of Hyannis, the tide of commercialism subsides occasionally to provide glimpses of Cape Cod's signature beauty. Make a southward detour for lovely **Centerville**, where relatively warm-watered **Craigville Beach** has drawn Christian "camp meetings" since the mid-19th century, and for affluent **Osterville**, a rarefied village surrounded by awe-inspiring seaside mansions.

Heading on toward Falmouth, take a side trip north to **Mashpee**, located amid Wampanoag tribal lands which in recent decades have been carved up by development. The **Old Indian Meetinghouse**, the oldest church building on the Cape, built in 1684, is well worth a look.

Falmouth is like a microcosm of Cape Cod life. The town green – a Revolutionary militia training ground – is among the prettiest on the Cape; it's ringed by fine old houses, including several charming B&Bs, and the **Falmouth Historical Society Museums**. Falmouth Harbor is filled with pleasure craft; swimmers and windsurfers favor the beaches and guest houses of Victorian-era **Falmouth Heights**, overlooking Nantucket Sound.

One of the nicest activities in Falmouth is to rent a bicycle and follow the old railroad bed, now a bike path, down to **Woods Hole**. This small town is devoted almost exclusively to maritime activities. Most travelers pass through here merely to board the ferry for Martha's Vineyard, a 45-minute voyage away. But Woods Hole itself warrants a stopover. The world-famous Woods Hole Oceanographic Institute maintains a visitor center to describe its fascinating research; visitors can also tour the Marine Biological Laboratory (reservations must be made in advance), and the small but intriguing National Marine Fisheries Service Aquarium. Though no larger than a couple of city blocks, this tiny town supports a number of superb casual restaurants, where the specialty, naturally, is seafood.

Left, not a shoppe for ye slimmers **Right**, a day's catch from Nantucket Sound.

MARTHA'S VINEYARD

Over the decades, Vineyard residents have grown blasé about the celebrities in their midst, and precisely because of that laissez-faire attitude, the roster just kept growing. World-renowned actors, musicians, writers, and public figures (including the late Jacqueline Onassis) have felt comfortable here. It took a Presidential visit – the Clintons' during the summer of 1993 – to shake things up a bit, but, despite the hordes lining the roadways, most people went about their business, and leisure, as usual.

Islanders have worked too hard to create and preserve a relaxed way of life to let a little glitz and glamour throw them. For many, the island represents a true escape from the pressures of city life and the stresses of high-powered careers. Though the price of admission may be high, once one has arrived, a kind of barefoot democracy prevails.

Like Cape Cod, Martha's Vineyard is a geological remnant from the last Ice Age. Two advancing lobes of a glacier molded the triangular northern shoreline, then retreated, leaving hilly moraines, low plains and many-fingered ponds. And Martha herself? She was the daughter of Thomas Mayhew, who in 1642 bought a large tract of land, including Nantucket Island, for just £40 – the equivalent today of $60. (Mayhew named Elizabeth Island after another daughter.)

The three protected harbor towns of the northeastern, or down-island portion, Vineyard Haven, Oak Bluffs, and Edgartown, were always more active and prosperous, and to this day represent the commercial half of the island, although the main order of business is no longer shipping and whaling, but tourism and summer homes. The sparsely populated "down-island" towns of West Tisbury, Chilmark, Menemsha, and Gay Head remain determinedly rural and non-ostentatious, despite a number of famous residents.

It may come as a disappointment to many visitors to find that, as a rule,

Martha's Vineyard's extensive beaches are not accessible to outsiders but have been reserved for homeowners; the major exception, beyond the placid Joseph Sylvia State Beach on the bay side, is South Beach, fronting the rolling Atlantic south of Edgartown.

A lively port: Long before the Cape Cod Canal provided a shortcut between Boston and ports south, boats had to travel around Cape Cod to make a coastal journey. As traffic on this route and those striking out to the West Indies increased, the harbor at the tip of the Vineyard grew in importance as a shelter and a source of supplies.

Known until 1870 as Holmes Hole, **Vineyard Haven** (the official name of the town is Tisbury, but everyone calls it by the name of its primary village) blossomed into a busy port during the 18th and 19th centuries, with both maritime businesses and farmers profiting from the constant movement of ships in and out of the port. Today, the homy Black Dog Tavern (with its offshoot bakery, store, and catalog business) en-

joys a similar relationship with the legions of vacationers who arrive by ferry from Woods Hole.

Vineyard Haven has a no-nonsense, matter-of-fact quality about it, with little of the preciousness of Edgartown or the cuteness of Oak Bluffs. Handsome houses dating from the years before the great fire of 1883 can be found on Williams Street, a block off Main Street. On Beach Street, near the water, is the contemporary **Luce House Gallery**, in an 1804 Federal House owned by the Dukes County Historical Society. The **Old Schoolhouse Museum**, located on Main Street, was built in 1829 to serve as the Tisbury school; it now contains island artifacts and whaling trade mementos collected by the Martha's Vineyard Preservation Trust.

Oak whimsy: Religion tinged with tourism produced an unusual community in **Oak Bluffs**, a town renowned for its engaging cottages built in "carpenter gothic" style.

In 1835, Methodists took to the backwoods out of Edgartown in search of a suitable site for a camp meeting, a place where the faithful could come for a short period of spiritual replenishment. They found a secluded circle of oak trees, named it Wesleyan Grove, and conducted the first summer camp meeting on the site. Twenty years later, there were more than 320 tents and many thousands of people. Small houses soon replaced the tents, laid out along circular drives that rimmed the large central "tabernacle" where the congregation assembled.

Today this camp meeting site is known as **Trinity Park**. Tiny gingerbread cottages are a riot of color and jigsaw carvery, with all manner of turrets, spires, gables and eaves. Yet the park remains remarkably serene and intimate. The huge cast iron-and-wood amphitheater in the center of the campground, built in 1870, still hosts community gatherings. Illumination Night, held every August, recreates the camp's traditional closing-night ceremony, when colorful glowing lanterns were strung up throughout the park. Circuit and Lake

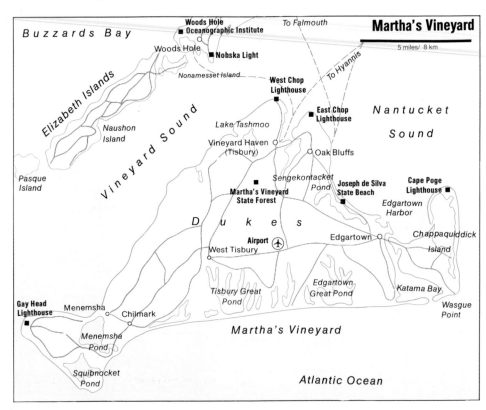

Streets mark the hub of town and the site of the **Flying Horses** (1876), the oldest merry-go-round in America.

Edgartown elegance: South of Oak Bluffs on Beach Road, Edgartown is the oldest settlement on Martha's Vineyard. In 1642, missionary Thomas Mayhew, Jr., son of the Watertown, Massachusetts, entrepreneur who bought the islands off the Cape for a pittance, arrived at Great Harbor, now **Edgartown**, and set about converting the island's native population. Relying on fishing or farming, the town grew at a slow pace until the 18th century, when it became a capital in the worldwide whaling trade, vying with Nantucket and, later, New Bedford. The captains who made their fortunes from the sea left behind a treasure: their elegant Federal and Greek Revival houses, especially those lining North and South Water streets.

The most dignified Edgartown residence is that built in 1840 by whale-oil magnate Dr Daniel Fisher, who once supplied all US lighthouses with Edgartown oil. His house sits on upper Main Street, next to the imposing Greek Revival **Old Whaling Church** of 1843, whose enormous pillars and soaring tower are a rare instance of monumental scale in Edgartown. Tucked behind is the **Vincent House** (1672), an example of the popular 17th-century Cape design. At the corner of Cooke and School streets is **The Vineyard Museum**, whose collections include whaling items, artifacts from daily Vineyard life and the famous French-made Fresnel lens, which until 1952 cast the warning beam from Gay Head Lighthouse.

A stone's throw away from Edgartown, across a narrow neck of the harbor, is **Chappaquiddick Island** which hit the world's headlines as a result of the 1969 accident in which Senator Edward Kennedy drove his car over a bridge on the island, drowning his 28-year-old passenger, Mary Jo Kopechne. The island's native name meant "The Separated Island," which it steadfastly remains, although the *On-Time III* regularly ferries cars (a few at a time) and clusters of pedestrians over the 200-

yard (183-meter) crossing. The main attraction on "Chappy," several miles from the ferry landing, is the **Wasque Reservation and Cape Poge Wildlife Refuge** at the island's eastern front.

Up-island escape: Should you tire of the enticing stores and restaurants to be found down-island, you need only retreat to the tranquility of up-island life (although the drive west from Edgartown, leading through forests of pine and oak, starts the transition to a Vineyard where nature still decisively holds the upper hand).

The 4,000-acre (1,640-hectare) **Martha's Vineyard State Forest** – laced with walking and bridle paths and containing the island's only youth hostel – brings the scent of pines to the outskirts of **West Tisbury Center**.

This modest and unassuming village traditionally has been a center of small industry (including woolen and flour mills). Quirky attractions such as the **Field Gallery** (where Tom Maley's fanciful sculptures frolic in a field) and the **Granary Gallery** at the Red Barn Emporium (showcasing the historic photos of summer regular Alfred Eisenstaedt, as well as contemporary work) draw more attention these days, but the county fair is still a high point of the summer.

Of the three parallel roads traveling from West Tisbury to Chilmark, Middle Road traverses the most rugged, interesting glacial terrain. At **Chilmark Center** is **Beetlebung Corner**, a stand of tupelo trees from which "beetles" (mallets) and "bungs" (wooden stoppers) were once made.

Nearby **Menemsha** is a tiny fishing village on Vineyard Sound, famed for its appearance in *Jaws* and prized for its Technicolor sunsets.

It is extraordinary but fitting that the most spectacular natural sight on Martha's Vineyard should be situated at its westernmost tip, looking away from the commotion of the domesticated island and out to the untamed sea. From Chilmark, follow the single hilly road that at several points offers breathtaking views of **Menemsha Pond** northward and **Squibnocket Pond** to the south. At the end, a lighthouse marks the western terminus of the island and the location of the stunning, ancient geologic strata that compose the cliffs at **Gay Head**. Clays of many colors – from gray to pink to green – represent eons of geological activity: fossils found amid the ever-changing contours of this 150-ft (46-meter) promontory have been dated back millions of years.

Gay Head is one of only two Native American communities in Massachusetts; it has been more successful than the Mashpee settlement in asserting its rights, and remains a cohesive social entity, over three centuries since the advent of colonizing forces.

On **Indian Hill Road**, heading back toward Vineyard Haven, is the site of **Christiantown**, settled by "praying Indians" in 1659; a plaque fixed to a boulder honors Thomas Mayhew's missionary efforts. At the end of the road, the **Cedar Tree Neck Wildlife Sanctuary** provides a commanding view of the Vineyard Sound, across to the Elizabeth Islands, and a fine spot for strolling and contemplating nature.

Left, seaside treat. **Right**, Gay Head lighthouse lens, Edgartown Museum.

NANTUCKET

In 1830 the whaling ship *Sarah* returned home to Nantucket Island, carrying 3,500 barrels of valuable whale oil after a voyage of nearly three years. On the island, stately mansions, decorated with silks and china from faraway lands, awaited the returning captains. Schools, hotels, a library and the commercial activity on Main Street were indications of a prosperous people.

These were the halcyon days of little Nantucket Island, the shining moment in its turbulent past. Although its fortunes soon declined, time has stood still on Nantucket, and the intimate scale and refined taste of its heyday have survived to the present day to endow the island with its charm, beauty and magnetic appeal.

Nantucket may never again know the excitement and adventure of the whaling trade, but its new industry – tourism – has brought an equal amount of fame and fortune. Like the earliest settlers, who came to escape the Puritan lifestyle, people today come to Nantucket to leave behind the harsh realities of life on the mainland.

Chasing the whales: Since its earliest days, Nantucket has been populated by determined and spirited people. The first colonists, who arrived from Massachusetts in 1659, were taught "onshore" whaling by the native Algonquins; they traveled out in open boats to chase and harpoon whales sighted from land. By the beginning of the 18th century, offshore whaling had begun and, with each generation of larger, more seaworthy craft, the whaling industry grew.

But the natives lost out. Although they sailed on whaling boats, their way of life on the island was irreversibly changed by the colonists. By 1855, disease and alcohol had taken the last of Nantucket's original residents.

By the time of the Revolutionary War, Nantucket had a fleet of 150 whaling ships. But Quaker pacifism and Nantucket's interest in London markets for whale oil divided islanders' loyalties,

and their ships suffered greatly at the hands of the Tories and Revolutionaries alike. No sooner had they rebuilt their fleet than the War of 1812 erupted; by the conflict's end, their whaling empire had once again been left battered and exhausted.

Tenacity brought Nantucket back to life. Nantucket ships again sailed throughout the world and brought back record quantities of oil from their catches. It was during this period that the town acquired much of its urbanity, but the islanders' prosperity was destined to be short-lived: the Great Fire of 1846 razed the port, and in the 1850s kerosene replaced whale oil. Too heavily dependent on whaling, Nantucket was left high and dry.

From a peak of around 10,000, Nantucket's population dropped to 3,200 in 1875. Those who remained applied their ingenuity to a new venture, one that thrives today and continues to capitalize on the gifts of the sea. Tourism took off toward the end of the 19th century, as the arrival of the steamboat

Preceding pages: processing cranberries. Left, jumping in the sand dunes is not encouraged. Right, Nantucket's harbor.

made the island more readily accessible from the mainland. Land speculators built hotels and vacation homes. Quaint Siasconset, linked to the town by a narrow-gauge railway building in 1884, was especially popular, drawing such luminaries as actress Lillian Russell. The railway is gone now (it was used for scrap metal during World War I), but tourism lives on.

An Indian word meaning "that faraway land," Nantucket isn't too far away for the thousands of people who visit each year by ferry and airplane. The winter population of 7,000 – lower than that recorded for the peak of the whaling era – increases sevenfold when the "summer people" take over the sidewalks of town and give it its cheery aspect.

In sharp contrast to Martha's Vineyard, Nantucket's mid-island moors and miles of beautiful, unspoiled beaches are open to visitors, most of whom use the preferred island mode of transportation: bikes (several shops stand ready to equip tourists near the ferry dock). Though smaller residential neighborhoods dot the island's coast, the harbor town of **Nantucket**, centrally located on the north shore, is unquestionably the focal point of the island.

The pleasures of town: One can spend days walking through town and always be sure of seeing something new. The community is a gem of 18th- and 19th-century architecture, from the dominant clapboard-and-shingle Quaker homes to the grandeur of the buildings lining Upper Main Street. And while the town may seem a maze of narrow streets, it is actually very ordered in its own cluttered way: early in the 18th century, its center was laid out in lots that ran roughly east-west from the harbor. Nevertheless, it is best to tour with a street map (available from the bike shops, or in the free local newspapers distributed on the ferry), for the twists and turns can prove disorienting.

The waterfront is certainly the spiritual center of town. Several wharves extend into the harbor, the most central of which – **Straight Wharf** – is an extension of Main Street. First built in

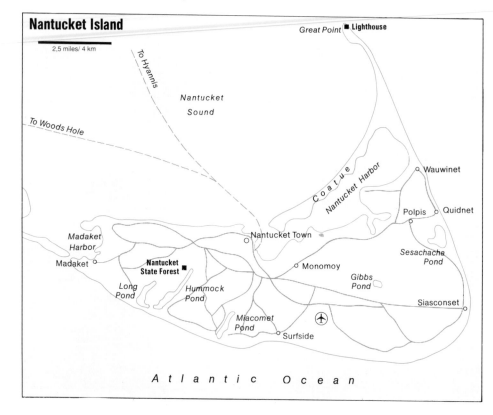

Nantucket Island

2,5 miles/ 4 km

Great Point ■ Lighthouse

To Hyannis

Nantucket Sound

To Woods Hole

Wauwinet

Coatue
Nantucket Harbor

Polpis ○ Quidnet

Madaket Harbor

Madaket ○

Nantucket Town

Sesachacha Pond

Nantucket State Forest ■

○ Monomoy

Long Pond

Hummock Pond

Gibbs Pond

Siasconset

Miacomet Pond

⊕

Surfside

A t l a n t i c   O c e a n

1723, rebuilt after the 1846 fire, and renovated in the late 1950s to accommodate shops and restaurants, it's now like a small village unto itself, surrounded by luxury yachts and sailboats, some of which are available for charter. (The untouched barrier beach of **Coatue** is an ideal destination.) **Old South Wharf** has also been spruced up and rendered tourist-friendly with boutiques and cafes; it's possible to rent tiny but picturesque wharfside cottages here.

Along Main Street up from Straight Wharf, a picturesque shopping district lines the gently rising cobblestone street. Although the square-mile (2.6 sq. km) **National Landmark Historic District** contains some 800 pre-1850 buildings, the red-brick facades lining Main Street are relatively "young," post-fire replacements. With its tree-lined, brick-paved sidewalks, Main Street is always a hub of activity in the summer months, offering every kind of distraction from collectibles to edibles. Among the more noteworthy emporia are the **Main Street Gallery** (actually, just off Main, on

South Water Street) and **Espresso**, a lively cafe with the look of a classic ice cream parlor.

Nantucket is justly proud of its history, especially its grand old homes and museums. The Nantucket Historical Association oversees more than a dozen properties: for a preview, and an excellent precis of island lore, visit the NHA's **Museum of Nantucket History** right on Straight Wharf.

An eye on the past: A walk down South Water Street to Broad Street leads past three important institutions. Located at the corner of Lower India Street, the **Greek Revival Nantucket Atheneum** (constructed by local architect Frederick Brown Coleman in 1847) represents the intellectual flowering that accompanied the island's era of prosperity: Ralph Waldo Emerson gave the inaugural address and was followed by the leading thinkers of the day. Now a public library, this temple of learning contains interesting exhibits relating to island history. On Broad Street, the **Whaling Museum** (housed in a former sperma-

ceti candle factory) commemorates Nantucket's seafaring days in a highly dramatic manner, with impressive displays. Nearby, the **Peter Foulger Museum**, also on Broad, mounts temporary exhibits deriving from the research conducted upstairs by the Nantucket Historical Association.

A bracing walk out of town, to the corner of South Mill and Prospect streets, leads to the **Old Mill** (1746), where, on windy days, visitors can watch corn kernels being ground into fine powder.

A few blocks away, at the corner of Vestal and Milk streets, is the **Maria Mitchell Science Center**, honoring the local savant – and Atheneum librarian – who discovered a comet at the age of 29 in 1847, garnering international acclaim; she went on to become the first woman admitted to the American Academy of Arts and Sciences, as well as the first female college professor in the United States (she taught astronomy at Vassar). The somewhat scattered complex comprises five facilities open to the public, including the **Mitchell House**, her childhood home; the **Hinchman House**, a natural history museum; the **Science Library**, located in a former school house; the **Loines Observatory**, located farther along Milk Street; and, on Washington Street, a small harborside **Aquarium** geared to children.

Further out on Vestal is the **Old Gaol**, built in 1805 and in use until 1933. It looks like a normal house on the outside but is shockingly crude within. But the island has never had much of a crime problem, and in any case prisoners were allowed to spend their nights at home.

The oldest house on Nantucket is the **Jethro Coffin House** (1686) on the northwest edge of town on Sunset Hill Lane. This plain saltbox design reflects the austere lifestyle led by the island's earliest settlers. In contrast, the three-story red-brick **Jared Coffin House**, at the corner of Centre and Broad, made its 1845 debut as the showiest dwelling on the island; within two years it became a hotel, and to this day it remains one of the island's finest inns.

Two more Coffin residences (the fam-

The Sankaty Head Lighthouse, Siasconset.

172

ily was so prolific, it accounted for half the island's population by the early 19th century) stand at No. 75 and No. 78 Main Street, rare examples of the brick Federal style of architecture.

Farther up Main Street are the "**Three Bricks**," architectural triplets built by wealthy whaler Joseph Starbuck for his three sons. Across the street, and worlds apart in style, stand the "**Two Greeks**," Greek Revival mansions built by Frederick Coleman for two Starbuck daughters. One, the **Hadwen House**, is maintained as a museum by the Nantucket Historical Association.

No. 99 Main Street, with its detailed and finely proportioned facade, is one of the most handsome wooden Federal style buildings on Nantucket; it was built by forebears of Roland Macy, who left the island to seek his fortune and founded a well-known namesake store.

Spits and moors: "Nantucket! Take out your map and look at it," urged Herman Melville in his whaling adventure classic *Moby Dick*. An inspection of the map reveals an island with hamlets and hideaways sprinkled across its 14-mile (23-km) length. Despite some mid-island development in recent decades, about one-third of the island is under protective stewardship, thanks to the intercession of the Nantucket Conservation Foundation; and although environmental restrictions limit activity on dunes, moors and other fragile areas, much of the land can be explored.

Stretching to the northeast from the town of Nantucket is a 6-mile (10-km) inner harbor, protected from Nantucket Sound by **Coatue**, a thin spit of land with flat white beaches accessible only by boat or four-wheel-drive vehicles (driven around the Head of the Harbor). This sweep of land, encompassing the **Caskata-Coatue Wildlife Refuge** spit, extends north to Great Point, where a lighthouse – a solar-powered 1986 replica of the 1818 original, swept away by a 1984 storm – warns boats away from the sandbars of Nantucket Sound.

Residential neighborhoods extend along the south side of the harbor. **Monomoy**, the nearest to town and the

most populous settlement, affords spectacular views from its bluffs.

From here, the Polpis Road leads across the rolling and delicate **Nantucket Moors**, packed with bayberry, beach plum, heather and other lush vegetation – a lovely green and flowering pink in summer, brilliant red and gold in the fall.

Wauwinet, a tiny community of cottages tucked amid the beach grass at the head of the harbor, is home to the ultra-elegant (and ultra-expensive) **Wauwinet House**, a finely refurbished 1850 hostelry within splashing distance of both ocean and harbor. (It's located on the "haulover" where fishing boats used to avoid the long trip around Great Point).

Tourists discovered **Siasconset** (pronounced "*Sconset*"), the easternmost and second-largest town on Nantucket, in the 1880s. Theater people from the mainland mingled with local fishermen; the resulting architecture ranges from Lilliputian cottages to large rambling shingle-style houses along the bluffs.

Nantucket's most popular beaches are located on the flat, windswept south shore, open to the cold, spirited waters of the Atlantic Ocean. At **Surfside Beach**, a colorful Victorian lifesaving station serves as the island's only Youth Hostel. Surfers favor the beach at **Cisco**, a bit more remote, at the end of Hummock Pond Road. **Madaket Beach**, at the southwestern tip of Nantucket, is popular for swimming, fishing, and, especially, sunset-gazing.

The northern coast east of **Madaket Harbor**, heading back toward town, offers the gentle surf of Dionis and Jetties beaches. The latter gets its name from its proximity to the **West Jetty**, which protects the channel leading into **Nantucket Harbor. Children's Beach**, tucked well inside the West Jetty, near **Steamship Wharf**, is especially placid and enhanced by a playground.

Overlooking the harbor from **Brant Point** is one of America's oldest lighthouses. Visitors departing by sea often toss the traditional penny into the water off Brant Point to ensure that they'll return to the shores of Nantucket.

Homes tend to be fairly luxurious.

WHALE WATCHING

Pegasus and Pepper, Batik and Gemini, Petrel and Ishtar make a great spectacle as they lunge, breach and flipper. You can see them by boarding one of the half-a-dozen large, handsome, white, whale-watching boats which, each day from Easter until the beginning of October, leave Commercial Wharf in Provincetown on a three-hour voyage.

Their destination is the Stellwagen Bank, a shallow underwater deposit of sand and gravel, to which, year after year, Pegasus and her friends, who are humpbacked whales, return after spending the winter in their West Indies breeding grounds. Experts recognize the different humpbacks, which often reach lengths of 40–50 ft (12–15 meters) and weights of 30 tonnes, by their distinctive body markings, especially those on their tail flukes.

Huge quantities of plankton and an infinite number of small sand eels are the magnets that attract to Stellwagen Bank the world's largest concentration of whales, both in numbers and in species. The vast majority of the 500 or so whales who visit here each year are humpbacks, but their number includes minkes, finbacks and a few right whales (so called because, being slow swimmers, they were the "right" whales to hunt). In addition to the whales, visitors are often fortunate enough to be entertained by pods of several hundred frolicking white-sided dolphins and to observe immense basking sharks.

It's rare for a visitor not to see a whale during a trip and, more often than not, the whale-watching boats approach to within 50 ft (15 meters) of six to 12 of these magnificent mammals. Nothing can be more dramatic than to watch a humpback lunging upwards from the depths to break the surface of the water with dozens of small fish hanging from its mouth.

The humpback is basically a bulk feeder who dives deep below the schools of sand eels and then lunges upwards through the school with its mouth open. In so doing, it engulfs large quantities of fish and water. Its rorquals (folds of skin that begin at the chin and stretch to the whale's navel) balloon up and probably double the capacity of the mouth. This allows the animals to capture hundreds, if not thousands, of fish with every lunge.

Other activities which are certain to thrill watchers are breaching, when the mammals jump out of the water, and flippering, when the whales roll onto their sides and lift their long white flipper out of the water before slamming it down hard on the surface.

Whale watching became popular in 1975 when Captain Al Avellar, who organized deep-sea fishing trips from Provincetown, had the idea that visitors to the Cape might enjoy watching the whales on Stellwagen Bank. He invited Charles Mayo, a marine biologist based in Provincetown, to act as a guide and so began an attraction which now annually draws more than 100,000 visitors.

On some boats the Provincetown-based Center for Coastal Studies provides a biologist who acts as guide and gathers scientific data. Whale watching at Provincetown has, with Yankee ingenuity, become a model for the marriage of science and commerce.

Whale watching boats which visit Stellwagen Bank are also based at Hyannisport, Gloucester, Boston and New Bedford. ■

ants of
e deep.

CENTRAL MASSACHUSETTS

New England's legacy of rural beauty and industry lives on Central Massachusetts. Whereas Boston belongs to the modern world of cosmopolitan cities and the Berkshires to the Gilded Age tradition of opulent leisure, the Commonwealth's midsection harkens back to an earlier, mostly agricultural era when the living was hard and plain, the rewards what ready hands and determined souls could create.

The vigor and sincerity of early Americans' social vision is on display from mid-May to mid-October at **Fruitlands Museums** in the little town of Harvard, an hour or so west of Boston via State Highway 2. In the mid-19th century, transcendentalist Amos Bronson Alcott, father of Louisa May Alcott (author of *Little Women*), left his Concord home with political activist Charles Lane and a group of followers to found an anti-materialist utopian community on the 18th-century Fruitlands farm.

Vegetarianism, asceticism and a philosophical return to nature were their mandates but, despite their inspiring view of the beautiful Nashua River Valley, the commune soon dispersed. Today, however, the farmhouse has been transformed into a transcendentalist museum with presentations on Alcott, Emerson, Thoreau and others; its tearoom offers the same view of the Nashua Valley, and is surrounded by several other small museums.

Some 19th-century utopian experiments enjoyed greater longevity than that of Fruitlands. The most notable was that of the chaste and fervent Shakers, who persisted in Harvard from the late 18th century until 1918 (other New England Shaker settlements are intact to this day, although the sect is now virtually extinct). Fruitlands' 1794 **Shaker House** contains their crafts and furnishings which bespeak a lifestyle of studied simplicity.

The **Indian Museum** boasts a fine collection of artifacts, and the **Picture Gallery** displays folk portraits by itinerant artists and landscapes by such Hudson River School disciples as Asher Durand and Frederick Church.

Continuing west on State 2 to Greenfield, and south on US Highway 202, through rolling hills verdant in spring and summer, an explosion of color come the fall, travelers skirt the northern reaches of the **Quabbin Reservoir**, 128 sq. miles (331 sq. km) of flooded valley that holds 412 billion gallons and supplies the drinking water to Greater Boston. Four towns were flooded in 1939 to create this great body of water; the Swift River Historical Society in New Salem preserves mementos of these vanished communities. More than a water source, Quabbin is prized as a place to fish, hike and admire the rare bald eagles that breed by the reservoir.

The pioneer heritage: The well-preserved pioneer town of **Old Deerfield**, off US Highway 5, has a fascinating history dating from its settlement by farmers in 1669. The Pocumtuck, who had been using the fertile valley to raise pumpkins, corn, and tobacco, were not

pleased to see their land usurped, and massacred the entire population (by then 125 strong) in 1675. That deterred settlers for the next seven years, but the lure of the land was irresistible, and the interlopers eventually won out, despite another raid in 1704 in which half the village was burned, some 100 colonists were abducted into slavery, and another 50 slaughtered.

Tomahawk marks can still be seen on one sturdy wooden door, but the town's lurid history is not what attracts most visitors. The draw is an extraordinary architectural cache: 13 carefully restored Colonial and Federal structures along "The Street," Deerfield's mile-long main thoroughfare, which once inspired John Quincy Adams to write: "It is not excelled by anything I have ever seen, not excepting the Bay of Naples."

The treasures inside, representing decades of changing decorative styles, easily equal the exteriors. Among the more interesting of the buildings open to the public are the **Ashley House** (1730), a former parson's home with intricately carved woodwork and antique furnishings; the **Asa Stebbins House** (1810) with early paintings, Chinese porcelain and Federal and Chippendale furniture; the **Dwight Barnard House** (1725), immediately recognizable by its handsome carved door, behind which is an 18th-century doctor's office; and the **Hall Tavern** (1760), where Historic Deerfield Inc. maintains its information center.

A cultural nexus: About 10 miles south of Old Deerfield, along the region designated as **Pioneer Valley** (which stretches from Vermont to Connecticut), is **Amherst College**, where stately fraternity houses flank a campus quadrangle that is a classic of early 19th-century institutional architecture.

The town of **Amherst** has long been a hotbed of intellectual vigor and social independence. Noah Webster, creator of the American dictionary, lived here, as did a reclusive genius of the English language.

Visitors to the **Emily Dickinson Homestead** can experience the spartan

Left, off duty **Right**, on duty at Old Deerfield Village.

environment that housed a sensitive, self-confined soul, who poured her emotions solely into her poetry.

Down State Highway 9 and across the Connecticut River is **Northampton**, which can also boast a taciturn celebrity. The 30th US President, Calvin Coolidge, began his law practice in Northampton and later died there. His reputation as a man of exceptionally few words once prompted a determined matron at a society banquet to coax him: "Mr President, I have a wager with a friend that I can persuade you to say more than two words." Coolidge's reply: "You lose."

Surrounded by colleges (Amherst, Hampshire, and U-Mass to the east, Mount Holyoke to the south, and Smith, right in town), Northampton has benefitted from the youthful, energetic company it keeps. Once drab and dull, it now boasts a lively mix of fashionable stores and international restaurants (from the popular Curtis & Schwartz deli to the *haute* Italian trattoria Spoleto), earning it the fond sobriquet of "Noho."

With a sophistication level equal to that of New York's Soho district, Northampton has attracted hundreds of artisans and artists, who showcase their wares at craft shops like the Ferrin Gallery and Pinch Pottery and at the fine-art Hart Gallery (where internationally renowned artists like Gregory Gillespie reveal their recent work).

The Smith College Museum of Art (one of the finest collections in the country, with a special focus on French impressionists) is on hand to lend inspiration, as is the splendidly landscaped campus; the college's **Lyman Plant House**, a delicate 1896 greenhouse, makes a lovely rainy-day retreat.

Bouncing back: Springfield is one of those large American cities that just seem to lack pizzazz – or at least it did, until recently. The problem was an insensitive highway project, I-91, that chopped up neighborhoods and cut the city off from its most valuable natural asset, the Connecticut River. Now its banks have been reclaimed for the populace, in the form of a refreshing

mherst
ommon.

Riverfront Park, where summertime concerts are held. Also gracing the shore is the **Basketball Hall of Fame**, a lively interactive museum dedicated to the game invented in 1891 by Springfield YMCA instructor Dr James Naismith, who nailed up a pair of peach baskets to keep his charges happily occupied; the game, they discovered, was even more absorbing once the bottoms of the baskets were removed. Visitors have an opportunity to experience the fast-paced thrills in the "Shoot-Out," where a conveyor belt moves participants along a line of hoops.

Among the other "firsts" Springfield is known for its role as the nation's original arsenal (George Washington chose the site in 1779). The **Springfield Armory National Historic Site**, home of the first American musket, now houses a museum featuring one of the largest collections of firearms in the world.

Springfield supports four more outstanding museums, all clustered around "the Quad" – the Springfield Museum Quadrangle on State Street. **The George**

Walter Vincent Smith Art Museum features oriental decorative arts, from Persian rugs to Japanese netsuke and Chinese cloisonne (the largest collection of the latter in the Western world). The **Science Museum** contains the first American-built planetarium and plenty of intriguing, hands-on exhibits. The **Connecticut Valley Historical Museum** showcases artifacts – from folk paintings to fine furniture – chronicling several centuries of regional life. The **Museum of Fine Arts** has an impressively broad collection, including portraits by the noted itinerant painter Rufus Porter; contemporary shows are also mounted.

Springfield's rich cultural life is reflected in the musical offerings, classical to popular, of the Springfield Symphony Orchestra, and in the sophisticated stagings of StageWest. And no visit to the city would be complete without a pilgrimage to the **Student Prince and Fort Restaurant**, a colorful 1935 redoubt of bier and sauerbraten.

Across the river, in **West Springfield**, **Townshend**.

are the 175-acre (71-hectare) fairgrounds for the **Eastern States Exposition**, New England's major agricultural fair and one of the largest in the nation. Every September, prize livestock and top-name talents entertain the crowds. Permanently ensconced on the grounds is the **Storrowton Village Museum**, a cluster of seven transplanted 18th- and early 19th-century buildings where traditional crafts are demonstrated.

Reliving the past: Some 30 miles (48 km) east of Springfield off US 20, **Old Sturbridge Village** – a recreated community encompassing 40 period buildings scattered over 200 acres (81 hectares) – offers a "you are there" take on early 19th-century rural life. Visitors are treated to illuminating explanations, couched in modern parlance, as the interpreters go about the business of farm and town life: tending animals, making tin lanterns, leading prayers or executing a will.

Though a delight any time of year, Old Sturbridge is especially captivating in winter, when the crowds are sparser and the harshness of New England weather that so shaped the early settlers' moral and physical fiber can be experienced firsthand. Of special interest is the **Pliny Freeman Farm**, where, depending on the season, workers in period dress engage in making soap, shearing sheep, and laboriously building stone walls. Concepts of political freedom and discourse grew, in part, from the emergence of a free and vibrant press, and the activities of the **Isaiah Thomas Printing Office** are designed to show how printed communication became an integral part of the new nation's growth.

Wonders of Worcester: A short drive past Sturbridge in the direction of Boston is **Worcester**, the state's second-largest city. Where would America be without Worcester? This gritty industrial city spawned the country's first park, first wire-making company, first steam calliope, first carpet loom, first diner, first Valentine, and (suitably enough) first birth-control pill, not to mention the beginnings of liquid-fuel

rocketry, female suffrage and the Free Soil Party, now known as the Republican Party. Notable residents have included abolitionist-composer Stephen Foster and socialist leader Emma Goldman; Sigmund Freud gave his only US lecture at Clark University.

The humorist Robert Benchley grew up in Worcester, as did the notorious 1960s radical Abbie Hoffman, and no doubt both owed their unfettered freedom of speech to publisher Isaiah Thomas, a Son of Liberty who fled Boston in advance of the British Army in 1770 and continued to publish his rabble-rousing revolutionary newspaper, the *Massachusetts Spy*, from Worcester. Thomas went on to become one of the wealthiest men in America, establishing the American Antiquarian Society on New York's Park Avenue in 1818; the original Worcester headquarters, on Salisbury Street, now serve as a research library.

The city, though left somewhat depressed in the wake of Masschusetts' industrial boom, is itself a trove of antiquarian delights. The **Worcester Historical Museum** is chockful of interesting memorabilia; the museum also maintains the splendid 1772 Georgian Salisbury Mansion. Awe-inspiring in its scope, the **Higgins Armory Museum** – the legacy of a local steel magnate – features a vast collection of medieval armor, as well as armaments dating back to 6th-century BC Greece.

The **Worcester Art Museum** is the second largest in New England and perhaps the most adventurous: its sponsorship of excavations at Antioch, Syria, in the 1930s yielded a stunning collection of 2nd-century AD Roman mosaics. The museum contains many other valuable antiquities along with fine collections of European and Eastern art. But perhaps most appealing is the extensive gallery of 17th-, 18th- and 19th-century American art, including paintings by Winslow Homer, John Singer Sargent and John Singleton Copley. In their portraits and landscapes, one can trace the gradual emergence of a distinctly American culture.

Racing is popular in the region.

184

THE SPORTING TRADITION

Ever since football was introduced to the nation on Boston Common in 1862 and basketballs were first stuffed into baskets in Springfield, Mass. in 1881, New England has been a trail-blazer in sports. Long before expansion became the buzz word, Boston was one of the very few cities in the nation to boast major league teams in baseball (Red Sox and Braves), basketball (Celtics), and ice-hockey (Bruins). The Braves decamped after 1952 and expansion led to the appearance in 1960 of the Patriots who, some claim, play football and in 1979 the Hartford Whalers from Connecticut entered the major ice-hockey arena.

Yet it seems the fate of New England fans, who lack nothing in loyalty and devotion, to nearly always be following losers. Only the Celtics have bucked the trend by winning 16 National Basketball titles, eight on the trot; but, their last pennant was in 1986.

In the 1986 baseball World Series the Sox were within a heart-beat of clinching the title, but they lost that game and the decisive seventh and the title. Four years later the Bruins succumbed 2–3 to the Edmonton Oilers in the third period of overtime in the seventh and last game of the Stanley Cup (the red ribbon of ice-hockey). Admittedly, the Sox were the first winners of the World Series and have clinched the title five times, and the Bruins have won the coveted Stanley Cup five times but the Sox last triumphed in 1918 and the Bruins in 1972.

Patience should, but does not, grow thin: there are always demi-gods to worship: Ted Williams and Carl Yastrzemski in baseball; Bobby Orr in hockey and Bob Cousy and Larry Bird in basketball.

Once and only once did the hapless Patriots reach the Super Bowl: that was in 1986 when the Chicago Bears trounced them 46–10. Macho New Englanders prefer to remember Rocky Marciano of Brockton, Mass. the heavyweight boxer who, when he retired in 1956, was the only world champion at *any* weight to have won *every* fight (49) of his professional career. And, long before him, a Boston boy, the legendary John L. Sullivan, was world heavyweight champion.

New England's sporting scene is enlivened by teams from its myriad colleges but, in the main, these have little impact nationally on major sports. Exceptions occur, such as Boston College (football and basketball), University of Connecticut (basketball), and Boston University and Harvard not infrequently contribute players to the US Olympic ice-hockey squad. And, in minor sports – squash, sailing and crew – New England college teams are often to the fore.

Since 1965 oarspeople from throughout the world flock to Cambridge at the end of October for the Head of the Charles regatta, the largest one-day regatta in the world.

Come the spring, thousands of singlet-clad runners, again from all over the world, line up at Hopkinton, Mass. for the start of the celebrated Boston Marathon. It's the world's oldest annual marathon, having begun in 1896, and is the only marathon to offer equal prize-money, in all classes, to both men and women. New Englanders support the race (John Hancock sponsors it) but New Englanders last came first in 1983 when Gregory Meyer of Wellesley won the Men's and Joan Benoit of Watertown the Women's race. ∎

The Boston Celtics in action.

185

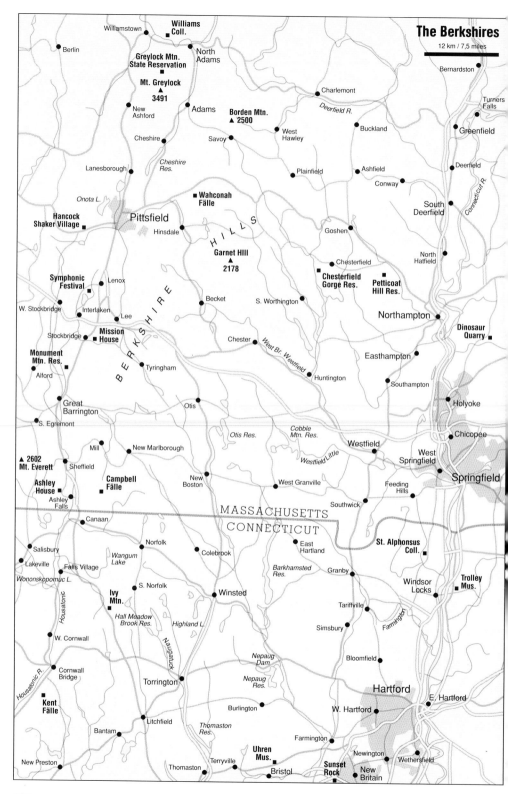

The Berkshires

12 km / 7,5 miles

Williamstown
Williams Coll.
Berlin
North Adams
Greylock Mtn. State Reservation
Charlemont
Bernardston
Mt. Greylock ▲ 3491
Turners Falls
New Ashford
Adams
Borden Mtn. ▲ 2500
Deerfield R.
Greenfield
Cheshire
Savoy
West Hawley
Buckland
Deerfield
Lanesborough
Cheshire Res.
Plainfield
Ashfield
Conway
South Deerfield
Onota L.
Wahconah Fälle
Goshen
North Hatfield
Hancock Shaker Village
Pittsfield
Hinsdale
HILLS
Chesterfield
Symphonic Festival
Lenox
Garnet Hlll ▲ 2178
Chesterfield Gorge Res.
Petticoat Hill Res.
W. Stockbridge
Interlaken
Becket
S. Worthington
Northampton
Lee
B E R K S H I R E
Dinosaur Quarry
Stockbridge
Mission House
Chester
West Br. Westfield
Easthampton
Monument Mtn. Res.
Tyringham
Huntington
Southampton
Alford
Otis
Holyoke
Great Barrington
S. Egremont
Otis Res.
Cobble Mtn. Res.
Westfield
Chicopee
Mill
New Marlborough
Westfield Little
West Springfield
Springfield
▲ 2602 Mt. Everett
Sheffield
Campbell Fälle
New Boston
West Granville
Feeding Hills
Ashley House
Ashley Falls
MASSACHUSETTS
CONNECTICUT
Southwick
St. Alphonsus Coll.
Canaan
Norfolk
East Hartland
Granby
Trolley Mus.
Salisbury
Colebrook
Barkhamsted Res.
Windsor Locks
Lakeville
Wangum Lake
Falls Village
Wononskopomuc L.
S. Norfolk
Winsted
Tariffville
Farmington
Housatonic
Ivy Mtn.
Hall Meadow Brook Res.
Highland L.
Simsbury
W. Cornwall
Naugatuck
Nepaug Dam
Bloomfield
Housatonic R.
Cornwall Bridge
Torrington
Nepaug Res.
Hartford
E. Hartford
Kent Fälle
Burlington
W. Hartford
Litchfield
Bantam
Thomaston Res.
Farmington
New Preston
Uhren Mus.
Newington
Wethersfield
Thomaston
Terryville
Bristol
Sunset Rock
New Britain

188

THE BERKSHIRES

Berkshire County, frequently called "the American Lake District," encompasses a landscape that provides almost every variety of beauty – valleys dotted with shimmering lakes, rolling farmlands punctuated by orchards and wheatfields, deep forests abundant with deer, powerful rivers that cascade into waterfalls under the bluest of New England skies.

Everywhere one turns in this westernmost county of Massachusetts, the horizon is piled and terraced with mountains. Though less dramatic than the White Mountains of New Hampshire or the Green Mountains of Vermont, these gentle ranges have nonetheless provided the Berkshire Hills with an insularity that has historically set them apart from the rest of the state.

The Dutch, who settled New York in 1626 and moved north into the Hudson Valley, were prevented from further advancement by the stony resistance of the Taconic Range. Similar difficulties were met by the English, who found their progress west from the Connecticut River Valley blocked by the Hoosac Mountains – a wall of granite later dubbed the Berkshire Barrier.

Contained within this natural barricade, the Berkshires remained a wilderness until 1725, when Matthew Noble traveled through its dense forests to build a cabin in what is now the town of Sheffield. In the years that followed, farmland was cleared and towns were established along the Housatonic River and its tributaries. During the 19th century, the Industrial Revolution brought prosperity to the Berkshires: its iron foundries melted ore for the country's first railroads, while marble quarried from its hills graced the dome of the Capitol in Washington, DC.

As big business lured succeeding generations to the cities and better land beckoned farmers farther west, the Berkshires receded into a sleepy silence. But city dwellers seeking pretty scenery and respite from summer heat have periodically rediscovered the Berkshires.

During the 1890s, for example, the county became a playground for such wealthy families as the Carnegies and Vanderbilts, who built their mansions in the hills surrounding Stockbridge and Lenox. More recently, visitors have come for the summer music festivals, the splendor of fall foliage, or the challenge of winter skiing.

The first settlers reached the Berkshires through the Housatonic Valley from Connecticut. The modern traveler can do the same, following US Highway 7 north along the Housatonic. Many of Berkshire County's best-known attractions are located along Route 7 (or just a short distance from it).

Colonel Ashley and the Cobble: Just inside the Connecticut border on Route 7A is **Ashley Falls**, a village surrounded by hayfields and dairy farms, its landscape reminiscent of a Constable painting. The village was named for Colonel John Ashley, a prominent lawyer and major-general of the Massachusetts militia during the Revolutionary War. The **Colonel John Ashley House**, built

Preceding pages: Church on the Hill, Lenox. Right, colonial "maids" re-enact history at the Colonel Ashley House.

in 1735, is the oldest structure standing in Berkshire County. It has been restored as a colonial museum, open from late May through Columbus Day.

Also located in Ashley Falls is **Bartholomew's Cobble**. This natural rock garden, with hiking trails that meander along the banks of the Housatonic, is a bird-watcher's paradise and an excellent place to search for the trilliums and trout lilies of early spring. It contains more species of fern than any other area in the continental United States.

Sheffield, established in 1733, is the oldest town in Berkshire County and boasts two of the best-preserved covered bridges in Massachusetts. Traffic still travels over the larger, a narrow, barn-red structure that spans the Housatonic just east of town, on the road to **New Marlborough**.

The Berkshires' true beauty lies in the backroads and small villages that are so much a part of its charm. New Marlborough and nearby **Mill River**, small communities that prospered in the heyday of the Industrial Revolution, are gems. At the Old Inn on the Green in New Marlborough, once a stagecoach stop en route from New York to Boston, visitors can dine on fresh lamb or breakfast on blueberry muffins.

The Great Wigwam: Great Barrington offers an excellent base from which to explore the towns and villages of the southern Berkshires. Although it does not have the obvious architectural charm of towns farther north such as Stockbridge and Lenox, Great Barrington does have a certain homey quality that is quite attractive.

The Housatonic River courses through the center of town, and it was here, at a natural ford in the river, that the Mohicans built their Great Wigwam. It was also here that William Stanley (later to found the General Electric Company) first successfully demonstrated the use of alternating current; in 1886, the town became one of the first communities in America to be lit by electricity.

Great Barrington has been home to a sizable African-American community since before the Civil War, when fugitive slaves journeyed to Massachusetts on the Underground Railroad. Socialist and scholar W.E.B. DuBois was born here in 1868.

At the far corner of the county, 2,000 ft (610 meters) up and teetering on the edge of New York State, is the tiny hill hamlet of **Mount Washington**. The smallest town in the Berkshires, Mount Washington offers some of the finest blueberry picking and fall-foliage viewing in New England.

Continuing along the Mount Washington road, the traveler arrives at **Bash Bish Falls**, a 275-ft (84-meter) natural waterfall where, legend has it, a Native American maiden jumped to her death after being spurned by her lover. When the moon is full, her ghost, it is said, may be seen walking through the mountain laurel to wade in the pool beneath the falls.

A literary heritage: North of Great Barrington is **Monument Mountain**, a craggy, hump-backed peak whose summit is a pleasant half-hour hike from the parking lot at its base. The mountain is a Berkshire literary landmark of considerable repute. The poet William Cullen Bryant sang its praises while practicing as a local attorney in the 1830s.

Monument Mountain is best known as the site of an extraordinary literary encounter between Herman Melville and Nathaniel Hawthorne. In 1850, the two writers were invited to join a hiking party organized by Dr Oliver Wendell Holmes, Boston essayist and father of Supreme Court justice. The party, numbering 10 in all, scaled the peak just as a thunderstorm unleashed a torrent of heavy rain. The group ran for shelter under a granite outcropping and waited out the storm while sipping champagne from a silver goblet.

Hawthorne and Melville met frequently after their day on the mountain, the scribe of the South Seas often traveling to Hawthorne's little red cottage in Lenox for refreshment and conversation. But the moody Hawthorne soon grew tired of the changeable Berkshire climate and, after only a brief stay, returned east to Boston. Melville, whose fondness for the region endured, remained another 10 years and wrote his masterpiece *Moby Dick*, while residing in the Berkshire Hills.

The Berkshires have, in fact, hosted a plethora of poets and writers over the years. Longfellow once hiked these trails, as did Emerson and Thoreau. Henry James regularly visited novelist Edith Wharton at The Mount, her grand Italianate 1890s mansion in **Lenox** (now open for touring, and the headquarters of the innovative theater troupe Shakespeare and Co.). It's here that she wrote *Ethan Frome*, set in the Berkshire town of West Stockbridge.

Route 7 is the most direct road to Stockbridge, but those with a little more time on their hands should consider the drive through the **Tyringham Valley**. From Great Barrington, take State 23 east to Monterey, then turn north onto Tyringham Road.

In the early years of this century, the beauty of the landscape transformed the valley into an artists' colony. Today, in summer, **Tyringham Art Galleries**, founded in 1953, continue to operate out of the fairy-tale Gingerbread House,

a former sculpture studio. The tiny village of **Tyringham**, where a community of Shakers settled in the 19th century, is charming and unspoiled, as is Lee, which appears frozen in time. State 192 heads west from Lee to Stockbridge.

Stately mission: Stockbridge was incorporated as an Indian mission in 1739. Its first missionary was John Sargeant, a young tutor from Yale who lived among the natives for 16 years. He slept in their wigwams, shared their venison and spoke their language, all the while introducing them to the colonists' ways. Eventually, Sargeant helped them establish a town, build homes and cultivate the land. Some among the Mohican tribe held public office, serving alongside whites in the town government.

The Stockbridge Mission was so successful that it became a model of cultural adaptation; however, the experiment was not to last. As more colonists moved into the area, the tribes were slowly deprived of their land. By 1783, the mission was history, and surviving Indians were forced to settle on the

astover
esort near
enox.

Oneida reservation in New York State. All that remains of the experiment is the **Mission House**, now a museum on Stockbridge's Main Street.

One century later, Stockbridge – as well as its sister city of Lenox, 7½ miles (12 km) north – gained a different kind of notoriety. The rich and super-rich discovered the Berkshire Hills, earning these communities a reputation for wealth and elegance. At first, the newcomers bought simple cottages and played at being country squires. But as "impressions" became important, neighbors built magnificent estates in which to pass the summer and fall months. Soon continental architecture crowded out the simplicity of the old colonial homes, and both towns became inland facsimiles of Newport, Rhode Island.

To name the wealthy people who spent time here is like reading from the pages of a turn-of-the-century *Social Register*. There were Harrimans, Stuyvesants, Westinghouses, Biddles, Vanderbilts, Carnegies and Sloans. Many of the old estates are gone now, rendered untenable by the institution of income tax and the advent of World War I. Some have been converted into private schools; others were destroyed by fire. A few, such as **Wheatleigh** and **Blantyre** in Lenox – survive as opulent country inns.

Rockwell's canvas: If the stately mansions and quaint shops located along State 102, the Main Street of Stockbridge, look familiar, it may be because their New England essence was captured on the canvases of that remarkable illustrator of American life, Norman Rockwell. Rockwell, who created more than 300 covers for the *Saturday Evening Post*, kept a studio in Stockbridge and made his home here for a quarter of a century, until his death in 1978. Located on State 183, a stunning new (1993) museum, designed by Robert A. M. Stern, showcases his *oeuvre* and even recreates his Stockbridge studio. No visitor, however sophisticated, should miss this display: reflecting a time when American ideals were simpler, Rockwell's portraits capture an age of innocence with humor and modesty.

The **Red Lion Inn**, located in the center of Stockbridge at the intersection of Route 7 and State 102, is surely the *grande dame* of New England country inns. Its flower-laden front porch, complete with rocking chairs, is a mecca for Berkshire travelers.

Naumkeag, 2 miles (3 km) north of Stockbridge, is a Norman-style mansion designed by Stanford White for Joseph Choate, US ambassador to Great Britain in 1899; the furnishings and gardens are unusually lavish. **Chesterwood**, the summer home of sculptor Daniel Chester French, is 3 miles (5 km) west of Stockbridge. It was here that he created his masterpiece, *The Seated Lincoln*, focal point of the Lincoln Memorial in Washington, DC. Casts of this work are displayed in the house, now a museum with a sculpture garden.

The sounds of music: Is it possible to vacation in the Berkshires without stopping in at **Tanglewood**, summer home of the Boston Symphony Orchestra? This 200-acre (81-hectare) estate, located on State 183, 1½ miles (2.5 km) west of Lenox, has been a haven for

performers, students and music lovers since the orchestra first began its outdoor concert series in 1931. The 6,000-seat Music Shed, designed by architect Eero Saarinen, has excellent acoustics; but many visitors prefer to pack their dinners, come early and picnic on the lawn. They need blankets and plenty of warm clothes to counter the cool night air. The BSO season begins in late June and runs through August, with concerts on Fridays, Saturdays and Sundays.

During the summer, near Tanglewood's lawn, a replica of the little red cottage where Hawthorne lived and wrote *The House of the Seven Gables* and *Tanglewood Tales* can be visited.

Tanglewood is only the best known of several summer festivals in the Berkshires. Travelers who wish to avoid crowds may find their musical tastes better served elsewhere. The **South Mountain Concerts**, featuring chamber music on weekends, take place on Route 7 one mile south of Pittsfield. Those who revel in Renaissance and Baroque music head for the Aston Magna Festival in Great Barrington. The festival was founded by harpsichordist Albert Fuller; performances on original instruments are given at St James Church several weekends in July.

When Ruth St Denis and Ted Shawn established the **Jacob's Pillow Dance Festival** in the early 1930s, modern dance was in its infancy, and many viewed the likes of Martha Graham and Merce Cunningham as a passing fad. Today, Jacob's Pillow – on State 8 in the quiet hilltown of **Becket**, southeast of Pittsfield – is a national institution.

Similarly impressive is the **Williamstown Theater Festival**, which consistently stages some of the finest summer theater in the country in Massachusetts' (and the Berkshires') northwestern corner. Running the gamut from Greek tragedy to Restoration comedy, from Chekhov to Coward, Pinter to Pirandello, the festival also boasts a superb company of actors, including many well-known names. At Stockbridge's **Berkshire Theater Festival**, whose main theater was designed by the architect

Ivy-covered academia at Williams College in Williamstown

194

Stanford White, the emphasis is on American classics. For fans of the Bard, there's **Shakespeare & Co.** at **The Mount** in Lenox, outdoor performances with an experimental bent.

Even operatic arias have found a foothold in the Berkshires. The **Berkshire Opera**, also in Lenox, offers seasonal performances in a lovely, old-world setting. The operas, in the Cranwell Opera House, are sung in English.

The simple Shakers: "Tis a gift to be simple," says the old Shaker hymn. A visit to **Hancock Shaker Village**, on US 20, 3 miles (5 km) west of Pittsfield, is testimony to the virtues of simplicity.

Originally called Shaking Quakers because of their dancing during religious ceremonies, the Shakers settled in Hancock during the late 1780s. Their life was based on the principles of community property, equality of the sexes, public confession of sins and separation from the outside world. Because members practised celibacy, converts (New Believers") were key. The Shakers frequently adopted orphans, many of whom subsequently elected to adopt the faith.

The community prospered through farming, printing, selling garden seeds and herbs and manufacturing their distinctively designed furnishings. The elegance and functionalism of Shaker architecture is exemplified by Hancock's famous 1826 round stone barn. It enabled one farmhand, standing at its center, to feed an entire herd of cattle.

Shakers lived in Hancock until the 1950s, when the community had dwindled to a few staunch survivors, celibacy and changing times having led to their decline. The village is open for tours from May 30 through August.

Returning to Route 7, the northbound traveler passes through **Pittsfield**, the Berkshire County seat and largest city (population 52,000) and the town that General Electric built. Although much of American industry has moved south, GE remains the city's largest employer.

The high country: Perched 14 miles (22 km) north of Pittsfield is **Mount Greylock**, at 3,491 ft (1,064 meters) the tallest peak in the Berkshires. Hardy travelers can ascend on foot, while those less energetic can drive to the summit via a steep and winding access road. From the top, Hawthorne looked down upon Williamstown – "a white village and a steeple set like a daydream among the high mountain waves."

Even today, Williamstown may be the loveliest of New England villages. It is home to **Williams College**, founded in 1793. Its finest attraction is the exceptional **Sterling and Francine Clark Art Institute**, located on South Street just west of the town center. Between World War I and 1956, the Clarks amassed a superb private collection of European and American paintings, including works by Botticelli, Goya, Gainsborough and Fragonard. But the museum is best known for its Impressionist collection, which includes Monet, Degas and Renoir.

From Williamstown, the **Mohawk Trail** (State Highway 2) winds west to east across the top of Berkshire County. An old Indian path-turned-roadway, it offers some of the most rugged and romantic scenery in the Berkshires.

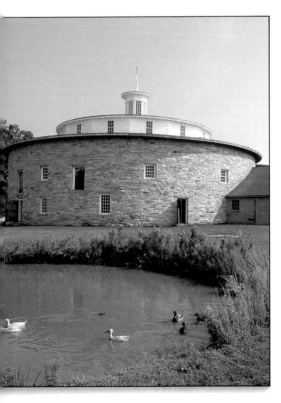

The stone barn at Hancock Shaker Village near Pittsfield.

CONNECTICUT

"Connecticut always looks as if the maid has just been in to clean," a long-time resident once remarked as he drove admiringly through the neat-as-a-pin village of Guilford. There, as in so many of Connecticut's picturesque colonial villages, the carefully kept white clapboard homes and manicured lawns evoke an image of quiet wealth, propriety and old school ties.

Indeed, this most southern of New England states has always had something of a conservative mien. The Puritans who settled here were staunch Congregationalists, little given to the radical ideas of Roger Williams or the autocratic piety of John Winthrop. They may have been farmers and seafarers, but they were primarily involved in commerce; they understood the value of a dollar and the importance of its proper investment.

Though generations have come and gone, this aspect of the Connecticut character has not changed. It has, however, been tempered with pride for the place and a heartfelt sense of its history.

Many visitors make the mistake of traveling non-stop through Connecticut (pronounced *kuh-ned-eket*) en route to vacations elsewhere in New England. Perhaps because its riches are so accessible, people tend to take them too much for granted. For those who exit from the highways and take to the back roads and small towns of Connecticut, there is a wealth of colonial heritage waiting to be explored.

With Long Island Sound as its southern border, Connecticut roughly forms a rectangle measuring 90 miles (145 km) from east to west and 55 miles (89 km) north to south. The Connecticut River, New England's longest, bisects the state; along with the Connecticut, the Thames and Housatonic rivers were vital in the settlement and later industrialization of the state.

The Constitution State: Adrian Block, a Dutch navigator, was probably the first to understand the possibilities of the region when he sailed along the coast and up the Connecticut River in 1614. Nineteen years later, the Dutch established a trading post near the future site of Hartford, naming their new colony Fort Good Hope.

Beaver and timber had attracted the Dutch first, but it was the British who, lured by fertile land and religious freedom, finally settled the region in 1635. By that time, the original colony of Massachusetts Bay was overcrowded, and newcomers arriving from England had to extend their search for arable land to the upper reaches of the Connecticut River. Added to economic causes were the personalities of strong-willed leaders such as the Reverend Thomas Hooker, who, unwilling to submit to the autocratic theocracy of the Massachusetts colony, chose to lead his congregation to an area beyond the reach of any colonial authority.

By 1636, settlements had been established in Hartford, Windsor and Weathersfield. Calling themselves the Hartford Colony, the three towns adop-

ted the Fundamental Orders of Connecticut on January 14, 1639. This document, sometimes called "the grandfather of the Constitution" is regarded by many historians as the world's first written constitution. From that historical first comes the legend on the license plates, "The Constitution State."

New settlements were organized along the shores of the Long Island Sound. Old Saybrook was first, followed by New Haven, Guilford and Stamford. Later towns, cleaving to the staunch Congregationalism of their settlers, took such Biblical names as Goshen, Sharon, Canaan and Bethlehem.

When the time came to fight in the American War for Independence, Connecticut soldiers were eager participants. No major battles were fought on Connecticut soil, but the state had its patriots. Among them were General Israel Putnam and Ethan Allen. Most famous was Nathan Hale, the Coventry, Connecticut schoolteacher who, when hanged by the British as a spy, uttered the immortal words: "I regret that I have only one life to give for my country."

With the end of the Revolution, Americans returned home to set about building their new nation. But Connecticut citizens quickly realized that they could not make their fortunes in farming. The stony, glacial soil that covered most of the region was poorly suited to cultivation. With the exception of the upper Connecticut valley, where tobacco is still grown under wide, cheesecloth tents, the land could support only small dairy farms and family fruit orchards.

Undeterred, Connecticut citizens turned to commerce, and from the years 1780 to 1840, the Yankee peddler reigned supreme. His sturdy wagon, loaded with tinware, soap, matches, yard goods and tools, was a familiar sight up and down the Atlantic seaboard, over the Appalachians into Detroit and St Louis, and even down to New Orleans. Success brought with it the demand for more and more products, and it was here that the Connecticut Yankees made their major contributions to the pioneering American economy.

Colonial piper in West Hartford.

Ever since the US Patent Office opened in 1790, Connecticut inventors have filed more patents per capita than any other state in the United States. Hats, combs, cigars, seeds, clocks, kettles, furniture and firearms – all came out of the factory stamped with the label "Made in Connecticut."

New products called for new systems of manufacture: Eli Whitney, inventor of the cotton gin, first introduced the use of standardized parts at his firearms factory in New Haven. With the introduction of interchangeable parts came the creation of the assembly line – and the rise of the Industrial Revolution. No longer would manufacturing rely on the talents of a few, skilled craftsmen. Mass production had entered the marketplace, and the American economy prospered accordingly.

Not surprisingly, industry made Connecticut's fortune. In Hartford, entrepreneur Samuel Colt gave his name to the Colt .45 revolver, the "gun that won the West." Winchester rifles were manufactured in New Haven, hats in Danbury,

clocks in Bristol and fine brass in Waterbury.

New industry meant new workers, and the late 19th and early 20th centuries saw waves of immigrants settle in such manufacturing centers as Bridgeport, New Haven and Torrington. While Connecticut may present a colonial face to the casual traveler, those who remain long enough appreciate the contributions of Italians, Germans, Portuguese and Eastern Europeans to the essential Connecticut character.

Connecticut's past is also its present, and today the state continues to rely on industry for its economic good fortune. Airplane engines are manufactured in East Hartford, helicopters in Stratford; nuclear submarines are designed and built in Groton.

Despite its industry, Connecticut has remained a largely rural enclave. With manufacturing concentrated along the South Shore and in Hartford, 75 percent of the state is given over to small towns and deeply forested woodlands. Narrow, winding roads lead the visitor from

After milking.

one charming village to another, to communities proud of their colonial heritage and seemingly untouched by modern times.

Capital of Connecticut: In any game of free association, the name of **Hartford** immediately elicits the response, "insurance." And, indeed, the skyline of Connecticut's capital city is dominated by the steel-and-glass skyscrapers of the nation's largest insurance companies. Today several dozen are located in the greater Hartford area, together employing approximately 10 percent of the total work force.

The first insurance policy, covering a shipowner's losses in the event his ship didn't make it safely back to port, was written in the 18th century. The early industry served the maritime trade, but as shipping declined during the 19th century, Hartford's canny insurance companies expanded their coverage to fire and casualty.

Hartford's reputation is well founded; from their earliest days, the insurance firms honored their commitments. In 1835, New York City suffered a disastrous fire that destroyed more than 600 buildings. Unable to pay the claims, many New York insurance companies folded. Not so the Hartford Insurance Company, however. Its president traveled to New York and personally guaranteed payment of every claim. Similar incidents in Boston and Chicago, as well as the 1906 San Francisco earthquake, bolstered the reputation of Hartford's insurance companies.

But Hartford is more than insurance companies. It is also Connecticut's oldest city, settled in 1635 by a group of Puritans from the Massachusetts Bay Colony. Its location on the navigable waterways of the Connecticut River has made Hartford a major force in the political, economic and social development of the region.

In 1662, a royal charter was drawn up uniting the colonies of Hartford and New Haven, and guaranteeing their independence. Sir Edmund Andros, appointed governor of Connecticut in 1687, had the charter revoked. In defiance of

Connecticut Classic 10-K road race, Danbury.

this move, the Hartford patriot John Wadsworth stole the charter and hid it in the trunk of an oak tree standing at the center of the town. Two years later, upon the accession of William III, Andros was recalled to England and the charter was reinstated.

A plaque at **Charter Oak Place**, in the south end of the city, marks the spot where the magnificent oak stood until 1856, when a windstorm felled it. Hartford's museums are filled with items supposedly made from the wood.

Any tour of the downtown area should begin with a visit to the **Old State House**, located at the intersection of Main Street and Asylum Avenue. The nation's oldest state house, it was the first public commission for architect Charles Bulfinch, who would later design the state capitols of Maine and Massachusetts. Neither quite compares to his Hartford creation, which stands as a supreme example of Federalist architecture.

Directly south of the State House, also on Main Street, is the Wadsworth Atheneum, the oldest continually oper-ating public art museum in America. Built in the Gothic Revival style, the Atheneum was erected to house the library and art gallery of Daniel Wadsworth. Numerous additions have been made since, and the museum's collection – which includes paintings by Goya, Rubens, Rembrandt and van Dyck, in addition to works by American masters such as Thomas Cole and John Singer Sargent – remains a proud part of the city's cultural heritage.

The **Connecticut State Capitol**, a Gothic wedding cake of turrets, gables, porches and towers, was designed by Richard Upjohn in 1879. Though some might question its good taste, there is no doubt that its ornate interiors of hand-painted columns, marble floors and elaborate stained-glass windows were designed to reflect the wealth and prosperity of the community it served. Located on Capitol Avenue overlooking **Bushnell Park** (which contains an enchanting 1914 carousel, open in summer), the Capitol is flanked by the **State Library**, which maintains an excellent

Hartford's Constitution Plaza at Christmas.

collection of Connecticut clocks and firearms; and the **Bushnell Memorial Auditorium**, a center for concerts, ballet, opera and theater.

More modern in concept, but respectful of the grace and dignity of its downtown district, is the Hartford Civic Center and Constitution Plaza. Completed in 1975, the **Civic Center** offers visitors a full range of convention services as well as being home to the Hartford Whalers ice hockey team.

Constitution Plaza, a 12-acre complex completed in the 1960s, provides Hartford with an open mall, a vast array of shops, office buildings and the starkly modern, elliptically shaped Phoenix Mutual Life Insurance Building, so familiar to the Hartford skyline.

Travelers Tower, the tallest building in the city, has an Observation Deck which offers an excellent view of the Hartford area. The Travelers Insurance Company was founded in 1683, when Colonel James Bolter insured his life for $5,000 to cover his lunchtime trip from home to the post office.

Mark Twain's home: Mark Twain, the riverboat pilot-turned-author, spent the happiest years of his life in Hartford. Although Twain, whose real name was Samuel Clemens, originally moved to Hartford in 1874 merely to be close to his publisher, he frequently sang the praises of his adopted city: "Of all the beautiful towns it has been my fortune to see, this is the chief... You do not know what beauty is if you have not been here."

Twain settled in Hartford soon after his marriage to Olivia Langdon, and it was in their home at 351 Farmington Avenue that they raised their three daughters, Clara, Jean and Susy. It was also in Hartford that Twain penned his most successful novels, including *The Adventures of Tom Sawyer*, *The Adventures of Huckleberry Finn* and *A Connecticut Yankee in King Arthur's Court*.

The family home was situated in **Nook Farm**, the intellectual center of Hartford settled in the second half of the 19th century. Twain's home is easily the largest, a great Victorian mansion de-

Dixieland comes to the Constitution State.

signed by Edward Tuckerman Potter in 1874. Exquisitely decorated by Louis Comfort Tiffany and his associates, the house very much reflects the character of its owner. Outdoor porches and balconies give the impression of a Mississippi riverboat, while the interiors are grand and whimsical. Of particular interest is the upstairs billiard room, where Twain did much of his writing.

The author remained in Hartford until 1891, when poor investments forced him to move to Europe or face bankruptcy. The family always intended to return, but after the sudden death of his daughter Susy in 1896, Twain could not bear to return to the site of their happiest memories. He sold the house in 1903.

Nook Farm is located just north of exit 46 on Interstate 84, less than 2 miles (3.5 km) from downtown Hartford. Now a busy residential area, it retains little of its pastoral charm, but both the Mark Twain Memorial, as the mansion is now called, and the nearby Harriet Beecher Stowe House have been expertly restored.

Timely Bristol: Hartford's environs include a number of historic towns and villages that provide worthwhile destinations for day trips.

Bristol, 18 miles (29 km) west, was the 19th-century clockmaking capital of the country, producing more than 200,000 clocks in a single year. The neighboring towns of **Terryville** and **Thomaston** were named for Eli Terry and Seth Thomas, craftsmen who at one time put a clock on every mantle in America. The **American Clock and Watch Museum** is located on Maple Street in Bristol, and houses a superb collection of the region's finest and most valuable time-pieces.

Farmington, a village situated on the Farmington River just 10 miles (16 km) west of Hartford, is considered by many to be one of the loveliest towns in New England. Certainly, its elegant 18th- and 19th-century mansions display a clarity of architectural detail seldom equaled in the area. **Hillstead Museum**, located at 35 Mountain Road, is a particular gem. Designed by architect

The roadside stand, a backroad tradition.

Stanford White, the Hillstead was originally conceived as a retirement home for a wealthy industrialist, Alfred Atmore Pope. A self-made man, Pope was a personal friend of the artist Mary Cassatt and a great admirer of the French Impressionist school of painters. Pope's home, which remains as it was in the early 1900s, reflects his taste in art. Scattered throughout the mansion are a number of familiar canvases. These include several paintings from Monet's "Haystack" series, Manet's *The Guitar Lady*, and Degas's *The Tub*. Whistler and Cassatt are also well represented.

Wethersfield, located on the Connecticut River just south of Hartford, is one of the oldest villages in the state. More than 150 of the 17th- and 18th-century homes in its downtown area have been preserved and restored. Take a look at the **1760 Congregational Meeting-house** on Main Street, then visit the combined **Webb-Deane-Stevens Museum**.

Hikers' Housatonic: The Housatonic River is a handsome river, crystal clear and freckled with trout – the kind of river that makes one want to roll up one's trousers and go wading. It rises in Vermont, flows through the Berkshire Hills of western Massachusetts and tumbles into Connecticut at the northwest corner of the state. As the river courses through the rustic communities of **Falls Village**, **West Cornwall** and **Cornwall Bridge**, the surging waters tear at the shoreline, creating small islands of pine trees and hardwoods.

To see the full beauty of this region, follow the river from **Kent** north on Route 7 to **Canaan**. Then head west on Route 44 to **Salisbury**. Hikers may want to follow the **Appalachian Trail** from Kent to Canaan. The Housatonic is a canoeists' river, and those who wish to spend a day on its waters will find a convenient rental service in Falls Village.

The Connecticut highlands, thickly wooded and crisscrossed with old stone walls left over from the days when farmers tried to till the soil, were settled somewhat later than the southern reaches

Ernie Tolx cooks planked shad in Old Saybrook.

206

of the state. The mountains made access difficult, and many of those who came soon packed their wagons and headed west for the more fertile regions of Ohio and Illinois.

With the discovery of iron ore in the Litchfield Hills during the 18th century, the valley enjoyed a brief period of prosperity. Forges, like the old furnace at Kent, produced pig iron until the discovery of coal in Pennsylvania made Connecticut's ironworks obsolete.

Visitors to present-day Kent, which is now an artists' colony, may examine the ruins of the Old Kent Furnace at the **Sloane-Stanley Museum** located on Route 7. Also on view is an extensive collection of early American wood and iron tools gathered by the writer and artist Eric Sloane.

North along the twisting and turning roadway of Route 7 from Kent are many well-preserved 18th- and 19th-century homes. In the especially picturesque village of West Cornwall, look for the covered bridge, erected in 1836 across the Housatonic.

The return journey down US 44 through Salisbury and **Lakeville** offers an even grander display of traditional 19th-century mansions. Open during the summer months, the **Holley-Williams House** in downtown Lakeville is an excellent example of a Classical Revival house built by one of the area's more prosperous "Iron Barons."

Lovely Litchfield: Approximately 15 miles (24 km) east of Kent lies the historic New England community of **Litchfield**. The Litchfield green, graced by the tall-steepled Congregational Church, forms the meeting point of the village's four main streets. Lining North and South streets are handsome, white, clapboard houses, which can be toured only on Open House Day in mid-July.

On South Street (Route 63) stands the **Tapping Reeve House**, behind which is a small building that housed the nation's first school of law. Visitors can see the desks where many a distinguished jurist learned his trade, among them Aaron Burr and John C. Calhoun, two vice presidents of the United States.

itchfield.

This simple schoolroom also graduated six cabinet members, 28 senators and more than 100 Congressmen.

Litchfield merchants prospered during the early days of the China trade when their money backed the sailing ships of Mystic and New Haven, but industry faltered when a new railroad bypassed the town center. Commerce was relocated to the more industrialized communities of Waterbury and Naugatuck. Litchfield was left as a sleepy town nestled in the past, and it remains one of the loveliest examples of 18th-century New England.

Cruising the Connecticut: Beginning as a mountain stream tumbling from its source near the New Hampshire-Canada border, the Connecticut River travels 410 miles (660 km) through four states and ends its journey to the sea as a broad and majestic tidal estuary. The Native Americans named it "Quinnituckett," which means "the long, tidal river." Throughout history, the Connecticut has linked valley residents with the outside world. A fertile floodplain has made this area a center for agriculture, and water power has generated energy for a variety of small industries.

A tour of the Connecticut Valley can begin near the river's mouth with a visit to **Essex**, founded in 1645 and a long-time center of maritime activity. Essex developed as an important shipbuilding center during the 18th century. *The Oliver Cromwell*, America's first warship, was launched in 1776 from its docks. Yachts and cabin cruisers still make their berths at various Essex marinas, where tall masts and yards of tackle lend the town a distinctly nautical air. Contained in its dockside museum is an exact replica of the *American Turtle*, the nation's first submarine. Invented by David Bushnell, a native of the nearby coastal town of **Old Saybrook**, it was employed in 1776 by Yankee forces to sink an English battleship during the blockade of New York Harbor. Though unsuccessful in its mission, the *Turtle* incorporated a number of engineering ideas that Robert Fulton later adopted in the design of the *Nautilus*.

Fall in Essex.

The **Old Griswold Inn** on Main Street has been in operation since 1776. The rare collection of maritime prints hanging in its tap room makes the inn worth a special visit.

Those who desire a firsthand glimpse of the Connecticut River may take an old-fashioned journey by steam locomotive and riverboat. Board the 1920s coaches of the Valley Railroad at Essex Depot, and ride along the river through the villages of **Chester** and **Deep River**. At Deep River, transfer to a riverboat similar to the hundreds of passenger ships that ferried travelers between Old Saybrook and Hartford more than a century years ago. The round trip takes about 2½ hours.

Those who continue their journey up the Connecticut Valley may cross the river by car ferry at Chester. It is a charming excursion that brings you to **Hadlyme**, home of the spectacularly eccentric **Gillette Castle**. William Gillette (1853–1937) was a much admired American actor whose portrayal of Sherlock Holmes brought him fame and fortune. Gillette was one of the first actors who took to wearing the deerstalker hat, the distinctive Holmes trademark; and it was he who uttered those memorable words onstage: "Elementary, my dear Watson."

Gillette was born and raised in Hartford and, when he decided to build the house of his dreams, the actor selected a hilltop aerie that commanded a breathtaking view of the Connecticut River and its surrounding countryside. Work began on the 122-acre (49-hectare) site in 1914, and it took five years and over $1 million before Gillette's architectural vision was completed.

The results were whimsical and bizarre. The stone-and-concrete castle is filled with hand-hewn oak furnishings and specialized gadgetry. Javanese mats line the walls, and light fixtures are fashioned from numerous bits of colored glass. Outside, Gillette was free to develop his favorite hobby: trains and locomotives. He constructed his very own railroad on the estate grounds and, although the tracks have long since been

dismantled, portions of the old roadbed make excellent hiking trails. Now a state park with excellent picnicking facilities, Gillette Castle is open daily from late May to mid-October.

Directly north of Gillette Castle, on Route 82, is the charming Victorian town of **East Haddam**. Still standing along the shoreline are the great rambling hotels (some of them now private homes) that served riverboat passengers during the 19th century. Before the introduction of the railroad, East Haddam was a point of embarkation for the many passengers who traveled by steamboat across the Long Island Sound to New York City.

The **Goodspeed Opera House**, which sits so majestically on the banks of the Connecticut River, is a reminder of the heyday of steamboat travel. Countless citizens paused here for a bit of entertainment before continuing their journey downriver. Beautifully restored, the Opera House presents musical revivals, as well as original productions, from April to December.

Coastal Connecticut: From the harbors of New Haven, New London, Mystic and Stonington, China clippers and Yankee whalers sailed out to seek their fortunes. Such associations may be merely historical, but people along Connecticut's coast still retain a fondness for salt air and a genuine love of the sea. Most towns have at least one marina, and on a clear summer's day the horizon of the Long Island Sound is filled with billowing sails.

For those planning to explore this region in depth, there are several routes available. The most efficient is the Connecticut Turnpike (Interstate 95 and 395), the major highway linking New York and Boston. But what one makes up in time is definitely lost in terms of charm. The more casual approach is the scenic Merritt Parkway which runs from New York to New Haven, where a convenient connection can be made with US Highway 1. Also known as the Post Road, this predominantly rural roadway meanders through most of the towns mentioned here.

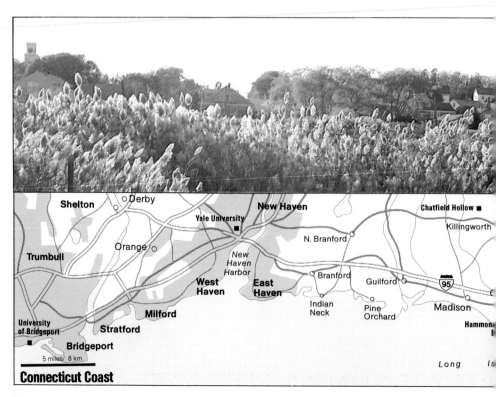

Connecticut Coast

5 miles/ 8 km

Greenwich, **Cos Cob**, **Stamford**, **Darien** and **Rowayton** – to the thousands of Connecticut residents who work in New York City, this is a railroad conductor's litany. About an hour away from Manhattan by train, the Connecticut suburbs are among the most luxurious bedroom communities in the nation. Many of New York's wealthiest business executives make their homes here, attracted by the pleasant, countrified locale.

This "Gold Coast" has an artistic streak, too, exemplified in the galleries and shops of newly trendy **South Norwalk**, dubbed "SoNo" for its emulation of New York's SoHo district. Once a gritty, run-down neighborhood, it's now a great place to while away a day pleasantly – especially if you spend part at the hands-on **Maritime Center** aquarium/museum.

Bridgeport, a major industrial center producing everything from clothes to electrical appliances, is an exception to the coast's general aura of ease and affluence. One fun note: the **Barnum Museum**, a showcase for big-top memorabilia.

Town and gown: New Haven, settled by Puritans in 1638, was an independent colony until 1662, when it merged with the Hartford settlement. In the early 19th century, the port brought prosperity to the town, and more than 100 ships regularly sailed along the coast to the West Indies and the Orient.

However, it was not until the Industrial Revolution that the town made the big leap to becoming a major manufacturing center. Eli Whitney first instituted a system of mass production in his firearms factory. Since that time, New Haven has pioneered such inventions as the steel fish hook, the meat grinder, the corkscrew and the steamboat.

New Haven is perhaps best known not as an industrial center, but as a center of learning. It is the home of **Yale University**, which dominates much of the city's cultural life. Founded in 1701 by a group of Puritan clergymen, Yale was originally located in nearby Saybrook. In 1716, the school was moved to

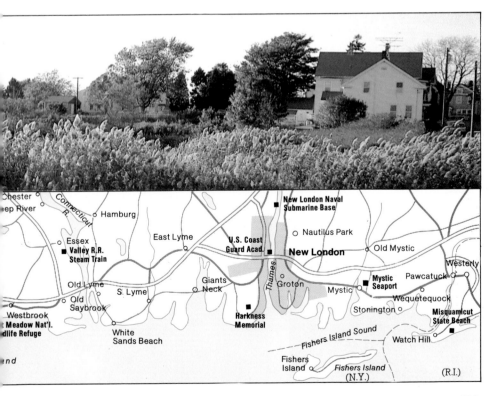

New Haven, and two years later it took the name of the wealthy merchant Elihu Yale, its benefactor.

Alma mater to famous personalities such as Eli Whitney, Nathan Hale and Noah Webster, Yale has pursued a policy of commissioning leading architects to design its buildings. But the dominant architectural style on the Yale campus is Gothic Revival, and there is more than enough greenery creeping up the walls to qualify the college as genuine Ivy League.

To make a thorough tour of Yale, inquire at the University's visitors' information office, located at the Old Campus' grand **Phelps Gateway** on College Street. Otherwise, even an abbreviated stroll should include visits to the excellent museums and libraries. Start from the **Beinecke Rare Book and Manuscript Library** on Wall Street, where an edition of the Gutenberg Bible is on display. Two blocks south is the **Yale University Art Gallery** which contains well over 100 paintings by patriot artist Jonathan Trumbull. The Gallery houses impressive collections of African and pre-Columbian art, as well as canvases by Manet, Van Gogh, Corot, Degas and Matisse.

Across the street stands the **Yale Center of British Art**, containing a vast collection of British paintings (including works by Constable and Turner), drawings and sculpture donated in 1966 by industrialist Paul Mellon.

Adjacent to the university is the **New Haven Green**, a 16-acre (6-hectare) common surrounded by a trinity of churches constructed in Gothic Revival, Georgian and Federal styles.

New Haven has rich cultural offerings available. The **Yale Repertory Theater** on campus and the **Long Wharf Theater** on the downtown waterfront mount some of the most interesting productions in the country. The New Haven Symphony Orchestra frequently performs at Woolsey Hall on the Yale campus.

Old communities: Up the coast from New Haven are two of the loveliest communities along this shore, the vil-

Left, Yale University, New Haven. Right, mission accomplished

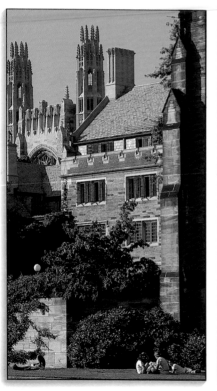

lages of Guilford and Madison. Of the two, **Guilford** is the older, having been settled in 1639 by the Reverend Henry Whitfield. His home on Old Whitfield Street is the oldest stone dwelling in New England; now called the **Henry Whitfield State Museum**, it is open to visitors mid-January to mid-December.

Guilford's town green, one of the purest in New England, is bordered by many of its original 17th- and 18th-century homes. Several of them are museums, including **Hyland House** (1660) and the **Thomas Griswold House** (1774), both on Boston Street.

Nearby **Madison** has some of the most beautiful summer and year-round homes in Connecticut. **Hammonasset Beach State Park**, just 2 miles (3 km) east, is the state's longest public beach.

Of all the towns on the Connecticut shore, **Old Lyme** can boast the richest artistic heritage. There was a time when "a sea captain lived in every house," but later the community came to be known primarily as an artists' colony, thanks in large part to Florence Griswold, the daughter of a sea captain and a devoted, if impecunious, patron of the arts. Her Lyme Street house, now the **Florence Griswold Museum**, contains a stunning array of works by her illustrious American Impressionist boarders, including such notables as Childe Hassam. Some were so moved by her *laissez-faire* hospitality, they left painted mementos on the doors, mantels and paneled walls.

Whales and submarines: New London, along with Nantucket and New Bedford, was one of the busiest whaling ports in the nation. In the early days of the 19th century, more than 80 ships sailed from its docks and many a vast fortune was accumulated by its merchants. Evidence of this wealth can be seen in **Whale Oil Row** on Huntington Street, where four Greek Revival mansions were built in the 1830s.

When oil was discovered in Pennsylvania in 1859, the whaling industry went into a sharp decline, and manufacturing became New London's chief occupation. But the city maintained its ties to

A ferry rosses lazy Connecticut River.

the sea and today is best known as the home of the **US Coast Guard Academy**. Located on State 32, just a mile north of I-95, the Academy is open to visitors daily from May to October.

Across the Thames River from New London stands the city of **Groton**, known as the "Submarine Capital of the World" – the manufacture of nuclear submarines is the town's major industry. Non-claustrophobes who wish to view the interior of a submarine may visit the *USS Nautilus* Memorial at the US Naval Submarine Base.

Mysterious Mystic: The village of **Mystic**, an old maritime community of trim white houses, sits at the tidal outlet of the Mystic River. For generations, Mystic was the home of daring mariners and fishermen, and was feared by the British during the Revolution as a "cursed little hornets' nest" of patriots.

The village teemed with activity during the Gold Rush days of 1849, when shipbuilders vied to see who could construct the fastest clipper ships to travel round Cape Horn to the boom town of

San Francisco. It was the *Andrew Jackson*, a Mystic-built clipper launched in 1860, that claimed the world's record – making the journey in 89 days and 4 hours, 9 hours faster than the famous *Flying Cloud*.

Today, Mystic is best known as the home of **Mystic Seaport**, a living replica of a 19th-century waterfront community during the heyday of sailing ships. Restoration of Mystic Seaport began in 1929 and, since that time, the project has expanded to include a complex of more than 60 buildings covering 17 acres (7 hectares). It's a big tourist draw, and a full day and plenty of stamina are required to tour the entire seaport properly.

The restoration imparts a vivid sense of how life was lived by Mystic's residents in the 1860s. Visitors are encouraged to wander along the wharves and streets of the village, and taste the old seafaring way of life.

Save time for a visit to the *Charles W. Morgan*, the last surviving vessel of America's 19th-century whaling fleet. Built in 1841, the *Morgan* plied the seas for more than 80 years and made 37 voyages, some of them lasting three or four years. Also board the *Joseph Conrad*, which was built in 1882 by the Danish as a training vessel, and now serves as a student dormitory; demonstrations of sail-handling and chantey singing are scheduled regularly aboard both ships.

It's also worth stopping at the **Stillman Building**, a museum housing an impressive collection of ship's figureheads, scrimshaw, ship models, logbooks and other artifacts.

Just up the road, near I-95, visit the **Mystic Marinelife Aquarium**, with extensive indoor and outdoor exhibits spanning seahorses to sea lions.

A few miles further east is the charming old whaling port of **Stonington**, huddled at the edge of the state near the Rhode Island border. Stonington was once the third-largest city in Connecticut and an important seaport. Although considerably reduced in circumstances, the village remains one of the prettiest coastal enclaves in New England.

Left, shad roe, a prime delicacy. Right, looking for lobsters.

RHODE ISLAND

The smallest state in the nation, ever since there were only 13, Rhode Island has nonetheless managed to hold on to a disproportionate share of wealth and clout. On the map, it may look more like an overgrown port than a genuine state, but that very sea-readiness accounts in large part for its long-term appeal.

Certainly, the turn-of-the-century millionaires who built their legendary summer "cottages" in Newport recognized natural wealth when they saw it: the dramatic vistas of the Rhode Island Sound, the refreshing westerly breezes wafting in to relieve summer doldrums. The mansions they left behind still gleam atop the cliffs, jewels left over from the Gilded Age.

Centuries earlier, the reclusive Reverend William Blaxton found the area equally attractive. Blaxton, who had been living contentedly as a hermit in what would soon become Boston , fled to Rhode Island when the Puritans he'd invited to share his peninsula proved too proselytizing.

Rhode Island's official founder was clergyman Roger Williams. Driven out of Salem in 1635 for preaching religious tolerance, Williams headed south to establish a settlement where all were free to practice their own faith: traveling by canoe with a cadre of followers, he arrived in what is now Providence. Anne Hutchinson followed in 1637, to be joined by other dissidents. In 1663 Charles II granted a charter to the rather wordily named Colony of Rhode Island and Providence Plantations – a name it still officially retains as a state.

Soon people from even farther afield flocked to Rhode Island's shores. A large number of Quakers, fleeing Puritan persecution, made Newport their home, and as early as the 18th century, Jews from Portugal and Holland settled here as well. In the ensuing centuries came Italians, Irish, Russians, Poles, French, Swedes, Greeks, Armenians, Chinese and Cape Verdeans. By 1960

Preceding pages: lavish Rosecliff Manor at Newport. Below, Newport marina.

Rhode Island was the most densely populated state in America, with 859,000 inhabitants crowded into 1,214 sq. miles (3,144 sq. km). Today, with a population in excess of 1 million, Rhode Island is a bustling, multicultural cross-section of New England life.

The Ocean State: As Rhode Island's license plate attests, Narragansett Bay dominates the state. Taking a dinosaur bite out of the New England coast, it gives the state a shoreline out of all proportion to its land area. Rhode Island is only 48 miles (77 km) long and 37 miles (60 km) wide, yet end to end it claims 400 miles (644 km) of coastline.

With such an abundance of water at their disposal, Rhode Islanders have long turned to the sea for their livelihood. Two of the nation's leading seaports in the early days of the republic were Providence and Newport. Using Rhode Island as a base, pirates raided merchant ships in the North Atlantic; the notorious Captain Kidd is rumored to have buried his cache of gold doubloons in Jamestown.

But Rhode Island is a land of contradictions. Despite the state's heritage as a sanctuary for pirates, Newport was the birthplace of the modern US Navy: President Chester Alan Arthur developed a new fleet – built of steel, rather than wood – there in the early 1880s, and enjoyed staging gun drills on the bay. (Though much of the Navy pulled out in the mid-1970s, the Naval War College, founded in 1884, remains.) Founded as a haven of religious liberty, it became a world-class slave trade center. Despite its considerable contributions to the success of the American Revolution, Rhode Island was the last holdout among states ratifying the US Constitution. Notorious for its exploitation of child labor, Rhode Island became a bastion of New Deal social ideals.

Until 1854, it couldn't even decide which city would be its capital. Each year the General Assembly packed up its belongings and moved lock, stock and barrel to one of the five locales contesting for the honor. Eventually, after a raucous battle in 1900, Provi-

estored sea aptains' omes on enefit treet, rovidence.

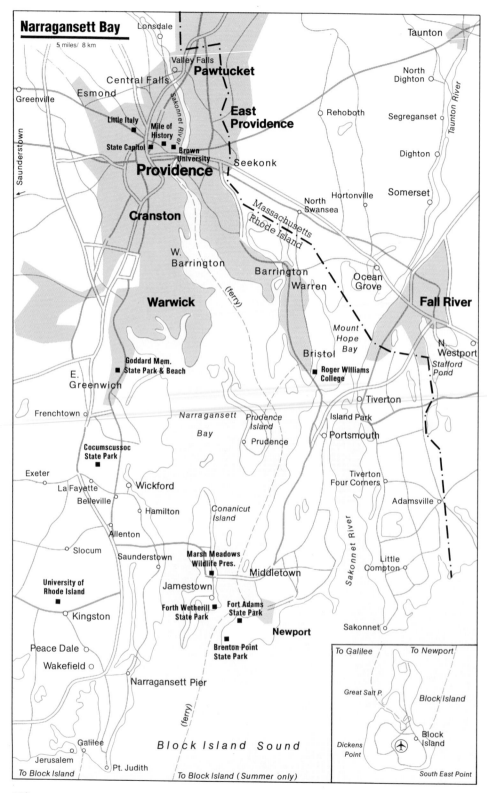

Narragansett Bay

5 miles/ 8 km

Lonsdale
Taunton
Valley Falls
Pawtucket
North
Dighton
Central Falls
Esmond
Greenville
Rehoboth
Segreganset
East
Providence
Little Italy   Mile of
History
Dighton
State Capitol
Brown
University
Seekonk
Providence
Hortonville
Somerset
North
Swansea
Cranston
Massachusetts
Rhode Island
W.
Barrington
Barrington
Ocean
Grove
Warren
Warwick
(ferry)
Mount
Hope
Bay
Fall River
Bristol
N.
Westport
Goddard Mem.
State Park & Beach
Roger Williams
College
Stafford
Pond
E.
Greenwich
Tiverton
Frenchtown
Narragansett
Bay
Prudence
Island
Island Park
Cocumscussoc
State Park
Prudence
Portsmouth
Exeter
Wickford
La Fayette
Belleville
Tiverton
Four Corners
Hamilton
Conanicut
Island
Adamsville
Allenton
Slocum
Saunderstown
Marsh Meadows
Wildlife Pres.
Middletown
Little
Compton
University of
Rhode Island
Jamestown
Forth Wetherill   Fort Adams
State Park   State Park
Kingston
Sakonnet
Newport
Peace Dale
Brenton Point
State Park
Wakefield
Narragansett Pier
(ferry)
To Galilee
To Newport
Galilee
Great Salt P.
Block Island
Jerusalem
To Block Island
Pt. Judith
Dickens
Point
Block
Island
Block Island Sound
To Block Island (Summer only)
South East Point

Saunderstown

Taunton River

Sakonnet River

Sakonnet River

dence won out over Newport. It remains the capital, but Newporters contend their city is truly the heart of the state.

If little Rhode Island is a land of contradictions, it is also a land of superlatives and firsts. Among the state's distinctions are: the world's widest bridge, in Providence; the only operational water-powered snuff mill in the United States, in Saunderstown; and, in Adamsville, the world's only known monument to a chicken (the prolific Rhode Island Red).

The state boasts the country's first synagogue, its first department store and its oldest enclosed shopping mall, built in the early 19th century. And lest it be forgotten, the first two-week paid vacation on record was spent in Rhode Island. In 1524, the Italian navigator Giovanni da Verrazano, on an exploratory mission for the King of France, was investigating the North American coast when he spotted Narragansett Bay. Verrazano was "so enthralled… he lingered for a fortnight."

Rhode Island, in the singular, is actually a misnomer. In fact, there are 35 islands within the state, the only one named after a Greek isle. Within and without Narragansett Bay are the four principal islands of Aquidneck, Block, Conanicut and Prudence; others include Hen, Hog, Rabbitt, Boat, Old Boy, Patience, Hope and Despair. In and about these islands, visitors enjoy boating, sailing, surfing and fishing.

Throughout the state – generously scattered through cities and towns like Providence, Wickford, Bristol, Little Compton and Newport – are lovely old homes representing the decorative ideals of several centuries. Despite the concentrated population, park lands are plentiful, too. And precisely because the state is so small –it takes less than two hours to drive from one end to the other – it's possible to enjoy its variegated offerings within a short time span. A visitor can walk historic city streets in the morning, picnic in an idyllic grove at noon and savor the delights of the seashore by moonlight.

Revitalized Providence: In its early days, **Providence** was the port of call for ships engaged in the lucrative triangular trade:New England rum for African slaves for West Indies molasses. In 1781, John Brown, one of four brothers whose family would dominate Providence for some years to come, sent the first of many ships to China. The maritime trade began to decline, however, following a series of international wars which resulted in embargoes and protectionism, and public interest and investment shifted toward industry. Techniques of factory production were pioneered and groundwork for the development of the region's textile industry was laid in 1789, with the construction of **Slater Mill** by Moses Brown. (Now fully restored as a historic site, the mill offers visitors a rare look into bygone industry at **Pawtucket**, north of Providence.)

As a major manufacturing center throughout the 19th century, Providence was dubbed "the cradle of American industry." Its huge plants were known worldwide – Brown & Sharpe (machinery and tools), Nicholson (files), Grinnel (sprinkler systems), Gorham (silver-

Ocean Drive, Newport, facing the Atlantic.

ware), Davol (rubber goods) and so on.

The 20th century brought hard times. With the Great Depression and the textile industry's exodus to the south, Providence lost its pre-eminence as an industrial center. Although no longer the giant it once was, Providence has enjoyed a revitalization of business in recent decades, and has in turn lavished restorative attention on its variegated downtown. Here, residents have grown accustomed to stumbling on a Victorian office building, or an old industrial complex jazzily accented in pink, purple or chartreuse, right next to a seedy remnant from the 1930s.

A two-legged tour: Given its maddening network of highways and one-way streets, Providence is a city best seen on foot. Begin at **Kennedy Plaza**. To the east stands the restored **Providence Station**, worth a visit for a glimpse back to the times when train travel was a grand affair. Across the plaza is the **Omni Biltmore Hotel**, a 1920s showpiece that deteriorated into a shabby eyesore until, in 1979, it was restored to first-class status.

Around the corner from Kennedy Plaza is the **Turk's Head Building**, a 1913 landmark with an ornate stone head over its entrance; and the **Customs House** (1856), with a dome and lantern that once welcomed ships returning from China.

Theater and architecture buffs will want to head toward the refurbished Ocean State Theater on Weybosset Street, now known as the **Providence Performing Arts Center**. This Hollywood extravaganza, built in the heyday of movie theaters, sports a great deal of gilt, a terra-cotta facade and a "Moorish sand castle" side entrance. Saved in the nick of time from total decay, it provides the city with a string of major performances and top stars throughout the year. Several blocks away is the **Lederer Theater**, home of the Trinity Repertory Company, one of the country's finest. Like the Arts Center, the Lederer has an ornate terra-cotta facade, along with a 3-story arched entrance, floral swags and a false balcony.

For shopping or snacking and a bit of history, visit the **Arcade** on Weybosset Street. This Greek Revival "temple of trade" and prototypal indoor shopping mall was built in 1828. Its three-story granite columns (said to be the second largest in America, after those at the Cathedral of St John the Divine in New York) were cut from single pieces of stone, which required 15 yokes of oxen to move.

A city of hills: Like Rome, Providence was built on seven hills. Most people remember three: College (officially, Prospect), Federal and Constitution. The other four – Tockwotten, Smith and two now-leveled hills – seem to have melted in the metropolitan sprawl.

Constitution Hill is almost impossible to miss because of the **State Capitol** which dominates its crest: this imposing 1891–92 McKim, Mead, and White structure is said to boast the second largest self-support dome in the world, and contains an historic portrait of George Washington by Rhode Island native Gilbert Stuart. On opposite sides of the downtown area, College and Fed-

The Arcade, a Greek Revival-style temple of trade.

eral hills are favored haunts of tourists and natives alike.

At the foot of College Hill, along the canal, stands **Market House**, a red-brick Colonial built in the 1770s. The wharves that fronted it are paved over now, and the building serves as a part of the **Rhode Island School of Design** (RISD, pronounced "*rizz-dee*") complex. But Market House was once the city's political nerve center. From its wharves in 1775, Rhode Islanders threw their own version of the Boston Tea Party. Instead of dumping tea into the river, they burned 300 pounds (136 kg).

Plaques on Market House and other downtown buildings record the high-water level of the 1815 storm that brought Providence to its knees with tides reaching nearly 12 ft (3.5 meters) above mean high-water level. The storms of 1938 and 1954 caused similar flooding in the city; today, the **Fox Point Hurricane Barrier**, south of Market House toward the mouth of the Providence River, stands as testimony to the devastation. A very unusual dam, its gates (usually open) face downstream and are closed only when a hurricane threatens.

On North Main Street, one block up the steep hillside from Market House, is the **First Baptist Meeting-House** (1775); designed by one of the Brown brothers, Joseph, it survives as a lovely example of the Colonial style.

The "Mile of History," as the Providence Preservation Society calls it, begins here. All along **Benefit Street** and adjacent blocks are more than 200 restored 18th- and 19th-century buildings (many are now private homes) originally built by sea captains and merchants; the old houses, churches and schools bear bronze plaques identifying their original owners and dates of construction. At twilight, gaslights and brick sidewalks, restored during the preservationist campaigns of recent decades, charmingly evoke the past.

For the benefit of the people: The **John Brown House**, built in 1786 at Power and Benefit streets, still lives up to John Quincy Adams' description as "the most magnificent and elegant private mansion that I have ever seen on this continent." Converted into a museum, it displays priceless antiques (including period furniture, paintings, pewter, silver, porcelain, and mementos of the China Trade); it also gives a good sense of early Providence life.

Farther north on Benefit Street is the **Sullivan Dorr Mansion**, owned in the 1830s and 1840s by state legislator Thomas Dorr, the leader of Dorr's Rebellion (1841–42). He and his supporters instituted a new state government – unrecognized by the existing government – when their reform efforts failed. Dorr was soon tried for treason and spent a year in jail.

Nearby is the **Sarah Whitman House**. Whitman, a poet, captured the heart of Edgar Allen Poe, but refused to marry him because he couldn't stay sober. The courtship reputedly took place in the stacks of the **Providence Atheneum**, the 1836 Greek Revival structure at 251 Benefit Street – itself worth a visit for its collections of rare books, prints, and paintings.

Benefit Street was once a twisting dirt path informally known as Back Street because it led around the back side of homes to the family graveyards. When at last a communal burial ground was marked out and ancestral bones duly transferred to it, Back Street was straightened out and "improved for the benefit of the people of Providence." Other streets have similar tales underlying their names; the Preservation Society guides who lead walking tours through this area can illuminate all the lore.

Competing with the historic houses on College Hill are the buildings of RISD – whose Museum of Art, at 224 Benefit Street, spans outstanding classical to contemporary work – and eversprawling **Brown University**. The heart of the College Hill shopping area is Thayer Street, four blocks east of Benefit, packed with interesting restaurants, bars, shops, and bookstores.

Old World enclaves: Continue south down Thayer Street to encounter one of Providence's best-kept secrets: **Fox Point**. Home to the city's Portuguese community, Fox Point speaks with an Old World accent. On holy days, celebrants parade with statues of the Virgin Mary while children dressed in their best suits and crinolines follow along. Early morning brings to Fox Point the tantalizing scent of Portuguese sweetbread wafting from small bakeries.

Perched on Federal Hill across the city is Providence's "**Little Italy**." Wander along Atwells Avenue and enjoy the aroma of crusty Italian breads, cheeses, pastas, herbs and spices. Some people come to stock up on traditional delicacies such as gorgonzola, Romano, homemade pork sausages and prosciutto, others for the restaurants, espresso shops and festive ambience. Without a doubt, Federal Hill is one of the friendliest parts of Providence.

Newport, domain of wealth: During World War II an anti-submarine net was strung across the entrance of the bay guarding Newport. It was effective. But then, the elite of the city had long been expert at protecting their privacy. In the halcyon days of the Gilded Age, New-

Brown University on College Hill.

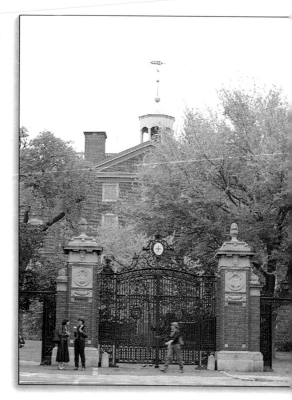

port was the domain of the very wealthy. Huge palaces built on expansive grounds were surrounded by mammoth fences and patrolled by guards and dogs. Now, however, a great many of these fiercely guarded fiefdoms are open to all comers, having become Newport's foremost tourist attractions.

Summering in Newport first became fashionable before the Revolution among Southern plantation owners intent on escaping the heat of Georgia and the Carolinas. After the Civil War, the nation's wealthiest families – Astors, Morgans, Fishers, Vanderbilts – discovered its charms. Arrivistes hoping to legitimize their newfound wealth with indisputable good taste tended to duplicate the palaces and chateaux that had so awed them on their grand tours of Europe. Edward Berwind, for instance, the son of poor German immigrants, managed to enter the ranks of this self-appointed aristocracy with **The Elms**, patterned after the Chateau d'Asnières outside Paris.

Extravagance became obligatory.

Harry Lehr hosted a formal dinner at which a monkey, complete with tuxedo and princely title, numbered among the guests. James Gordon Bennett, the man who bought a Monte Carlo restaurant when it refused him a table, rode stark naked in his carriage through Newport's streets. The Coogans invited everyone who was anyone to a grand ball to celebrate the completion of their "summer cottage." When no one showed up, the Coogans simply walked out – leaving all the food, drink and furniture – never to return.

Golden Age grandeur: Although there is so much else to see and do in Newport, a trip must include a tour of at least some of the mansions, the most impressive of which line Bellevue Avenue and Ocean Drive. Although literally hundreds of these establishments existed during Newport's Golden Age, only 70 remain now. Most are no longer occupied by private individuals; many now house schools and charitable institutions. The Newport Preservation Society pays the grand sum of $1 a year to rent **The Breakers**. Considered the most magnificent of the Newport cottages, this Italian Renaissance palace, completed in 1895, took only two years to build. Cornelius Vanderbilt II commissioned American architect Richard Morris Hunt to design the mansion, whose 70 rooms are extravagantly adorned with marble, alabaster, gilt, mosaic, crystal and stained glass. The Grand Salon was constructed in France, and later dismantled and shipped to Newport, where it was reassembled.

Marble House, another of Hunt's designs, was built for William K. Vanderbilt and styled after the Grand et Petit Trianons of Versailles. And the list goes on: the coal-rich Edward Julius Berwind commissioned The Elms; Mrs Hermann Oelrichs hired Stanford White to design **Rosecliff**, an imitation of Versailles' Grand Trianon; China-trade merchant William S. Wetmore built **Chateau-sur-Mer** in 1852, and Hunt renovated it in 1872; Mrs Astor, the grande dame of New York society, held court at **Beechwood Mansion**.

Strollers can examine the backyards

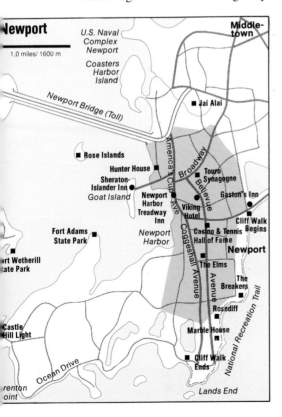

of the Bellevue Avenue mansions from the Cliff Walk, a 3½-mile (5.5-km) path that overlooks Rhode Island Sound. Crusty local fishermen saved this path for public use by going to court when wealthy mansion owners tried to close it. Visitors who do not wish to walk the length of this path can start at the end of Narragansett Avenue and reach the water by way of the **Forty Steps**; or wander down to **Brenton Point State Park** on the island's southernmost tip, an ideal place to watch gulls, picnic or just enjoy a sunset.

For a visual feast of Newport's great architectural wealth, tour **The Point** and the **Historic Hill**, the oldest colonial sections of the town. Among the historic buildings worth seeking out are the white clapboard **Trinity Church** (1725–26) on Queen Anne Square, said to be based on the designs of Christopher Wren; Hunter House, a 1748 Georgian home considered an outstanding example of colonial American architecture; **Touro Synagogue** (1763), America's first, also of Georgian style; the **Old Colony House** (1739), seat of the state's first government; and the **Redwood Library and Atheneum** (1748–50), inspired by Roman temple architecture and thought to be the oldest continuously used library building in the US.

Yachting and other pastimes: Newport is the scene of many yachting events. The prestigious America's Cup was held in Newport waters 24 times from 1851 through 1983, when the Cup was lost (for the first time) to the Australians. The 685-mile (1,102-km) Bermuda-Newport Race, held every other year, begins here, and the grueling Single-Handed Transatlantic Race, which starts in Plymouth, England, ends in Newport. To many, Newport is the yachting capital of the world. A stroll along the docks reveals a decidedly salty air. Watch boats being prepared and sails stitched in lofts along the wharves; admire the handsomely fitted craft tied up at yacht club slips.

Wandering inland, head for the **International Tennis Hall of Fame**, housed in the **Newport Casino**, America's most

Newport harbor.

exclusive country club when it was built in 1880; its grass courts hosted the first Men's US Lawn Tennis Association tournament, played in 1881. (Today they're open to the public.) Also in this complex is the **Casino Theater**, designed by Stanford White, where various performing arts events are mounted.

Peruse the offerings of the **Newport Art Museum** on Bellevue Avenue, an 1862 Richard Morris Hunt mansion in the "Stick Style," and meander past the **Old Stone Mill**, a landmark variously said to have been left behind by the Phoenicians, Vikings, Portuguese, Irish – or, more likely, a Colonial farmer. It's also worth taking a side-trip to nearby Portsmouth to visit the Green Animals Topiary Gardens, a fanciful Victorian estate where 80 sculpted trees and shrubs represent everything from an ostrich to a camel.

Newport is also surrounded by fine beaches. The choice ranges from First, Second and Third beaches in **Middleton** (north of Newport) to the more exclusive Bailey's, Hazard's and Gooseberry.

As night falls, brush off the sand and head for the waterfront. The parade of strollers on **Bowens Wharf** resembles a prep-school reunion. Most action centers on the bars, cafes and restaurants along Thames Street, where the fresh seafood comes accompanied by sea breezes. Restaurants and bars typically come and go, but Newport's better eateries – such as the White Horse Tavern, the Cooke House, and Le Bistro – have enjoyed unusual longevity. The White Horse, for instance, is a contender for the title of oldest tavern in the US.

During the summer, Newport hosts a number of major outdoor music events, such as Ben and Jerry's Newport Folk Festival and the JVC Jazz Festival, both of which take place in August at **Fort Adams State Park**. While there, take a look at the **Museum of Yachting**, which examines the pursuit through the centuries and across continents. For a bucolic detour, venture eastward, across the Sakonnet River, to wander through the "old money" summer colonies of **Tiverton Four Corners** and **Little**

Compton, where you can picnic – or opt for a tour and tasting – at lovely **Sakonnet Vineyards**.

The island off Rhode Island: When Rhode Islanders want to get away from it all, they head for **Block Island**, a 3-by-7 mile (5-by-11 km) island some 12 miles (19 km) south of Narragansett Bay. Whereas Newport is packed to the gills with hotels, shops, restaurants, and tourists, Block Island remains a hideaway holding its own, quite successfully, against developers and fast-food chains.

Block is the least accessible of the state's islands: although regular or chartered planes fly out of Westerly, R.I., and points in Connecticut (a 10-minute hop), most people take the ferry, a 70-minute trip from Galilee, R.I., or two hours from New London, Connecticut.

Greeting arrivals are fine beaches, popular fishing grounds, tranquility and the romantic allure of aging Victorian hotels with huge verandas and a sense of bygone splendor. Dutch settler Adrian Block discovered the island in 1614; the landscape has changed so little, he would in all probability still recognize it today.

The island's claim to fame in maritime annals is the large number of shipwrecks off its coast. Thousands of luckless captains saw their vessels come to misery along the coast of New England, and a great many were wrecked on the submerged rocks and sandbars around "The Block." Scavenging goods from the holds of wrecked ships became such a lucrative trade that some islanders helped engineer more wrecks by setting up lanterns and flares to confuse the ships. Many island place names commemorate the wrecking trade; at **Cow Cove**, for instance, a cargo of cows from a wrecked ship waded ashore, and on **Calico Hill**, bolts of cloth collected from another disaster were hung out to dry in the sun.

Life in the early days was hard. In the turbulent years of the late 17th century, the island was constantly under siege from pirates. During the Revolution, islanders – cut off from the mainland – nearly stripped Block Island of its trees building houses and ships.

Yachts brave the waters en route to Block Island.

228

Tourism arrived in 1842, when the first hotel was opened, and a party of ten men checked in. The Spring House opened its doors 10 years later and is still accommodating visitors to this day. To spend time in this antique of a summer hotel, with its rambling corridors and simply furnished rooms, is to be caught in a time warp. From its perch high on a hill, one can gaze out over the Atlantic Ocean and breathe the beneficent sea air just as wealthy tourists from New York and Baltimore once did.

Beaches and bluffs: The island has several fine sand beaches. The waves are lively at **Surfers Beach**, as its name suggests; **State Beach** and others on the east are calmer and attract the most visitors. The westerly strands are windswept and, more often than not, deserted. One trek not to be missed is the hike to **Mohegan Bluffs**. Here, the entire Mohegan tribe met its doom at the hands of the Manasees, who either enslaved them or drove them over the 200-ft (60-meter) cliffs.

Fishing for flounder and other species in **New Harbor** (formerly Great Salt Pond) can absorb an entire day, as can wandering along the roads and over the hills, looking for wildflowers and Indian relics. Shops in **Old Harbor**, the island's only town, sell the usual souvenirs as well as local specialties, such as candles, jellies and wool watch caps. A good way to explore is by bicycle; rentals are available at reasonable rates at several concessions.

Back on the mainland, take a short detour to **Jamestown** on Conanicut Island. The southern tip of the island offers New England scenery at its most picturesque. Among other notable sights, don't miss **Mackerel Cove**, the **Beavertail Lighthouse** and the view from Fort Wetherhill.

From Jamestown, follow US 1A along the coast. From **Narragansett**, an elegant resort town during the 19th century, proceed south to **Scarborough State Beach**, popular with Rhode Island's teenage crowd. The sheltered beach at **Galilee** is a perfect spot for passing a languid summer afternoon.

Mohegan Bluffs, Block Island.

VERMONT

Vermont is a great green slice of high ground, a measured wedge of American Pie left over, wrapped up and set aside as a souvenir of the homemade, agrarian utopia America once aspired to be.

Fatally vertical, down-west and up-stream, "the land in-between" was a rocky byroad up and away from the parade route of national destiny. Vermont had its brief, booming share of speculators, cash-croppers, side-wheelers, mother lodes and iron horses. But there was always something wildly tentative about the sweep and dash of its struggle to keep up with the American pageant, something mildly eccentric in its slapdash network of railways, turnpikes and fine rural academies.

Even before the hill towns could settle down properly, the westward exodus kicked in: the farmers' offspring were only too eager to abandon their flinty fields and frowzy home towns in search of more welcoming ground. For all its overlay of tradition, Vermont is a land of transience and experiment, a bottom land repeatedly reclaimed by nature, a country outstripped by the bigger wheels of progress, a land still imperfectly subjugated to human priorities.

The Civil War: "Put the Vermonters ahead and keep the column well closed up," said General John Sedgewick at the Battle of Gettysburg. The price of such military strategy was high, for the Civil War decimated Vermont. No other state gave as large a share of its sons to the cause of Union. The year 1865 marked the beginning of its decline in population, which until 1960 grew gradually older and smaller.

The Civil War provided Vermont with one unexpected boon. Mrs Lincoln chose to spend the summer in Manchester in 1863, putting the area on the map (President Lincoln planned to join his family there in 1865, but fate had other plans). Other visitors soon discovered the subtler pleasures of what the 19th-century British historian Lord Bryce described as "the Switzerland of North America."

"Setting and viewing," fishing and strolling among the green hillsides became *de rigueur* during America's Gilded Age; Manchester, Burlington and Woodstock were simply the great places to summer and be seen summering.

At the height of the season, the population approached its pre-war numbers. By putting up city folk, boiling and peddling "sweet water" (maple syrup) and enclosing more of their land for pasturage, some Vermont farmers found a way to lead a somewhat softer life. Some of their neighbors, like marble baron Redfield Proctor and William Dean Howell's fictive paint king, Silas Lapham, simply turned the fallow land over and made a mint out of bedrock mined by cheap foreign labor. But by the time the railways gave way to the automobile, tourism had become the state's unofficial No. 1 industry.

America's playground: "Vermont, Designed by the Creator for the Playground of the Continent," read a 1911 brochure published by Vermont's state publicity bureau, the first such in the nation. "De-

Preceding pages: the Green Mountains. Left, time to think. Right, Peacham welcomes visitors to its Fall Foliage Festival.

velopment" became the 20th-century battle cry, and roadside attractions outflanked each other from Brattleboro to Morses Line. Natives and visitors alike started grumbling in the 1930s, when rolling pastures and grassy meadows quietly gave way here and there to a lakeside resort, a new rambling "summer cottage," another country club or (finally) the slim interstate highway. Stories began to circulate, about the farmer and his 12-gauge shotgun versus a brigade of the Conservation Corps and their back-hoe. But the lawmakers in Montpelier didn't notice until, nearly overnight in the early 1950s, the ski industry blew land taxes through the rooftop. Suddenly the land of milk and honey was overflowing with New Yorkers from solstice to solstice. The real boom had finally begun.

In 1965, Vermont lost its distinction as the state with more cows than people. Today, few natives make a decent living off the land. But the new gentry – the second-homers with condos or splendid country estates, complete with Morgan

horse and 30 head of sheep – are determined to reconstitute and preserve their township's special flavor, its fallow charm, its pastoral innocence, from late-comers. They have formed a shaky coalition with their neighbors – the disgruntled patricians, pillars of their community; refugees from the 1960s, back-to-land artisans of the post-industrial era; the seventh-generation Vermonters, whose trailer homes, pick-up trucks and snowmobiles are emblems of hardscrabble endurance. This is the backwoods elite – the holy alliance keeping the lobbyists and the developers at bay.

One of the toughest anti-pollution stances in the nation, a dizzying array of zoning ordinances, new wilderness designations, a "no off-premise billboards" mandate and even a touch of urban renewal have kept Vermont a superior place to live. Ironically, these factors, together with the protective attitude of its residents, have also made it one of the best places to visit.

The Connecticut River Valley: The long, lazy Connecticut River forms the entire boundary between the states of Vermont and New Hampshire. Covered over by a hydroelectric dam at the southernmost end, Vermont's first permanent settlement – Fort Dummer, founded in 1752 – has been reduced to a mere marker on the shore. A few miles north, however, **Brattleboro**, the town it was meant to protect, is still thriving after two centuries of colorful history. Rising from the Connecticut River Valley in a chain of ledges facing Wantastiquet Mountain, the town enjoyed resort status from 1846 to 1871, when a local physician parlayed its pure springs into a "water cure." During the same period, Jacob Estey, with a workforce of 500, produced reed organs, the parlor fixture every respectable 19th-century homemaker dreamed of owning.

"Winter has chased all these really interesting people south," lamented Rudyard Kipling from his Dummerston homestead on the Brattleboro town line, during an era when gypsies and itinerant artisans dared to cross just this far into peddler country. In the 1960s and '70s, a new wave of adventurous folk **Brattleboro.**

washed upstream and settled right in. The back-to-the-land crowd, not just wandering hippies but dedicated communards, sunk their roots deep into the community, and though it's now their children who sport tie-dyes and flowing hair about town (the baby-boom generation seems to have melded into the general populace), the hippies managed to set up an economic infrastructure with surprising staying power. They – and a general populace whose tastes have come around – support natural foods markets, alternative shops, and a worker-owned restaurant, the **Common Ground**, which after several decades of broad-based success – even the business crowd lunches here – seems less a restaurant than a cultural touchstone.

Naulahka, the ship-shaped manse where Kipling wrote the first two *Jungle Books* and *Captain Courageous* in the 1890s, has been recently restored by Great Britain's Landmark Trust and, although not open to the general public, is offered for rent by the week. Kipling, an Englishman born in India, came here on his honeymoon in 1892 (his bride's parents had settled in Brattleboro after taking the cure) and he immediately warmed to the life of a country sqire; he even enjoyed playing golf in the snow, with balls painted red. His grand airs, however, didn't endear him to the locals, and in 1896 when a property dispute with his roguish brother-in-law hit the headlines, destroying his rural idyll, he and his wife fled, never to return.

Towns with personality: US 9 to the west of Brattleboro leads to **Marlboro** – hilltop home of experimental Marlboro College, which every summer hosts the world-renowned Marlboro Music Festival – and the ski resort towns of **Wilmington** and **West Dover**. The latter two towns are somewhat overdeveloped in places (in the 1950s, the burgeoning Mount Snow ski resort, then the largest, turned these hamlets into veritable boom towns); still, they harbor a number of fine inns and restaurants.

Just far enough south to have escaped development – to date – are the rural villages of **Jacksonville** (where the

Fly fishing for trout on the Battenkill River.

North River Winery has begun to attract discerning tourists), and **Whitingham**, home to several lakes popular for fishing and swimming, and the 1801 birthplace of Mormon leader Brigham Young. A small marker on Stimpson Hill hails him as "A Man of Much Courage And Splendid Equipment."

State 30 northwest out of Brattleboro follows the **West River**, past a picturesque covered bridge, to the postcard-perfect town of **Newfane**. Its broad common is lined with shady elms and surrounded by stately Greek Revival public buildings – a white-columned courthouse with Congregational church to match, flanked by a grange, two outstanding inns famous for their culinary offerings (the **Four Columns** and **Old Newfane Inn**), and some worthwhile antique stores. A flea market held summer weekends in a field north of town since the late 1960s has become something of an institution, and a draw for locals and visitors alike.

Further up Route 30 are the equally appealing, low-key villages of **Town-shend** and **Jamaica**, with plenty of unspoiled parkland – including the beach at the West River reservoir behind the Townshend Dam – to explore en route.

A small town directly north of Brattleboro on US 5, **Putney** predated the social experiments of the 1960s by a good 150 years: in the early 18th century, it was the site of a short-lived but sensational commune espousing free love. The countryside is still populated in part by '60s protesters, some clustered in communes of several decades' duration. Many artists and craftspeople ply their trades in Putney; look for handcrafted signs announcing sculpture and woodworking studios, potteries, and the **Green Mountain Spinnery**, where visitors can watch fleece from local sheep being scoured and carded, and take home some naturally dyed skeins.

Once a bustling crossroads – the first bridge to span the Connecticut was constructed here, as well as America's first canal (built in 1792) – **Bellows Falls** is a fairly typical Vermont mill town. The Falls were long the favorite fishing

Purity and light: the Common in Newfane.

ground of the Abenakis, and mysterious petroglyphs, of unknown dates and significance, decorate boulders beside the waters where, swore one early settler, "shad and salmon swarmed so thick a person could walk across the Connecticut on their backs." A pleasant way to view the countryside along the riverbank, especially during foliage season, is via the diesel-powered vintage cars of the Green Mountain Flyer.

Scenic backroads dotted with antique shops connect Bellows Falls with Grafton and Chester to the northwest. Purchased in its entirety and renovated by the Windham Foundation, **Grafton** is a preserved-in-amber Greek Revival town eerily close to its appearance in the early 1800s: visitors wander about in blissful disbelief, sampling a slice of cheddar at the Granton Cheese Company, and perhaps claiming a rocker on the porch of the 1801 Old Tavern, whose guests have included notables from Thoreau and Kipling to Ulysses S. Grant and Teddy Roosevelt. **Chester** is a curious little strand of Victoriana on the Williams River. One especially ornate building houses the **National Survey Charthouse**, which publishes maps and operates a retail store. An 1850s stone village-within-a-village features 30 homes faced in gneiss ledgestone.

Precision Valley: A center of invention during the 19th century and today home of a thriving machine tool industry, the towns of **Springfield** and **Windsor** form Precision Valley, a living testament to Yankee ingenuity. The **American Precision Museum** on Windsor's Main Street is chock-full of all the gadgets, whatsits and thingamabobs that not only made the region famous, but helped the North win the Civil War. Windsor is also famed as the birthplace of Vermont, because it is here that delegates met in 1777 to establish the Free and Independent Republic of Vermont, draw up a constitution and create a Council of Safety to protect the new country as much from the other 12 states as from the Crown. The **Windsor-Cornish Covered Bridge**, spanning the Connecticut River to lovely Cornish, New Hamp-

shire, is the longest covered bridge in the United States.

"I live in New Hampshire so I can get a better view of Vermont," explained artist Maxfield Parrish from his home in Cornish. He did sneak a considerable piece of that view into most of his paintings, notably **Mount Ascutney**, which looms south of Windsor. The largest monadnock in New England, Ascutney is home to a ski resort and conference center which mounts cultural events in the summer months.

Vermont's largest ski area is **Killington** in Sherburne Center, which quickly eclipsed Mount Snow, expanding to cover six peaks. With a 4,241-ft (1,296-meter) gondola available for sightseers as well as skiers, the resort is active year-round – the skiing often lasts into June, and then mountain bikes take over. Although the access road is hideously cluttered, there are lots of worthwhile eateries about, including Hemingway's, considered to be one of the top restaurants in the country. It's said that a 1763 picnicking party to Killington Peak gave

the state its name: instead of quaffing the champagne they brought for refreshment, Rev. Samuel Peters broke it on a rock and christened the region "Verd Mont" ("Green Mountain" in French).

Nearby **Plymouth** spawned the US's most taciturn president. The **Coolidge Birthplace and Homestead** serves as a hilltop shrine to silent Cal – that self-styled "Puritan in Babylon," and the only President born on the Fourth of July. When President Harding died on August 3, 1923, and Vice-President Coolidge needed to be sworn in, the news had to be conveyed to the Coolidges by hand; true to form, the family did not have a phone.

Wonders of Woodstock: Woodstock's older money can, from time to time, be heard to lament inroads made by what one observer has called the "suburban gold-coast mink-and-manure set." Upscale shopping sprees along the refurbished downtown blocks of Cabot and French streets may have replaced placid strolls up Mount Tom as the fashionable summer pastime, but in general the en-

Early season powder at Killington.

lightened despotism of Laurence Rockefeller has preserved the tone of the town much as it must have been in the 1930s, when he met his future wife, Mary French, while summering here.

A passion for maintaining a graceful balance between society and nature has long been the keynote to Woodstock's renown. Mary's grandfather, Frederick Billings, returned from his lucrative law practice in San Francisco in the 1890s to become a pioneer in reforestation and a zealous model farmer. The slopes of **Mount Tom** and **Mount Peg** and the restored **Billings Farm Museum** are testaments to his love for rural Vermont. Growing up on the elder Billings' farm in the 1830s, George Perkins Marsh – later to become a noted linguist and diplomat – drafted a landmark treatise, *Man and Nature*, which, over a century after its publication, remains the ecologist's New Testament.

For further glimpses of Woodstock's past, visit the **Woodstock Historical Society** headquarters, nine rooms of period furnishings in an 1807 house.

The Rockefellers' **Woodstock Inn & Resort** on the green remains the place to stay – and the Robert Trent Jones golf course and Suicide Six ski area offer year-round amusements. On the other side of the green, a covered bridge leads to **Mountain Avenue**, a redoubt of old summer cottages, and a park at the base of Mount Tom. Trails to the summit overlook a guided floral walk through the Rockefeller estate, and the Vermont Institute of Natural Science maintains the fascinating Vermont **Raptor Center**, a habitat for 26 species of owls, hawks, and eagles unable to survive in the wild.

The hills surrounding Woodstock are horse country. Since 1926, the Green Mountain Horse Association in South Woodstock has been a mecca for well-heeled equestrians, and nearby stables offer unusually expert training.

At the fairgrounds in **Quechee** to the east, polo matches are played on Saturday afternoons during the height of the summer season. In town, Irish artisan Simon Pearce has transformed The Mill at Quechee, an abandoned flannel factory, into a most inviting complex featuring his distinctive glasswork (glassblowers can be observed at work on weekdays) and a delightful restaurant overlooking the mill pond.

To the east, **Quechee Gorge** is billed by local boosters as "Vermont's Little Grand Canyon."

Visionaries, religious and commercial: A major crossroads since the days when railroads ruled interstate traffic, **White River Junction** still serves as an Amtrak stop and marks the intersection of Interstates 91 and 89. One reason to stop by is the Catamount Brewing Co., which offers tours and tastings.

"A man can easily hear strange voices," said Kipling of the lonely Vermont winter, "the Word of God rolling between the dead hills; may see visions and dream dreams…" Joseph Smith, founder of the Church of Jesus Christ of Latter-day Saints, was born in 1805 atop **Dairy Mill Hill**, about a mile outside of **South Royalton**, where Mormon followers maintain a 38½-ft (11.5-meter) obelisk and a museum.

Over the river and up State 110 hide

Mrs Santa Claus at Woodstock's Wassail Parade.

the towns of **Tunbridge** – cozy site of the world's smallest World's Fair since 1761, a country treat in mid-September – and **Chelsea**, a rural trading post where time has stood still for a century.

Heading westward, seek out the village of **Brookfield**, the geographical center of the state and perhaps the most unspoiled four corners in New England. In 1812, a 320-ft (98-meter) **Floating Bridge**, supported by 380 tarred barrels, was built across the pond at the center of town, and it survives to this day – as part of State 65 – accommodating one car at a time; it's also popular for fishing. One of the last ice harvests in the East is now the occasion for an annual festival on the lake, held the last Saturday in January.

Between Brookfield and Barre is the town of **Graniteville**, site of the **Rock of Ages Quarry**, one of the largest granite quarries in the world. Mining began in the early 19th century, soon after the War of 1812, and boomed with the influx of skilled immigrant stoneworkers between 1880 and 1910. Fed up with poor wages and working conditions (many died of silicosis), the granite workers managed to elect a Socialist mayor – many decades before liberal Burlington was ready to do the same. Today, the Rock of Ages firm owns nearly all of the quarries on and around Graniteville's Millstone Hill, which provide the nation with one-third of its memorial stones. The operation has long been a tourist-oriented showcase, with free access to the polishing and sculpting factory, and optional tram tours skirting the fully operational quarry a mile up the hill. Free granite specimens off the scrapheap make weighty souvenirs.

For a more evocative tour, though, visit **Barre's Hope Cemetery**, where the workers commemorated their own, with often touching artwork.

The smallest capital: Home to about 8,200 people, **Montpelier** is the smallest state capital in the nation. And – with the green ridge of **Hibbard Park** rising behind its gold-leaf dome – the **Vermont State House** has to be the most charming of the 50.

Brookfield's extraordinar[y] floating bridge.

Originally, Vermont's capital rotated through the state, but with the completion of the original nine-sided building in 1808, the seat of power settled here. When an imposing stone successor, built in 1838, was gutted by fire in 1857, the Doric portico and native granite walls withstood the flames to form a shell for the present structure. The Senate Chamber is rightfully considered the most beautiful room in the state.

The "Steamboat Gothic" **Pavilion Hotel** – "the Grand Old Lady of State Street," where so many lawmakers bedded down for the January–April session (following an agrarian calendar, legislators go about their ordinary lives the rest of the year) – was demolished in 1966. However, a skillful replica now occupies its place beside the State House Lawn and houses a collection of Vermont icons which once decorated the capitol building. This, the **Vermont Historical Society Museum**, is a must-see mishmash of Green Mountain artifacts, including the last cougar shot in Vermont and Ethan Allen's blunderbuss.

If you spot an unlikely number of chefs' hats about town, it's because Montpelier is also home to the **New England Culinary Institute**, a highly regarded training school that maintains two excellent public restaurants – the casual Elm Street Cafe and formal Tubbs – as well as an irresistible bakery.

Mountain country: Some 20 miles west of Montpelier, the Green Mountain range attains heady heights irresistible to skiers – mountain climbers and bikers, too. South of I-89, the towns of **Waitsfield** and **Warren** support two ski areas, the rustic, but challenging **Mad River Glen**, and more developed and extensive **Sugarbush**. Both towns are full of the pleasures – inviting restaurants and cozy inns – that outdoors enthusiasts enjoy in their off-hours. Waitsfield boasts an unusual cinema, the Art Deco **Edison's Studio Movie Palace**, which offers cafe-style service and seating in overstuffed love seats. Spectators are also welcome at two summertime sporting venues, the **Sugarbush Polo Club** (the original players, in 1962, used ski poles and a

eft, State apitol, Montpelier. ight, Robert urns stands uard in arre.

volleyball) and the **Mad River Valley Cricket Club**. To get an unusual perspective on the countryside, consider a vintage airplane ride or soaring excursion out of the Warren-Sugarbush Airport, or try horse-trekking at the **Vermont Icelandic Horse Farm**.

In Waterbury, midway between these peaks and Mount Mansfield to the north, a number of gourmet entrepreneurs have set up shop. **Vermont Distillers**, "the smallest (legal) distillery in the US," produces vodka, gin, and spicy Tamarack liqueur. And a pair of "flatlander" entrepreneurs have found a great use for Vermont's abundant ice and milk: the **Ben & Jerry's Homemade Ice Cream Factory** on Route 100 in Waterbury is now the second-largest tourist attraction in Vermont, offering tours (with tastings) daily. Just up the road, you can watch cider being pressed in season, and sample some, at the **Cold Hollow Cider Mill**, and stop for a nibble at the **Green Mountain Chocolate Co.**, a confiserie run by former White House pastry chef Albert Kumin.

Even before the advent of skiing in the 1930s, when the Civilian Conservation Corps cut the first of Mount Mansfield's precipitous trails, ensuring Stowe's ascendancy as "the Ski Capital of the East," Stowe enjoyed a reputation as a stylish summer place. Three grand hotels were built in the mid-1800s, of which only the 1833 **Green Mountain Inn**, at the center of town, survives. Ralph Waldo Emerson had a bracing vacation at the Summit House, where, he recounts, his "whole party climbed to the top of the [mountain's] nose and watched the sun rise over the top of the White Mountains of New Hampshire." Hikers still favor this craggy human profile, and two shortcuts are popular: for a fee, the 4½-mile (7.5-km) **Auto Road**, a century-old toll road rising from the Inn at the Mountain, offers an easy way to ascend to the "nose," and an 8-passenger gondola, the world's speediest, makes fast work of the 4,393-ft (1,338-meter) "chin," the state's highest point. A good restaurant, the Cliff House, awaits in a cleft below the chin.

The Black River Valley near Craftsbury, Orleans County.

On adjoining **Spruce Peak**, the **Stowe Mountain Resort** also operates an alpine slide and the world's first alpine in-line skate park, opened in 1993.

Summer or winter, sports opportunities abound, particularly along the **Stowe Recreation Path**, created in the 1980s through community donations and effort. Ideally suited for skiers, cyclists, skaters, wheelchair racers, runners, walkers and stroller-pushers, the 5.3-mile (8.5-km) paved path skirts the West Branch river from town all the way out to the Topnotch resort, passing a number of appealing inns, restaurants, and shops en route. Other notable Stowe inns, such as the Trapp Family Lodge (founded by the Baroness Maria Von Trapp of Sound of Music fame) are tucked away in the wooded hills; in summer, the meadows of the Trapp Family Lodge are alive with the sound of concerts and equestrian shows.

Another big summertime draw is the mid-August classic car rally, and in mid-January, during the Stowe Winter Carnival, the whole town parties. As the Federal Writers' Project put it decades ago, "Stowe is a 'smart' place to be seen and many snowtime visitors are not skiers."

Wintertime visitors hoping to fit in a visit to the nearby ski area of **Smuggler's Notch** (so named for its role during the War of 1812) are in for a rude surprise: the connecting road is closed in winter, and those who've traveled it in summer will understand why. Hundred-foot cliffs and giant boulders crowd the narrow, winding roadway – a popular staging point for mountaintop hikes.

On the other side, the Smuggler's Notch ski resort, encompassing three peaks (one offers ski access back to Stowe), is popular with families for its well-thought-out children's programs. In summer the attraction is an assortment of water slides – so far, the only such amusements in the state. The town closest to the resort, **Jeffersonville**, has a number of shops and restaurants that will appeal to the sophisticated.

About 8 miles (13 km) east, the sleepy town of **Johnson** has been all but taken

'all gathering ɪt Peacham.

over by the **Vermont Studio Center**, a working retreat for artists and writers that attracts many prominent instructors. From mid-July through the foliage season, the **Lamoille Valley Railroad** offers sightseeing excursions from Morrisville to Johnson and Hardwick, aboard four 1917 coaches.

The Northeast Kingdom: Head southeast on State 15 to enter a remote and remarkable region. The Kingdom – that is, the Northeast Kingdom – is a nearly 2,000-sq.-mile (over 5,000-sq.-km) swath of crystal lakes and climax forests, a region known for greater natural wealth and homegrown poverty than any other area in the state. The counties of Caledonia, Essex and Orleans are sparsely populated and virtually without industry, except for a scattering of lake resort towns, paper company holdings in the far east corner, and various businesses in St Johnsbury, the Kingdom's unofficial capital. *Where the Rivers Run North* is the title Orleans writer Howard Frank Mosher gave his collection of short stories (it spawned an ac-

claimed locally produced movie in 1994) in honor of a region known for its backwater quirks.

Craftsbury Common and **Greensboro** are among the more moneyed summer communities hidden in theses hills. The former has become a magnet for serious athletes – the Craftsbury Center Sports Resort offers dorm-style accommodations and year-round instruction in sports – and the latter remains a peaceful retreat favored by writers and other intelligentsia (the local general store stocks the *New York Times*).

Increasingly beset by competition from development and government regulation, Vermont's dairy industry has fallen on hard times of late. Not so the 500-odd farms involved with the Cabot Creamery Co-operative in **Cabot**; founded in 1919, the co-op thrives to this day, and offers factory tours, starting with a video recounting the history of farming in the region and ending with tastings of its outstanding Vermont cheddar. Nearby **Danville** hosts another organization of unlikely survivors: the

Lake Willoughby.

American Society of Dowsers counts among its members hundreds of firm believers in the powers of the divining rod. Their headquarters, housed in a red clapboard hall, doubles as a store, and their annual fall gathering attracts curious observers.

The city of **St Johnsbury** itself remains a vibrant pocket of Victorian charm. From the bank buildings downtown to the Fairbanks mansion on the Plains overlooking the valley, the stamp of architect Lambert Packard and his wealthy patrons is visible everywhere. Thaddeus Fairbanks started making the world's first platform scale here in the 1830s, and he and his sons reinvested the fruits of their precision instrument into the quality of civic life. The St Johnsbury Atheneum/Art Gallery, built in 1871–73, is a tastefully combined library, music chamber and exhibition space dominated by the huge skylit panorama *Domes of the Yosemite* by Hudson River School artist Albert Bierstadt. This is one of the oldest intact art collections in the country ("Welcome to the nineteenth century," reads a sign at the entrance) and one of the most inviting. With a collection of more than 3,000 stuffed fauna and its own vintage planetarium, the Romanesque Fairbanks Museum and Planetarium is a little bastion of natural history erected by the Fairbanks family in 1890.

About 10 miles (6 km) north of St Johnsbury, the still relatively undiscovered ski area of **Burke** deserves its promotional billing as "Vermont's Northern Star." With a challenging array of trails, and affordable lift tickets, it's one of the best deals in the Northeast. It also serves as an outdoor campus for Burke Academy, which has consistently turned out Olympians.

Every summer, hordes of joyous pilgrims descend on the small town of **Glover** to partake in the Bread and Puppet Theater's "Domestic Resurrection Circus," a pageant and festival put on by the radical theatre group founded by Peter Schumann in 1963 to illustrate the horrors of war and wonders of life. The date is not publicized, so as to

Left. old postcard view of the Atheneum in St Johnsbury. **Right**, farmer at Norwich.

Vermont, Athanaeum, St. Johnsbury.

minimize crowds (they come by the hundreds anyway), but details can be obtained by calling or visiting the Bread and Puppet Museum, an amazing barnful of fantastical creatures.

Brownington's **Old Stone House Museum** was assembled between 1827 and 1830 by "Uncle" Alexander Twilight, claimed by Middlebury College as the first black college graduate, Class of 1823. This Old Athenian rural academy houses the Orleans County Historical Society, and each of its 11 rooms is devoted to a particular township.

Once a fashionable watering hole on the Canadian frontier, the vast **Lake Memphremagog** lost most of its following in the 1920s with the retirement of the *Mountain Maid* and *Lady of the Lake* steam liners, but none of its international charm. **Newport**, "the Border City," is a fair-sized town noted for its easy mingle of Canadian day-trippers, contented locals and southerly summers strung along Cape Elizabeth Bluffs at the lake's eastern shore. Smelt, smallmouth bass and wall-eyed pike are all common catches over the Derby Line.

To the west, State 242 climbs from Jay to the ski area of **Jay Peak**, where a 60-passenger aerial tramway runs year-round, transporting skiers and sightseers to its 3,861-ft (1,177-meter) summit. The views into Canada are great.

The northwestern corner: The northwest corner of Vermont's border with Canada, between Alburg and Morses Line, was a favorite route for smugglers in the steamboat era. But the notorious smuggling center of **Highgate** was known primarily for its springs (which supposedly had curative powers) up until Prohibition, when bootleggers began running their nag brigades and motorcades right into Franklin County.

Over the years since 1609, when Samuel de Champlain discovered the body of water that now bears his name (and spotted a Loch Ness-like monster which has as yet eluded capture), the islands at its northern end have been compared to every place from the Isle of Man to the Louisiana bayou. Just fertile enough to support a few orchards and

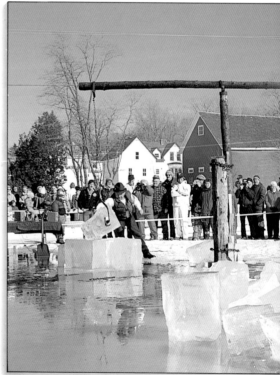

some grazing Jerseys, and just far enough out of the way to have withstood development, the Four Brothers Islands – **Alburg**, **Isle La Motte**, the **Two Heroes** and **Grand Isle** – stretch for 30 beautiful miles (48 km) south to the widest reach of **Lake Champlain**. "Vermont's Cape Cod" is strewn with arcadian preserves, lakeshore drives and sleepy little towns. From a visitor's perspective, Isle La Motte is perhaps the most satisfying of the islands, with its exquisite marble deposits, "the oldest coral reef in the world" (a leftover from 10,000 years ago, when the Atlantic Ocean covered the Champlain Valley, it's littered with sunken steamboats and bobbing scuba buoys), and the **St Anne's Shrine**, honoring America's first French settlement (1664).

Franklin County was the center of Vermont's rise to eminence as a dairy state. Although the principal town, **St Albans**, lacks the vivacity it enjoyed as a major railyard on the way to Montreal, it does host a Vermont Maple Festival in mid-April which officially denotes the long-awaited end of winter. And it was also once the scene of the Civil War's most northerly skirmish: in 1864 a band of Confederates seized the town, robbed the banks and hightailed it to Canada. There they were caught and brought to trial; however, their exploits were excused as "legitimate" acts of war.

Ever Greater Burlington: "The most miserable of one-horse towns," complained the young wife of an Army recruiting officer stationed here in the 1840s. "Startling incidents never occur in Burlington. None ever occurred there, and none probably ever will." Things have livened up considerably along "New England's West Coast" since then. By the Civil War, fiercely competitive steamboat lines and a busy lumber trade were beginning to make **Burlington** a plucky little inland port of entry. By the turn of the century, the wharves were teeming with businessmen, seekers of pleasure and ships' crews.

Today, a cadre of trendy restaurants and the lively **Church Street Marketplace**, a pedestrian mall lined with

Gliding near Burlington.

sidewalk cafes and gentrified shops, have further improved Burlington's outlook. But the view remains the same. From Battery Park or the Cliffs, the sunset over Lake Champlain and the Adirondacks is still – as novelist William Dean Howells maintained – "superior to the evening view over the Bay of Naples," and "parties of pleasures" are again threatening to outnumber the workaday commuters who board the evening ferry to Port Kent, New York. In fact, the dock itself has become a tourist attraction, with a lively bar and sailboards to rent, sailboats to charter.

A growing influx of industry – notably, IBM – and the new metropolitan tone mingle to make the core of Vermont's "Queen City" (population 40,000) a commercial and cultural nexus that keeps turning up on polls as being one of the US's "most livable cities." Thanks in part to the presence of the **University of Vermont** (called "UVM" for its Latin name, *Universitas Viridis Montis*), the city enjoys a year-round array of cultural events, including annual Mozart and Shakespeare festivals. The Flynn Theater for the Performing Arts, a 1930 Art Deco movie palace, hosts an impressive line-up of dance, music and theatre.

There's a lot worth doing within Burlington's widening metropolis. When the city's famous woolen industry moved south, the nearby city of **Winooski** (straddling its namesake river) went completely bottom up. But in 1978, the huge mill was revamped and refitted with an alluring bay of shops as the Champlain Mill Mall. Nearby, St Michael's Playhouse, on the campus of **Saint Michael's College**, has been mounting professional summer theatre performances since 1951. Circling back into Burlington from the north, stop in at the **Ethan Allen Homestead Trust**, a restored 1787 farmhouse, for exhibits that not only recount the exploits of this beloved native son but shed light on 5,000 years of local history.

About 7 miles (11 km) south of the city is the **Shelburne Museum**, which has to be seen to be believed. Neither a "living museum" nor a fusty historical collection, it's a 45-acre complex reflecting the tastes of one very passionate and well-funded collector. Electra Havemeyer Webb developed an eye for Americana and folk art long before anyone else was paying attention, and managed to amass some 80,000 exemplary objects – 37 buildings full in all, with some train cars, a carousel and a Lake Champlain side-wheeler, the *Ticonderoga*, thrown in for good measure. It takes more than a casual stroll to do the collection justice; hence admission, though pricy, is good for two days.

Shelburne's other landmark is the Webbs' 100-room Queen Anne–style "cottage" on the lake. Carved from 22 lakeside farms by Frederick Law Olmsted, designer of New York City's Central Park, this 1,000-acre estate is now a model ecological farmstead, **Shelburne Farms**, where tours are offered in summer. The **Shelburne House** itself has been restored and is open to the public as a luxury restaurant.

Charlotte, a few miles south of Shelburne, is home to the unusual Vermont

Pumpkins at Cambridge General Store.

248

Wildflower Farm, a 6-acre preserve and learning center that offers delightful strolling.

Galloping into the hills: Vermont spawned the world-famous Morgan horse, a barrel-chested steed which, as one celebrant boasted, "can outrun, outpull, and outlast any other breed, just as you would expect a Vermont horse to do." The UVM **Morgan Horse Farm**, in the village of **Weybridge**, is a working farm with training demonstrations and guided tours, May through October.

Middlebury, a few miles southeast, is the ideal university town, a verdant campus of grand, well-spaced 19th-century buildings, accompanied by a lively community of shops and restaurants. The Vermont State Craft Center at **Frog Hollow** showcases the traditional and contemporary work of more than 300 of the state's most talented artisans.

Poet Robert Frost spent his summers writing in a log cabin in **Ripton**, not far from **Bread Loaf**, home of the prestigious Bread Loaf Writers' Conference. The mile-long **Robert Frost Interpretive Trail**, beginning at his home, the Homer Noble Farm, leads to the Breadloaf campus by way of the cabin, which has been left untouched. For some magnificent scenery, continue on State 125, through steep **Lincoln Gap**, and drive southward through the unspoiled towns lining this stretch of State 100, which bisects the state vertically, and not always so prettily.

The lakes region: The region west of Vermont's second-biggest city, **Rutland**, was a popular summer spot in the Victorian era, but faded after World War II, when the trains stopped coming. Rediscovered in recent decades by starry-eyed innkeepers and their guests, pretty towns like **Middletown Springs** (a one-time spa) and **Fair Haven** are making a comeback, offering little more than old-fashioned B&B hospitality and plenty of unspoiled countryside to roam.

Hubbardston is where Vermont's only Revolutionary War battle was fought, and in Castleton, Vermont's first college was founded in 1787. Though they're minuscule in comparison to Lake

Spring colors near Rutland.

Champlain, **Lake Catherine** and **Lake Bomoseen** are flanked by state parks and offer sandy beaches.

Rutland itself is rather drab, but it does harbor a hidden gem: **Wilson's Castle**, an improbably opulent mid-1800s mansion with 32 rooms, 12 fireplaces and such elegant appointments as a Louis XVI crown jewel case, with manicured walkways covering 115 acres (46 hectares). The nearby town of **Proctor** is the home of the **Vermont Marble Exhibit**, offering a glimpse of the Vermont Marble Company factory, a sculptor at work, and marble samples from around the world, including the local product – some of which can be seen lining the sidewalks of the more prosperous towns in the region. The abandoned quarries make tempting swimming holes, too, if you can wrest the location from a local source.

So bucolic is this region today that visitors may have a hard time empathizing with 19th-century journalist Horace Greeley, who grew up on a West Haven farm, left to apprentice in a Poultney printing shop, and escaped to found the *New York Tribune*. "The moral I would deduce from my experience," he wrote, "is simply this. Our farmers' sons escape their fathers' calling whenever they can, because it is mad, a mindless, monotonous drudgery, instead of an ennobling, liberalizing, intellectual pursuit."

A pre-eminent summer place: It was during this era that the tide began to turn. For all the former farmhands drawn to the metropolis, city-dwellers began to catch on to the attractions of open spaces and fresh air. Franklin Orvis gave the local tourist industry a boost in 1849 when he began taking in summer guests at his father's house, located next to the famed 1769 **Marsh Tavern** in **Manchester**, where Ethan Allen and his "Green Mountain Boys" had plotted the Tories' overthrow. The hotel kept expanding bit by bit until it became the grand Equinox (named for the mountain which presides over the town).

Meanwhile, Frank's younger brother, Charles, had a clever idea, too – why not teach the leisured class to catch their

Chicken farmer.

supper along the banks of the abundant Battenkill River? Less than 10 years after he sold his first bamboo flyrod, Manchester had become the place to get away from it all.

By the mid-20th century, the Equinox had deteriorated into white elephant-hood, but in the early 1980s it was restored to showplace luster, along with its 18-hole golf course. And the Orvis Company has prospered all the while: today it operates a thriving mail-order business, and the store – with its history-of-the-art museum next door – draws visitors from around the world, as do the company's three-day fly-fishing courses. Orvis's success inspired other upscale companies (Ralph Lauren, Esprit, *et al*) to open their own outlets here, so the shopping opportunities are unsurpassed in the state.

All this brisk commerce notwithstanding, Manchester Village remains as tranquil and elegant as ever, with its marble-slab sidewalks and showy summer homes, many of them creatively converted into inns and restaurants.

And although Lincoln never made it to the Equinox (several other presidents did), Mary Lincoln and son Robert cherished fond memories of the mountains; they later returned to build an estate, **Hildene**, which now opens its richly appointed rooms to antiquity-lovers and its 412-acre (167-hectare) grounds to cross-country skiers and summer strollers. Another pleasant place to visit in town is the **Southern Vermont Art Center**, with contemporary indoor exhibits, outdoor sculptures, and a well-marked botany trail.

Rockwell country: The Williams Department Store in the picturesque, marble-paved village of **Dorset**, about 6 miles (10 km) north of Manchester, is perhaps Vermont's most authentic country store, stocking everything from talc to timber. The town is also home to the **Dorset Playhouse**, a rustic barn that served as Vermont's first summer playhouse, and to a writers' colony.

South of Manchester on US 7A, **Arlington** is a former Revolutionary capital and one-time home to five *Sat-*

Classic Vermont scene, near Peacham.

urday Evening Post artists. The Norman Rockwell Exhibition displays a large number of *Post* covers and lesser-known prints, in which local uncles and grandmas figure largely; some former subjects actually serve as museum guides. Local author Dorothy Canfield Fisher needs no introduction to Vermonters: in a series of down-home novels and her glorious *Vermont Tradition: The Biography of an Outlook on Life*, Fisher celebrated the spirit of fairness and community that imbues the state. The **Martha Canfield Library**, named after Dorothy's grandmother, holds a rich store of the author's memorabilia.

From battleground to Bohemia: The 1777 skirmish commemorated by the **Bennington Battle Monument**, a 306-ft (93-meter) blue limestone obelisk erected in 1887–91, actually took place a few miles west, where General John Stark and 1,800 ragtag troops forced the Redcoats back across the Walloomsac River in Hoosick Falls. However, it was a colonial supply dump on this site that General John Burgoyne was after, and his failure to attain it proved a turning point in the entire British campaign.

For an interesting trove of local artifacts, from Revolutionary War mementos to vintage toys, visit the **Bennington Museum & Grandma Moses Gallery**. The self-taught painter's endearing primitives of rural life are exhibited in the schoolhouse she attended as a child in Eagle Bridge, New York.

Old Bennington sprawls east toward Bennington proper, home of **Bennington College**, among the country's most progressive – and expensive – schools. The older part of town, free of commerce but for the occasional inn, is like an immaculate open-air museum along Monument Avenue. Wander about the green and visit the Old First Church, with its unusual three-tiered steeple. Beside it, in the Old Burying Ground, lie the founders of Bennington, five Vermont governors, and Robert Frost, whose epitaph epitomizes the feisty loyalty endemic to true Vermonters, whether native-born or transplanted: "I had a lover's quarrel with the world."

Left, mountain biking, Putney. Right, Bennington College.

SKI FEVER

Skiing is believed to have got its start 4,000 years ago in Scandinavia, and it was Scandinavian immigrants who introduced the sport in New Hampshire's logging camps in the 1870s. The Norwegian-speaking Nansen Ski Club was founded in Norway Village near Berlin about 1872; it got together with six other clubs to found the US Eastern Amateur Ski Association in 1922, and survives to this day.

Ski fever spread to the college circuit after Fred Harris founded Dartmouth's Outing Club in 1909; Dartmouth college librarian Nathaniel Goodrich accomplished the first recorded descent of Mount Mansfield in Stowe (Vermont's highest peak) in 1914. This was all without trails, of course, much less the "up-ski" devices – rope tows, J-bars, and ultimately aerial trams, gondolas, and high-speed quads – that came decades later. The sport was essentially confined to "touring" (comparable to today's cross-country), jumping off wooden chutes (in the 1920s, the southern Vermont town of Brattleboro hosted the first US National Ski Jumping Championships) and the odd foray into the woods. In 1926 Appalachian Mountain Club hutmaster Joe Dodge was the first to hurtle down Mount Washington's Tuckerman Ravine, and Austrian instructor Toni Matt first schussed its headwall in the infamous Inferno Race of 1939.

By then, skiing was well on its way to popularity. In 1929, fresh from a Switzerland ski trip, 23-year-old Katharine Peckett had opened the country's first organized ski school at her family's resort in Sugar Hill, New Hampshire. In January 1931, the Boston and Maine Railroad ran the first of what would be 10 years of ski trains up to New Hampshire; it's estimated that 40,000 would-be skiers clambered aboard in the first three years. Then, in 1934, New England's first rope tow was constructed at Gilbert's Hill, in Woodstock, Vermont, and was soon copied throughout the region.

The sport was dormant during the gas-rationing of the early 1940s, but the US was busy training a native corps of experts: the 10th Mountain Division "Ski Troops" came home from World War II with skills and expectations equal to those of their European peers. Area after area sprouted up in the late '40s and '50s, among them Vermont's Mount Snow, Smuggler's Notch, Stratton, and Killington (to date, the largest development in New England, straddling seven peaks, including Pico).

It was at Killington, in the mid-'60s, that the Graduated Length Method was introduced, easing the way for the general public to approach this often intimidating sport: tyros could start out on short skis, gradually increasing the length as their prowess improved. Subsequent breakthroughs in equipment further widened skiing's appeal.

Just to keep the challenge fresh, though, a Stratton bartender came up with an innovation in the mid-'60s that has changed the landscape of skiing, and promises to do so for decades to come. Jake Carpenter started experimenting with "snurfing" – as the underground sport of snowboarding was then called – secretly at night, after his shift. It would take years, but his Burton snowboard company would become a leader in the field, revolutionizing the sport with a thrilling new hybrid and, in the process, creating a "rad" new skiing subculture. ∎

D^R D^R

PATENTED
& GALL

HA
STO

NEW HAMPSHIRE

Once every four years, New Hampshire trundles out of general obscurity to perform one of the classic song-and-dance acts of American politics. The New Hampshire presidential primary is the first in the nation, the supposed diviner of political fortunes and, for many, a make-or-break event.

Though typically disdainful of such ephemeral trivia as fame and public attention, the people of New Hampshire jealously guard their self-appointed right to keep the nation's elections reasonably honest. Vermont (New Hampshire's perennial competitor for glories about which no one else much cares) once hinted that it might steal the primary limelight by sneaking its elections in before New Hampshire's. Retaliation was swift and decisive: New Hampshire passed a law stipulating that its primaries will be held on "the Tuesday preceding the date on which any other New England state shall hold a similar election." So there.

Crafty Massachusetts made its move in 1975, waiting until only a few months before the 1976 primaries began, to announce that it would vote on the same day as New Hampshire, the second Tuesday of March. New Hampshire promptly pushed its date up to the last Tuesday in February, even though this resulted in the inconvenience of voting in the primaries one week and then getting back together for Town Meeting Day the next (the two events had formerly been something of a political double-header). Though it's highly unlikely that many New Hampshirites lie awake nights worrying over the fact that the rest of the nation is reminded of their existence only once every four years, the Presidential primary is their moment center stage and they intend to keep it.

Politics in New Hampshire is definitely a participatory (and contact) sport. New Hampshire's state legislature, the General Court, is the third-largest governing body in the English-speaking world. The United Kingdom's House of Commons has 630 members; legislators in both houses of the US Congress total 485; New Hampshire manages to get by with 24 senators and 400 representatives (roughly, one for every 3,000 residents).

Much of the state's business, however, is conducted by that venerable, fundamentally American institution, the Town Meeting. Each Town Meeting Day, every eligible voter with an opinion on any part of that year's agenda has the opportunity to speak his or her piece and cast a vote. This is politics in the revolutionary vein which first shaped the nation. Without the camouflage of cloakroom deals, press-conference equivocation or media hype, the Town Meeting is pure, simple democracy, out in the open and accessible to immediate response, whether praise or scorn. The signatures of only 10 voters are required to place an issue on the agenda. It's not a very efficient system, but it is difficult to corrupt.

It's no surprise, then, that New Hampshire is something of an acid test for

Presidential hopefuls. Most of the voters are amateur politicians themselves, and they are not easily fooled. They're also pretty accurate in anticipating the nation's mood. Since its first primary in 1952, New Hampshire has picked the candidates nominated by both parties 9 out of 10 times. In the great majority of the contested elections in the nation's history (George Washington ran unopposed), New Hampshire has voted for the winner.

All this hands-on governmental process both reflects and, no doubt, fosters the feistiness that is deeply ingrained in the state's collective temperament. New Hampshire has yet to institute a general sales tax or state income tax. Instead, it rather deviously allows outsiders to make sizable donations by deriving over half of its general-fund revenue from tax-free liquor sales, state-run gambling and other "sin taxes." And New Hampshire's constitution retains (in its Bill of Rights) the right of revolution when "all other means of redress are ineffectual."

This is not to suggest that New Hampshire is a haven for rampant radicals. In fact, the state is decidedly right-of-center on most issues, yet fervently independent. Though predominantly Republican, New Hampshire has voted for Democratic presidential candidates about one-third of the time in recent decades. The Republican predominance is kept in check by a nearly equal (if not entirely opposite) force of registered Independents. Public opinion falls mostly between the two poles represented, on the one hand, by the arch-conservative viewpoint of the *Manchester Union-Leader*, which is distributed statewide and, on the other, by the more liberal *Concord Monitor*, which is not.

Yankee ingenuity: The rugged individualism which typifies the people of New Hampshire is intricately bound up in both their land and their history. The first settlers came not to escape religious or political pressures, as was the case in many of the other original colonies, but simply to have a little space in which to apply their Yankee ingenuity productively. They encountered and

An old-fashioned toboggan ride.

eventually subdued a land that was obstinate and rugged – with thin, "cold" soil, fresh crops of rock pushing through the surface each year, a forested wilderness that had to be cleared before settlements and farming were possible and, long, hard winters. The Indians, if initially welcoming, soon learned that the arrival of these foreigners was no blessing and began to retaliate.

The main assets of the region at the beginning of the colonial period were the deepwater port and surrounding shores of what is now Portsmouth; and the tall, straight pines, which became highly prized in the construction of ships. Fisheries established along the coast prospered from the sale of salt cod and other catches, hauled from the Atlantic as far north as the Grand Banks off Newfoundland.

The impetus behind these first forays was provided by Sir Ferdinando Gorges, head of the council established by King James to govern all of New England, and Captain John Mason, an early governor of Newfoundland. They obtained grants to an ill-defined territory lining the coast from the Naumkeag to the Sagadahock rivers and extending roughly 60 miles (100 km) inland. With capital obtained from English shareholders in their Laconia Company, Gorges and Mason proposed a variety of commercial enterprises and promised healthy dividends to investors.

The venture never really paid off. Lack of supplies limited the scheme's progress, the company eventually collapsed and the settlers simply divided the land up among themselves and proceeded to amass their own fortunes, without giving much thought to the niceties of property laws.

At first, relations with the Indians, primarily Abenakis and Pennacooks, were harmonious and mutually rewarding. In exchange for coats, shirts, kettles and other goods, and in anticipation of assistance in repelling assaults by other tribes and of a market for their furs, the Indians granted the settlers access to the land between the Piscataqua and Merrimack rivers, including the rich fishing

*oungsters
⌐ne up for a
╳i lesson at
Jaterville
alley.*

bases of the Isles of Shoals. In principle, the Indians were to retain the right to hunt, fish and farm in the area.

The original deal was reasonably fair to both parties. Soon, however, the settlers became more ambitious. They built dams which obstructed the migration of salmon along the rivers, conducted lumbering operations which frightened off game, introduced livestock which wandered into and consumed the Indians' crops and clogged the waterways with sawdust from mills. Realizing that they had been taken, the tribes of New England banded together in 1675 and unleashed "King Philip's War," named for Philip, chief of the Wampanoags. For one year, they raided settlements and garrisons, and the turmoil continued, on a lesser scale, for nearly a century.

Throughout this period, New Hampshire's commercial reputation and prosperity rested primarily on its supplies of mast pines. Soaring 150–200 ft (46–61 meters), as much as 6 ft (2 meters) in diameter and up to 1,000 years old, these massive shafts of wood required as many as 100 oxen to haul them from the forest. But they were invaluable to the expanding fleets of England's merchant marine. The best of them were reserved solely for the use of the King, providing in due course one of many motives leading to the Revolution.

Settlement and Revolution: Strong-willed settlers, gradually pushing their way inland from Portsmouth and up the Connecticut River from the south, laid claim first to the lush valleys, then to the harsher hillsides and finally to the forbidding mountains in the north. The first man to lend the colony some cohesion was John Wentworth, a prosperous merchant appointed by the King in 1717 to govern the province of New Hampshire. Though hardly an altruist (his land grants always reserved a portion for himself, a token 500 acres/250 hectares), he did begin the process – later carried on by his son and nephew – of stabilizing the province, encouraging settlement and promoting commerce. Largely through their enthusiasm for gracious living, the Wentworths helped

Old-style shopping.

transform Portsmouth into a genteel oasis, traces of which are still evident.

For most of the settlers, however, life was anything but genteel. When not warring with the Indians, they cleared land, produced crops without much help from either climate or terrain and, by sheer obstinance, endured. Matters were not improved by the unresponsiveness of their government, and when the Revolution came, New Hampshire joined early in the fight, moved not so much by political fervor as by a general acknowledgment that change could hardly be for the worse. Savvy in the ways of guerrilla warfare after a century of skirmishes with the Indians, New Hampshire's militia were particularly skilled at battle tactics which the orderly British were ill-equipped to combat.

Despite its active involvement in all the major campaigns of the war, New Hampshire, alone of the 13 original colonies, was spared the task of fighting the British within its own boundaries.

Among its Revolutionary credits, New Hampshire was the first colony to assert its independence from England (establishing its own government on January 5, 1776) and the first to suggest the idea to the Continental Congress in Philadelphia (in 1775). Late in 1774, alarmed by an edict from the King forbidding the shipment of gunpowder to the colonies, and informed that a British ship was on the way to fortify Fort William and Mary near Portsmouth, 400 New Hampshire rebels invaded the garrison, locked up the British guard and stole 100 barrels of gunpowder, later put to good use at Bunker Hill.

Following the Revolution, the people of New Hampshire went back to the task of coming to terms with their land. The push inland was by now extending up into the White Mountains, already rich with Native American myth and soon to generate new legends of the courageous settlers. Revolutionary fervor gave way to the more tiresome task of transferring high ideals to workable practice. Given the combination of a terrain ill-suited to plantation farming and an innate resistance to the idea of constraint, New

Riding low.

Hampshire resolved the issue of slavery for itself by effectively abolishing it early in the 19th century. An unfortunate pragmatism, however, kept the only New Hampshire-born US president, Franklin Pierce, from advocating abolition throughout the country. He argued that slavery was morally wrong, but that the issue should be decided by the states practicing it.

By the middle of that century, it was becoming evident that New Hampshire's weak soil and short summers could not support competitive agriculture. Farmland was abandoned as people moved West in hopes of greater success. Textile mills were established and logging operations continued, but the most notable shift in New Hampshire's economy resulted from the discovery that it possessed one asset that promised a good return for relatively little investment or labor: scenery.

The summer people: By the 1850s, "summer people" were a well-established industry. Executives on holiday, retired librarians with a nest-egg set aside, and an assortment of temporary bohemians came to sit on farmhouse porches in rocking chairs, dine in the lavish resort hotels newly built in splendid surroundings, or hike the expanding network of trails through the hills and mountains. Others, professedly more serious in intent, came to paint, sculpt or write. Among them were essayist Ralph Waldo Emerson, novelists Nathaniel Hawthorne and Willa Cather, sculptor Augustus Saint-Gaudens, and playwright Thornton Wilder.

Over the decades, the ranks of summer people have steadily swelled and spilled over into other seasons as well. Autumn draws connoisseurs of vibrant foliage which reaches its peak in early October to the north, then proceeds south. And New Hampshire's heavy snowfalls provide for superb skiing. The state boasts over a dozen ski areas; Cannon, Loon, Wildcat and Waterville Valley are among the largest, each with a vertical rise in excess of 2,000 ft (600 meters). Wildcat boasts cozy gondolas-for-two, and Cannon a roomy aerial

Protecting the pumpkins as harvest approaches.

tram; both run through the summer for sightseers.

New Hampshire's river, streams and lakes are kept well stocked with game fish: brook trout, smallmouth and largemouth bass, salmon, pickerel, perch, whitefish and shad, among others. Hunters – and, more often these days, photographers – track deer, hare and rabbit, porcupines, raccoons, gray squirrel, ruffed grouse, pheasant and migratory birds. The lucky few might spot a lynx or wildcat.

In addition to the White Mountain National Forest (of which nearly 700,000 acres/283,000 hectares are situated in New Hampshire, roughly 40,000 acres/ 16,000 hectares in Maine), there are 32 state parks in New Hampshire, with some 1,000 campgrounds in the 11 largest. Depending on location, these parks offer swimming, boating, fishing, cross-country and downhill skiing, snow-mobiling, hiking, camping and picnic facilities.

Local enterprise has also resulted in an impressive crop of roadside attrac-tions – compact amusement parks, mini-ature golf courses, water slides and just about anything else that might by some stretch of the imagination be termed "entertainment." Although not always in the best taste, and rarely sophisti-cated, they do at least ensure that no one can complain of a lack of activities, and most are fun.

Beauty and elegance: Although New Hampshire's primary appeal is its quiet country life and serene beauty, there are a number of special spots that warrant hitting the road. There are particularly elegant flourishes of nature, such as the Old Man of the Mountain, the Flume, the notches and Mount Washington; there are examples of human ingenuity and history, like the Cog Railway, Can-terbury Shaker Village and Mystery Hill. And there are such local specialties as covered bridges. More than half of the covered bridges in New England are in New Hampshire, including the nation's longest – the 460-ft (140-meter) span crossing the Connecticut River from Cornish – and very likely the shortest: a

12-ft (3.5 meter) expanse on a private estate in Alstead.

From the outset, New Hampshire has appealed to visitors not so much as a place in which to do or see anything in particular, but as a place simply to be. It is the ambience of the state that attracts, more than any roster of sites.

Isolated until relatively recently, with few links to international industry, New Hampshire was slow to receive and absorb developments originating elsewhere. This cultural sluggishness has now paid off: while so much of the country has progressed into a wasteland of "miracle miles" and economic frenzy, many parts of New Hampshire have retained a calmer, more dignified pace and quality.

Here, there are still long, slow days to sit idle on a shaded porch or inside by the fire; evenings with the stars clear overhead and the startling silence of the countryside; neighbors with the time and inclination to chat about how the snow (or rain or heat) this year is nothing like it was back in '78 (or '42 or last year); old farms with pastureland arching down to a barn with a pond beside it; small towns where everybody is on a first-name basis with everybody else; and forests where the only signs of the 20th century are the visitors themselves.

New Hampshire's town fairs feature ox-pulls and taffy-pulls, exhibits of handmade quilts, the rapid-fire patter of auctioneers hawking antiques, beans baked in a pit in the ground, homespun games involving baseballs and milk bottles and a prize for the best pig.

The industrious Merrimack Valley: Driving north from Boston, the first site worth a detour off Interstate 93 (after it crosses the border into New Hampshire) may, appropriately enough, also be the oldest. America's Stonehenge in North Salem, long known as **"Mystery Hill,"** has purportedly been carbon-dated to about 2000 BC. Though considerably scaled down from its British namesake – its circle of standing stones measure only 3 feet (1 meter) tall – the site is thought to have served much the same purpose as Stonehenge: as a giant calendar tracing celestial movements. Within the circle are a series of stone buildings and passageways, altars, walls, chambers and carvings which have been attributed, variously, to ancient Greeks, Phoenicians, Celts, and Native Americans, or more recent settlers of a mystical or perhaps mischievous bent – take your pick. The identity of the builders and the purpose the site served remain matters of pure speculation. Indeed, much of its charm derives from the fact that questions outnumber answers: your guess is as good as anyone's.

Further north on I-93 is **Manchester**, one of several New Hampshire cities (including Nashua to the south) that, as centers of textile manufacturing, attracted large numbers of French-Canadian immigrants to work in the mills. Manchester still retains its vast red brick mill buildings and much of its French-Canadian legacy, including a large bilingual population and the nation's most comprehensive archives of material on French-speaking Canadians, L'Association Canado-Américaine, founded by a Manchester grocer in 1918. For a

precis of local history, visit the Manchester Historical Association, three floors of old-fashioned exhibits spanning Indian relics to a Victorian parlor.

The **Currier Gallery of Art** features fine collections of European and American paintings, New England decorative arts, and contemporary crafts; it also offers modern architecture buffs access to the **Zimmerman House**, a 1950 design by Frank Lloyd Wright..

Some 15 miles (24 km) north of Manchester is **Concord**, where the gold-domed State House, the centerpiece of the downtown area, is fronted by statues of New Hampshire's political luminaries (Daniel Webster, Franklin Pierce, General John Stark and others) striking imperial poses in bronze.

Its entrance topped by a Daniel Chester French sculpture, the grand **Museum of New Hampshire History** houses the collections of the New Hampshire Historical Society, from furniture and folk art to tools and toys. Among the highlights is an original Concord Coach, the 19th-century vehicle known as "the coach that won the West." Also worth a visit is the **League of New Hampshire Craftsmen gallery** (New Hampshire was the first state officially to support its artisans, with the establishment of the New Hampshire Commission of Arts and Crafts in 1931), and the **Christa McAuliffe Planetarium**, dedicated to the New Hampshire teacher/astronaut who perished in 1986 aboard the US's first civilian space shuttle. A fitting tribute to her dream, this highly interactive museum features the most advanced digital planetarium projection system in the world, capable of simulating space travel in three dimensions.

Located in its namesake town, about 17 miles (27 km) north of Concord, **Canterbury Shaker Village** is an eloquent testament to the ingenuity and gentle faith of the Shakers, one of the religious sects that sought asylum in the New World. Devoted to orderliness, community, productive labor and such progressive notions as sexual equality and industrial innovation, the Shakers established communal "families," here **Tugboats in Portsmouth.**

and elsewhere, blending religious discipline with craftsmanship and business acumen to produce spiritual and fiscal prosperity. They believed all should be made welcome, a commitment that continues today as docents, rather than family members, greet each visitor.

The 1½-hour tours of the Village provide a glimpse of the skill and faith of this remarkable community. Crafts on display (some reproductions of which are available for purchase) include basketry, tinsmithing, wood-working and "the sewing arts." In addition, there is the simple grandeur of Shaker architecture, a host of intriguing inventions and a restaurant offering Shaker specialties.

A sliver of seacoast: A little more than 40 miles (65 km) east of Concord is **Portsmouth** – the state's major seaport, situated at the northernmost edge of its narrow 18-mile (28-km) coast, and the nation's third oldest settlement (after Plymouth and Jamestown). The **Strawbery Banke Museum** (the English settlers named their 1623 colony for the profusion of wild strawberries that greeted them) is an ongoing restoration project that recaptures the look and feel, and some of the activities, of this old seaport neighborhood encompassing some three dozen buildings and covering 10 acres (4 hectares) A handful of restored and refurnished homes, ranging from humble to grand, illustrate changes in architectural style from the 18th and the early 19th centuries. Some feature displays of construction and restoration techniques; others await restoration as funding permits.

Several of the lesser abodes serve as workshops for artisans whose work harks back to the past: open on a revolving schedule, there are studios for a cabinet-maker, cooper, potter and weaver. Here, also, one of the oldest boat shops in America continues to produce dories, skiffs and other vessels, employing archaic copper clench nails. Strawberry Banke is literally an open-air museum: tours are self-guided and open-ended, permitting visitors to proceed at their own pace.

Several other worthy historic manses

Restored home at Strawberry Banke, Portsmouth.

are scattered about this enchanting, compact town, full of appealing shops and noteworthy restaurants. A popular 2½-mile (4-km) walking tour links a half-dozen historical houses, including the 1763 Moffatt-Ladd House. Also well worth a visit, near I-93, is the **Port of Portsmouth Maritime Museum & Albacore Park**. The "albacore" in question is not a tuna but a grounded 1952 submarine, 205 feet (62-meter) long, which for two decades carried a crew of 55 in sardine-like quarters.

For a more pleasant experience on the water, consider a cruise to the **Isles of Shoals** 6 miles offshore, "barren piles of rock" charted in 1614 by Captain John Smith and long haunted by pirates and other nefarious outcasts. Improbably enough, an arts colony blossomed here at the turn of the century, after poet Celia Thaxter, the daughter of an innkeeper, created a miraculous garden on Appledore which inspired no less than 400 paintings by the noted American Impressionist Childe Hassam.

The "Quiet Corner": More than one local booster is not keen on the marketing monitor often used for the southwestern corner of the state ("Might as well come right out and call it boring," grouses one), but there's no question that it fits. Crowned by **Mount Monadnock**, a rocky 3,165-ft (968-meter) peak whose 360° views attract record numbers of climbers (the ascent is surpassed in popularity only by Mount Fuji), this is a region of meandering back roads past prim white churches, innumerable antique stores, and historic inns.

In **New Ipswich**, the **Barrett House** (*circa* 1800), a Gothic Revival summer house maintained by the Society for the Preservation of New England Antiquities, is a remarkable trove, retaining all its original furnishings.

The small town of **Rindge** hosts the interdenominational **Cathedral of the Pines**, a war memorial chapel with a set of Norman Rockwell bas-reliefs. Peterborough, home to the McDowell Colony, the country's most prestigious artists' retreat, inspired Thornton Wilder's famous play, *Our Town*.

Harrisville.

Bucolic **Harrisville** has perfectly preserved its 19th-century mill-town mien; a self-guided tour of its beautifully proportioned brick buildings (one is now a renowned weaving center) is a lovely way to travel back in time.

The region's largest town is **Keene**, where manufacturing companies flourished at the turn of the century. Some of its Hampshire pottery, along with some of the nation's earliest glassworks, can be seen on exhibition in the **Colony House Museum**.

Along the Connecticut River: In **Charlestown**, about 22 miles (35 km) northwest of Keene, the **Fort at Number 4** recreates a 1746 settlement which, in its day, was the northernmost frontier of colonization. Within its stockade, interpreters demonstrate such crafts as candle-dipping, weaving and the molding of musket balls and, at certain dates, re-enact skirmishes.

Some 10 miles (16 km) farther north, in **Cornish**, is the **Saint-Gaudens National Historic Site** – the summer residence, garden and studios of Augustus Saint-Gaudens, one of America's most celebrated classical sculptors.

Another 15 miles (24 km north) is **Hanover**, home of **Dartmouth College**. One of the bastions of Ivy League tradition, Dartmouth was founded in 1769, primarily for "the education and instruction of youth of the Indian tribes in this land." The college retains much of its colonial appearance while accommodating such modern touches as the **Hood Museum of Art**, with galleries spanning many cultures over the centuries, and the **Hopkins Center** with an impressive performing arts roster.

Hanover is very much a college town, and for that very reason full of interesting shops and restaurants. Possibly the best in the state is D'Artagnan, housed in a restored Colonial tavern 10 miles (16 km) away in the small town of **Lyme**. For the extraordinary sight of a row of magnificent Charles Bulfinch mansions, it's worth pressing on another 7 miles (11 km) to Orford.

Lake country: At the center of the state, north of Concord, is New Hampshire's

Dartmouth College, Hanover.

"Lake Country," where **Lake Winnipesaukee** sprawls in convoluted splendor with 183 miles (294 km) of shoreline and 274 islands, the centerpiece of a cluster of lakes and ponds scattered among rolling hills. According to legend, Winnipesaukee means "the smile of the Great Spirit," the name given it by Chief Wonotan on the occasion of his daughter's marriage to a young chief from a hostile tribe. Wonotan regarded the overcast sky on their wedding day as a bad omen. but just as the two lovers were departing, the sun broke through the clouds and sparkled over the lake.

Weirs Beach (named for the weirs, or fishnets, which Indians once stretched across a narrow channel there) brings a touch of Atlantic City to Winnipesaukee's western shore, with its boardwalk, arcade, marina, and elaborate miniature-golf links. Other attractions include two water-slide parks and the *MS Mount Washington*'s 3¼-hour cruises.

Wolfeboro, on the eastern side, can lay claim to being the oldest summer colony in the nation. In 1769, John Wentworth, the last of New Hampshire's colonial governors, built a summer home here, and comfortable old money has been following his example ever since. For glimpses of a lost way of life, visit the **Wolfeboro Historical Society Museum**, which includes an 18th-century house, a 19th-century firehouse, and an 1820 schoolhouse. In nearby **Wakefield**, two sisters who are inveterate doll collectors have opened a charming **Museum of Childhood**, complete with an 1890s schoolroom.

Looking down over the lake from the north, **Castle in the Clouds**, near **Moultonboro**, stands as an imposing monument to one man's rather megalomanaical vision of bucolic tranquility. Built by eccentric millionaire Thomas Gustave Plant, this 1910 mansion is set in a 5,200-acre (2,100-hectare) estate with waterfalls, ponds, streams, miles of forest trails and magnificent views out over the surrounding countryside. Among the seasonal activities are camping, nordic skiing and western-style horseback riding. While in Moulton-

Two views of Weirs Beach, Lake Winnipesaukee.

boro, visit the **Old Country Store**, which doubles as an informal regional museum. This, and other towns north of the lake, offer a refreshing respite from the commercialism that has claimed the western shore. Particularly pretty is the predominantly early 19th-century village of **Center Sandwich**, with several appealing crafts and antiques shops.

About 8 miles (13 km) southwest, a visit to the **Science Center of New Hampshire** is sure to intrigue: exhibits include a nature preserve for injured animals unable to survive in the wild. Here's a rare opportunity to observe bears, owls, perhaps even a bobcat.

A walk on the wild side: Continuing north, travelers now begin their ascent into the **White Mountain National Forest**, a vast tract encompassing the **Franconia Range**, clustered along an east-to-west axis, and the **Presidentials**, running northeast and culminating in New England's tallest peak, **Mount Washington**. Long a forbidding wilderness, the White Mountains have evolved into an enormously popular region, with

an ambience as distinct as the landscape. Here, hikers can enjoy the serenity of seemingly endless stretches of untrammeled (though no longer quite so forbidding) nature. The region also supports a thriving tourist industry, contained – by law and convenience – in pockets along the major highways. All the rest is reserved (and preserved) for backwoods purists.

A typical trail will lead from a parking lot along the highway directly into the forest, over gradually inclining terrain. Trails are well marked, with color-coded blazes cut into tree trunks at regular intervals, so there's little risk of taking a wrong turn. Eventually, towering trees give way to twisted dwarf pines and lichen-encrusted boulders. Above the tree line are the summits, from which adventurers may gaze down over the world spread at their feet, savoring that peculiar sense of accomplishment that comes from finding oneself on top of the world.

Most of these peaks are not, for all their massive beauty, too demanding.

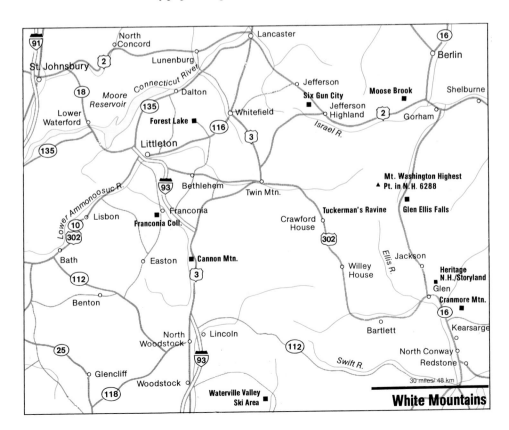

Many summits can be reached with an hour or so of fairly leisurely walking. One of the most rewarding excursions (in terms of view obtained relative to energy expended) is the short (45-minute) romp up **Mount Willard**, along an old bridle path. Those reaching the summit are rewarded with a magnificent panorama of **Crawford Notch** – a particulary splendid view at sunrise.

There are too many trails – some 1,200 miles (1,900 km) all told – to attempt even a partial description here; the White Mountain National Forest Headquarters and the Appalachian Mountain Club can provide further information. The AMC also maintains a network of "huts" (some are fairly large) offering bunk lodgings and hearty meals; they're often booked up months in advance, so reserve well ahead.

Franconia Notch: Just off I-93 north of Lincoln, **The Flume**, an 800-ft (243-meter) gorge with granite walls attaining 90 ft (27 meters), was reportedly discovered in 1803 by 93-year-old Aunt Jess Guernsey, who happened upon it while out fishing. Unfortunately, it's no longer quite as she found it – viewing platforms have been added to accommodate the busloads of sightseers – but some hint of the awe this natural wonder must have inspired remains.

Northward, pull into the parking lot at **Profile Lake** for a glimpse of the **Old Man of the Mountains**. Noteworthy not so much for its size – it measures 40 ft (12 meters) from top to bottom – as for the fine detailing of its features, the Old Man has generated a sense of reverence over the years. The jutting brow, regal nose, lips slightly pursed as if in meditation and sharp line of the bearded chin – all conspire to produce not merely a likenesss, but a real sense of character. As Nathaniel Hawthorne described it in his story *The Great Stone Face*: "all the features were noble, and the expression was at once grand and sweet, as if it were the glow of a vast, warm heart, that embraced all mankind in its affection, and had room for more."

Though credit for its discovery has been ascribed, rather presumptuously,

Left, the "Old Man of the Mountains." **Right**, resting on Foss Mountain.

to a road-survey team in 1805, no doubt the region's Indians were acquainted with the Old Man long before then. According to some sources, they saw in it the features of Manitou, the Great Spirit, and reserved for their chiefs the right to view it – and, even for them, only in times of crisis. Legend has it that the face was not always as stern as it now appears, but became so through sorrow over the conflicts and cruelty of the human race.

Directly to the north is **Cannon Mountain** (named for a cannon-shaped rock perched on its ridge). An easy means of ascent is offered by the Aerial Tramway (a 1980 replacement for the 1938 original) at its base. Also located here is the fascinating **New England Ski Museum**, with historical paraphernalia (such as hand-crafted wooden skis from the 19th century) and various audio-visual exhibits.

Two charming villages await just past the notch. **Franconia** was home to poet Robert Frost in 1915–20, and the Frost Place ("R. Frost" still marks the mailbox of Route 116) preserves assorted memorabilia and hosts a changing roster of worthy successors amenable to giving readings. The small town of **Sugar Hill**, once a magnet for summer manses, is still a mecca for maple-lovers, who flock to feast on unlimited "seconds" at Polly's Pancake Parlor. The **Sugar Hill Historical Museum** contains relics of 19th-century resort life.

A few miles north of Franconia, US 302 veers eastward, through **Bethlehem** (another handsome town full of dazzling summer homes, some turned B&B) and southeast toward **Bretton Woods**, nestled on the western flank of magnificent Mount Washington.

An "awful" peak: Hawthorne (who played an important role in promoting and preserving the region) accurately pointed out that the White Mountains, and particularly the Presidential Range, are "majestic, and even awful, when contemplated in a proper mood, yet by their breadth of base and the long ridges which support them, give the idea of immense bulk rather than of towering

Homestead Country Inn, Sugar Hill.

height." **Mount Washington**, at 6,288 ft (1,197 meters), is high enough to qualify as the tallest summit north of the Carolinas and east of the Rockies, and its sheer bulk is impressive, at least from the bottom. To appreciate its height, one must tackle the peak.

There are three ways to "climb" Mount Washington: on foot, by car (from **Gorham**, on the eastern side), or by train. The first option is, of course, the preference of outdoors enthusiasts, but the ascent is not easy and, even in summer, can be extremely dangerous, even deadly; be sure to check on conditions before heading out. The summit bears several chilling markers commemorating those who, like 23-year-old Lizzie Bourne in September 1855, died of exposure only a few hundred yards of the top. The destination she sought, a rustic hotel called the **Tip Top House**, survives as a small museum; visitors can marvel at the cramped dormitories, where travelers bunked down on crude beds cushioned with moss.

Climatically, the summit is classified as arctic. Its topographic isolation results in alarmingly abrupt changes in weather, including blizzards even in summer. The highest-velocity winds ever recorded – 231 miles (372 km) an hour – were measured here in 1934, and some of the buildings that are part of a year-round weather observatory (founded in 1932) are tethered to keep them from blowing away.

Visitors have access to the **Sherman Adams Summit Building**, surrounded by a deck with 70-mile (112-km) views, and within it the small but fascinating **Mount Washington Observatory Museum**, which focuses on mountaineering history and on the summit's unusual ecology.

Those not up to the climb can avail themselves of the remarkable 1869 **Cog Railway**, a testament to American ingenuity in the pursuit of diversion. The train serves no more noble purpose than that of carting tourists 3½ miles (5.5 km) up and down the mountain, but it does so with an admirable inventiveness. The average grade is 25 percent, the steepest

The Mount Washington Cog Railway

37.4. Relying on a failsafe rack-and-pinion system, the railroad was devised by Sylvester March, a local inventor who hoped to capitalize on the tourist trade attracted to the mountain. He obtained a charter to build the railroad from skeptical Concord legislators (they offered him the right to extend it all the way to the moon) and completed it in three years. It was the first railroad of its kind and has since been emulated, though outdone only once by an even steeper version in the Swiss Alps.

Just beyond the access road to the Cog Railway stands one of the few remaining symbols of New Hampshire's heyday as the home of numerous luxury resorts. Its genteel grandeur still intact, the colossal **Mount Washington Hotel**, which opened in 1902, continues to welcome well-heeled visitors in a manner to which most people could all too easily become accustomed. Circled by a 900-ft (274-meter) veranda set with white-wicker chairs, and topped with red-tiled turrets, this elongated white-stucco wedding-cake contains some 174 rooms (many marked with plaques commemorating famous former residents) and a voluminous lobby with 23-ft (7-meter ceilings supported by nine sets of columns and illumined with crystal chandeliers. Without leaving the hotel grounds, guests can enjoy golf (on an 18-hole PGA course), swimming (indoor or out), tennis (12 clay courts),and horseback riding. Though the lovely formal dining room has yet to catch up with an admittedly trend-crazy age, diners can at least console themselves with the thought that, because of the room's intentionally octagonal design, they'll never be relegated to a corner table. And with a band playing throughout the dinner hour, they can work in some dancing as well.

If a spectacular setting and impeccable service aren't allure enough, the Mount Washington also has a place in history. The hotel was the site, in 1944, of the Bretton Woods Conference, at which representatives of 44 nations established the gold standard, instituted the International Monetary Fund and

the World Bank and stabilized currencies in the aftermath of World War II.

Cradle of tourism: From Bretton Woods, US 302 cuts south through **Crawford Notch**, a narrow pass named for two notable early entrepreneurs. The notch was "discovered" in 1771 (more or less accidentally) by Timothy Nash, who was tracking a moose at the time. When Nash informed Governor Wentworth of his discovery, the disbelieving governor offered to grant him a tract of land including the notch if Nash could bring a horse through it and present the animal, intact, at Portsmouth; he was even willing to provide the horse. Nash met the challenge – incidentally opening up the White Hills (as the mountains were then called) to a steady influx of settlers, and eventually tourists.

Among the first to anticipate and capitalize on the area's potential were Abel Crawford and his son, Ethan Allen Crawford. They blazed the first path to the summit of Mount Washington (in 1819), advertised both it and their services as tour guides and established inns to accommodate their clients and other travelers – thereby masterminding the White Mountains' debut as a tourist attraction. Both men were as rugged as the mountains. In his 80s, Abel is said to have hiked five mountainous miles each morning to his son's house for breakfast. He was 75 when he made the first ascent of Mount Washington on horseback. Known as the "Giant of the Hills" – he was nearly 7 feet (2.1 meters) tall – Ethan was fond of wrestling bear and lynx and could carry a live buck home on his shoulders.

About 20 miles (32 km) southeast of Crawford Notch, the bustling town of **North Conway** is doing its best to steal some of the mountains' thunder. An odd amalgam of historic structures, rather tacky modern "resorts," and discount outlets (doubly attractive, given New Hampshire's lack of sales tax), this commercial strip is prone to peak-season bottlenecks; be forewarned. One reason to venture into town is to take a 1-hour, 11-mile (18-km) journey on the vintage **Conway Scenic Railway**, based at an

A Jackson farm in winter.

1874 Victorian railroad station in the center of town.

Without some such motivation, however, it might make more sense to veer north, rather than south, on State 16, and spend a few pleasant hours in the "cross-country capital" of **Jackson**, which communally maintains a 90-mile (150-km) network of trails. Its many delightful restaurants are just as appealing in summer, and **Jackson Falls**, a series of cascades trickling toward town past glacial "potholes," decidedly more so. Those traveling with children might enjoy a stopover at **Story Land in Glen**, a small-scale amusement park guaranteed to delight the 10-and-under set.

Just up the road from Jackson is **Pinkham Notch**, home to the pristine Wildcat ski area, set amid national forest (the gondola welcomes sightseers), and opposite it, the Appalachian Mountain Club's Pinkham Notch Visitor Center, which offers lodgings, workshops, and trail information. Every spring, skilled skiers make the arduous pilgrimage to shoot the headwall at **Tuckerman's Ravine**, a natural snow bowl affording a precipitous descent; others climb up just to watch.

It's on this side of Mount Washington that it's possible to drive up – provided your car's in fighting trim. The 8-mile (13-km) climb up the **Mount Washington Auto Road**, via endless switchbacks, can be hell on radiators, the return journey tough on the best of brakes. For those who'd rather spare their vehicles the ordeal (and forgo the campy "This Car Climbed Mount Washington" bumper-sticker), there's also a van shuttle service from the base.

The North Country: This isolated, sparsely populated region is one of New Hampshire's better-kept secrets. The landscape is as stunning as any in the state, if less than inviting during the long months of winter. Vast stretches of forest cover most of the region and provide its primary industry – logging. A lacework of lakes, rivers, ponds and streams offers a delicate counterpoint to the craggy hills and mountains. It is up here that the Connecticut River has its source, in a string of lakes just a few miles from the northern tip of the state, in a corner so out of the way that its allegiance was not decided, nor its boundary with Canada fixed (and then, by force), until 1840.

There is one grand old resort up here: **The Balsams at Dixville Notch**, a sprawling 1866 establishment with some 233 rooms and recreational facilities (golf, tennis, skiing, trout-fishing, canoeing, riding) spread out over an area the size of Manhattan Island; it even has its own small ski area. Not the least among its appeals are the groaning buffets set out three times a day, featuring some surprisingly polished and ambitious cuisine. Little wonder that subsequent generations, braving the long journey, keep coming back.

From here northward to Canada, it's a world of forest, water, scattered hunting camps and occasional towns hugging quiet highways, a world well suited to (and perhaps requiring) an exploring spirit. Those prepared to explore an environment such as this one don't need a guide to tell them how to go about it.

Mother and daughter, Canaan.

MAINE

Even by New England standards, Maine – beyond its heavily trafficked southern coast – remains a mysterious wilderness. Larger in area than the other five New England states combined, but less populous than any one of them, the "Pine Tree State" (nine-tenths of it are covered with forest) bears little resemblance to its comfortably settled neighbors. Winters here can be an endurance test: some joke that Maine has only two seasons, winter and July.

It's little wonder, then, that residents pride themselves on their rugged independence and turn a bemused eye on the strange habits of "summer people" – or "rusticators," as they're sometimes still called. The term dates back to the late 19th century, when the first brave tourists came to reconnoiter this uncharted territory.

Henry David Thoreau explored the Mount Katahdin region in 1846 and came back raving about its savage beauty. "What is most striking in the Maine wilderness is the continuousness of the forest," he mused in Katahdin. "It is even more grim and wild than you had anticipated, a damp and intricate wilderness." Despite the inroads of civilization, vast stretches still fit the description, offering nature-lovers of a Thoreauvian bent the opportunity truly to get away from it all.

For those who prefer to encounter nature on their own terms, with a certain modicum of creature comforts, old-fashioned "camps" are still scattered along remote lakes interspersed among rugged mountains. Long prized by skilled canoeists and kayakers, Maine's wild waterways have been harnessed for the sport of white-water river rafting. The ocean waters may prove too chilly for all but the most stalwart of swimmers, but sailboats, including majestic restored windjammers, ply the crenulated coastline – only 400 miles (640 km) as the gull flies, but 3,500 miles (5,600 km) if all the coves, inlets, and peninsulas were magically ironed out.

Drowned valleys and Red Paint: Traditionally, the Maine coastline has been the focus of the state's commercial and cultural activity. Geologists refer to it as a "drowned" coastline: the original coast sank thousands of years ago, its valleys becoming Maine's harbors, its mountains the hundreds of islands that cling to the shoreline from the New Hampshire border to New Brunswick, Canada. While the coastline was sinking, receding glaciers exposed vast expanses of granite, which not only gave Maine's mountains their peculiar pink coloration, but provided setters with a valuable source of building material.

The first known residents, 11,000 years ago, were paleolithic hunters and fishers who lived along the coast. Other tribes followed, including a race known as the Red Paint People because lumps of red ochre (powdered hematite), thought to have been part of a religious sacrament, have been found in their grave sites. The earliest European explorers, in the 15th and 16th centuries, were greeted by the Abenaki tribe, whose

name means "easterners" or "dawn-landers."

John Cabot visited Maine in 1497–99 (his explorations established all future British claims to the land), but it wasn't until after Captain John Smith sounded "about 25 excellent harbors" in 1614 that the "Father of Maine," Sir Ferdinando Gorges, was granted a charter to establish British colonies. Rival French explorers also claimed parts of Maine and Canada, and territorial disputes eventually led to the French and Indian Wars of the 18th century. Maine became a part of the Commonwealth of Massachusetts and remained so until 1820, when it became, as residents still like to call it, the State of Maine.

The South Coast: The best way to see Maine is to start at the southern tip and head northeast along the old coastal highway, US 1. (Interstate 95 is bigger and faster, for those who have a specific destination in mind, but utterly lacking in scenery.) Although, geographically, the coast represents only a tiny fraction of the state, 45 percent of Maine resi-

dents call it home, and the overwhelming majority of visitors to "Vacationland" (Maine's license plate slogan) are also headed for the shore.

The southernmost segment, extending from **Kittery** to Freeport, attracted the earliest settlers and to this day is the most heavily traveled, blending historic enclaves with built-up beaches and discount shopping malls. Just across the New Hampshire border from Portsmouth, Kittery's **Portsmouth Navy Yard** – the nation's first, founded in 1806 – is still active; the **Kittery Historical and Naval Museum** documents the shipyard's history, from the construction of *Ranger* (the first ship ever to fly the Stars and Stripes, under the command of John Paul Jones) to a more recent focus on submarines. Nearby Fort McClary was first fortified in 1715 and rebuilt repeatedly right up until the 1898 Spanish-American War. All that remains is the 1844 hexagonal wooden blockhouse, and the granite seawall – a scenic vantage point from which to view racing yachts in Portsmouth Harbor.

The Old Gaol at York.

Maine

30 miles/ 48 km

York was a center of dissent during the Revolutionary era. The local chapter of the Sons of Liberty decided to hold their own tea party when a British ship carrying tea anchored in York Harbor. Being Mainers, however, they were much too practical to waste all that good tea by dumping it in the harbor – they hijacked it instead.

The Yorks epitomize that odd blend of historical preservation and beach-oriented tourism typical of the lower Maine coast. The Old York Historical Society maintains seven historic buildings, including the **John Hancock Warehouse** (a contemporary wrote that the signer of the Declaration of Independence was "more successful in politics than in business"), the 1759 **Jefferds Tavern** and the **Old Gaol**, built in 1719, thought to be the oldest public building in the US. With its 2-ft (60-cm) thick fieldstone walls and tiny windows bordered with sawteeth, the jail served its purpose right up until 1860. It has now been restored to its 1790s appearance, complete with dungeon.

The other side of York, physically and philosophically, is **York Beach**, a narrow mile-long strip of fine sand, lined with every imaginable type of fast-seafood shack and family-entertainment facility. The **Cliff Walk** off York Harbor's boardwalk affords beautiful views of the coastline, and of Cape Neddick's 1879 **Nubble Light**.

To the north is **Perkins Cove**, a quaint fishing village that is now part of **Ogunquit** (whose Indian name meant "beautiful place by the sea"). Boston painter Charles Woodbury "discovered" the area in the late 19th century, and the word soon spread to other artists, including Edward Hopper and Maurice Prendergast. Where the artists wandered, the gentry soon followed. Today, tourists crowd the countless small galleries and eateries that have taken over the fishing shacks. The **Museum of Art of Ogunquit** displays locally produced work, including a sampling by such renowned summer residents as Reginald Marsh. **Marginal Way**, a 1-mile (1.6-km) seaside walk along the cliff is still

Perkins Cove, Ogunquit.

quite scenic, in spite of its popularity.

Ogunquit itself is a bustling summer colony so thronged with visitors that a quartet of reproduction trolleys offer the easiest way to get around (parking is tight). On fine summer days, the magnet is the 2½-mile (4-km) beach. Night spots abound, and a perennial pleaser is the **Ogunquit Summer Playhouse**, a highly regarded straw-hat theatre founded in 1933; Tallulah Bankhead, Bette Davis, and Helen Hayes all trod these boards.

To escape the bustle of town, try a contemplative – and educational – walk amid the 3,100-acre (1,252-hectare) **Rachel Carson Wildlife Refuge**. The pioneering ecologist spend many summers exploring these fertile wetlands.

Once the shipbuilding center of York County, the town of **Kennebunk** has long since turned its attention to tourism: the commercial center of **Kennebunkport**, Dock Square, is practically impenetrable in summer, but worth pressing through for a visit to the Kennebunkport Book Port, specializing in Maine and maritime titles and housed in a 1775 brick warehouse that served, variously, as a boardinghouse, post office, harness shop, fish market, and artists's studio. The town's legacy shines on in its stately elms and handsome white houses. To get a closer look at these buildings (a few of which are open to the public), take the architectural walking tour conducted by the **Brick Store Museum**, an old general store now devoted to exhibits about local history. Among the sights not to be missed is the unmistakable 1826 **Wedding Cake House**, festooned with elaborate carved wooden scrollwork. Legend has it that a sea-bound captain who married in haste had it built to compensate his wife for the lack of a cake at their rushed ceremony. For intimations of a slower-paced age, visit the **Seashore Trolley Museum**, which showcases some 200 vintage streetcars; about 40 still run regularly, around a 2-mile (3-km) track through the woods.

Further up the coast is **Old Orchard Beach**, a turn-of-the-century seaside resort popular among French Canadi-

Sign of a sea-going heritage.

ans. The 7-mile (11-km) beach is flanked with motels and condos and, at the Ocean Pier, an amusement park and waterslide complex. Eastward, just south of Portland on **Cape Elizabeth**, is the oldest lighthouse on the eastern seaboard, the **Portland Head Light**, commissioned by President George Washington in 1791. The Museum at Portland Head Light documents the history of lighthouses from early Egypt up to the present, when satellites have led to the decommissioning of towers such as this one. With its sweeping views of the bays, it's still immensely scenic – much as it was in Henry Wadsworth Longfellow's day. The Portland-born poet often walked here from town to chat with the keeper and draw inspiration from the surroundings. His *Wreck of the Hesperus* drew on an actual shipwreck off Peak's Island in 1869.

The phoenix of Maine: The state's most populous city (with only about 65,000 residents, or 125,000 in the metropolitan area), **Portland** presides over Casco Bay. Founded as Casco in the middle of the 17th century, the city soon became a center of international commerce. Located more than 100 miles (160 km) closer to Europe than any other major US seaport, and blessed with a sheltered, deep-water harbor, it presented itself as a natural port for trade.

Yet Portland's success has often been choppy and beset by sudden storms. Three times the city was burned completely to the ground – by Indians in 1675, by the British in 1775 and by accident in 1866. Three times the city rose quickly from its ashes, improved and rejuvenated. After the last fire, it was reconfigured. Streets were widened, and an elaborate network of municipal parks instituted. The city stands today as one of the best planned urban centers in the world – all the more so with the revitalization, in recent decades, of the atmospheric **Old Port Exchange** district, a salty warren of old brick buildings and cobbled streets, packed with sophisticated shops and restaurants.

Portland remains a thriving cultural crossroads, known for its innovative

Two Lights State Park near Portland.

dance and theater troupes. (Theater stood a better chance here after the repeal of a Puritan statute holding that plays "have a pernicious influence on the minds of young people and greatly endanger their morals by giving them a taste for intrigue, amusement and pleasure.") Portland also houses two outstanding art museums: the majestic **Portland Museum of Art**, designed by I.M. Pei and strong on such locally inspired artists as Winslow Homer, and a small gem, the **Payson Gallery of Art** at Westbrook College, which features works by Van Gogh, Degas, and other first-rank artists in a stark yet intimate setting.

Several Portland neighborhoods warrant strolling – especially the the **Western Promenade**, a parade of 19th-century architectural styles. The 1859–63 **Morse-Libby House**, a brownstone Italian villa popularly known as the Victoria Mansion, is by far the most elaborate dwelling in town – perhaps oppressively so, with its intensive adornment, but a fascinating study in any case. The 1785–86 **Wadsworth-Longfellow House**, built by the poet's grandfather, a Revolutionary War officer, is as austere as the Victoria Mansion is frilly, and a refreshing counterpart. The best way to view the city in its entirety is to climb the **Portland Observatory**, a cupola built in 1807 by Captain Lemuel Moody to keep tabs on incoming ships.

Spread out below are the **Calendar Islands** – so named because John Smith reported that there were 365 of them, when in fact they number only 136. Cruises to the various islands leave from Portland's State Pier Wharf. The islands range in size from a few square yards of exposed rock to fully functional suburbs like **Peaks Island**; they tend to get wilder and more beautiful, the farther out to sea. Though rumors of pirate booty have been bruited about for centuries, none – at least on record – has been found so far. Portland's residents and visitors find treasure enough in these peaceful retreats, ideal for biking and picnicking.

Following in Bean's boots: The little town of **Freeport**, on the Bay, attracts

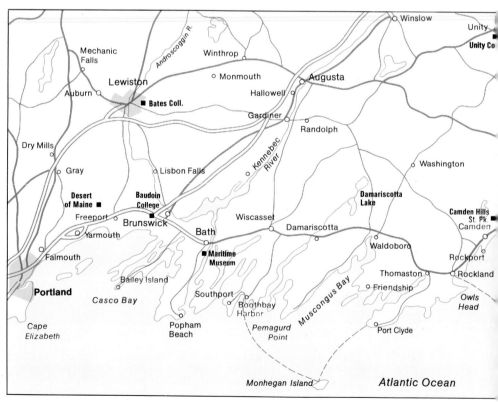

customers from around the world – all because, in 1912, a young man named Leon L. Bean decided to build a better hunting boot. In his initial circular, he offered the new, improved waterproof boot with a money-back guarantee. Legend has it that 90 out of the first 100 pairs fell apart: the soles separated from the leather uppers. True to his word, Bean replaced the defective boots with pairs of a newer, improved design and – after absorbing the loss – began building the legendary **L. L. Bean** empire that he controlled until his death in 1967.

Bean lived long enough to see his store, built in 1951, grow from a humble hunting and outdoors outfitter to a purveyor of casual fashion and recreational sporting goods. The back-to-the-land movement of the 1960s and '70s, along with a boom in mail-order sales, soon prompted expansion into a three-story department store, open 24 hours. Though a boon to the local economy, Bean's has had the unfortunate side effect of inspiring imitators, so that the entire village is now overrun with discount outlets –

tasteful, for the most part, but nonetheless intrusive. In the final irony, Bean's original customer base, the liberally inclined baby boomers, have begun to shun the enterprise because of his daughter's ultra-conservative stance. Ardent shoppers continue to throng here nonetheless; doing the outlets has become one of Maine's more popular sports.

A rather peculiar attraction in this area is the **Desert of Maine**, a former farm that was overcultivated, then logged, eventually losing all its topsoil. Sand took over, eventually engulfing entire trees... Amateur mineralogists and children alike will enjoy this overgrown sandbox.

The midcoast: Brunswick is best known as the home of **Bowdoin College.** Founded in 1794, Bowdoin was originally slated to be built in Portland, but the college's benefactors found that that city offered too many "temptations to dissipation, extravagance, vanity and various vices of seaport towns" for impressionable young minds. Nathaniel Hawthorne and Henry Wadsworth

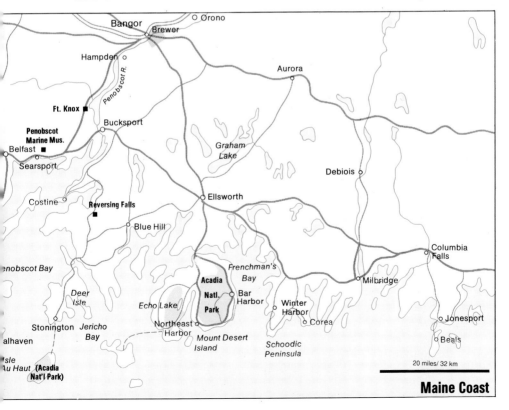

Maine Coast

Longfellow were classmates in 1825; Harriet Beecher Stowe wrote her 1852 masterpiece *Uncle Tom's Cabin* in Brunswick after having a vision while listening to her husband preach at the town church.

The **Pejepscot Historical Society Museums** (the Indian name for the Androscoggin River meant "crooked like a snake") provides a good overview of 19th-century life in this region, and the campus harbors two worthwhile museums. The college's **Museum of Art** houses a small but astute sampling of paintings by such notables as Start, Copley, Homer, Eakins and Wyeth. The **Peary-MacMillan Arctic Museum** heralds the accomplishments of Polar explorers Robert E. Peary and Donald MacMillan, who achieved their objective in 1909. Etched over the doorway is the Latin inscription Peary carved over his shipboard bunk after frostbite claimed most of his toes on a failed 1899 mission: *Inveniam viam aut faciam* ("I shall find a way or make one"). It's also possible to visit the house Peary built on **Eagle Island**, via cruises out to Bailey Island; inquire at the museum.

East of Brunswick on US 1 sits **Bath**, once the state's shipbuilding center, and the nation's fifth-largest seaport. For a time during the 19th century, Maine's shipyards were responsible for one-third to one-half of all ships on the high seas. Timber cut north of Augusta was floated down the Kennebec River to Bath, where the riverbank slopes perfectly for laying keels into the water. The era of the wooden ships ended, however, on the day the iron hull was invented. Not ready to give up a lucrative business, Bath constructed the Bath Iron Works, today one of the country's busiest producers of Navy ships. The shipyard is off-limits to civilians (except for occasional open houses), but a good view of the towering cranes and other equipment can be obtained from the **Carleton Bridge** over the Kennebec.

The history of shipbuilding in Bath and other coastal towns is preserved in a beautiful riverside complex, the **Maine Maritime Museum & Shipyard**. Exhibits on nautical tools and gadgets cap-

ture the flavor of seafaring days, while a working boatyard demonstrates techniques of different stages of shipbuilding. For a small additional fee, visitors can cruise up the Kennebec to view the Iron Works. The museum also maintains an authentic 142-ft (43-meter) Grand Banks schooner, the *Sherman Zwicker*, which can be boarded, when in port, for a glimpse of the seafaring life.

The town of Bath has much the same atmosphere as Portland's Old Port Exchange, with restaurants lined up along Front Street and Elm Street. Also worth a curious peek is the **Shelter Institute**, a school for amateur home-builders interested in maximizing energy efficiency and minimizing costs; the brick storefront showcases some of the success stories.

Directly south of Bath is **Popham Beach State Park**, featuring an unfinished 1861 fort and a 4½-mile (7-km) stretch of sand, one of the prettiest in the state. This was also the site of a failed 1607 colony, of which no trace remains.

Wiscasset claims, with some justifi-

eft,
aunching
e *Arleigh*
urke at Bath
on Works.
ight,
outhwest
arbor.

cation, to be the "prettiest village in Maine." It's certainly a contender, with its many grand houses, several of them built by prosperous sea captains. Two are open to visitors: the Federal-era **Nickels-Sortwell House**, maintained by the Society for the Preservation of New England Antiquities, and **Castle Tucker**, a prim 1807 Federal aggrandized in 1860 by Captain Richard H. Tucker. The 1852 **Musical Wonder House** is an aptly named mansion packed with vintage music boxes, player pianos, and other automata from around the world – often playing against one another in improbable euphony.

One of the most picturesque sights in town, oddly enough, is a pair of scuttled World War I schooners, the *Hesper* and the *Luther Little*, mouldering in the mudflats near the town landing. Another offbeat tourist attraction is the **Old Lincoln County Jail and Museum**, an 1811 hoosegow with granite walls up to 41 inches (over 1 meter) thick. Considered a model of humanity in its day, because prisoners were af-

forded individual cells, this grim repository was used right up until 1913, and has the sailors' graffiti to prove it.

Although certainly subdued compared to the commercial excesses of the south coast, **Boothbay Harbor** is decidedly touristy. In summer, tens of thousands of visitors throng the streets of this former fishing village to inspect the shops, sample seafood delicacies and charter boats to explore offshore islands with names such as the **Cuckolds** and the **Hypocrites**. There are yacht and golf clubs, flower shows, auctions and clambakes to pass the time. Antique buffs should look into the **Boothbay Railway Village**: in addition to a rideable narrow-gauge railroad, the large outdoor museum features a turn-of-the-century small-town barbershop, bank and country store, as well as an antique automobile museum.

South of Damariscotta on State 130 is **Pemaquid Point**, a rocky peninsula whose Indian name meant "long finger." Early explorers couldn't miss it, and in fact there's some evidence to

Ornamented window in Boothbay Harbor.

support a claim – unsubstantiated as yet – that a settlement here may have predated Plymouth. It's known that Pemaquid's settlers provided the Pilgrims with supplies to survive their first harsh winter in the New World; lacking a chronicler like Governor William Bradford, however, Pemaquid's history was never recorded, so details remain hazy.

Its cellar holes filled in by 19th-century farmers, the existence of this "Lost City" was entirely unknown until the early 1960s, when Helen Camp, a Rutgers University professor, noticed clay pipes and other detritus in a freshly plowed field. She alerted the Smithsonian Institute; the state bought the land and began excavations. Some 40,000 artifacts have been unearthed so far. The more remarkable ones – such as a 16th-century German jug – are displayed in the state-run museum, **Colonial Pemaquid Restoration**, alongside a diorama recreating the settlement.

Admission to the museum also includes **Fort William Henry**, a 1907 replica on the site of several unsuccessful stockades. The 1630 original was burned by pirates, and a 1677 replacement, thought impregnable, was captured and destroyed in 1689 by the French Baron de Castin (for whom the town of Castine was named) and his Indian cohorts. A Fort Frederick was built here in 1729, but during the Revolution locals leveled it, lest it fall into the hands of the British.

At the tip of this peninsula stands the **Pemaquid Point Lighthouse**, built in 1824. With powerful surf constantly breaking on the rocks, the point is a favorite spot for painters and photographers, as well as families who enjoy poking around the tide pools. The **Fishermen's Museum**, located next to the lighthouse in the old keeper's residence, displays a large variety of fishing and lobstering equipment, ship models, and information on Maine's 61 surviving lighthouses.

An island in time: An early European explorer, David Ingram, astounded Europe with tales – most rather tall – of the marvelous peoples and cities he encoun-

emaquid
oint
ighthouse.

tered on a journey from the Gulf of Mexico to Canada. Lured by such promising reports, a group of Germans settled **Waldoboro** in 1748, with, as a plaque at the center of town attests, "the promise and expectation of finding a prosperous city, instead of which they found nothing but wilderness." Another Ingram allusion, to "a great island that was backed like a whale," was naturally dismissed as fantasy.

This time, though, he'd been telling the truth. The cliffs of **Monhegan**, 12 miles (19 km) south of Port Clyde, do indeed lend the island the appearance of a whale. And yet an otherworldly air still pervades this 700-acre (283-hectare) isle, little changed in the past century. Cars have made no inroads, and virtually all of the cottages – including two out of the three hotels – not only lack electricity, but like it that way. A magnet first for fishing fleets (the abundantly stocked waters attracted European fleets as early as 1605, and possibly the Vikings six centuries earlier) and later artists (the most famous sum-

mer resident is painter Jamie Wyeth), most of the island remains undeveloped. Visitors are free to explore the **Cliff Trail** circling the island, and the **Cathedral Woods Trail**, where the island children are in the habit of constructing tiny "fairy houses" out of twigs and moss. Monhegan is served by ferries from both Boothbay Harbor and Port Clyde (the latter vessel is a rugged mailboat named the *Laura B.*), and though it's possible to make the round-trip in one day, an overnight is advised for those who wish to ease back into a less stressful age. Traditionally, departing visitors are given bouquets of some of the 600 species of wildflowers scattered throughout the island meadows.

Penobscot Bay: On the west end of Penobscot Bay is the town of **Rockland**, once a great limestone producer and now the world's largest distributor of lobsters. Thanks to the 1935 bequest of "Aunt" Lucy Farnsworth, a frugal spinster who lived in but three rooms of her family mansion and left the town $1,300,000 to start a museum, Rockland

Marriage, Maine-style.

has a world-class collection of art. The **William A. Farnsworth Library and Art Museum** counts among its holdings many noted 19th- and 20th-century works, including sculpure by Louise Nevelson, who grew up in a Bath lumberyard, and paintings by all three Wyeths – N.C., Andrew, and Jamie. Andrew Wyeth still summers in nearby **Cushing**, where the weathered house featured in his signature painting *Christina's World* still stands, the site of many a reverential pilgrimage (it's now owned by the Farnsworth museum, which also possesses the painting itself).

A ferry out of Rockland serves the large, mostly old-money island of **Vinalhaven**, where abandoned granite quarries (the stone went into Boston's Museum of Fine Arts, among other edifices) make fine swimming holes and the paved roads are ideal for day-tripping bicyclists. Right in town, take note of the curious 19th-century **Odd Fellows Hall**, now home to iconographic painter Robert Indiana.

Just off Vinalhaven is **Hurricane Is-land**, where the Outward Bound School offers participants – from teens to senior citizens – "the hardest, most miserable, most wonderful days of your life." This dubious endorsement describes a rugged travel-and-camping program involving old-style pulling boats, which can be rowed as well as sailed.

To view an interesting assortment of vehicles, airborne and otherwise, visit the **Owl's Head Transportation Museum**, housed in a spiffed-up hangar at the Owl's Head airport south of Rockland. The collections range from vintage bicycles to a 1910 Harley, a Model T Ford and a Model F plane (a Wright Brothers prototype). On summer weekends, some of the displays are taken off their blocks and sent for a spin.

Up the coast, Rockport is home base to a fleet of windjammers. These two- or three-masted schooners, sails billowing in the wind, are a throwback to an earlier era, and a wonderful way to discover the coast as the earliest explorers encountered it. Weekend and weeklong excursions may be booked aboard

Sunset cruise from Camden.

more than a dozen venerable vessels, including the *Stephen Taber*, believed to be the oldest sailboat in continuous use. At the Rockport Apprenticeshop, a school for boat-builders, visitors can watch ongoing work from an observation loft.

Rockport is also a summer mecca for shutterbugs attending the Maine Photographic Workshops; they can be spotted prowling the town, snapping up picturesque tableaux, or exploring new technological frontiers at the Kodak- and Apple Computer-sponsored **Center for Creative Imaging** in the neighboring town of Camden.

Camden ("Where the Mountains Meet the Sea") has enjoyed a long reign as the ultimate in genteel summering spots. It was here, as a chambermaid at the gracious **Whitehall Inn**, an 1834 home turned hotel in 1901, that Rockland native Edna St Vincent Millay first began to polish her poetry, and even recite some aloud (one of the guests, noting her talent, arranged for a scholarship to Vassar). At the summit of 800-ft (244-meter) **Mount Battie**, now accessible on foot or via a toll road, she observed:

All I could see from where I stood
Was three long mountains and a wood;
I turned and looked another way,
And saw three islands in a bay.

A modern statue of the poet stands watch in a waterfront park overlooking the Megunticook River falls which once powered a half-dozen woolen mills; it's a pleasant place to catch one's breath amid the hubbub of town. Camden is once again in full flower as a summer destination, and the port is packed with restaurants and shops. Many of the grander "cottages" gracing the hilltops have become luxurious B&Bs.

Much quieter than Camden, **Belfast** is starting to attract some fun shops to its Victorian brick storefronts, and its fine houses, too, are turning B&B. **Searsport**, lined with dazzling white sea captain's homes (nearly 300 lived here in the 19th century), calls itself "the antiques capital of Maine," and the pickings are indeed unusually good. Between 1770 and 1920, this one town

Looking down on Camden.

produced more than 3,000 vessels, and evidence of its rich history, along with China Trade treasures, can be found at the **Penobscot Marine Museum**.

Bangor, once the center of Maine's timber and paper industries, has declined along with the pine trees. Although an important hub, it has neither the cultural attractions of Portland nor the charm of the smaller towns nearby.

Detours "Down East": Intent on getting to the justly famed Desert Island, many tourists never veer from US 1 and thus miss one of the most scenic areas in all of Maine. The peninsulas along the eastern side of Penobscot Bay well warrant some leisurely poking around.

Established as a trading post by the Plymouth Pilgrims, **Castine** became one of the most hotly contested chunks of property in New England: changing hands nine times, it was owned by the French, Dutch, British, and, eventually, Americans (it was a Tory outpost during the Revolution, and the British managed to take it over again after the War of 1812). Plaques around town, as well as a free walking-tour brochure distributed by the Castine Merchants' Association, will fill in the details, but it's enough to wander around, beneath a canopy of well-tended elms, taking in the array of fine white houses. Some belong to the Maine Maritime Academy (one of five such schools nationwide which train merchant marines). Their 1952 troop ship, the decommissioned *State of Maine*, is a floating classroom; tours are offered in summer.

Take a detour off this detour to make a circuit of **Deer Isle**, where the principal occupations are lobstering and fishing, and tourists, though welcome, won't find themselves catered to unduly. On the eastern side of the isle is the prestigious **Haystack Mountain School of Crafts**, whose 1960 "campus" is a cluster of small modern buildings perched precipitously on a piney bank overlooking **Jericho Bay**; visitors are admitted during specified afternooon hours, and for evening lectures and concerts.

For a true getaway, take the mailboat from the picturesque port of **Stonington**

to the sparsely inhabited 2,800-acre (1,130-hectare) **Isle au Haut**. Half is privately owned, the other half part of the **Acadia National Park** (most of which is situated on Mount Desert Island). For those who wish to stay over, a small, somewhat costly B&B has been opened in the former lighthouse; campers who think to reserve months ahead can take shelter in a handful of lean-to structures maintained by the Park.

Heading northeast to hook up with US 1 again, one passes through **Blue Hill**, long the choice of blueblood summerers who didn't care for the showy social season in Bar Harbor. This lovely town attracts craftspeople (especially potters), musicians and restaurateurs, so the pleasures are varied. One early citizen was the cleric Jonathan Fisher, who served here from 1796 to the mid-19th century and was a man of many enthusiasms. One of his primitive landscapes hangs at the **Farnsworth Museum**, and the 1814 **Parson Fisher House**, which he built himself, is full of his handiwork, from furniture and maps to the wooden clock he made while at Harvard, decorated with phrases from the five languages he spoke.

Ponds and precipices: Spotting the 17 exposed pink granite peaks of this island in 1604, Samuel de Champlain described the place as "*l'île des monts deserts*" – and the French pronunciation still holds, more or less, so be sure to accentuate the final syllable, as in "dessert." The tallest peak, 1,530-ft (466-meter) **Cadillac Mountain**, is the highest point along the Atlantic coast north of Rio de Janeiro, and affords glorious 360° views stretching inland as far as Mount Katahdin and seaward to encompass myriad smaller islands – a particularly lovely vista when bathed in the orange glow of sunset. It's possible to hike or bike up, but the gently graded access road makes driving a snap, so save your energy to scale some less populated summits. Try the **Precipice Trail**, outfitted with handrails and ladders, up **Champlain Mountain**, or the Jordan Cliffs walk from **Jordan Pond House** (the place for tea and popovers

Left, fisherman. Right, souvenirs of Acadia.

since the 1870s) up **Penobscot Mountain**, stopping near the top for a dip in **Sargent Pond**.

The reason there's so much territory to explore is that 35,000 acres (1,414 hectares) of the 16 by 13-mile (26 by 34 km) island belongs to **Acadia National Park**, which draws over 5 million visitors a year. "Society" discovered this remote spot in the mid-19th century, inspired in part by Hudson River School painter Thomas Coles. By the time the stock market crashed in 1928, millionaires arriving by steamboat and yachts had constructed more than 200 extravagant "cottages." (Only a few survive, some as institutions or inns: many were destroyed in 1947's devastating fire.)

Fortunately, Harvard University president Charles W. Eliot had the foresight to initiate the park in 1916, and many of his peers contributed parcels. John D. Rockefeller threw in 11,000 acres (4,400 hectares) crisscrossed with 50 miles (80 km) of bridle paths he built to protest the admission of horseless carriages onto the island in 1905. The trail network makes for great mountain-biking, cross-country skiing, and just plain walking.

Car traffic is kept under control by a permit system covering the 22-mile (35-km) **Park Loop Road**, which makes a circuit of all the more scenic spots along the eastern coast; the reasonably priced permits are good for a week, and among the sites worth stopping for are Cadillac Mountain, **Schooner Head** (climb down to look for a cave abloom with sea anemones), **Thunder Hole** (where the pounding ocean creates impressive sound effects), and peaceful **Otter Cove**. Also on this side of the island is **Bar Harbor**, the island's main town – a bit overcommercialized, but boasting a pretty town green, a marvelous Art Deco cinema, and some exceptional crafts stores, along with appealing restaurants.

On the other side of **Somes Sound**, the only fjord on the East Coast, the landscape is just as lovely and a bit less traveled. Visit the spectacular seaview **Thuya Gardens**, and stop in **Southwest Harbor** to try your hand at the "touch tanks" and "mystery barrels" in

Bar Harbor.

the ramshackle **Oceanarium**. Next door, you can enjoy a freshly boiled lobster al fresco at **Beal's Lobster Pier**.

The far east: In Washington County – also known as "Sunrise County" for its easterly location – tourism takes a back seat to lobstering and growing blueberries and Christmas trees. The patient will be rewarded with a vision of the true Maine, much as it looked 50 years ago. It's worth a detour to visit the small, unspoiled fishing town of **Winter Harbor**, and, to the south, **Schoodic Peninsula**, a little-visited portion of Acadia National Park with fine views of Cadillac Mountain across the bay.

Machias, about 35 miles (60 km) farther east on US 1, was once a haven for pirates and smugglers. It was also the site of the first naval battle of the Revolutionary War. In June 1775, a month after the Battle of Lexington, the *Margaretta* set anchor off Machias to stand guard over a freight ship collecting wood with which to build British barracks in Boston. After debating their course of action at **Burnham Tavern** (now restored and open as a museum), the townspeople rounded up two smaller ships and successfully attacked. *Margaretta*'s captain died of his wounds when brought back to the tavern, but the crew, nursed back to health there, vowed revenge – and followed through, with subsequent attacks and conflagrations.

Lubec is the easternmost town in the United States, and the easternmost American soil is **West Quoddy Head**, graced with a candycane-striped 1858 lighthouse surrounded, in summer, by wild roses and day lilies. A walking trail leads from here, along a 50-ft cliff, to **Quoddy Head State Park**. Having come this far, don't miss **Campobello Island**, only a bridge away from Lubec but officially in Canada. Franklin Delano Roosevelt summered here from the age of one (in 1883) to 1921, when he was crippled by polio. After a self-guided tour of the house, which remains as the family left it, visitors can enjoy 8 miles (13 km) of walking trails, including a 2-mile (3 km) stroll along the ocean.

The County: Tucked into Maine's north-

"Lobster from the Black Lagoon" – a Maine advertisement

eastern corner, **Aroostock County** – larger than Connecticut and Rhode Island combined – is a gentle landscape, a patchwork of potato farms and rolling hills. Swedish immigrants came here to establish homesteads in the 1870s; their history is recounted in the **New Sweden Historical Society Museum**, housed in a replica of the original Kapitoleum (meetinghouse). In the towns along the St John River, French is more apt to be heard than English – a legacy of the French colonists who settled Nova Scotia in the 17th century but were ejected by the British during the French and Indian Wars and took refuge here. Longfellow chronicled their exodus in his epic poem *Evangeline*; further background can be gleaned at **Acadian Village** in **Van Buren**, a complex of authentic and replica structures representing Acadian culture from the 17th through 19th centuries. The border town of **Fort Kent** retains its 1839 wooden fort, built to fend off the British.

The North Woods: Much of the northernmost part of Maine consists of millions of acres of softwood forest, owned by a couple of dozen corporations who sometimes admit visitors onto their gravel logging roads for a fee. For an overview of the logging boom that swept the area in the mid-19th century, when papermakers turned to timber in lieu of rags, visit the **Lumberman's Museum** in **Patten**, whose 10 buildings of exhibits include a reconstructed 1860s cabin.

To the west, via State 159, is **Baxter State Park**, the legacy of Percival Baxter, who served as governor from 1920 to 1925. Unsuccessful in his efforts to get the state legislature to purchase and protect this land, he bought and donated a total of 201,018 acres (81,211 hectares) himself between 1930 and 1962, and deeded them to the state, requiring only that the tract remain "forever wild." The park contains 45 peaks over 3,000 ft high, including 5,267-ft (1,605-meter) **Baxter Peak**, the tallest of Mount Katahdin's three peaks and the second highest point in New England. Baxter is connected to nearby Pamola Peak by a narrow, mile-long

Baxter State Park reminds visitors to preserve the wilderness.

strip of rock known as the **Knife Edge**. Only a few feet wide in spots, the Knife Edge is an acrophobe's nightmare – 3,000 feet (915 meters) straight down on one side, 4,000 feet (1,200 meters) on the other. Would a person fall straight down to the bottom? No, a park ranger reassures: they'd bounce a couple of times. Don't try to cross in high winds.

Pamola Peak is named for the Native American god Pamola, said to have the wings and talons of an eagle but the arms and torso of a man. In *The Maine Woods*, Thoreau warned of Pamola's legendary ire for mortals who reach the top of **Katahdin**, thus entering the territory of the gods. Those who attempt to scale Katahdin – particularly up the most difficult trails, Cathedral and Dudley, which present the most rugged rock-climbing possible without benefit of ropes and pitons – might well wonder whether Thoreau was right.

Running northward from the northwest corner of Baxter State Park, the **Allagash Wilderness Waterway** provides 92 miles (150 km) of the most scenic canoeing available in the United States; the trip takes a week to 10 days. South of the park, the **Penobscot River**'s West Branch offers some of the state's most hair-raising whitewater rafting, throught granite-walled **Ripogenus Gorge**. And to the west of the park, accessible only by boat or float plane, is the preserved-in-amber 19th-century logging town of **Chesuncook**, of which Thoreau wrote: "Here immigration is a tide which may ebb when it has swept away the pines." Logged out and left to recover, this lovely little village welcomes outdoors-oriented guests eager to leave the 20th century behind.

Several dozen such "camps," unchanged for decades, are tucked away in this region pocked with lakes and ponds, where the fish are plentiful and moose and black bear still roam. Many are clustered around **Moosehead Lake**, the largest body of freshwater in New England, with 320 miles (512 km) of shoreline. The *SS Katahdin*, a restored 1914 steamship, tours the lake out of **Greenville** on the southern shore, and the

A roadside blueberry stand near Rockport.

Moosehead Marine Museum, which operates the ship, contains fascinating displays on Greenville's history, from frontier town to logging capital to turn-of-the-century tourist destination. Another great way to get a full grasp of this mammoth lake is to take a float-plane tour; several operators offer "fly-and-canoe" packages.

About 20 miles (32 km) southwest of Greenville as the crow flies (or thrice that distance by car), **The Forks** has turned into a major tourist attraction in recent decades, attracting thousands of amateurs eager to try whitewater rafting along the Kennebec and Dead rivers. Suitable for anyone over the age of 10 and in reasonably good health, these thrilling descents take only a day and alternate roiling rapids with placid floats.

The western lakes and mountains: Another 30 miles (42 km) southwest – the actual distance will be about twice that, because of scarce roads – **Kingfield** has been a magnet for sporting types since the mid-18th century. It also fostered a family of homegrown geniuses, whose accomplishments are showcased in the **Stanley Museum**. The twins, F. O. and F. E., invented the Stanley Steamer, which wowed enthusiasts at the first New England auto show in 1898 and set a land-speed record of 127 miles (203 km) an hour in 1906. Three restored, working samples are garaged in this Georgian-style schoolhouse, which the family built for the town in 1903.

Also on display are the photographs of their younger sister, Chansonetta, who had an eye for rural customs now all but forgotten.

About 8 miles (13 km) north, **Carrabassett** is home to Maine's largest ski area, **Sugarloaf**; with more than 700 condos, it also constitutes New England's largest self-contained ski village. An 18-hole Robert Trent Jones golf course and abundant wilderness trials for hiking and mountain-biking make Sugarloaf a year-round destination.

About 30 miles (42 km) west is **Rangeley**, also popular with outdoors enthusiasts for more than a century, and the unlikely home of one-time Freud

Timber is a mainstay of the Maine economy.

protégé Wilhelm Reich. His renegade theories on sexual energy ended in his ignominious death in jail – the victim, many believe, of an overzealous Food & Drug Administration. Some of the "orgone energy accumulators" he built stand at his remote home and laboratory, Orgonon. The tour is fascinating, the view of Rangeley Lake inspiring.

The **Norlands Living History Center** in **Livermore**, about 50 miles (80 km) south, offers a rare opportunity to time-travel back to 19th-century farm life. Most visitors content themselves with a two-hour tour, but true aficionados can sign up for a weekend "live-in" program, in which they'll enact historic characters associated with the farm – and carry out all their chores. **West Paris**, about 12 miles (19km) west, might prove more attractive to those with "get rich quick" inclinations: Perham's of West Paris, founded in 1919, is a rockhound's mecca, not just for its store, but for the chance to poke around in the five quarries it owns within 10 miles (16 km). Gem-quality tourma-

line – striated in a watermelon-like color scheme – is fairly common in these hills, and even gold is not unheard of.

Byron, north of Rumford, is said to have been the site of the first US gold strike, but California stole its thunder.

Passing through **Rumford**, take a look at the **Strathglass Park Historic District**, a model mill village built in 1901–02. It's so attractive that would-be homeowners still compete to buy the hillside duplexes.

Bethel gained prominence as a spa town when Dr John Gehring attracted to his clinic many Harvard academicians suffering from nervous disorders. The hotel he built in 1913 on the pretty town green, the **Bethel Inn**, is still a restorative treat. Also in town, the **Moses Mason House**, an 1813 Federal manse mantained by the Bethel Historical Society, is a must for fans of American primitive painting: the itinerant muralist Rufus Porter decorated the entryway and second-floor landing with, respectively, a seascape and forest tableau.

North of town, the **Sunday River** ski resort is trying mightily to catch up with Sugarloaf, and its growth since the 1980s – when many of New England's ski areas started suffering a decline – has been phenomenal. To the west of Bethel, the **Telemark Inn**, a 1900 stone lodge secluded at the end of a mountain road, offers supremely peaceful cross-country skiing half the year, and llama-assisted mountain treks the rest.

To the south, lovely **Kezar Lake** is ringed by opulent summer houses, some of them tranformed into inns, and the various villages of **Waterford**, scattered amid the **Oxford Hills**, present an unspoiled reminder of the era when vacation "amenities" consisted largely of cool water, lots of trees, and fresh air. **Willowbrook** at Newfield, a reconstituted late 19th-century village between the southern end of Sebago Lake and the New Hampshire border, captures many of the pleasures of this slower, gentler time, from horse-drawn sleighs to bicycles built for two, from a classic ice cream parlor to a musty general store. In Maine, none of these pleasures is necessarily confined to the past tense.

Left, wild lupins. **Right**, dusk at Pemaquid Point.

INSIGHT GUIDES
Travel Tips

FOR THOSE WITH MORE THAN A PASSING INTEREST IN TIME...

Before you put your name down for a Patek Philippe watch *fig. 1*, there are a few basic things you might like to know, without knowing exactly whom to ask. In addressing such issues as accuracy, reliability and value for money, we would like to demonstrate why the watch we will make for you will be quite unlike any other watch currently produced.

"Punctuality", Louis XVIII was fond of saying, "is the politeness of kings."

We believe that in the matter of punctuality, we can rise to the occasion by making you a mechanical timepiece that will keep its rendezvous with the Gregorian calendar at the end of every century, omitting the leap-years in 2100, 2200 and 2300 and recording them in 2000 and 2400 *fig. 2*. Nevertheless, such a watch does need the occasional adjustment. Every 3333 years and 122 days you should remember to set it forward one day to the true time of the celestial clock. We suspect, however, that you are simply content to observe the politeness of kings. Be assured, therefore, that when you order your watch, we will be exploring for you the physical—if not the metaphysical— limits of precision.

Does everything have to depend on how much?

Consider, if you will, the motives of collectors who set record prices at auction to acquire a Patek Philippe. They may be paying for rarity, for looks or for micromechanical ingenuity. But we believe that behind each $500,000-plus

bid is the conviction that a Patek Philippe, even if 50 years old or older, can be expected to work perfectly for future generations.

In case your ambitions to own a Patek Philippe are somewhat discouraged by the scale of the sacrifice involved, may we hasten to point out that the watch we will make for you today will certainly be a technical improvement on the Pateks bought at auction? In keeping with our tradition of inventing new mechanical solutions for greater reliability and better time-keeping, we will bring to your watch innovations *fig. 3* inconceivable to our watchmakers who created the supreme wristwatches of 50 years ago *fig. 4*. At the same time, we will of course do our utmost to avoid placing undue strain on your financial resources.

Can it really be mine?

May we turn your thoughts to the day you take delivery of your watch? Sealed within its case is your watchmaker's tribute to the mysterious process of time. He has decorated each wheel with a chamfer carved into its hub and polished into a shining circle. Delicate ribbing flows over the plates and bridges of gold and rare alloys. Millimetric surfaces are bevelled and burnished to exactitudes measured in microns. Rubies are transformed into jewels that triumph over friction. And after many months—or even years—of work, your watchmaker stamps a small badge into the mainbridge of your watch. The Geneva Seal—the highest possible attestation of fine watchmaking *fig. 5*.

Looks that speak of inner grace *fig. 6*.

When you order your watch, you will no doubt like its outward appearance to reflect the harmony and elegance of the movement within. You may therefore find it helpful to know that we are uniquely able to cater for any special decorative needs you might like to express. For example, our engravers will delight in conjuring a subtle play of light and shadow on the gold case-back of one of our rare pocket-watches *fig. 7*. If you bring us your favourite picture, our enamellers will reproduce it in a brilliant miniature of hair-breadth detail *fig. 8*. The perfect execution of a double hob-nail pattern on the bezel of a wristwatch is the pride of our casemakers and the satisfaction of our designers, while our chainsmiths will weave for you a rich brocade in gold *figs. 9 & 10*. May we also recommend the artistry of our goldsmiths and the experience of our lapidaries in the selection and setting of the finest gemstones? *figs. 11 & 12*.

How to enjoy your watch before you own it.

As you will appreciate, the very nature of our watches imposes a limit on the number we can make available. (The four Calibre 89 time-pieces we are now making will take up to nine years to complete). We cannot therefore promise instant gratification, but while you look forward to the day on which you take delivery of your Patek Philippe *fig. 13*, you will have the pleasure of reflecting that time is a universal and everlasting commodity, freely available to be enjoyed by all.

Should you require information on any particular Patek Philippe watch, or even on watchmaking in general, we would be delighted to reply to your letter of enquiry. And if you send

fig. 1: The classic face of Patek Philippe.

fig. 4: Complicated wristwatches circa 1930 (left) and 1990. The golden age of watchmaking will always be with us.

fig. 6: Your pleasure in owning a Patek Philippe is the purpose of those who made it for you.

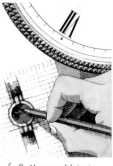

fig. 9: Harmony of design is executed in a work of simplicity and perfection in a lady's Calatrava wristwatch.

fig. 2: One of the 33 complications of the Calibre 89 astronomical clock-watch is a satellite wheel that completes one revolution every 400 years.

fig. 5: The Geneva Seal is awarded only to watches which achieve the standards of horological purity laid down in the laws of Geneva. These rules define the supreme quality of watchmaking.

fig. 7: Arabesques come to life on a gold case-back.

fig. 10: The chainsmith's hands impart strength and delicacy to a tracery of gold.

fig. 11: Circles in gold: symbols of perfection in the making.

fig. 3: Recognized as the most advanced mechanical regulating device to date, Patek Philippe's Gyromax balance wheel demonstrates the equivalence of simplicity and precision.

fig. 8: An artist working six hours a day takes about four months to complete a miniature in enamel on the case of a pocket-watch.

fig. 12: The test of a master lapidary is his ability to express the splendour of precious gemstones.

PATEK PHILIPPE
GENEVE
fig. 13: The discreet sign of those who value their time.

your card marked "book catalogue" we shall post you a catalogue of our publications. Patek Philippe, 41 rue du Rhône, 1204 Geneva, Switzerland, Tel. +41 22/310 03 66.

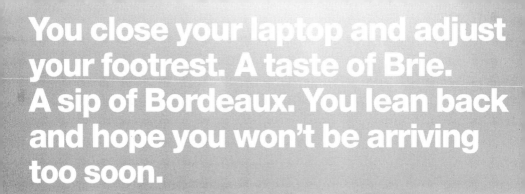

You close your laptop and adjust your footrest. A taste of Brie. A sip of Bordeaux. You lean back and hope you won't be arriving too soon.

That depends on how far you're going.

The fact that Lufthansa flies to 220 global destinations comes as a surprise to some. Perhaps we've been too busy with our award-winning service to tell everybody that we are one of the world's largest airline networks. A network that can offer you fast and convenient connections to anywhere. A network that offers rewards with Miles and More, one of the world's leading frequent flyer programmes. And above all, a network that makes you feel at home, however far you're going. So call Lufthansa on 0345 252 252 and we'll tell you the full story.

Lufthansa

TRAVEL TIPS

GETTING ACQUAINTED

MASSACHUSETTS

Known as: The Bay State.

Motto: *Ense Petit Placidam Sub Libertate Quietem* (By the sword we seek peace, but peace only under liberty)

Origin of name: May derive from an Algonquian Indian village meaning "place of big hills"

Entered Union: February 6, 1788, as the sixth of the 13 original states

Capital: Boston

Area: 10,555 sq. miles (27,337 sq. km)

Highest point: Mount Greylock in the Taconics

Population: 6 million

Population density: 570 people per sq. mile (220 per sq. km)

Economy: Manufacturing (industrial machinery, such as textile-, shoe-, and paper-making machinery, office equipment, and engines; electronic equipment, especially high-technology electronic components; and precision instruments, notably scientific measuring devices.) The Boston area is a center for advanced research and for the production of high-technology electronic items.

Annual visitors: 33 million

Top attractions: vacation areas of Cape Cod, with Provincetown artists' colony, and nearby Martha's Vineyard and Nantucket islands. In summer, the Berkshire Music Festival at the Tanglewood estate in Lenox. The Freedom Trail, Museum of Fine Arts and Boston "Pops" concerts, all in Boston.

Historical sites: Plymouth Rock, where the Pilgrims are said to have landed in 1620, and Plimoth Plantation, a reconstruction of the first Pilgrim community, in Plymouth; Saugus Iron Works National Historic Site, including a re-creation of the first integrated iron works in North America (begun 1646); Boston National Historical Park, encompassing several noted buildings such as Faneuil Hall and Old North Church; Minute Man National Historical Park, containing the sites in Lexington and Concord of the first fighting of the American Revolution; and Salem Maritime National Historic Site. Homes of Paul Revere, in Boston; of Christian Science founder Mary Baker Eddy, in Lynn; of the poet and essayist Ralph Waldo Emerson, in Concord; and of the poet Emily Dickinson, in Amherst. Adams National Historic Site, in Quincy, includes the home of Presidents John Adams and John Quincy Adams as well as other noted members of the Adams family, and John Fitzgerald Kennedy National Historic Site, in Brookline, contains the birthplace of President Kennedy.

Climate: Temperate, but colder and drier in the west. Pittsfield, in the west, has an average annual temperature of about 7.2°C (about 45°F); Boston, in the east, about 10.8°C (about 51.5°F); and Nantucket, about 9.7°C (49.5°F).

Local Government: 14 counties, 39 chartered cities and its 312 incorporated towns

National representation: 2 senators and 10 representatives to Congress.

Famous citizens: Samuel Adams, Louisa May Alcott, Emily Dickinson, Ralph Waldo Emerson, John Hancock, Nathaniel Hawthorne, Oliver Wendell Holmes, Edgar Allen Poe, Paul Revere, Henry David Thoreau

CONNECTICUT

Known as: The Constitution State, because its delegates played a crucial role in drawing up the US Constitution in 1787

Motto: *Qui Transtulit Sustinet* (He who transplanted still sustains)

Origin of name: Probably derived from an Algonquian Indian term probably meaning "place of the long river"

Entered Union: January 9, 1788, as the fifth of the original 13 states.

Capital: Hartford

Area: 5,544 sq. miles (14,358 sq km)

Highest point: Mount Frissell, 2,380 ft (725 meters)

Population: 3.29 million

Population density: 593 people per sq. mile (229 per sq. km),

Economy: Hartford a major insurance centre. Also aircraft engines, helicopters, submarines, and firearms.

Top attractions: Beautifully preserved old towns and villages. The indented shore of Long Island Sound and the wooded Litchfield Hills in the northwest are among the major resort areas in the state. Mark Twain House, Hartford. Yale University's Art Gallery and Peabody Museum, New Haven. Barnum Museum, Bridgeport. Gillette Castle, Hadlyme. 120 state parks and recreation areas, the most popular being Gillette Castle State Park, in Haddam; Hammonassett Beach State Park, in Madison; Sherwood Island State Park, in Westport; and Dinosaur State Park, in Rocky Hill.

Historical sites: Fort Shantok State Park, near Norwich, includes the site of an old Mohegan Indian village; Groton Monument, in Groton, honors revolutionary war patriots killed by the British; and the Nathan Hale Homestead, in South Coventry, has furnishings of the famous revolutionary officer's family. Mystic Seaport, in Mystic, features a recreation of a 19th-century whaling town.

Climate: Moderate. Winters just below freezing;

summers warm and humid. Average yearly temperature along the coast is 10.6°C (51°F), and in the northwest 7.2°C (45°F); for most of the rest of the state the yearly mean temperature ranges between 8.3°C and 9.4°C (47°F and 49°F).

Local Government: 169 cities and towns

National representation: 2 senators and 6 representatives to Congress

Famous citizens: Phineas T. Barnum, Samuel Colt, Katharine Hepburn, J. Pierpoint Morgan, Harriet Beecher Stowe, Mark Twain, Noah Webster, Eli Whitney

RHODE ISLAND

Known as: The Ocean State

Motto: Hope

Origin of name: Unknown. Perhaps reminded an early explorer of Rhodes in Greece. Or perhaps derived from the Dutch for "red" after the color of its soil.

Entered Union: May 29, 1790, as the last of the 13 original states

Capital: Providence

Area: 1,545 sq. miles (4,002 sq. km)

Highest point: Jerimoth Hill, 812 ft (247 meters)

Population: 1 million

Population density: 649 people per sq. km (251 per sq. km)

Economy: Manufacturing (fabricated metals, precision instruments, apparel and textiles, printed materials, rubber and plastic items, industrial machinery, primary metals, electronic goods, transportation equipment, chemicals, and processed foods)

Annual visitors: 29 million

Top attractions: sand beaches, boating and fishing opportunities, and Newport mansions such as The Breakers (1895). Noted resorts are Block and Conanicut islands and the city of Newport.

Historical sites: two Newport buildings, the Friends Meetinghouse (begun 1699) and Touro Synagogue National Historical Site, including America's oldest synagogue (built in 1763). Many other colonial structures.

Climate: Changeable. Summer temperatures are moderated by proximity to the ocean, but winters are quite cold. Providence has an average January temperature of about -2°C (about 28°F) and an average July temperature of about 22°C (about 72°F); Block Island has a mean January temperature of about -1°C (about 31°F) and a mean July temperature of about 21°C (about 70°F).

Local Government: 5 counties, 8 cities and 31 towns

National representation: 2 senators and 2 representatives to Congress

Famous citizens: George M. Cohan, Nelson Eddy, Christopher and Oliver La Farge.

VERMONT

Known as: The Green Mountain State

Motto: Freedom and unity

Origin of name: from the French *vert* (= green) and *mont* (= mountain)

Entered Union: March 4, 1791, as the 14th state

Capital: Montpelier

Area: 9,615 sq. miles (24,903 sq km)

Highest point: Mount Mansfield, 4,393 ft (1,339 meters)

Population: 562,800

Population density: 59 per sq. mile (23 per sq. km)

Economy: once agricultural, now relies increasingly on tourism

Annual visitors: 7.9 million

Top attractions: Outdoor sports, especially hiking, camping, skiing. Summer vacation centers include the Lake Champlain area and the village of Woodstock. Ski resorts include Big Bromley, Jay Peak, Killington, Magic Mountain, Mount Snow, Stowe, Stratton, Sugarbush. There are 46 state parks. Green Mountain National Forest is a popular recreation area.

Historical sites: Birthplace of President Chester A. Arthur, in Fairfield, and the birthplace of President Calvin Coolidge, in Plymouth. The Bennington Battle Monument, commemorating the American victory over the British at Bennington in 1777, and a monument, near Sharon, marking the birthplace of the Mormon leader Joseph Smith.

Climate: temperate, with considerable variations in temperature. Heavy snow in mountains. Saint Johnsbury, in the northeast, has an average January temperature of about -8.1°C (about 17.5°F) and an average July temperature of about 20.8°C (about 69.5°F); Rutland, in the central part of the state, has a mean January temperature of about -5.8°C (about 21.5°F) and a mean July temperature of about 20.8°C (about 69.5°F).

Local Government: 14 counties, 9 cities, and 237 organized towns

National representation: 2 senators and 1 representative to Congress

Famous citizens: Ethan Allen, Calvin Coolidge, Admiral George Deweys

NEW HAMPSHIRE

Known as: The Granite State

Motto: Live free or die

Origin of name: Named in 1629 by Captain John Mason of Plymough Council for his home county in England.

Entered Union: June 21, 1788, as the ninth of the 13 original states

Capital: Concord

Area: 9,351 sq. miles (24,219 sq. km)

Highest point: Mount Washington, 6,288 ft (1,917 m)

Population: 1.1 million

Population density: 119 people per sq. mile (46 per sq. km)

Economy: Manufacturing (industrial machinery, precision instruments, and electronic equipment) and services (including tourism)

Top attractions: mountains (especially Mount Washington), forests and lakes such as the large White Mountain National Forest and Lake Winnipesaukee. Camping, hiking, swimming, fishing, and boating

Historical sites: Old Fort Number 4, in Charlestown, a reconstruction of a mid-18th-century fort; the Shaker Village (1792), in Canterbury; Strawbery Banke, in Portsmouth, a restoration project with houses dating from 1695; and the Saint-Gaudens National Historic Site, near Lebanon, including the studio and home of the sculptor Augustus Saint-Gaudens. The Daniel Webster birthplace, near Franklin. The Franklin Pierce homestead, near Hillsboro;. The Horace Greeley birthplace, in Amherst.

Climate: Very varied because of mountains and ocean. Concord has an average July temperature of about 21°C (about 70°F) and a mean January temperature of about -6°C (about 21°F); atop Mount Washington the average July temperature is about 10°C (about 50°F) and the mean January temperature about -14°C (about 6°F). In April 1934, winds of 231 mph (372 km/h) were recorded on the summit of Mount Washington.

Local Government: 10 counties and 221 towns

National representation: two senators and two representatives to Congress.

Famous citizens: Mary Baker Eddy, Robert Frost, Horace Greeley, Daniel Webster

MAINE

Known as: The Pine Tree State

Motto: *Dirigo* (I direct)

Origin of name: Called after ancient French province.

Entered Union: March 15, 1820, when it was separated from Massachusetts to form the 23rd state

Capital: Augusta

Area: 35,387 sq. miles (91,653 sq. km)

Highest point: Mount Katahdin, 5,268 ft (1,606 meters)

Population: 1.23 million

Population density: 35 people per sq. mile (13 per sq. meter)

Economy: services (including tourism) and manufacturing (paper and paper products, footwear and other leather goods, lumber), plus fishing, agriculture, and forestry

Annual visitors: 8 million

Top attractions: Acadia National Park, mostly on Mount Desert Island, which includes rugged coastal areas. Mount Katahdin, in Baxter State Park, is the northern terminus of the Appalachian National Scenic Trail

Historical sites: Saint Croix Island International Historic Site, near Calais, encompasses the site of a short-lived French settlement of 1604–5. In Burnham Tavern (1770), in Machias, Americans plotted the capture (1775) of the British warship Margaretta in the first naval encounter of the American Revolution. The Wadsworth-Longfellow House, in Portland, was the childhood home of the poet Henry Wadsworth Longfellow.

Climate: On the coast, a maritime climate. Winter temperatures are much milder than those inland, and summer temperatures are cooler. In the north, extremely cold with high snowfall. In 1925, Maine's lowest recorded temperature, -44.4°C (-48°F), was observed. The south is the warmest part of the state.

Local Government: 16 counties, 22 cities and 424 towns

National representation: 2 senators and 2 representatives to Congress

Famous citizens: Longfellow, Sir Hiram and Hudson Maxim, Edna St Vincent Millay.

PLANNING THE TRIP

WHAT TO BRING

Clothing styles in New England vary from state to state, and then from region to region. Styles in New Hampshire, Maine, Vermont and the Berkshires in Massachusetts tend to be casual and geared towards outdoor life. The standard attire in most other New England cities in Massachusetts, Connecticut and Rhode Island is more traditionally oriented.

To cover all occasions, bring a variety of clothing from sportswear to formal attire. For men, a jacket and tie, although not necessarily a suit, is standard dress for more formal restaurants and may in fact be required; women have more latitude, in terms of pants versus dresses, but be warned that even youth-oriented bars and nightclubs may have odd "dress code" rules regarding jeans. Some warm clothing, such as sweaters, jackets, and windbreakers, should be packed even during the summer, when evening temperatures tend to dip, especially in the mountains and along the coast. Winters necessitate heavy outerwear, including hats, scarves, gloves, and boots.

ENTRY REGULATIONS

A passport, a passport-size photograph, a visitor's visa, evidence of intent to leave the United States after your visit and, depending upon your country of origin, an international vaccination certificate, are required for entry into the United States by foreign nationals. Vaccination certificate requirements vary, but proof of immunization against smallpox or cholera may be necessary.

Canadian and Mexican citizens, as well as British residents of Canada and Bermuda, are normally exempt from these requirements, but it is always wise to check for specific regulations on international travel in your home country at time of visit.

HEALTH

Though statistically rare, Lyme disease (borne by deer ticks hiding in high grass) is a potentially life-threatening condition, so precautions are in order. When hiking in grass or brush, wear light-colored pants tucked into socks, and spray the clothing with a DEET-based insecticide. Inspect your skin afterward: if a tick has attached itself, disinfect the area with alcohol and visit a doctor or clinic immediately. An undetected bite may result in a red-ringed rash; again, see a doctor. For further details, contact the Lyme Borreliosis Foundation (tel: 203-871 2900). Poison ivy is only temporarily discomfiting, but can be avoided by keeping an eye out for the shiny three-leaf clusters and washing immediately upon accidental contact.

CURRENCY

The use of American dollars travelers' checks is advised; they can be used for payment and are easily cashed in most hotels, restaurants and stores throughout New England. More importantly, however, they can be replaced if lost or stolen. Despite the small fee, generally 1 percent of the cash value of the checks, travelers' checks are a good way to avoid unnecessary problems and complications.

Visitors to New England may encounter problems exchanging foreign currency. A large number of banks throughout New England offer foreign-exchange service, but the practice is not universal (and a passport is required). Banks generally close between 3pm and 5pm on weekdays, by 1pm on Saturday and are closed on Sunday.

SPECIAL NEEDS

Federal regulations regarding handicapped accessibility have made some inroads, but the work is by no means complete. Larger facilities, especially those of recent vintage, should pose no problem. Many B&Bs, mindful of their elderly clientele, have also done adaptive retrofitting. If in doubt, call ahead. Broader questions may be directed to the Information Center for Individuals with Disabilities at (800) 562-5015.

USEFUL ADDRESSES

The following state tourist agencies can provide ample information on attractions, restaurants, lodgings, recreational options, and seasonal events; they can also refer you to local chambers of commerce, as needed.

Connecticut Department of Economic Development, Tourism Division, 865 Brook St, Rocky Hill, CT 06067, (203) 258-4293.

Maine Publicity Bureau, 97 Winthrop St, Hallowell, ME 04347, (207) 582-9300.

Massachusetts Office of Travel and Tourism, 100 Cambridge St, Boston, MA 02202, (617) 727-3201.

New Hampshire Office of Vacation Travel, Box 856, Concord, NH 03301, (603) 271-2598.

Rhode Island Department of Economic Development, Tourist Promotion Division, 7 Jackson Walkway, Providence, RI 02903, (401) 277-2601, (800) 556-2484.

Vermont Travel Division, Agency of Development and Community Affairs, 134 State St, Montpelier, VT 05602, (802) 828-3233.

TIME ZONES

New England is within the Eastern Time Zone, which is 1 hour ahead of Chicago and 3 hours ahead of California. On the last Sunday in April the clock is moved ahead 1 hour for Daylight Saving Time, and on the last Sunday in October the clock is moved back 1 hour to return to Standard Time.

Without Daylight Saving Time adjustment, when it is noon in New England, it is:
7am in Hawaii
9am in San Francisco
11am in Chicago
12pm in New York and Montreal
5pm in London
6pm in Bonn, Madrid, Paris and Rome
7pm in Athens and Cairo
8pm in Moscow
12am in Bangkok
1am (the next day) in Singapore and Hong Kong
2am (the next day) in Tokyo
3am (the next day) in Sydney

PUBLIC HOLIDAYS

During the holidays listed below, some or all state, local and federal agencies may be closed. Local banks and businesses may also be closed.

January 1: New Year's Day
Third Monday in January: Martin Luther King Jr. Day
Third Monday in February: Presidents' Day – celebrating Lincoln's and Washington's birthdays
Third Monday in April: Patriots' Day (Massachusetts only)
Last Monday in May: Memorial Day
July 4: Independence Day

First Monday in September: Labor Day
Second Monday in October: Columbus Day
November 11: Veteran's Day
Fourth Thursday in November: Thanksgiving
December 25: Christmas Day

GETTING THERE

BY AIR

Most major US carriers service the New England states. Logan International Airport in Boston is the 15th-busiest airport in the world, and smaller airports – many of them served by Delta – are scattered throughout New England, near larger cities such as Hartford, Bangor, and Burlington.

Some 15 international airline companies serve New England. If traveling with one of those airlines that do not serve Boston, travelers can route a trip through New York where there are many connecting flights to the New England area, as well as regular hourly shuttles to Boston (shuttle tickets may be purchased just prior to boarding). Visitors should consult a travel agent before choosing a flight. A variety of discount fares and special deals are usually offered.

BY RAIL

Amtrak (tel: 1-800-368 8725) offers efficient rail services to New England from Washington, DC, and New York, routing through Connecticut and Rhode Island and terminating in Boston; another route extends from New Haven, Connecticut, to St Albans, Vermont. Various commuter trains serve smaller towns, and seasonal trains – such as a ski train out of Portland, Maine, and the Cape Codder to Hyannis in summer – cater to tourists.

BY BUS

Greyhound and other bus companies, such as Peter Pan and Bonanza, provide service to New England. Many bus terminals, however, tend to be in "problem areas," thus necessitating caution when traveling to and from stations.

BY CAR

A number of well-maintained interstate highways (ranging from four to eight or more lanes) make covering New England's distances easy. To get an idea of the range, picture a radius from Boston to Burlington, in northwestern Vermont – a trip which, on Routes 93 and 89, would take only about four hours. That radius, extended across New England, would cover all but the northernmost regions of Maine (beyond Bangor). Travel on secondary roads is more time-consuming, but all the more scenic. However, beware of dirt roads – usually represented by a broken line – in mud season

(typically, March into May), and also make note of mountain roads which may be closed in winter.

PRACTICAL TIPS

SECURITY & CRIME

The best policy in case of emergency is to dial the police at 911 (toll-free; no coin needed at pay phones). State the nature of the emergency, and clearly give your name and address or location. Another option, time permitting, is to turn to the inside front cover of a local telephone directory, which lists emergency numbers.

Many parts of New England are best enjoyed on foot and it is generally safe to walk the streets. But as with newcomers to any place, it pays to exercise extra caution when moving about sightseeing, shopping, and so forth. Keep a firm grip on bags (shoulder straps could be slashed) and, when in a restaurant, don't sling them over the back of a chair.

Whenever possible, travel with another person, especially at night. Women, in particular, should avoid being alone in less populated areas and exercise extreme caution when entering a building or elevator alone.

When not driving, lock your car and never leave luggage, cameras or other valuables in view. Lock them in the glove compartment or in the trunk. At night, park in lighted areas. Also, when returning to your parked car, have your car keys ready before you reach the car. If in doubt about the safety of a neighborhood or parking garage, walk down the middle of a street or traffic lane.

Never leave your luggage unattended. While waiting for a room reservation, a cab or a rental car, always keep your property in plain view. Check to see that your door is locked when you go out, and never leave money or valuables in your room, even for a short time. If you are in transit, see if you can check your luggage with the front desk of a hotel, restaurant, or department store; many train and bus stations also have coin-operated lockers.

Do not carry more cash than you need. Whenever possible, use credit cards and travelers' checks; be discreet when paying cash for your purchases.

MEDICAL SERVICES

It's not cheap to get sick in the United States. Make sure you're covered by medical insurance while traveling in New England.

If cost is a concern, turn first to clinics offering free or pro-rated care (look under "Clinics" in the Yellow Pages). Major hospitals have 24-hour emergency rooms. You may have a long wait before you get to see the doctor, but the care and treatment are thorough and professional.

WEIGHTS & MEASURES

Given below are the US equivalents of metric units:
1 inch (in) = 2.54 centimeters (cm)
1 foot (ft) = 0.305 meters (m)
1 mile = 1.609 kilometers (km)
1 square mile = 2.69 square kilometers
1 US gallon = 3.785 liters
1 ounce (oz) = 28.35 grams (g)
1 pound (lb) = 0.454 kilograms (kg)

ELECTRICITY

Most wall outlets have 110-volt, 60-cycle, alternating current. If you plan to use European-made electrical appliances, be sure to step down the voltage with a transformer.

BUSINESS HOURS

Most offices are open 9am–5pm Monday–Friday; many businesses have free 800 numbers (some in operation 24 hours), and virtually all employ voice-mail or answering machines. Fax machines are also ubiquitous.

POSTAL SERVICES

Post-office hours vary in central big-city branches and in smaller cities and towns. Hotel personnel will be able to answer questions about the business hours of the nearest post office. If you do not know where you will be staying in a particular town, you can receive mail simply by having it addressed to you, care of General Delivery at the main office in that town. But you must pick up such mail personally. Check with postal officials about charges and the variety of mail delivery services available.

Stamps may also be purchased from vending machines installed in hotel lobbies, in shops and airports, and at bus and train stations.

To facilitate quick delivery within the States, include the five-digit zip code when addressing communications. Zip code information may be obtained from any post office.

TELEGRAMS & FAX

Western Union and International Telephone & Telegraph (ITT) will take telegram and telex messages by phone and payment can be made by credit card; check the local phone directory or call local information for the toll-free (800) numbers of their offices (for information on 800 numbers, dial 1-800-555-1212). All but the smallest of hotels and B&Bs can offer access to a fax machines; there's generally a charge for outgoing faxes, but incoming faxes are usually free.

TELEPHONES

Public telephones are generally located in hotel lobbies, restaurants, drugstores, street corners, garages, convenience stores and other general locations throughout New England. Long distance call rates decrease after 5pm, decrease further after 11pm and are lowest on weekends. Several countries can be dialled directly from many areas in New England, without operator assistance. For all specific information concerning telephone rates and conveniences, simply call the local operator ("0") and inquire. All 800 numbers are toll-free.

GETTING AROUND

Boston is the only New England city boasting a subway system (the MBTA, or "T" for short); the cost is low (especially compared to other cities), the transit rapid, and the experience generally quite pleasant. The "Boston Passport," offering 1, 3, or 7 days of unlimited rides, can be purchased at the Boston Common Visitor Information Center at 147 Tremont St, or call 617-722 5218 for further information. The Association for Public Transportation advocacy group, publishes an excellent and comprehensive low-cost guide called Car-Free in Boston, available at newsstands and bookstores, or call (617) 482-0282 to order a copy; it actually covers, in lesser detail, all of New England.

Tourist information and useful literature may be obtained from the tourist board of each specific state. (See *Useful Addresses*)

A car offers the most popular and convenient means of getting around New England. Although the network of airplanes, buses, trains, ferries, and taxis is quite reliable, having your own car is the easiest way to get around (except, perhaps, in the congested heart of Boston), and it also offers the greatest leeway for getting off the beaten path.

Visitors wishing to rent or lease a car after arriving in New England will find offices of all the major US firms, including Hertz (800-654 3131), Avis (800-331 1212) and Budget (800-527 0700) at airports and other locations convenient to tourists. Toll-free arrangements can be made in advance.

Call around, referring to the Yellow Pages ("Automobile Renting & Leasing"), for the best rates. Sometimes local rental firms may offer lower rates, especially for lower-quality cars (several franchise chains, such as Rent A Wreck, have sprung up to cater to just this market). But be sure to check insurance coverage provisions before signing anything.

Most automobile rental agencies require drivers to be at least 21 years old (sometimes 25), and to hold a valid driver's license and a major credit card; some will accept a cash deposit, sometimes as high as $500, in lieu of a credit card. Foreign travelers may need to produce an international driver's license or a license from their own country. Liability is not included in the terms of your lease, so advertised rates usually do not include additional fees for insurance. Also check with an airline, bus or rail agent or travel agent for special package deals that provide rental cars at reduced rates.

MOTORING ADVISORIES

In general, state laws apply to the New England driver. Each state has specific laws and special regulations regarding parking, speed limits and the like; most are clearly posted. Check with the tourism board if in doubt.

New England states maintain their interstate highway system in fine condition. Highway speed is generally limited to 55 miles (89 km) per hour, although along some stretches in certain states – check the roadside signs – a maximum of 65 miles (105 km) is permitted. On interstates, you may find your fellow drivers will be cruising along at about 10 miles more per hour than the posted limit, on the presumption that such an offence is likely to get them no more than a warning. Join them at your own risk: Enforcement, if sporadic, can be strict, with high penalties.

Rotaries, especially in Boston, pose a particular challenge. The official rule is that the cars already in the circle have the right of way in exiting, but this rule is rarely observed in practice. It's best to proceed cautiously, whether entering or exiting.

Unless otherwise posted, a right-hand turn at a red light is permitted throughout New England. On sighting a school bus that has stopped to load or unload children, the driver must stop completely before reaching the bus and may not proceed until the warning signals on the school bus have been switched off, or until directed to do so.

Hitchhiking is discouraged; so is picking up hitchhikers. Car-jackings are exceedingly rare, but a growing threat. If you are planning to drive, learn what areas of cities to avoid before starting out. Ask questions of your rental clerk when you arrive, or check with tourist offices before taking a drive.

WHERE TO STAY

New England provides an especially diverse set of accommodation alternatives. The options vary in terms of location, price, amenities, atmosphere and orientation.

Perhaps the most uniquely New England type of lodging is the famed country inn. If you are tired of the monotony of motels and hotels, and willing to forego certain conveniences (such as an in-room phone or TV) for more simple pleasures, country inns are a wonderful option. They can be stereotyped only to the degree that they provide year-round good lodging and regional fare – some quite sophisticated – throughout the New England states. They range from weathered farmhouses with huge fireplaces and relaxing music, like Vermont's Inn at Sawmill Farm, to the grand elegance of Wheatleigh in Lenox, Massachusetts, to the golf courses, shops and pools of the Spalding Inn Club located in Whitfield, New Hampshire. Other country inns offer many or all of these attractions, and often more; the common traits they share are high-quality service and hospitality.

Of course New England also offers the more traditional types of lodging – from Holiday Inns to full-service grand hotels like Boston's Ritz Carlton, from numerous roadside motels to low-budget bed and breakfast inns and youth hostels. Among the large chains that have hotels throughout New England are: Best Western, (800) 528-1234; Comfort Inn, (800) 4-CHOICE; Days Inn, (800) 325-2525; Econolodge, (800) 424-4777; Hilton, (800) HILTONS; Holiday Inn, (800) HOLIDAY; Howard Johnson, (800) 654-2000; Hyatt Regency, (800) 233-1234; Marriott, (800) USA-WKND; Quality Inn, (800) 228-5151; Radisson, (800) 333-3333; Ramada, (800) 2RAMADA; Red Roof Inn, (800) THE ROOF;

Sheraton, (800) 325-3535; Stouffer's, (800) ; Super 8, (800) 800-8000; Susse Chalet, (800) 258-1980; Westin, (800) 228-3000.

A very approximate guide to current room rates (standard double), subject to change, is: $ = under $100; $$ = $100–150; $$$ = $150–200; $$$$ = over $200. "B&B's" (bed and breakfast) supply a complimentary full breakfast, often quite sophisticated. "MAP" (Modified American Plan) rates include breakfast and dinner; "FAP" (Full American Plan) all three meals.

CONNECTICUT

CLINTON
Captain Dibbell House, 21 Commerce St, 06413 (I-95, Exit 63S), tel: (203) 669-1646. 3 rooms. $ B&B. A subdued 1866 Victorian; perennial gardens.

EAST HADDAM
Bishopsgate Inn, 7 Norwich Rd, 06423, tel: (203) 873-1677. 6 rooms. $ B&B. An 1818 shipwright's home with 6 fireplaces.

ESSEX
Griswold Inn, 36 Main St, 06426, tel: (203) 767-1776. 25 rooms. $$. A haven for wayfarers since 1776.

FARMINGTON
The Barney House, 11 Mountain Spring Rd, 06032, tel: (203) 677-9735. 7 rooms. $ B&B. An imposing 1832 mansion with formal gardens and Victorian greenhouse.

The Farmington Inn, 827 Farmington Ave, 06032, (203) 677-2861. 72 rooms. $–$$. A handsomely renovated motel with traditional decor.

GLASTONBURY
Butternut Farm, 1654 Main St, 06033, tel: (203) 633-7197. 5 rooms. $ B&B. A 1720 colonial with herb gardens and period antiques.

GREENWICH
Homestead Inn, 420 Field Point Rd, 06830 (I-95, Exit 3), tel: (203) 869-7500. 23 rooms. $$ B&B. A 1799 farmhouse lavished with Victoriana.

Stanton House Inn, 76 Maple Ave, 06830 (I-95, Exit 4), tel: (203) 869-2110. 25 rooms. $ B&B. A turn-of-the-century mansion designed by Stanford White.

HARTFORD
The Goodwin Hotel at Goodwin Square, 1 Haynes St, 06103, tel: (203) 246-7500, (800) 922-5006. 124 rooms. $$$. A luxury urban inn in the heart of town.

IVORYTON
Copper Beech Inn, 46 Main St, 06442 tel: (203) 767-0330. 13 rooms. $$–$$$. Luxuriously appointed 1890 home; 9 rooms come with jacuzzi.

KENT
Flanders Arms, Route 7, 06757, tel: (203) 927-3040. 5 rooms. $ B&B. A tastefully decorated 1738 Colonial.

LAKEVILLE
Wake Robin Inn, Sharon Rd (Route 41), 06039, tel: (203) 435-2515. 40 rooms. $$. A Georgian colonial on 15 acres.

LITCHFIELD
Litchfield Inn, Route 202, 06759, tel: (203) 567-4503. 31 rooms. $$. Central location is a plus at this traditionally decorated Colonial-style inn.

Tollgate Hill Inn, Tollgate Rd and Route 202, 06759, tel: (203) 567-4545. 20 rooms. $$ B&B. A 1740 Federal inn supplemented by a renovated schoolhouse.

MADISON
Madison Beach Hotel, 94 West Wharf Rd, 06443, tel: (203) 245-1404. 35 rooms. $–$$. An old-fashioned wooden hotel, right on the sound.

MYSTIC
The Inn at Mystic, Routes 1 and 27, 06355, tel: (203) 536-9604. 64 rooms. $$$. Choose from motel units or elegant rooms in the Colonial Revival mansion.

The Steamboat Inn, 73 Steamboat Wharf, 06355, tel: (203) 536-8300. 6 rooms. $$–$$$$. Dramatic spaces right on the water.

The Whaler's Inn, 20 E Main St (Route 1), 06355, tel: (203) 536-2506, (800) 243-2588. 45 rooms. $–$$. Several 19th-century homes, clustered near the docks.

NEW CANAAN
The Roger Sherman Inn, tel: (203) 966-4541. 12 rooms. $$$. A comfy 1740 country inn.

NEW HAVEN
The Inn at Chapel West, 1201 Chapel St, 06511, tel: (203) 777–1201. 10 rooms. $$$. A restored 19th-century urban inn.

Park Plaza Hotel, 155 Temple St, 06510, tel: (203) 772-1700. 300 rooms. $$. Big and fully modernized; outdoor pool.

NEW LONDON
Lighthouse Inn, Lower Blvd, 06320 tel: (203) 443-8411. 51 rooms. $$. Restored 1902 mansion with private beach.

Queen Anne Inn, 265 Williams St, 06320, tel: (203) 447-2600. 9 rooms. $ B&B. Fanciful Victorian inn.

NEW PRESTON
Boulders Inn, Route 45, 06777, tel: (203) 868-7918. 17 rooms. $$$$ MAP. An 1895 stone mansion overlooking Lake Waramaug.

Hopkins Inn, Hopkins Rd, 06777, tel: (203) 868-7295. 11 rooms. $. An 1847 Federal house with Alpine touches and lake views.

The Inn on Lake Waramaug, North Shore Rd, 06777, tel: (203) 868-0563. 23 rooms. $$. A modernized and expanded 1790s lakeside colonial inn with lots of family activities.

NOANK
The Palmer Inn, 25 Church St, 06340, tel: (203) 572-9000. 16 rooms. $$. A grand turn-of-the-century seaside mansion.

NORTH STONINGTON
Randall's Ordinary, Route 2, 06359 tel: (203) 599-4540. 15 rooms. $$. Colonial inn on the National Register of Historic Places.

NORFOLK

Manor House, Maple Ave, 06058, tel: (203) 542-5690, (800) 488-5690. 10 rooms. $–$$ B&B. An opulent 1898 Tudor summer home.

NORWALK

Silvermine Tavern, Silvermine and Perry avenues, 06850, tel: (203) 847-4558. 10 rooms. $$. A 1785 country inn set by a waterfall.

NORWICH

Norwich Inn and Spa, 607 West Thames St, 06369, tel: (203) 6-2401. 65 rooms. $$. A turn-of-the-century inn with world-class spa.

OLD LYME

Bee & Thistle Inn, 100 Lyme St, 06471, tel: (203) 434-1667. 11 rooms. $$. A 1756 home, set peacefully beside a river.

Old Lyme Inn, Lyme St, 06471, tel: (203) 434-1667. 13 rooms. $$. An 1850s Victorian mansion.

OLD MYSTIC

Red Brook Inn, 2750 Gold Star Highway, 06372, tel: (203) 572–0349. 11 rooms. $$. A pair of classic colonials on 7 acres.

OLD SAYBROOK

Saybrook Point Inn & Spa, 2 Bridge St, 06475, tel: (203) 395-2000, 1-800-243 0212. 62 rooms. $$$. Spiffily nautical, with a spa, pool, and water views.

POMFRET

Cobbscroft, Routes 44 and 169, 06258, tel: (203) 928-5560. 4 rooms. $ B&B. A white clapboard inn in a pristine town.

The Inn at Gwyn Careg, Route 44, 06230, tel: (203) 928-7758. 12 suites. $$$. A 1760 Colonial on 30 acres; spectacular gardens.

POMFRET CENTER

Karinn, 330 Pomfret St, 06259, tel: (203) 928-5492. 4 rooms. $ B&B. An 1885 inn and former girls' school, restored with eclectic flair.

PUTNAM

Felshaw Tavern, Five Mile River Rd, 06260, tel: 9203) 928-3467. 2 rooms. $ B&B. The original 1742 tavern, where revolutionaries supped.

RIDGEFIELD

Stonehenge Inn, Route 7, 06877, tel: (203) 438-6511. 16 rooms. $$. Colonial-style lakeside inn.

West Lane Inn, 22 West Lane, 06877, tel: (203) 438-7323. 20 rooms. $$ B&B. A colonial home with all the comforts.

SALISBURY

Under Mountain Inn, 482 Undermountain Rd, 06068, tel: (203) 435-0242. 7 rooms. $$. British hospitality in an 18th-century farmhouse

White Hart Inn, Routes 44 and 41, 06068, tel: (203) 435-0030. 23 rooms. $$. A century-old landmark at the center of a timeless town.

SIMSBURY

Simsbury 1820 House, 731 Hopmeadow St, 06089, tel: (203) 658-7658. 34 rooms. $$. A Colonial Revival manor, presiding over a pastoral hilltop.

The Simsbury Inn, 397 Hopmeadow St, tel: (203) 651-5700, (800) 634-2719. 100 rooms. $$–$$$$. A stylish new hotel with elegant traditional touches.

THOMPSON

Lord Thompson Manor, Route 200, 06277, tel: (203) 923-3886. 8 rooms. $$. An English manor house preserved from the Gilded Age

TOLLAND

The Old Babcock Tavern, 484 Mile Hill Rd (Route 31), 06084, tel: (203) 875-1239. 4 rooms. $ B&B. A circa 1720 ordinary, full of fireplaces.

WASHINGTON

Mayflower Inn, Route 47, 06793, tel: (203) 868-9466. 24 rooms. $$$$. The ultimate in country luxury, on 28 secluded acres.

WATERBURY

House on the Hill, 93 Woodlawn Terrace, 06710, tel: (203) 757-9901. 5 rooms. $$ B&B. An 1888 Victorian, furnished to the hilt.

WESTBROOK

Water's Edge Inn & Resort, 1525 Boston Post Rd, 06498, tel: (203) 399-5901, (800) 222-5901. 120 rooms. $$. A handsome new hotel, plus condos, overlooking a small stretch of private beach.

WEST CORNWALL

Hilltop Haven, Dibble Hill Rd, 06796, tel: (203) 672-6871. 2 rooms. $$. A stone house perched over the village, with lovely views.

WESTPORT

The Cotswold Inn, 76 Myrtle Ave, 06880, tel: (203) 226-3766. 4 rooms. $$$–$$$$. A pampering new inn which resembles an old one.

Inn at Longshore, 260 Compo Rd South, 06880, tel: (203) 226-3316. 12 rooms. $$. An old-fashioned inn on the sound.

The Inn at National Hall, 2 Post Rd West, 06880, tel: (203) 221-1351. 15 rooms. $$$$. An elegant new inn fashioned from a 19th-century Historic District building on the banks of the Saugatuck.

WOODBURY

Merryvale, 1204 Main St South, 06798, tel: (203) 266-0800. $ B&B. A 1789 home, decorated in an English country style, in Connecticut's "antiques capital."

WOODSTOCK

The Inn at Woodstock Hill, 94 Plaine Hill Rd, 06267, tel: (203) 928-0528. 19 rooms. $–$$. An 1816 Christopher Wren-style home, with rooms awash in country chintz.

MAINE

NB: Many of Maine's hotels and inns are open only in summer.

BAILEY ISLAND

The Driftwood Inn & Cottages, 04003, tel: (207) 833-4361. 29 rooms. $$ MAP. An old seaside inn, with a saltwater swimming pool.

BANGOR

Phenix Inn, 20 Broad St, 04401, tel: (207) 947-3850. 36 rooms. $. A restored 1873 downtown hotel.

BAR HARBOR

Bass Cottage in the Field, 04609, tel: (207) 288-3705. 10 rooms. $. Closed winter. A well-priced guest house with vestiges of glory days past.

Breakwater 1904, 45 Hancock St, 04609, tel: (207) 288-2313. 6 rooms. $$$–$$$$ B&B. A 39-room mock-Tudor mansion.

Cove Farm Inn (B&B), Crooked Rd, 04644, tel: (207) 288-5355. 9 rooms. $. A pastoral retreat with a personable local host.

Manor House Inn, 106 West St, 04609, tel: (207) 288-3759, (800) 437-0088. 14 rooms. $–$$. Closed winter. A Victorian inn surrounded by gardens.

Nannau-Seaside Bed & Breakfast, Lower Main St, 04609, tel: (207) 288-5575. 4 rooms. $–$$ B&B. Closed winter. A 1904 Shingle-style summer cottage set by the water.

The Tides, 119 West St, 04609, tel: (207) 288-4968. 3 rooms. $$$ B&B. Closed winter. An 1887 Greek Revival manor by Frenchman's Bay.

BETHEL

Bethel Inn & Country Club, Village Common, 04217, tel: (207) 824-2175, (800) 654-0125. 65 rooms. $$$–$$$$ MAP. A rambling yellow clapboard 1913 country inn, with tennis, golf, and a lake for water sports.

The Hammons House, 04217, tel: (207) 824-3170. 3 rooms. $ B&B. An 1850 home built by a congressman.

Holidae House, Main St, 04217, tel: (207) 824-3400. 5 rooms. $ B&B. A bargain, considering the bountiful breakfast.

Summit Hotel & Conference Center, Sunday River Resort, 04217, tel: (207) 834-3000, (800) 543-2SKI. 230 rooms. $–$$. A new slopeside condo-hotel with year-round heated outdoor pool.

Sunday River Inn, RFD 2, Box 1688, 04217, (207) 824-2410: 23 rooms. $$ MAP. A handsome ski dorm with its own cross-country center.

Telemark Inn, RFD 2, Box 800, 04217, (207) 836-2703. 5 rooms. $ B&B. A secluded 1900 stone mansion; llama treks offered.

BOOTHBAY HARBOR

The Green Shutters Inn and Cottages, Bay St, 04538, tel: (207) 633-2646, (800) 272-1028. 22 rooms. $ MAP. A comfy family resort featuring bountiful food and home baking.

Linekin Bay Resort, 04538, tel: (207) 633-2494. 70 rooms. $$ FAP. An old-fashioned seaside resort with complimentary sailing instruction.

Spruce Point Inn and Lodges, Grandview Ave, 04538, tel: (207) 633-4152, (800) 553-0289. 74 rooms. $$$–$$$$ MAP. A turn-of-the-century inn on a 100-acre peninsula.

BLUE HILL

Blue Hill Farm Country Inn, 04614, tel: 9207) 374-5126. 14 rooms. $ B&B. A rural retreat on 48 acres.

The Blue Hill Inn, Union St, 04614, tel: (207) 374-2844. 11 rooms. $$–$$$ MAP. An 1830s inn in a lovely village.

John Peters Inn, Peters Point (off Route 176), 04614, tel: (207) 374-2116. 14 rooms. $–$$ B&B. A columned 1815 mansion with a commanding view of the bay.

BRUNSWICK

Bethel Point Bed and Breakfast, Bethel Point Rd 2387, 04011, tel: (207) 725-1115. 3 rooms. $ B&B. An 1830s house on Hen Cove.

CAMDEN

Camden Harbor Inn, 83 Bayview St, 04843, tel: (207) 236-4200. 20 rooms. $$–$$$ B&B. A porch-encircled 1874 Victorian.

The Camden Maine Stay, 22 High St, 04843, tel: (207) 236-9636. 8 rooms. $ B&B. A Federal house serving elegant breakfasts.

Edgecomb-Coles House, 64 High St, 04843, tel: (207) 236-2336. 6 rooms. $$ B&B. An 1890s summer home with water views.

The High Tide Inn on the Ocean, Route 1, 04843, tel: (207) 236-3724. 30 rooms. $–$$. A pleasant motel complex near the beach and harbor.

Maine Stay Inn, 22 High St, 04853, tel: (207) 236-9636. 8 rooms. $–$$ B&B. An 1802 house with period furnishings.

Norumbega, 61 High St, 04843, tel: (207) 236-4646. 13 rooms. $$$–$$$$ B&B. An 1880s Victorian stone "castle" overlooking the bay.

The Reunion Inn, 49 Mechanic St, 04843, tel: (207) 236-1090. 3 rooms. $–$$. Contemporary comfort at the center of town.

Whitehall Inn, 52 High St, 04843, tel: (207) 236-3391. 50 rooms. $$ MAP. A venerable 1834 home, turned inn in 1901; local poet Edna St Vincent Millay gave her first reading here.

Windward House, 6 High St, 04843, tel: (207) 236-9656. 5 rooms. $–$$ B&B. Antiques, an English garden, and all-out breakfasts.

CAPE ELIZABETH

Inn by the Sea, 40 Bowery Beach Rd (Route 77), 04107, tel: (207) 799-3134, (800) 888-4287. 43 rooms. $$$$. A superb new resort connected by boardwalk to Crescent Beach.

CAPE NEDDICK

Wooden Goose Inn, Route 1, 03902, tel: (207) 363-5673. 7 rooms. $$ B&B. Closed January. A Victorian inn serving sumptuous breakfasts and teas.

CARABASSET VALLEY

Sugarloaf/USA, 04947, tel: (207) 237-2000, (800) THE LOAF. Over 400 rooms. New England's largest ski village attracts hikers, mountain-bikers, and golfers when the snow subsides.

CASTINE

The Castine Inn, 04421, tel: (207) 326-4365. 20 rooms. $ B&B. Closed winter. A 1898 clapboard inn with harbor views and a distinguished restaurant.

The Pentagoet Inn, Main St, 04421, tel: (207) 326-8616, (800) 834-1701. 20 rooms. $$$ MAP. A turreted Victorian beauty with *prix-fixe* feasts.

Village Inn, Main St, 04421, tel: (207) 326-9510. 4 rooms. $ B&B. Nothing-fancy rooms, but there's a wonderful in-house bakery.

CENTER LOVELL

Quisisana, 04016, tel: (207) 925-3500. 40 rooms. $$$$ MAP. A lakeside music-lovers' retreated, founded in 1917.

Westways on Kezar Lake, Route 5, 04016, tel: (207) 928-2663. 7 rooms. $$$ MAP. A baronial corporate retreat built in 1928.

CHEBEAGUE ISLAND

Chebeague Island Inn, 04107, tel: (207) 846-5155. 21 rooms. $–$$ B&B. A classic summer hotel, accessible by water taxi from Yarmouth.

CHESUNCOOK

Chesuncook Lake House, tel: (207) 745-5330. 12 rooms, 3 cabins. $$ MAP. Focal point of an 1864 logging village, accessible only by water or air.

DAMARISCOTTA MILLS

Mill Pond Inn, Route 215, tel: (207) 563-8014. 6 rooms. $ B&B. A 1780 clapboard house in a sleepy mill village.

DEER ISLE

The Pilgrim's Inn, 04622, tel: (207) 348-6615. 13 rooms. $$–$$$ MAP. A 1793 inn with seaside cottages.

EAST BOOTHBAY

Five Gables Inn, Murray Hill Rd, 04544, tel: (207) 633-4551, (800) 451-5048. 15 rooms. $–$$ B&B. A spiffed-up 1865 guesthouse by the bay.

EASTPORT

Weston House, 26 Boynton St, 04631, tel: (207) 853-2907. 5 rooms. $ B&B. This 1802 Federal manse, at the easternmost town in Maine, once hosted John James Audubon.

FREEPORT

The Bagley House, 04032, tel: (207) 865-6566, (800) 765-1772. 4 rooms. $ B&B. A 1772 Colonial in the country, 10 minutes from town.

Harraseeket Inn, 162 Main St, 04032, tel: (207) 865-9377, (800) 342-6423. 54 rooms. $$–$$$$. Luxury in a town of bargains.

FRYEBURG

Admiral Peary House, 9 Elm St, 04037, tel: (207) 935-3365. 4 rooms. $–$$ B&B. The Arctic explorer lived here in 1877–79, long before the addition of a hot tub and clay tennis court.

The Oxford House Inn, 105 Main St, 04037, tel: (207) 935-3442. 5 rooms. $ B&B. A turn-of-the-century house with a noted restaurant.

GEORGETOWN

Grey Havens Inn, Reid Park Rd, 04548, tel: (207) 371-2616. 14 rooms. $–$$ B&B. A Shingle-style 1904 inn on an oceanfront hillside.

GRAND LAKE STREAM

Weatherby's, 04637, tel: (207) 796-5558. 16 rooms. $$ MAP. Closed winter. A white clapboard lodge surrounded by cottages, by a world-renowned fishing hole.

GREENVILLE

Greenville Inn, Norris St, 04441, tel: (207) 695-2206. 12 rooms. $. A lumber baron's opulent 1895 mansion, overlooking Moosehead Lake.

HANCOCK

The Crocker House Country Inn, Hancock Point Rd, 04640, tel: (207) 422-6806. 20 rooms. $ B&B. On the water, just beyond the tourist tide.

Le Domaine Restaurant and Inn, Route 1, 04604, tel: (207) 422-3395. 7 rooms. $$$ MAP. An unpretentious, authentic *auberge*.

HULLS COVE

Inn at Canoe Point, 04644, tel: (207) 288-9511. 5 rooms. $$–$$$ B&B. A secluded Tudor mansion dramatically perched on a rocky point near Bar Harbor.

ISLE AU HAUT

The Keeper's House, 04645, tel: (207) 367-2261. 4 rooms. $$$$ MAP. A turn-of-the-century lighthouse keeper's house, on an island off Stonington.

ISLEBORO

Dark Harbor House, 04848, tel: (207) 734-6669. 7 rooms. $$–$$$ B&B. A waterside 1890s mansion on an island accessible by ferry.

KENNEBUNKPORT

Bufflehead Cove, 04046, tel: (207) 967-3879. 5 rooms. $–$$ B&B. A turn-of-the-century summer home overlooking the Kennebunk River.

Captain Jefferds Inn, Pearl St, 04046, tel: (207) 967-2311. 15 rooms. $–$$ B&B. Closed winter. An antique-filled 1804 Federal home, with three carriage-house suites.

Captain Lord Mansion, 04046, tel: (207) 967-3141, (800) 522-3141. 16 rooms. $–$$$ B&B. An elegant 1812 inn topped by an octagonal cupola.

The Colony, Ocean Ave and Kings Rd, 04046, tel: (207) 967-3331. 139 rooms. $$–$$$$ FAP. A coastal grand hotel built in 1914.

Flakeyard Farm, South Main St, 04046, tel: (207) 967-5965. 2 rooms. $ B&B. A 1737 Georgian house within walking distance of Dock Square.

Green Heron Inn, Ocean Ave, 04046, tel: (207) 967-3315. 11 rooms. $–$$ B&B. Plain and pleasant lodgings; outstanding breakfasts.

The Inn at Harbor Head, Pier Rd, 04046, tel: (207) 967-5564. 5 rooms. $$–$$$ B&B. Luxury lodgings and gourmet breakfasts, alongside quaint Cape Porpoise harbor.

Old Fort Inn, Old Fort Avenue, 04046, tel: (207) 967-5353, (800) 826-3678. 16 rooms. $$–$$$$. Closed winter. Country decor in a converted barn and brick carriage house.

The White Barn Inn, Beach St, tel: (207) 967-2321. 24 rooms. $$–$$$$. *Relais et Châteaux*-level luxury.

KINGFIELD

The Herbert Hotel, 04947, tel: (207) 265-2000, (800) THE-HERB. 33 rooms. $. This columned hotel, heralded upon its 1918 debut as "a Palace in the Wilderness," is now the unofficial heart of town.

Three Stanley Avenue, 04947, tel: (207) 265-5541. 6 rooms. $ B&B. Comfy, country-style rooms, and possibly the state's best regional restaurant.

KITTERRY POINT

Harbour Watch Bed and Breakfast, 6 Follett Lane, 03905, tel: (207) 439-3242. 4 rooms. $ B&B. Closed winter. A 1750s white clapboard house situated at the southernmost point in Maine.

MACHIASPORT
The Gutsy Gull, Main St and Phinney Lane, 04655, tel: (207) 255-8633. 5 rooms. $ B&B. An 1850s sea captain's house beside the Machias River.

MONHEGAN ISLAND
The Island Inn, Ocean View Terrace, 04852, tel: (207) 596-0371. 45 rooms. $ MAP. Turn-of-the-century simplicity on a painter's dream of an island.
Tribler Cottage, 04852, tel: (207) 594-2445. 5 rooms. $. Plain and appealing accommodations, some with kitchen.

MOUNT DESERT
Seal Cove Farm, Star Route 304, 04660, tel: (207) 244-7781. 3 rooms. $ B&B. A small working farm, appealing to families.

NEWAGEN
Newagen Seaside Inn, Route 27, 04522, tel: (207) 633-5242. 50 rooms. $$$–$$$$ B&B. Summer only. An old-fashioned inn, with saltwater and freshwater pools, at the tip of Southport Island.

NEWCASTLE
The Newcastle Inn, River Rd, tel: (207) 563-5685, 1-800-323 8669. 15 rooms. $$–$$$ MAP. A traditional inn, serving contemporary candlelit dinners.

NEW HARBOR
Gosnold Arms, Northside Rd, 04554, tel: (207) 677-3727. 25 rooms. $$ MAP. Shoreside rusticity since 1925.

NORTHEAST HARBOR
Asticou Inn, Route 3, 04662, tel: (207) 276-3341. 51 rooms. $$$$ MAP. A cultured carryover from Bar Harbor's heyday as Society's summer playground.
Harbourside Inn, 04664, tel: (207) 276-3272. 14 rooms. $–$$$$. A Shingle-style 1889 inn beside Acadia National Park.

OAKLAND
Bear Spring Camps, Route 1, 04963, tel: (207) 397-2341. 32 rooms. $ MAP. Lakeside cottages prized for serious fishing.

OGUNQUIT
The Anchorage, 55 shore Rd, 03907, tel: (207) 646-9384. 220 rooms. $–$$$. A modern waterside resort with classic detailing.
Cliff House Resort, Bald Head Cliff (off Route 1), 03907, tel: (207) 361-1000. 164 rooms. $$$. Set on 70 acres with ravishing ocean views.
The Dunes on the Waterfront, Route 1, 03907, tel: (207) 646-2612. 36 rooms. $–$$. Closed winter. A 1930s cottage complex on the tidal Ogunquit River; swimming dock, with rowboats.
Gorges Grant Hotel, 239 Route 1, 03907, tel: (207) 646-7003, (800) 646-500. 56 rooms. $–$$. A sleek contemporary hotel with traditionalist furnishings.
The Morning Dove, 30 Bourne Lane, 03907, tel: (207) 646-3891. 3 rooms. $–$$ B&B. A lovingly decorated 1860s farmhouse.
Sparhawk Resort, Shore Rd, 03907, tel: (207) 646-5562. 12 rooms. $$–$$$. A luxury motel with beach views and private decks.

ORLAND
Alamoosook Lodge, 04472, tel: (207) 469-6393. 6 rooms. $ B&B. A comfy lakeside inn.

PORTLAND
The Inn at Park Spring, 135 Spring St, 04101, tel: (207) 744-1059. 7 rooms. $ B&B. A charming 19th-century townhouse, near the Portland Art Museum.
Pomegranate Inn, 49 Neal St, 04101, tel: (207) 772-1006, (800) 356-0408. 8 rooms. $$ B&B. An art-filled home in Portland's residential West End.
The Portland Regency in the Old Port, 20 Milk St, 04101, tel: (207) 774-4200, (800) 543-7804. 95 rooms. $$. A snazzily rehabbed 19th-century armory, centrally located.

PROUTS NECK
Black Point Inn, 510 Black Point Rd, tel: (207) 883-4126, (800) 258-0003. 80 rooms. $$$$ FAP. An 1870s resort, on a peninsula favored by Winslow Homer.

RANGELEY
Country Club Inn, 04970, tel: (207) 864-3831. 20 rooms. $$ MAP. Picture-window views of the lake; swimming pool and golf course.
Rangeley Inn and Motor Lodge, Main St, 04970, tel: (207) 864-3341, (800) MOMENTS. 50 rooms. $–$$. An old-fashioned lakeside inn, with some modern motel units.

ROCKPORT
Samoset Resort, 220 Warrenton St, 04856, tel: (207) 594-2511, (800) 341-1530. 150 rooms. $$–$$$$. A full-scale, seaside golf resort.
Sign of the Unicorn, 191 Beauchamp Ave, 04856, tel: (207) 236-4042. 4 rooms. $ B&B. A comfy home, with children's loft.

ROCKWOOD
The Birches, 04478, tel: (207) 534-7305. 33 rooms. $ B&B; MAP/FAP available. A rustic 1940s lakeside lodge with log cabins.
Maynard-in-Maine, 04478, tel: (207) 534-7702. 13 rooms. $, or $$ MAP. Closed winter. A classic hunting camp, founded in 1919.

SARGENTVILLE
Oakland House, Herricks, 04673, tel: (207) 349-8521, (800) 359-RELAX. 33 rooms. $$–$$$ MAP. An 1889 complex with waterside cottages.

SEARSPORT
The Homeport Inn, Route 1, 04974, tel: (207) 548-2259. 11 rooms. $ B&B. A cupola-topped 1860s captain's house in the "antiques capital" of Maine.

SOUTH BROOKSVILLE
Buck's Harbor Inn, 04617, tel: (207) 326-8660. 7 rooms. $ B&B. Turn-of-the-century charm in a quiet seaside town.

SOUTH CASCO
Migis Lodge, 04077, tel: (207) 655-4524. 32 rooms. $$$–$$$$ FAP. Closed winter and spring. An old-fashioned 100-acre lakeside resort.

SOUTHWEST HARBOR
The Claremont, 04679, tel: (207) 244-5036. 41 rooms. $$–$$$ MAP. Mount Desert Island's oldest grand hotel, built in 1884.

SPENCER LAKE

Falcon Lodge, tel: (800) 825-8234. 8 rooms. $$$$. Remote and pricy, a luxurious retreat for those who prefer to "rough it" in style.

SPRUCE HEAD

Craignair Inn at Clark Island, 04859, tel: (207) 594-7644. 23 rooms. $ B&B. Closed February. A cheerful shorefront inn near a nature preserve.

STOCKTON SPRINGS

The Hichborn Inn, Church St, 04981, tel: (207) 567-4183. 4 rooms. $ B&B. An Italianate mansion in an old ship-building village.

STONINGTON

Captain's Quarters Inn and Motel, 04681, tel: (207) 367-2420. 15 rooms. $. Waterside lodgings in a scarcely touristed harbor town.

STRATTON

Widow's Walk, Route 27, 04982, tel: (207) 246-6901. 6 rooms. $ B&B. A quirky 1892 Queen Anne mansion, popular with hikers on the last leg of the Appalachian Trail.

SULLIVAN HARBOR

Island View Inn, Route 1, 04689, tel: (207) 422-3031. 7 rooms. & B&B. Closed winter. A shingled turn-of-the-century "cottage" with private beach and views of Mount Desert.

SUNSET

Goose Cove Lodge, Deer Isle, 04683, tel: (207) 348-2508. 22 rooms. $$$ MAP. Closed winter. An informal family resort in a remote natural setting.

TENANTS HARBOR

The East Wind Inn and Meeting House, 04860, tel: (207) 372-6366. 26 rooms. $–$$ MAP. Harborside, in an unspoiled fishing village.

TOPSHAM

Walker-Wilson House, 2 Melcher Place, 04086, tel: (207) 729-0715. 4 rooms. $ B&B. An 1803 Federal "four-square" house.

VINALHAVEN

Tidewater Motel, Main St, 04863, tel: (207) 863-4618. 11 rooms. $. A harborside motel on a moneyed island ideal for biking.

WATERFORD

Lake House, Routes 35 and 37, 04088, tel (207) 583-4182. 5 rooms. $–$$ B&B. A centuries-old staging inn in an historic spa town.

WELD

Kawanhee Inn Lakeside Lodge, Lake Webb, 04285, tel: (207) 778-4306. 22 rooms. $. Closed winter. A fishing lodge with classic cottages.

WILSONS MILLS

Bosebuck Mountain Camps, Route 16, 03579, tel: (207) 243-2945. 11 rooms. $$ FAP. Closed winter. A fishing camp set amid a 200,000-acre lumber tract.

WISCASSET

Squire Tarbox Inn, R. R. 2, Box 620, 04578, tel: (207) 882-7693. 11 rooms. $$–$$$ B&B or MAP. A colonial country farmhouse, with delicious home-grown provisions.

YORK

Dockside Guest Quarters, Harris Island Rd, 03909, tel: (207) 363-2868. 22 rooms. $–$$. A classic 19th-century seacoast home flanked by cottages.

YORK BEACH

ViewPoint Inn, 229 Nubble Rd, 03910, tel: (207) 363-2661. 10 rooms. $$$. On the rocky shore, with views of Nubble Light.

YORK HARBOR

Stage Neck Inn, off Route 1A, 03911, tel: (207) 363-3850, (800) 222-3238. 60 rooms. $$–$$$. A contemporary seaside resort known for low-key luxury.

York Harbor Inn, Route 1A, 03911, tel: (207) 363-5119, (800) 343-3869. 32 rooms. $–$$. A fresh seaside inn which accrued around a 1637 sail loft.

MASSACHUSETTS

AMHERST

The Lord Jeffrey Inn, On the Common, 01002, tel: (413) 253-2576. 50 rooms. $–$$. A traditionalist Colonial Revival-style inn at the center of town.

BARNSTABLE

Ashley Manor, 3660 Route 6A, 02630, tel: (508) 362-8044. 6 rooms. $$ B&B. A 1699 Colonial mansion shielded behind massive private hedges.

Beechwood, 2839 Route 6A, 02630, tel: (508) 362-6618. $$ B&B. A 1853 Victorian with deep porches shaded by massive beech trees.

Charles Hinckley House, 8 Scudder Lane, 02630, tel: (508) 362-9924. 5 rooms. $$ B&B. Period rooms in an 1809 Federal house; lavish breakfasts.

Crocker Tavern Bed and Breakfast, 3095 Route 6A, 02630, tel: (508) 362-5115. $ B&B. A 1750 ordinary, tastefully renovated.

BOSTON

Boston Harbor Hotel, 70 Rowes Wharf, 02109, tel: (617) 439-7000, (800) 752-7077. 230 rooms. $$$$. A modern beauty with Old World charm, perched on the harbor.

The Bostonian Hotel, 4 Faneuil Hall Marketplace, 02110, tel: (617) 523-3600, (800) 343-0922. 152 rooms. $$$$. A mix of modern and historic, overlooking Quincy Market.

Boston Park Plaza Hotel, 64 Arlington St, 02117, tel: (617) 426-2000, (800) 225-2008. 966 rooms. $$. A huge hotel at the hub of the Hub.

Copley Plaza Hotel, 138 James Avenue, 02116, tel: (617) 267-5300, (800) 678-8946. 373 rooms. $$$$. A 1912 grand hotel with plenty of romance.

Copley Square Hotel, 47 Huntington Avenue, 02116, tel: (617) 536-9000, (800) 225-7062. 143 rooms. $$. Centrally located; affordable.

Eliot Hotel, 370 Commonwealth Avenue, 02115, tel: (617) 267-1607. 100 rooms. $$. Convenient to both Back Bay and the Fenway.

Four Seasons, 200 Boylston St, 02116, tel: (617) 338-4000. 288 rooms. $$$$. The standard-setter for luxury.

The Lenox Hotel, 710 Boylston St, 02116, tel: (617) 536-5300, (800) 225-7676. 222 rooms. $$.

Well situated for shopping, with Copley Place and Newbury Street on either side.

Le Meridien, 250 Franklin St, 02109, tel: (617) 451-1900, (800) 543-4300. 326 rooms. $$$$. A modern hotel built atop a Renaissance Revival 1922 bank; fabulous French service.

The MidTown Hotel, 220 Huntington Avenue, 02115, tel: (617) 262-1000, (800) 343-1177. 159 rooms. $$. One of Boston's better deals, with an outdoor pool.

Newbury Guest House, 29 Newbury St, 02116, tel: (617) 536-0290. $$. An 1881 townhouse/inn right on the "street of dreams."

The Omni Parker House, 60 School St, 02108, tel: (617) 227-8600 or 1-800-843 6664. 535 rooms. $$$. Hawthorne, Whitier, Emerson and Longfellow used to conduct literary salons at this grand hotel soon after it opened in 1854.

The Ritz-Carlton Hotel, 15 Arlington St, 02117, tel: (617) 536-5700, (800) 241-3333. 278 rooms. $$$$. White-glove elegance, with the lovely Public Garden at its doorstep.

Swissotel Boston, 1 Avenue de Lafayette, 02110, tel: (617) 451-2600, (800) 621-9200. 500 rooms. $$$$. Modern luxury, convenient to the financial and theatre districts, as well as the Common.

Terrace Townehouse, 60 Chandler St, 02116, tel: (617) 350-6520. 4 rooms. $$. Dazzlingly decorated rooms in the South End.

Tremont House, 225 Tremont St, 02116, tel: (617) 426-1400, 1-800-331 9998. 281 rooms. $$. Nicely refurbished, in the thick of the theatre district.

BREWSTER

Bramble Inn, 2019 Main St, 02631, tel: (508) 896-7644. 12 rooms. $$. Three houses (1792–1861) with distinctive decors.

Brewster Farmhouse Inn, 716 Main St, 02631, tel: (508) 896-3910, (800) 892-3910. 5 rooms. $$ B&B. A Greek Revival home redecorated in a breezy California style; gourmet breakfasts.

The Captain Freeman Inn, 15 Breakwater Rd, 02631 tel: (508) 896-7481, (800) 843-4664. 12 bedrooms. $$$ B&B. A luxurious 1866 Victorian with spacious rooms (some feature private jacuzzis) and outdoor pool.

High Brewster, 964 Satucket Rd, 02631, tel: (508) 896-3636. 9 rooms. $$$. A 1738 homestead on 31/2 peaceful acres overlooking a mill pond.

Old Sea Pines Inn, 2553 Main St, 02631, tel: (508) 896-6114. A 1907 Shingle-style mansion that once served as a girls' boarding school; the modern annex is wheelchair-accessible.

CAMBRIDGE

The Charles Hotel, 1 Bennett St, 02138, tel: (617) 864-1200, (800) 882-1818. 299 rooms. $$$. Airy, neo-traditional rooms, some overlooking the name-sake river; right in Harvard Square.

The Inn at Harvard, 1201 Massachusetts Avenue, 02138, tel: (617) 491-2222, (800) 528-0444. 113 rooms. $$. Graham Gund designed this intimate four-story inn encircling a peaceful atrium.

CENTERVILLE

The Inn at Fernbrook, 481 Main St, 02632, tel: (508) 775-4334. 5 rooms. $$. An elegant 1881 estate with a sweetheart garden designed by Frederick Law Olmsted.

CHATHAM

The Captain's House Inn of Chatham, 371 Old Harbor Rd, 02633, tel: (508) 945-0127. 16 rooms. $$$ B&B. Luxurious traditional decor; silver-service tea in the garden room.

Chatham Bars Inn, Shore Rd, 02633, tel: (508) 945-0096. $$$$ MAP. A 1914 private hunting lodge turned grand hotel, now grander than ever.

The Cranberry Inn at Chatham, 359 Main St, 02633, tel: (508) 945-9232, (800) 332-4667. 14 rooms. $$ B&B. An 1830s redecorated with an eye to spaciousness and luxury.

Moses Nickerson House, 364 Old Harbor Rd, 02633, tel: (508) 945-5859, (800) 628-6972. $$ B&B. An 1839 captain's house with lavish gardens and rooms.

Pleasant Bay Village Resort Motel, 1191 Orleans Rd, 02633, tel: (508) 945-1153, (800) 547-1011. 58 rooms. An unmotelish complex with elaborate gardens.

Wequasset Inn, Pleasant Bay, 02163, tel: (508) 432-5400, (800) 352-7169. 103 rooms. $$$. A country club-like setting, with tennis courts, pool, bay beach.

CONCORD

Colonial Inn, 48 Monument Square, 01742, tel: (508) 369-9200. 47 rooms. $$. A 1716 inn on Concord's town common.

Hawthorne Inn, 462 Lexington Rd, 01742, tel: (508) 369-5610. 7 rooms. $$ B&B. In the historic district, opposite Hawthorne's Wayside.

CUMMINGTON

Cumworth Farm, Route 112, 01026, tel: (413) 634-5529. 6 rooms. $ B&B. A hip-roofed farmhouse in the unspoiled countryside.

Swift River Inn, 151 South St, 01026, tel: (413) 634-5751. 22 rooms. $$. This historic 600-acre farm makes a luxurious country retreat.

Windfields Farm, Windsor Bush Rd, 01026, tel: (413) 684-3786. 2 rooms. $ B&B. Closed early spring. An 1830 Federal farmhouse adjoining a 1,500-acre Audubon sanctuary.

CUTTYHUNK

Allen House Inn, 02713, tel: (508) 996-9292. 14 rooms. $$. An unassuming country inn on an island untouched by development.

DENNIS

Isaiah Hall B&B Inn, 152 Whig St, 02638, tel: (508) 385-9928, (800) 736-0160. 11 rooms. $. Stars from the Cape Playhouse favor this charming 1857 home.

EAST FALMOUTH

Bed & Breakfast of Waquoit Bay, 176 Waquoit Highway, 02536, (508) 457-0084. 4 rooms. $ B&B. A 1920s bungalow set beside the peaceful Child's River.

EASTHAM

Over Look Inn, 3085 Route 6, 02642, tel: (508) 225-1886, (800) 356-1121. $$ B&B. Scottish hospitality in a colorful 1869 Victorian near the Salt Pond Visitors Center.

Whalewalk Inn, 220 Bridge Rd, 02642, tel: (508) 225-0617. 13 rooms. $$ B&B. An 1830s Greek Revival captain's house, decorated with breezy panache.

EAST ORLEANS

Nauset House Inn, 143 Beach Rd, 02643, tel: (508) 255-2195. 14 rooms. $ B&B. An 1810 farmhouse (with a turn-of-the-century conservatory) on the moors near magnificent Nauset Beach.

EAST SANDWICH

Wingscorton Farm (B&B), 11 Wing Blvd, 02537, tel: (508) 888-0534. 6 rooms. $$ B&B. A 1758 Federal working farmstead with original paneled bedrooms.

EDGARTOWN

Charlotte Inn, 27 S. Summer St, 02539, tel: (508) 627-4751. 26 rooms. $$$$. An exquisite country inn encompassing 5 buildings (18th-century to new) romantically decorated in various styles.

Colonial Inn, 38 N Water St, 02539, tel: (508) 627-4711, (800) 627-4701. 42 rooms. $$$. Nicely updated and centrally located, this shingled 1911 hotel is as vital as ever.

Harbor View Hotel, 131 N. Water St, 02539, tel: (508) 627.4333, (800) 225-6005. 124 rooms. $$$$. A lavishly renovated 1891 shingled grand hotel, with heated pool, near Lighthouse Beach.

Point Way Inn, 104 Main St, 02539, tel: (508) 627-8633, (800) 942-9569. 15 rooms. $$$$ B&B. A cozy, convivial 1840 Federal sea captain's house.

FALMOUTH

Coonamesset Inn, Jones Rd and Gifford St, 02540, tel: (508) 548-2300. 24 rooms. $$. A fixture since the turn of the century, and the social hub of town.

Mostly Hall (B&B), 27 Main St, 02540, tel: (508) 548-3786. 6 rooms. $$ B&B. An 1849 plantation-style mansion (built by a seafarer to please a homesick wife) with large, handsome, high-ceilinged rooms and friendly, knowledgeable hosts.

FALMOUTH HEIGHTS

Peacock's Inn on the Sound, 313 Grand Ave South, 02540, tel: (508) 457-9666.$$ B&B. An 1880 shingled cottage on a bluff overlooking the Sound.

GAY HEAD

The Outermost Inn, Gay Head, 02535, tel: (508) 645.3511. 7 rooms. $$$. A handsome modern house with country comforts and staggering sea views.

GLOUCESTER

Bass Rocks Ocean Inn, 103 Atlantic Rd, 01930, tel: (508) 283-7600. 48 rooms. $$. A motel looking straight out to sea.

GREAT BARRINGTON

Elling's Guest House, Route 23, 01230, tel: (413) 528-4103. 4 rooms. $ B&B. A cozy 1742 frame house.

Round Hill Farm, 17 Round Hill Rd, 01230, tel: (413) 528-3366. 4 rooms. $–$$ B&B. A pair of hilltop horse farms; an 1820s dairy barn houses two luxury suites.

The Windflower Inn, Egremont Star Route 65, 01230, tel: (413) 528-2720. 13 rooms. $$$ MAP. A turn-of-the-century country estate.

HARWICH PORT

The Augustus Snow House, 528 Main St, 02646, tel: (508) 430-0528, (800) 339-0528. $$ B&B. Victorian splendor in a 1901 Queen Anne mansion near the Sound.

Beach House Inn, 4 Braddock Lane, 02646, tel: (508) 432-4444, (800) 870-4405. 12 rooms. $$. All the comforts of home (air-conditioning, color TV), right on the beach.

HYANNIS

Sea Breeze Inn, 397 Sea St, 02601, tel: (508) 771-7213. 14 rooms. A cheerful inn a short stroll from the Sound.

The Simmons Homestead Inn, 288 Scudder Ave, 02601, tel: (508) 778-4499, (800) 637-1649). 10 rooms. $$. An 1820s captain's house done up with playful animal motifs.

LENOX

The Apple Tree Inn, 224 West St, 01240, tel: (413) 637-1477. 11 rooms. $$–$$$$. A 22-acre hilltop estate with heated pool, within earshot of Tanglewood.

Blantyre, Route 20, 01240, tel: (617) 637-3556. 23 rooms. $$$$. An opulent mock-Tudor mansion on 85 manicured acres.

Canyon Ranch, Bellefontaine, Kemble St, 01240, tel: (413) 637-4100, (800) 742-9000. 120 rooms. $$$$. New England's most elaborate spa occupies an 1890s cottage modeled on Le Petit Trianon.

Cliffwood Inn, 25 Cliffwood St, 01240, tel: (413) 637-3330. 7 rooms. $$$ B&B. An 1890 colonial mansion with outdoor swimming pool.

Garden Gables, 141 Main St, 01240, tel: (413) 637-0193. 12 rooms. $$ B&B. Country charm in a 1780s, and one of Lenox's better deals.

Gables Inn, 103 Walker St, 01240, tel: (413) 637-3416. 18 rooms. $$$. Edith Wharton stayed at this lavish Victorian mansion while building her own.

Rookwood Inn, 19 Stockbridge Rd, 02140, tel: (413) 637-9750. 19 rooms. $$ B&B. An 1886 "painted lady" at the center of town.

The Village Inn, 16 Church St, 01240, tel: (413) 637-0020, (800) 253-0917. 30 rooms. $$–$$$. A 1771 inn, comfortably furnished.

Walker House, 74 Walker St, 01240, tel: (413) 637-1271. 8 rooms. $$ B&B. A cultural mecca; private recitals.

Wheatleigh, West Hawthorne, 01240, tel: (413) 637-0610. 17 rooms. $$$$. An 1893 Italian palazzo on 22 acres.

MARBLEHEAD

Harbor Light Inn, 48 Washington St, 01945, tel: (617) 631-2186. 12 rooms. $–$$$ B&B. A formally decorated 18th-century house.

Spray Cliff on the Ocean, 25 Spray Avenue, 01945, tel: (508) 744-8924, (800) 626-1530. 7 rooms. $$–$$$ B&B. A 1919 Tudor mansion near the beach.

MARSTONS MILLS
Inn at the Mills, 71 Route 149, 02648, tel: (508) 428-2967. A beautifully decorated 1780 house overlooking a private pond.

MENEMSHA
Beach Plum Inn, off North Rd, 02552,, tel: (508) 645.9454. 11 rooms. $$$$. An airy white farmhouse with gardens descending toward the harbor.

Menemsha Inn and Cottages, off North Rd, 02552, tel: (508) 645.2521. 15 rooms. $$. Peaceful simplicity, on 10 green acres with water views.

NANTUCKET
The Four Chimneys Inn (B&B), 38 Orange St, 02554, tel: (508) 228-1912. 10 rooms. $$ B&B. A surprisingly opulent 1835 B&B with a Japanese garden.

Jared Coffin House, 29 Broad St, 02554, tel: (508) 228-2400. 60 rooms. $$$. A grand 1845 mansion, and several adjoining buildings, constitute a popular island inn.

Martin's Guest House (B&B), 61 Centre St, 02554, tel: (508) 228-0678. 13 rooms. $ B&B. Reasonably priced, this 1803 mariner's home is one of the prettiest and most congenial of the many historic B&Bs in town.

Robert B. Johnson AYH-Hostel, Surfside, tel: (508) 228-0433. 50 beds. $. Separate-sex dorm rooms in an 1874 lifesaving station.

The Summer House, Ocean Ave, Siasconset, tel: (508) 257-4577. 8 cottages. $$$$. A cluster of rose-covered (and renovated) fishing shacks overlooking the sea.

The Wauwinet, 120 Wauwinet Rd, Wauwinet, tel: (508) 228-0145, (800) 426-8718. 35 rooms. $$$$. A fabulously refurbished 1850 hotel: luxurious, secluded, and very expensive.

Wharf Cottages, New Whale St, 02554, tel: (508) 228-4620. 25 cottages. $$$$. Small but stylish, and right on the water.

NEWBURYPORT
The Clark Currier Inn, 45 Green St, 01950, tel: (508) 465-8363. 6 rooms. $ B&B. An 1803 shipbuilder's home in the Federal mode.

The Morrill Place Inn, 209 High St, 01950, tel: (508) 462-2808. 10 rooms. $ B&B. A Federalist mansion, lavishly decorated.

Windsor House, 3 Federal St, 01950, tel: (508) 462-3778. 6 rooms. $$ B&B. A 1786 house with a British bent.

NEW MALBOROUGH
Old Inn on the Green, Gedney Farm, 01230, tel: (413) 229-7924, (800) 752-1896. 14 rooms. $$–$$$$. Antique-furnished rooms in a ca. 1760 stagecoach inn, plus luxury suites in a former Normandy-style cow barn.

NORTHAMPTON
The Hotel Northampton, 36 King St, 01060, tel: (413) 584-3100. 72 rooms. $$. A handsome 1926 hotel in the heart of town.

NORTHFIELD
Northfield Country House, School St, 01360, tel:

(413) 498-2692. 7 rooms. $ B&B. A grand turn-of-the-century summer home.

OAK BLUFFS
The Oak House, Seaview Ave, tel: (508) 693-4187. 10 rooms. $$$ B&B. A lavish Queen Anne house overlooking Nantucket Sound.

OLD DEERFIELD
Deerfield Inn, Main St, 01342, tel: (413) 774-5587. 23 rooms. $$. A traditionally appointed inn surrounded by historic houses.

The Tea House, Main St, 01342, tel: (413) 772-2675. 2 rooms. $ B&B. An 1840 Colonial with luxurious rooms and elaborate breakfasts.

OSTERVILLE
East Bay Lodge, 199 East Bay Rd., 02655, tel: (508) 428-5200, (800) 933-2782. 18 rooms. $$. Traditional elegance in a seaside bastion of old money.

PLYMOUTH
The Governor Bradford Motor Inn, 98 Water St, 02360, tel: (508) 746-6200. 94 rooms. $$. A motel right on the historic (and heavily trafficked) harbor.

Jackson-Russell-Whitfield House, 26 North St, 02360, tel: (508) 746-5289. 3 rooms. $ B&B. A charming 1782 home with antique furnishings.

The John Carver Inn, 25 Summer St, 02360, tel: (508) 746-7100. 79 rooms. $. An immaculate modern hotel, near the sights.

PROVINCETOWN
Captain Lysander Inn (B&B), 96 Commercial St, 02657, tel: (508) 487-2253. 12 rooms. $. An 1850s captain's house in the sedate West End.

Watermark Inn, 603 Commercial St, 02657, tel: (508) 487-0165, (800) 734-0165. $$$ B&B. A dazzling, architect-designed contemporary seaside inn in P-town's quiet East End.

White Horse Inn, 500 Commercial St, 02657, tel: (508) 487-1790. An 18th-century captain's house inn shaped by Provincetown's 20th-century artistic history.

ROCKPORT
Addison Choate Inn, 49 Broadway, 01966, tel: (508) 546-7543. 8 rooms. $$ B&B. Lovely summery decor and a quiet in-town setting.

Eden Pines Inn, Eden Rd, 01966, tel: (508) 546-2505. 8 rooms. $$ B&B. A cliffside mansion with dramatic ocean views.

Linden Tree Inn, 26 King St, 01966, tel: (508) 546-2494, (800) 794-2494. 18 rooms. $ B&B. A captain's home with reasonably priced rooms and an innkeeper who loves to bake.

Seacrest Manor, 131 Marmion Way, 01966, tel: (508) 546-2211. 8 rooms. $$ B&B. Closed winter. A comfortable inn with gardens looking out to the sea.

Seaward Inn, Marmion Way, 01966, tel: (508) 546-3471. 38 rooms. $–$$ B&B, $$–$$$ MAP. Closed winter. A welcoming summer house on a beautifully landscaped seaside ledge.

Yankee Clipper Inn, 96 Granite St, 01966, tel: (508) 546-3407, (800) 545-3699. 27 rooms. $$$. A Georgian mansion on an ocean promontory, an 1840 neo-classic mansion designed by Charles Bulfinch, plus a modern waterwide addition; heated saltwater pool.

SALEM
Hawthorne Hotel, 18 Washington Square West, 01970, tel: (508) 744-4080. 89 rooms. $–$$$. A centrally located 1920s hotel: the high floors have harbor views.

SANDWICH
Dan'l Webster Inn, Main St, 02563, tel: (508) 888-3622, (800)444-3566. 47 rooms. $$. A large luxury hotel on the site of an historic tavern.
The Inn at Sandwich Center, 118 Tupper Rd, 02563, tel: (508) 888-6958. 5 rooms. $ B&B. A 1750s saltbox, with bright, airy bedrooms.
Isaiah Jones Homestead, 165 Main St, 02563, tel: (508) 888-9115. 5 rooms. $$ B&B. Victorian opulence and candle-lit country breakfasts.
Summer House, 158 Main St, 02563, tel: (508) 888-4991. 5 rooms. $ B&B. An 1835 Greek Revival house with large, airy bedrooms.
The Village Inn at Sandwich, 4 Jarves St, 02563, tel: (508) 833-0363. 8 rooms. $ B&B. An 1837 Federal home decorated in a spare, fresh style.

SHEFFIELD
Staveleigh House, South Main St, 01257, tel: (413) 229-2129. 5 rooms. $ B&B. An 1821 parson's home, on spacious grounds beside the Housatonic.

SOUTH LEE
Merrell Tavern Inn, Main St (Route 102), 01260, tel: (413) 243-1794. 10 rooms. $$. An authentically restored 1794 stagecoach tavern, in a rural riverside setting.

SOUTH SUDBURY
Longfellow's Wayside Inn, Wayside Inn Rd, 01776, tel: (508) 443-8846. 10 rooms. $. A mid-18th century tavern, close to Boston and reasonably priced.

STOCKBRIDGE
The Inn at Stockbridge, Route 7, 01262, tel: (413) 298-3337. 8 rooms. $$ B&B. A formal Georgian-style "cottage" near Tanglewood.
The Red Lion Inn, tel: (413) 298-5545. 108 rooms. $$. A grand old inn (since 1773) at the center of a Normal Rockwell town.

STURBRIDGE
Publick House Historic Resort, 01566, tel: (508) 347-9555. 125 rooms. $$. A cluster of historic houses, plus a modern annex, close by Old Sturbridge Village.

TRURO
Little America AYH-Hostel, Castle and Meetinghouse Roads, 02666, tel: (508) 349-3889. 42 beds. $. A white clapboard house (a former Coast Guard Station) only a few hundred yards from a pristine beach.

UXBRIDGE
Charles Capron House, 2 Capron St, 01569, (508) 278-2214. 3 rooms. $. An 1865 mill owner's abode along the Blackstone Canal, an historic Industrial Age preserve scarcely touched by tourism.

VINEYARD HAVEN
Deux Noisettes, 114 Main St, (508) 693.0253. 4 rooms. $$ B&B. A handsome 1840 Greek Revival house with spacious bedrooms, each with fireplace.

WEST DENNIS
The Beach House, 61 Uncle Stephen's Rd, 02670, tel: (508) 398-4575. 7 rooms. $ B&B. Bright and airy, and right on the beach.
Lighthouse Inn, 4 Lighthouse Rd, 02670, tel: (508) 398-2244. ·60 rooms. $$$ MAP. An old-fashioned seaside resort comprising cottages and a 1855 lighthouse-turned-inn.

WEST FALMOUTH
The Inn at West Falmouth, 66 Frazar Rd (off Route 18A), 02574, tel: (508) 540-6503. 9 rooms. $$$. A luxuriously renovated 1900 Shingle-style summer house with tennis court, small heated pool, and views of Buzzards Bay.

WEST HARWICH
The Commodore Inn, 30 Earle Rd, 02671, tel: (508) 432-1180. 26 rooms. $$. A very nearly seaside motel with pretty country decor.

WEST TISBURY
Breakfast at Tiasquam, off Middle Rd, 02575, tel: (508) 645.3685, (800) 696-3685. $$$ B&B. A modern Cape custom built as an inn, and loaded with skylights; rural location.
Lambert's Cove Country Inn, Lambert's Cove Rd, 02575, tel: (508) 693-2298. 15 rooms. $$. A 1790s farmhouse on 7 pastoral acres with an English garden.

WILLIAMSTOWN
Field Farm Guest House, 554 Sloan Rd, 01267, (413) 458-3135. 5 rooms. $ B&B. A 1948 American Modern mansion on over 250 acres of conservation land.
The Orchards, 222 Adams Rd, 01267, tel: (413) 458-9611, (800) 225-1517. 49 rooms. $$$. A modern hotel with antique appointments.
River Bend Farm, 643 Simonds Rd, 01267, tel: (413) 458-5504. 5 rooms. $ B&B. A 1770 colonial, painstakingly restored.
Steep Acres Farm, 520 White Oaks Rd, 01267, tel: (413) 458-3774. 4 rooms. $ B&B. On a 50-acre hilltop, with orchards and animals.

WORCESTER
The Beechwood Inn, 363 Plantation St, 01605, tel: (508) 754-5789. 58 rooms. $$. A handsome new hotel overlooking the lake.

YARMOUTH PORT
Lane's End Cottage, 268 Main St, 02675, tel: (508) 362-5298. 3 rooms. $ B&B. A 300-year-old full Cape in a quiet wooded setting.
Wedgewood Inn, 3 Main St, 02675, tel: (508) 362-5157. 6 rooms. $$. An imposing 1812 Federal home, at once formal and romantic.

NEW HAMPSHIRE

ANDOVER

The English House, Main St, 03216, tel: (603) 735-5987. 7 rooms. $ B&B. Off the beaten track; afternoon tea.

BEDFORD

Bedford Village Inn, 2 Old Bedford Rd, 03102, tel: (603) 472-2602, (800) 852-1666. 14 rooms. $–$$. Luxury suites, with four-posters beds and marble bathrooms, carved out of a three-story barn.

BETHLEHEM

Adair, Route 302, 03574, tel: (603) 444-2600. 8 rooms. $$–$$$ B&B. A 1927 mansion with 200 acres encompassing gardens and tennis courts.

The Bells (B&B), Strawberry Hill St, 03574, tel: (603) 869-2647. 5 rooms. $ B&B. A 1892 Victorian manse with fanciful, pagoda-like trim.

The Mulburn Inn, Main St, 03574, tel: (603) 869-3389. 7 rooms. $ B&B. A Tudor mansion built for Woolworths in 1913.

BRETTON WOODS

The Mount Washington Hotel and Resort, Route 302, 03575, tel: (603) 278-1000, (800) 258-0330. 174 rooms. $$$–$$$$ MAP. A grand hotel preserved in all its glory since 1902.

CANAAN

The "Inn" on Canaan Street, Rd 1, Box 92, Canaan St, 03741, tel: (603) 523-7310. 5 rooms. $ B&B. A lakeside Federal home serving luscious breakfasts.

CENTER HARBOR

Red Hill Inn, Route 25B, 03226, tel: (603) 279-7001. 21 rooms. $–$$ B&B. This red-brick summer home once belonged to the inventor of the soda fountain.

CENTER SANDWICH

Corner House Inn, Main St, 03227, tel: (603) 284-6219, (800) 232-7829. 4 rooms. $ B&B. A Victorian cottage in a Currier & Ives town.

CHOCORUA

Stafford's-in-the-Field, 03817, tel: (603) 323-7766, (800) 446-1112. 14 rooms. $$–$$$ MAP. A rural farmhouse offering hospitality since the 1880s.

CONCORD

Wyman Farm, RFD 13, Box 163, 03301, tel: (603) 783-4467. 3 rooms. $ B&B. An 18th-century Cape on a 60-acre hilltop.

CORNISH

The Barbarry House, 70 Saint-Gaudens Rd, 03745, tel: (603) 675-2802. 5 rooms. $ B&B. A Colonial farmhouse once owned by Saint-Gaudens' son; period antiques and perennial gardens.

DIXVILLE NOTCH

The Balsams Grand Resort Hotel, 03576, tel: (603) 255-3400, (800) 255-0600. 233 rooms. $$$$ FAP. A fabulous 19th-century hotel, set in its own natural preserve.

EATON CENTER

The Inn at Crystal Lake, Route 153, 03832, tel: (603) 447-2120. 11 rooms. $–$$ B&B. An 1884 Victorian in a sleepy lakeside village.

ROCKHOUSE

Rockhouse Mountain Farm Inn, 03832, tel: (603) 447-2880. 15 rooms. $$ MAP. Closed winter. A family resort on a 450-acre farm, since 1946.

ENFIELD

Shaker Inn, Lower Shaker Village, Route 4A, 03748, tel: (603) 632-7800. 20 rooms. $–$$. Spacious, Shaker-accoutred rooms in the Great Stone Dwelling.

ETNA

Moose Mountain Lodge, Moose Mountain Lodge Rd, 03570, tel: (603) 643-3529. 12 rooms. $$$ FAP. A classic 1938 ski lodge, with stone hearth and dizzying views.

FITZWILLIAM

Amos A. Parker House, Route 119, 03447, tel: (603) 585-6540. 5 rooms. $ B&B. A formal 18th-century home with superb gardens.

Fitzwilliam Inn, Route 119, 03447, tel: (603) 585-9000. 28 rooms. $. This 1796 stagecoach inn offers nonpricy, atmospheric lodgings.

FRANCESTOWN

Inn at Crotched Mountain, Mountain Rd, 03043, tel: (603) 588-6840. 13 rooms. $$ MAP. An 1822 inn with lovely views.

FRANCONIA

Bungay Jar Bed & Breakfast, Easton Valley Rd, 03580, tel: (603) 823-7775. 6 rooms. $–$$ B&B. An imaginatively retrofitted 18th-century barn on 8 private acres with fabulous views.

Franconia Inn, Easton Rd, 03583, tel: (603) 823-5542, (800) 4RELAXX. 34 rooms. $$$ MAP. A 19th-century inn with 117 acres to explore on foot, by ski, or on horseback.

Lovett's by Lafayette Brook, Route 1, 03583, tel: (603) 823-5522. 31 rooms. $$ MAP. A 1784 main house surrounded by cottages, some with fireplaces.

GLEN

The Bernerhof, Route 302, 03838, tel: (603) 383-4414, (800) 548-8007. 11 rooms. $–$$ B&B. A Victorian inn with some modern improvements, such as double whirlpools.

GORHAM

Appalachian Mountain Club, (603) 466-2727. 10 dorms. $–$$ MAP. The AMC operates two roadside dorms and six high-mountain "huts" in the White Mountain National forest; reservations required.

GREENLAND

The Captain Folsom Inn, 480 Portsmouth Ave, 03849, tel: (603) 436-2662. 6 rooms. $ B&B. A Colonial tavern turned Federal country mansion, 10 minutes from Portsmouth.

HANCOCK

John Hancock Inn, Main St, 03449, tel: (603) 525-3318. 11 rooms. $–$$ B&B. One bedroom in this Colonial hostelry boasts a mural by itinerant painter Rufus Porter.

HANOVER

Hanover Inn, Main St, 03755, tel: (603) 643-4300, (800) 443-7024. 92 rooms. $$$–$$$$. An integral part of the Dartmouth campus, with rockers on a long porch overlooking the common.

HARRISVILLE

The Harrisville Squires' Inn, Keene Rd, 03450, tel: (603) 827-3925. 5 rooms. $. An 1840s farmhouse of 50 acres, near the historic milltown.

HAVERHILL

Haverhill Inn, Dartmouth College Highway, 03765, tel: (603) 989-5961. 4 rooms. $ B&B. An 1810 Federal house with fireplaces and canopy beds.

HENNIKER

Colby Hill Inn, The Oaks, 03242, tel: (603) 428-3281. 16 rooms. $–$$ B&B. A rambling late 18th-century inn with a perennial garden where pheasants roam.

HOLDERNESS

The Manor on Golden Pond, Route 3, 03245, tel: (603) 968-3348, (800) 545-3141. 29 rooms. $$$–$$$$ MAP. A 1903 stone mansion with a clay tennis court, swimming pool, and private beach.

JACKSON

Eagle Mountain Resort, Carter Notch Rd, 03846, tel: (603) 383-9111, (800) 527-5022. 94 rooms. $–$$. The furnishings may be reproduction, but this porch-wrapped 1879 grand hotel is a pleasant reminder of summers past.

Inn at Thorn Hill, Thorn Hill Rd, 03846, tel: (603) 383-4242, (800) 289-8990. 19 rooms. $$–$$$ MAP. Stanford White designed this gambrel-roofed summer house, on a secluded slope with views of Mount Washington.

The Wentworth Resort Hotel, Route 16A, tel: (603) 383-9700, (800) 637-0013. 62 rooms. $–$$. An 1869 grand hotel adjoining an 18-hole golf course.

Whitney's Inn at Jackson, Route 16B, 03846, tel: (603) 383-6886, (800) 252-5622. 37 rooms. $$ MAP. A comfy inn geared to families, at the foot of Black Mountain, a small-scale ski area.

Wildcat Inn & Tavern, Route 16A, 03846, tel: (603) 383-4245, (800) 228-4245. 12 rooms. $–$$ B&B. Charming if tiny suites in the social center of town.

JAFFREY

Benjamin Prescott Inn, Route 124, 03452, tel (603) 532-6637. 11 rooms. $. A sprawling 1820 house, set amid a dairy farm.

LITTLETON

The Beal House Inn, 247 West Main St, 03561, tel: (603) 444-2661. 13 rooms. $ B&B. A Federal-style farmhouse full of antiques.

MARLBOROUGH

Thatcher Hill Inn (B&B), Thatcher Hill Rd, 03455, tel: (603) 876-3361. 7 rooms. $$. A 1794 farmstead perched high on a peaceful hilltop.

NEW LONDON

New London Inn, 140 Main St, 03257, tel: (603) 526-2791, (800) 526-2791. 30 rooms. $ B&B. An 1792 inn with eclectic decor and an inventive chef/innkeeper.

Pleasant Lake Inn, Pleasant St, 03257, tel: (603) 526-6271, (800) 626-4907. 13 rooms. $. A 1790 inn on 5 pastoral lakeside acres.

NORTH CONWAY

Stonehurst Manor, Route 16, 03860, tel: (603) 356-3113. 24 rooms. $$. A turn-of-the-century mansion with outdoor pool, hot tub, and tennis court.

NORTH SUTTON

Follansbee Inn, Route 114, tel: (603) 927-4221. 23 rooms. $ B&B. A cozy lakeside inn with 500 acres of woods to roam or ski.

NORTH WOODSTOCK

The Woodstock Inn, Main St, 03262, tel: (603) 745-3951. 19 rooms. $–$$. Three Victorian inns in a bustling tourist town.

ORFORD

White Goose Inn, Route 10, 03777, tel: (603) 353-4812. 10 rooms. $. Country-elegant decor and toothsome breakfasts.

PORTSMOUTH

Governor's House, 32 Miller Ave, 03801, tel: (603) 431-6546. 4 rooms. $–$$ B&B. An opulently appointed former governor's manse.

Inn at Christian Shore, 335 Maplewood Avenue, 03801, tel: (603) 431-6770. 5 rooms. $ B&B. An antique-appointed 1800 Federal house in a historic district.

The Inn at Strawbery Banke, 314 Court St, 03801, tel: (603) 436-7242. 7 rooms. $ B&B. An 1800 captain's house adjoining the historic preserve.

Martin Hill Inn, 404 Islington St, tel: (603) 436-2287. 6 rooms. $ B&B. An 1820 house with solicitous hosts and lavish breakfasts.

Sise Inn, 40 Court St, 03801, tel: (603) 443-1200, (800) 232-INNS. 34 rooms. $$. A 1881 Queen Anne inn with luxurious amenities.

SHELBURNE

Philbrook Farm Inn, North Rd, tel: (603) 466-4841. 23 rooms. $$ MAP. Run by the same family since 1861, this charming country inn offers an escape from the 20th century.

SNOWVILLE

Snowvillage Inn, 92 Stuart Rd, 03849, tel: (603) 447-2818. 15 rooms. $$$. Austrian motifs pervade this high-perched aeirie.

SUGAR HILL

The Hilltop Inn (B&B), Route 117, 03585, tel: (603) 823-5695. 7 rooms. $–$$ B&B. A homey 1895 Victorian.

Sugar Hill Inn, Route 117, 03850, tel: (603) 823-5621, (800) 54-VISIT. 16 rooms. $–$$ B&B. An 18th-century country inn.

SUNAPEE

Dexter's Inn and Tennis Club, Stage Coach Rd, 03782, tel: (603) 763-5571, (800) 232-5571. 17 rooms. Closed winter. $$–$$$ MAP. A secluded yellow clapboard 1801 house with 3 all-weather courts and an outdoor pool.

The Inn at Sunapee, Burkehaven Hill Rd, 03782, tel: (603) 763-4444, (800) 327-2466. 16 rooms. $ B&B. A hilltop inn with wraparound porch, swimming pool, and tennis courts.

Seven Hearths, Route 11, 03782, tel: (603) 763-5657, (800) 237-2464. 10 rooms. $$ B&B. An 1801 farmhouse, imaginatively refurbished.

TAMWORTH

The Gilman Tavern, Main St, 03886, tel: (603) 323-8940. 6 rooms. $. Packed with museum-quality Americana.

The Tamworth Inn, 03886, tel: (603) 323-7721, (800) 933-3902. 18 rooms. $–$$ B&B. A gracious 1833 inn in a classic village.

TEMPLE

The Birchwood Inn, Route 45, 03084, tel: (603) 878-3285. 7 rooms. $ B&B. An 1800 brick inn with Rufus Porter murals.

WATERVILLE VALLEY

Waterville Valley Resort, 03215, tel: (603) 236-4501. Over 700 rooms. $–$$$$. A resort complex cupped in a high valley, with skiing in winter, hiking, tennis, and other sports the rest of the year.

WEST CHESTERFIELD

The Chesterfield Inn (B&B), Route 9, 03466, tel: (603) 256-3211, (800) 365-5515. 13 rooms. $$.

WHITEFIELD

Spalding Inn and Club, Mountainview Rd, 03598, tel: (603) 837-2572. 48 rooms. $ B&B. A full-scale resort with golf course, tennis courts, and heated pool.

WOLFEBORO

Wolfeboro Inn, 44 North Main St, 03894, tel: (603) 569-3016, (800) 451-2389. 43 rooms. $$$. A luxury lakeside inn since 1812.

RHODE ISLAND

BLOCK ISLAND

The Hotel Manisses and The 1661 Inn, 02807, tel: (401) 466-2063. 39 rooms. $–$$$$. Victorian inns with ocean views.

NARRAGANSETT

The Richards, 144 Gibson Ave, tel: (401) 789-7746. 4 rooms. $ B&B. An 1884 stone mansion with private access to the rocky coast.

NEWPORT

Cliffside Inn, 2 Seaview Avenue, 02840, tel: (401) 847-1811. 10 rooms. $$$. An 1880 Victorian villa, carved into dramatic quarters.

Elm Tree Cottage, 336 Gibbs Avenue, 02840, tel: (401) 489-1610, (800) 882-3ELM. 5 rooms. $$$$ B&B. A "cottage" only in the Newport sense, one block from the water.

The Francis Malbone House, 392 Thames St, tel: (401) 846-0392. 9 rooms. $$–$$$$ B&B. A 1760 Colonial brick mansion on the harborfront.

Ivy Lodge, 12 Clay St, 02840, tel: (401) 849-6865. 8 rooms. $$–$$$ B&B. A Victorian home designed by Stanford White.

The Melville House, 39 Clarke St, 02840, tel: (401) 847-0640. 7 rooms. $ B&B. A 1750 Colonial on Historic Hill.

The Victorian Ladies, 63 Memorial Blvd, 02840, tel: (401) 849-9960. 11 rooms. $$–$$$ B&B. A pair of vintage lovelies, done up in the style of the period.

PROVIDENCE

The Old Court, 144 Benefit St, 02903, tel: (401) 751-2002. 10 rooms. $$. An 1863 rectory retrofitted as a Victorian-style inn.

Omni Biltmore Hotel, Kennedy Plaza, 02903, tel: (401) 421-0700, (800) THE-OMNI. 246 rooms. $$–$$$$. A turn-of-the-century grand hotel, nicely restored.

WEEKAPAUG

Weekapaug Inn, 02891, tel: (401) 322-0301. 62 rooms. Summer only. $$$$ FAP. A classic inn sheltering well-heeled families since 1938.

WESTERLY

Shelter Harbor Inn, Route 1, 02891, tel: (401) 322-8883. 24 rooms. $$ B&B. Once a working farm, now a luxury getaway.

VERMONT

NB: Many Vermont inns take a break between foliage and the holidays, and again during "mud season," so check first if you plan to visit in the late fall or early spring.

ARLINGTON

Arlington Inn, Route 4, US 7, 05250, tel: (802) 375-6532. 13 rooms. $$. An elegant Greet Revival mansion.

AVERILL

Quimby Country Lodge and Cottages, 05901, tel: (802) 822-5533. 20 rooms. $$–$$$ FAP. A 19th-century family-oriented resort overlooking Forest Lake.

BARTON

Fox Hall, Willoughby Lake, 05822, tel: (802) 525-6930. 9 rooms. $ B&B. A turreted turn-of-the-century mansion with lake views and access (canoes and sailboards provided).

BENNINGTON

Four Chimneys Inn, 21 West Rd, 05201, tel: (802) 447-3500. 6 rooms. $$. French Provincial decor in a grand old manse.

BOLTON VALLEY

The Black Bear, Mountain Rd, 05477, tel: (802) 434-2126. 24 rooms. $$. Cozy countrified decor in a lodge located amid the Bolton Valley Resort.

Bolton Valley Resort, 05477, tel: (802) 434-2131, (800) 451-3220. 146 rooms. $–$$. This Alpine-style family ski resort, with a sports center and 6,000 acres of mountainous wilderness, makes an affordable summer getaway as well.

BRANDON

Brandon Inn, Route 7, 05733, tel: (802) 247-5766. 35 rooms. $–$$. Victorian splendor in a town off the tourist circuit.

BRIDGEWATER CORNERS

The October Country Inn, Upper Rd, 05035, tel: (802) 672-3412. 10 rooms. $$ MAP. A cozy farmhouse on a back road.

BROOKFIELD
Green Trails Inn, 05036, tel: (802) 276-3412. 15 rooms. $ B&B. A sprawling inn and lodge, with cross-country/hiking trails.

BRATTLEFIELD
Latchis Hotel, 50 Elliot St, 05301, tel: (802) 254-6300. 35 rooms. $. A 1938 Art Deco hotel, right in town.

CHESTER
The Inn at Long Last, Main St, 05143, tel: (802) 875-2444. 32 rooms. $$$ MAP. A lively village inn; rooms are apt to have literary themes.

CHITTENDEN
Mountain Top Inn, Mountain Top Rd, 05737, tel: (802) 483-2311, (800) 445-1200. 52 rooms. $$$$ MAP. A big, comfy family resort deep in the countryside; outstanding Nordic skiing.
Tulip Tree Inn, Chittenden Dam Rd, 05737, tel: (802) 483-6213. 8 rooms. $ $$ MAP. An electricity magnate's 1920s retreat; five rooms feature jacuzzis.

COLCHESTER
Marble Island Resort, 150 Marble Island Rd, 05446, tel: (802) 864-6800. A tasteful modern complex with an enviable lakeside setting.

CRAFTSBURY
The Craftsbury Inn, Route 14, 05826, tel: (802) 586-2848. 10 rooms. $ B&B, $$ MAP. Country comfort, with wraparound verandas overlooking lavish gardens.

CRAFTSBURY COMMON
The Craftsbury Center, 05827, tel: (802) 587-7767, (800) 729-7751. 40 rooms. $–$$ MAP. Dorm-style accommodations, with skilled training available in various outdoor sports.
The Inn on the Common, Main St, 05827, tel: (802) 586-9619, (800) 521-2223. 16 rooms. $$$$ MAP. Luxurious decor and ambitious cuisine serve dinner party-style.

DANBY
Silas Griffith Inn, 05739, tel: (802) 293-5567. 17 rooms. $ B&B. An 1891 lumber baron's mansion, with pool.

DORSET
Barrows House, Route 30, 05251, tel: (802) 867-4455. 28 rooms. $$$–$$$$ MAP. An 18th-century house with homy touches.
Cornucopia of Dorset, Route 30, 05251, tel: (802) 867-5751. 5 rooms. $$–$$$ B&B. Prettily appointed rooms; marvellous breakfasts.
Dorset Inn, 05251, tel: (802) 867-5500. 34 rooms. $$ MAP. One of the state's oldest – and reliably enjoyable – inns, opened in 1796.
Marble West Inn, Dorset West Rd, 05251, tel: (802) 867-4155. 8 rooms. $–$$ B&B. A marble-columned 1840s Greek Revival manse, elegantly decorated.

DUMMERSTON
Naulahka, 19 Terrace St, 05301, tel: (800) 848-3747. Rudyard Kipling's rural estate, rented by the week.

ENOSBURG FALLS
Berkson Farms, 05450, tel: (802) 933-2522. 4 rooms. A century-old, 200-head dairy farm featuring home-grown breakfasts; guests are welcome to help with chores, from milking to sugaring.

ESSEX JUNCTION
Inn at Essex, 70 Essex Way, 05452, tel: (802) 878-1100, (800) 288-7613. 97 rooms. $$. A neo-traditional hotel with outstanding cuisine (provided by the New England Culinary Institute); convenient to Burlington.

FAIR HAVEN
Vermont Marble Inn, On the Town Green, 05473, tel: (802) 265-8383. 13 rooms. $$$ MAP. A ca. 1876 Italianate marble mansion in a quiet corner of the lakes region.
Maplewood Inn, Route 22A, 05473, tel: (802) 265-2039, (800) 253-7729. 5 rooms. $$$. A former dairy farm with fanciful decor and hearty breakfasts.

FAIRLEE
Rutledge Inn & Cottages, 05045, tel: (802) 333-9722. 41 rooms. $$ MAP. A family-style cottage complex on Lake Morey.

GRAFTON
The Old Tavern at Grafton, 05146, tel: (802) 843-2231, (800) 843-1801. 35 rooms. $$. An 18th-century stagecoach inn in a lovingly restored town.

GREENBORO
Highland Lodge, 05841, tel: (802) 533-2647. 21 rooms. $$ MAP. An 1860s farmhouse turned family-style inn, with a lake for summer fun, cross-country trails for winter.

HIGHGATE SPRINGS
The Tyler Place on Lake Champlain, Box 203, 05460, tel: (802) 868-3301. 50 rooms. Closed winter. $$$–$$$$ FAP. A family "camp" since the 1930s.

JAMAICA
Three Mountain Inn, 180 Main St, 05343, tel: (802) 874-4140. 15 rooms. $$$ MAP. A 1790 inn, with a handsome keeping room and clever additions.

KILLINGTON
Cortina Inn, Route 4, 05751, tel: (802) 773-3331, (800) 451-6108. 98 rooms. $$$. Surprisingly lush and spacious rooms; indoor pool.
The Inn at Long Trail, Route 4, 05751, tel: (802) 775-7181, (800) 325-2540. 19 rooms. $$ MAP. A rustic ski inn built around a huge boulder, which intrudes, picturesquely in the dining room and Irish Pub.
Inn of the Six Mountains, Killington Rd, 05751, tel: (802) 422-4302, (800) 228-4676. 103 rooms. $$$. A modern hotel with a Rockies feel; everything, including the central fieldstone hearth, is lavishly overscale.
The Mountain Meadows Lodge, Thundering Brook Rd, 05751, tel: (802) 775-1010. 18 rooms. $–$$ MAP. A large lakeside farmhouse, with extensive cross-country trails.
Trailside Lodge, Coffee House Rd, 05751, tel: (802) 422-3532. 33 rooms. $$ MAP. A friendly dorm with hot tub and bar.

LONDONBERRY
Village Inn at Landgrove, Landgrove, 01548, tel: (802) 824-6673, (800) 669-8466. 20 rooms. $ B&B, $$–$$$ MAP. A rambling family inn with tennis courts, pool, and cross-country trails.

LOWER WATERFORD
Rabbit Hill Inn, 05848, tel: (802) 748-5168, (800) 762-8669. 19 rooms. $$ MAP. A Greek Revival stagecoach inn with ultra-romantic rooms, a superb restaurant, and lots of pampering personal touches.

LUDLOW
The Governor's Inn, 86 Main St, 05149, tel: (802) 228-8830, (800) GOVERNOR. 8 rooms. $$$ MAP. Victorian decor and solicitous hospitality.

LYNDONVILLE
Wildflower Inn, Darling Hill Rd, 05851, tel: (802) 626-8310. 20 rooms. $–$$ B&B. A cheerfully renovated 1796 farmhouse (with modern carriage house annex) great for families; there's a petting zoo, pool, and beautiful views.

MANCHESTER
Birch Hill Inn, West Rd, 05254, tel: (802) 362-2761. 6 rooms. $$ B&B or MAP. A late 18th-century hilltop house; home cooking.

1811 House, 05254, tel: (802) 362-1811. 14 rooms. $$ B&B. A Federal manse that has been an inn for most of its history.

The Equinox, Route 7A, 05254, tel: (802) 362-5700. 175 rooms. $$$$. A grand old hotel, beautifully refurbished and maintained as a sister property to Scotland's Gleneagles.

Village Country Inn, Route 7A, 05245, tel: (802) 362-1792. 30 rooms. $$$ MAP. A rambling old inn with romantic French country decor.

Wilburton Inn, River Rd, 05254, tel: (802) 362-2500. 32 rooms. $$ B&B. A railroad baron's turn-of-the-century brick mansion.

MIDDLEBURY
Middlebury Inn, 14 Court House Square, 05753, tel: (802) 388-4961, (800) 842-4666. 75 rooms. $–$$. An 1825 inn (plus 1827 annex and modern motel extension) overlooking the village green.

Swift House Inn, 25 Stewart Lane, 05753, tel: (802) 388-2766. 20 rooms. $–$$. An 1815 Federal house; the Carriage House features spacious suites.

MIDDLETOWN SPRINGS
Middletown Springs Inn, On the Green, 05757, tel: (802) 235-2198. 10 rooms. $–$$ B&B. A pink-and-white gingerbread Victorian, with cheerful decor.

Priscilla's Victorian Inn, South St, 05757, tel: (802) 235-2299. 6 rooms. $ B&B. A Victorian home with impressive porches and parlors.

MONTPELIER
The Inn at Montpelier, 147 Main St, 05602, tel: (802) 223-2727. 19 rooms. $–$$. A pair of adjoining Federal mansions make a restful in-town retreat.

NEWFANE
The Four Columns Inn, 230 West St, 05345 tel: (802) 365-7713. 15 rooms. $$–$$$. A Greek Revival inn beside one of New England's most photogenic greens.

NORTH HERO ISLAND
Shore Acres Inn and Restaurant, RR1, Box 3, 05474, tel: (802) 372-8722. 23 rooms. $. A sedate lakeside hotel with a vast veranda affording a 40-mile view.

NORTHFIELD
The Northfield Inn, 27 Highland Ave, 05663, tel: (802) 486-8558. 8 rooms. $–$$ B&B. A turn-of-the-century inn in a town off the tourist track.

PERU
Johnny Seesaw's, Route 11, 05152, tel: (802) 824-5333. 30 rooms. $ B&B, $$ MAP. A rustic 1920s dancehall turned quintessential skiers' inn.

PUTNEY
Hickory Ridge House, Hickory Ridge Rd, 05346, tel: (802) 387-5709. 7 rooms. $ B&B. An 1808 brick Federal manor on 12 pastoral acres.

QUECHEE
Quechee Bed & Breakfast, 53 Woodstock Rd, 05059, tel: (802) 295-1776. 8 rooms. $$ B&B. Surprisingly spacious quarters carved out of a 1795 house.

The Quechee Inn at Marshland Farm, Clubhouse Rd, 05059, tel: (802) 295-3135, (800) 235-3133. 24 rooms. $$$ MAP. A 1793 farmstead in a bucolic riverside setting.

ROCHESTER
Harvey's Mountain View Inn, 05767, tel: (802) 767-4273. 10 rooms. $$ MAP. A mountaintop farmhouse with children's activities and a pool.

Liberty Hill Farm, Liberty Hill Rd, 05767, tel: (802) 767-3926. 7 rooms. $ MAP. A working farm, fun for families.

SHELBURNE
Shelburne House, Harbor Rd, 05482, tel: (802) 985-9498. 24 rooms. $$$$ MAP. Lila Vanderbilt's turn-of-the-century mansion set amid a grandiose farm beside Lake Champlain.

SHOREHAM
The Shoreham Inn, 05770, tel: (802) 897-5081, (800) 255-5081. 11 rooms. $ B&B. A personable village farmhouse, with sophisticated hosts.

SIMONSVILLE
Rowell's Inn, 05143, tel: (802) 875-3658. 6 rooms. $$ MAP. An 1820 stagecoach inn, catering to nostalgic adventurers.

SOUTH LONDONDERRY
The Londonderry Inn, 05155, tel: (802) 824-5226. 25 rooms. $. A comfy country inn, offering a welcoming hearth in winter, a refreshing outdoor pool in summer.

SOUTH NEWFANE
Inn at South Newfane, 05351, tel: (802) 348-7191. 6 rooms. $$ MAP. Pretty country decor, a pool and pond, and over 100 acres to roam.

SOUTH WOODSTOCK
Kedron Valley Inn, Route 106, 05071, tel: (802) 457-1473. 28 rooms. $$$. Heirloom quilts line the walls and dress up the prettily decorated rooms; the restaurant is exceptional.

STOWE

Fiddler's Green Inn, Mountain Rd, 05672, tel: (802) 253-8124. 7 rooms. $. A homey 1820 lodge with a congenial host.

Green Mountain Inn, Main St, 05672, tel: (802) 253-7301, (800) 455-6629. 62 rooms. $–$$$. A rambling 1833 inn, nicely restored.

The Inn at the Mountain, Route 108, 05672, tel: (802) 253-3000. $$$–$$$$. A tastefully decorated motel-and-condo complex at the foot of Mt. Mansfield, surrounded by state forest.

The Spruce Peak Inn, Mountain Rd, 05672, tel: (802) 253-4010, (800) 639-3390. 2 dorms. $ MAP. Basic bunk-bed lodgings in a Civilian Conservation Corps hostel built in the '30s; with two hearty meals, the best bargain in New England.

Stowehof Inn, Edson Hill Rd, 05672, tel: (802) 253-9722, (800) 422-9722. 45 rooms. $$$. A hilltop hotel with intentionally eccentric decor and an outdoor pool with the best view in town.

Ten Acres Lodge, Luce Hill Rd, 05672, tel: (802) 253-8511, (800) 826-7000. 13 rooms. $$. An 1826 farmhouse with all the modern comforts, including an outdoor hot tub.

Topnotch at Stowe Resort and Spa, Mountain Rd, 05672, tel: (802) 253-7638. 105 rooms. $$$$. A luxury establishment with a world-class spa, plus tennis and stables.

Trapp Family Lodge, Luce Hill Rd, 05672, tel: (802) 253-8511, (800) 826-7000. 93 rooms. $$$$. A modern replacement for the original lodge, lost to fire; 2,000 acres with skiing and walking paths.

VERGENNES

Basin Harbor Club, 05491, tel: (802) 475-2311, (800) 622-4000. 121 rooms. Closed winter. $$$ FAP. A classic lakeside summer colony, full of timeless pleasures.

WAITSFIELD

Inn at Round Barn Farm, E. Warren Rd, 05673, tel: (802) 496-2276. 6 rooms. $$ B&B. A luxuriously retrofitted farmhouse; the unusual barn houses a lap pool.

Knoll Farm Country Inn, Bragg Hill Rd, 05673, tel: (802) 496-3939. 4 rooms. $$ FAP. A functioning farmhouse on 150 acres; home-grown meals, and a pond for swimming or skating.

The Lareau Farm Country Inn, Route 100, tel: (802) 496-4949, tel: (800) 833-0766. 14 rooms. $ MAP. Authentic farmhouse atmosphere (complete with menagerie).

Mad River Barn, Route 17, 05673, tel: (802) 496-3340, (800) 834-4666. 15 rooms. $$ MAP. A 1948 ski lodge with a vintage game room.

WATERBURY

Inn at Blush Hill, Blush Hill Rd, 05676, tel: (802) 244-7429, (800) 736-7522. 6 rooms. $ B&B. An exemplary B&B, with cheerful rooms and gourmet breakfasts in a 1790s keeping room.

WEATHERSFIELD

The Inn at Weathersfield, Route 106, 05151, tel: (802) 263-9217. 12 rooms. $$$ MAP. A magical 18th-century country inn, with the promise of romance at every turn.

WEST DOVER

Inn at Sawmill Farm, Country Club Rd, 05356, tel: (802) 464-3131. 21 rooms. $$$$. An old farmstead jazzed up with bold decorative touches; country elegance at its best, plus superb regional cuisine.

Trail's End, Smith Rd (off Route 100), tel: (802) 464-2727, (800) 859-2585. 15 rooms. $–$$$. A gloriously updated ski lodge, with an outdoor pool and clay tennis court; some suites have fireplaces and whirlpools.

WEST GLOVER

Rodgers' Dairy Farm, RFD 3, Box 57, 05875, tel: (802) 525-6677. 5 rooms. $ FAP. A working farm deep in the countryside.

WEST TOWNSEND

Windham Hill Inn, 05359, tel: (802) 874-4080. 15 rooms. $$ MAP. An 1825 farmhouse, cum cross-country center, set way back in the country.

WESTON

The Inn at Weston, Route 100, 05161, tel: (802) 824-5804. 19 rooms. $$. A pair of early 19th-century farmhouses with crisp country decor.

The Wilder Homestead Inn, Lawrence Hill Rd, 05161, tel: (802) 824-8172. 7 rooms. $. An 1827 Federal brick mansion with original stenciling.

WILMINGTON

Trail's End, Smith Rd, 05363, tel: (802) 464-2727. 18 rooms. $–$$$ B&B. Lovely rooms and suites branch off from a cathedral-ceiling living room with fieldstone hearth.

WOODSTOCK

The Applebutter Inn, Happy Valley Rd, 05091, tel: (802) 457-4158. 4 rooms. $ B&B. A Federal house full of fluffy comforters; yummy breakfasts.

Jackson House, 37 Route 4 West, 05091, tel: (802) 547-2065. 14 rooms. $$–$$$ B&B. A lovingly restored 1890s clapboard house; five-course breakfasts, and *hors-d'oeuvres* with champagne.

Three Church Street, 3 Church St, 05091, tel: (802) 457-1925. 11 rooms. $ B&B. A gracious early 19th-century house near the common, with a tennis court and pool; well priced for this level of elegance.

Woodstock Inn & Resort, 14 The Green, 05091, tel: (802) 457-1100, 1-800-223 7637. 143 rooms. $$$$. Laurance Rockefeller's homage to country inns past, full of Americana.

FOOD DIGEST

WHAT TO EAT

New England's culinary standing has made a stratospheric leap in just the past decade. Once bemoaned as the land of "the bean and the cod," Boston started the region's culinary renaissance rolling with a core group of world-class chefs who trained their sous-chefs so well that their ranks kept expanding. Where once the highest quality one could expect was provincial and stodgy, now the offerings are fresh and flavorful, easily the equal of sophisticated fare anywhere.

New England's chefs have not only come up with brilliant new uses and combinations for the area's renowned bounty (especially seafood), they've developed their own network for securing new native delicacies, from farmstead cheeses to locally raised game birds. If you've never tried the classics – lobster bisque, shad roe, Indian pudding, Boston cream pie – by all means track them down. But be prepared for some surprises. New England's ingenious cooks – from executive chefs at the four-star hotels to the hardworking chef/owners at country inns – are having a field day year-round now with seasonal specialties, and their lucky customers are in for an ever-changing array of treats.

Price ranges are approximate, and subject to revision, but for a three-course meal for one (excluding beverages, tax and tip), the following guidelines may prove helpful: $ = under $15, $$ = $15–28, $$$ = $28–40, $$$$ = over $40. Meal tax varies from state to state, but it is customary to tip 15 to 20 percent on the pre-tax total. The more expensive establishments generally accept credit cards, but call ahead to check just in case. Most restaurants, except for the clearly casual, appreciate reservations (some even require them), as well as appropriate dress.

WHERE TO EAT

CONNECTICUT

AVON
Avon Old Farms Inn, Routes 44 and 10, tel: (203) 677-2818. $$$. One of the country's oldest inns (1757); Yankee/Continental fare in a suite of atmospheric rooms.

BROOKLYN
The Golden Lamb Buttery, 499 Wolf Den Rd (off Route 169), tel: (203) 744-4423. May–December. Reservations required. $$$. American nouvelle in an eccentric yet extravagant country setting.

CANAAN
The Cannery, 85 Main St (Routes 44 and 7), tel: (203) 824-7333. $$–$$$. "American bistro" innovations.

CENTERBROOK
Fine Bouche, 78 Main St, tel: (203) 567-8561. $$$. Classically influenced French cuisine, offered *prix fixe*.
8 Westbrook Restaurant, 8 Westbrook Rd., tel: (203) 767-7085. American nouvelle in airy rooms overlooking a millpond.

CHESTER
Restaurant du Village, 59 Main St, tel: (203) 526-5301. Dinner only. $$$$. Superb formal French fare in a country auberge.

EAST LYME
The Flanders Fish Market, 22 Chesterfield Rd (Route 161), tel: (203) 739-8866, (800) 638-8189. $. This humble little roadside restaurant dishes up ultra-fresh fish.

ESSEX
The Black Seal, 29 Main St, tel: (203) 767-0233. $$. Contemporary grazing, with nautical touches.
Griswold Inn, 36 Main St, Essex; tel: (203) 767-1776. $$–$$$. Traditional American fare; test your capacity at the Sunday hunt breakfast.

FARMINGTON
Apricots, 1591 Farmington Avenue, tel: (203) 673-5404. $$$. Hartford's favorite New American restaurant, just outside town.

GREENWICH
Bertrand, 253 Greenwich Ave, tel: (203) 661-4618. $$$$. French classicism; singled out by *Condé Nast* as one of the fifty finest restaurants in the nation.
La Grange, The Homestead Inn, 420 Field Point Rd, tel: (203) 869-7500. $$$$. Exquisite classical French cuisine.

IVORYTON
Copper Beech Inn, 46 Main St, tel: (203) 767-0330. $$$$. Classic French cuisine in a setting of studied elegance.

LITCHFIELD
The Litchfield Food Company, West St, tel: (203) 567-3113. $–$$. A bakery/deli/cafe; great grazing.
Tollgate Hill Inn, Tollgate Rd and Route 202 and Tollgate Rd, tel: (203) 567-4545. $$$. The superb New American cuisine belies the stark and lovely simplicity of this 1745 tavern.
West Street Grill, 43 West St, tel: (203) 567-3885. $$–$$$. Trendy in black-and-white, this citified bistro serves brilliant regional fare.

MANSFIELD DEPOT
Mansfield Depot Restaurant, 57 Middle Turnpike (Route 44), tel: (203) 429-3663. Robust American fare in a renovated railroad station.

MYSTIC

Flood Tide Restaurant, The Inn at Mystic junction Routes 1 and 27, tel: (203) 536-9604. $$$. Contemporary continental; water views.

Seamen's Inne, 65 Greenmanville Rd, tel: (203) 536-9649. Seafood. $$. American seafood; convenient to Mystic Seaport.

NEW HAVEN

Louis' Lunch, 261 Crown St, tel: (203) 562-5507. $. Home of the original hamburger (served on toast, sans frills).

Bruxelles Brasserie and Bar, 220 College St, tel: (203) 777-7752. $$. A lively bistro with a theatre motif.

Sally's Pizza, 237 Wooster St, tel: (203) 624-5271. The hands-down local favorite.

NEW MILFORD

The Bistro Cafe, 31 Bank St, tel: 203) 355-3266. $$$. Classic French and contemporary American.

Maison LeBlanc, Route 7, tel: (203) 354-9931. $$$. Classic, country, and nouvelle French, fireside in an 18th-century home.

NEW PRESTON

Boulders Inn, Route 45, tel: (203) 868-0541. $$$. Tasty extrapolations of hearty Continental fare, with a view of the lake.

Doc's, Flirtation Ave and Route 45, tel: (203) 868-9415. $–$$. This rustic cafe serves California-style pizzas and other evolved Italian delights.

Hopkins Inn, 22 Hopkins Rd., tel: (203) 868-7295. $$–$$$. Specializing in Austrian and Swiss dishes (and pretty vistas of the lake).

The Inn on Lake Waramaug, North Shore Rd, tel: (203) 868-0563. $$$. The cuisine is more experimental than the traditionalist decor would suggest.

NOANK

Abbott's Lobster in the Rough, 117 Pearl St, tel: (203) 536-7719. Summer only. $. A classic lobster shack on the water.

NORTH STONINGTON

Randall's Ordinary, Route 2, tel: (203) 599-4540. Reservations required. $$$. Authentic 17th-century hearth cookery.

NORWALK

Silvermine Tavern, 194 Perry Avenue, tel: (203) 847-455. $$$. American classics in an old inn beside a mill pond.

OLD LYME

Old Lyme Inn, 85 Old Lyme St, tel: (203) 434-2600. $$$$. Dazzling seasonal dishes served with aplomb.

OLD SAYBROOK

Saybrook Point Inn, 2 Bridge St, tel: (203) 395-2000, (800) 243-0212. $$$. Traditionalist decor, contemporary fare, water views.

POMFRET

Vanilla Bean Cafe, 450 Deerfield Rd. (Routes 44, 97, and 169), tel: (203) 928-1569. $. A congenial bistro in a 150-year-old barn.

SALISBURY

White Hart Inn, Village Green (Routes 44 and 41), tel: (203) 435-0030. Julie's Sea Grill for creative seafood, and there's the tap room for lighter fare.

SIMSBURY

Evergreens, 397 Hopmeadow St, tel: (203) 651-5700. $$$. Simsbury's newest inn serves New American in a neo-traditional setting.

Hop Brook, 77 West St (Route 167), tel: (203) 651-0267. $$$. Contemporary comfort foods in a 300-year-old grist mill.

One-Way Fare, 4 Railroad St, tel: (203) 658-4477. $$. Boisterous fun food in a former railroad station.

Simsbury 1820 House, 731 Hopmeadow St, tel: (203) 658-7658. $$$. Delectable nouvelle inventions amid restful traditional trappings.

SOUTH NORWALK

Pasta Nostra Trattoria, 116 Washington St, tel: (203) 854-9700. $$. A convivial contemporary cafe.

Water Street, 50 Water St, tel: (203) 854-9640. $$. Contemporary American in a turn-of-the-century glass warehouse.

SOUTH WOODSTOCK

The Harvest at Bald Hill, Routes 169 and 171, tel: (203) 974-2240. $$$. Daring international fare in a classic country barn.

STONINGTON

The Boatyard Cafe, 194 Water St, tel: (203) 535-1381. $$. A waterside cafe with priceless sunsets.

The Harborview, Water Street at Cannon Square, tel: (203) 535-2720. $$$. Classical French cuisine.

STRATFORD

Stick to Your Ribs Texas Barbecue, 1785 Stratford Avenue, tel: (203) 377-1752. $. A southern staple, transplanted north.

TORRINGTON

Harvest Roasterie, 2407 Winstead Rd, tel: (203) 496-9796. $$. No pretension, a stripped-down decor, and absolutely delectable updated classics.

Le Rochambeau Restaurant, 46 E Matin St, tel: (203) 482-6241. $$$. French/Continental; game in season.

VERNON

Rein's New York-Style Delicatessen, Route 30 (I-84, Exit 65), tel: (203) 875-1344. The most authentic – and tasty – noshing north of Manhattan.

WASHINGTON

Mayflower Inn, Route 47, tel: (203) 868-9466. $$$. The "country American" cuisine is far, far from rustic – every bit as rarefied, in fact, as this fine country inn.

WASHINTON DEPOT

The Pantry, Titus Sq, tel: 9203) 868-0258. $–$$. A gourmet shop cum cafe, in a charming town.

WEST CORNWALL

Freshfields, Route 128, tel: (203) 672-6601. $$$. New American cuisine, beside Mill Brook.

West Cornwall Grill, 9 Railroad Plaza, tel: (203) 672-2219. $$$. Freshness and simplicity are the key words here.

WESTBROOK

Water's Edge Inn & Resort, 1525 Boston Post Rd, tel: (203) 399-5901, (800) 222-5901. Excellent New American cuisine, with a view of the Sound.

WOODBURY

Carole Peck's Good News Cafe, 694 Main St, tel: (203) 266-GOOD. $$. A cheerful spot focused on local bounty and luscious desserts.

WOODSTOCK

The Harvest at Bald Hill, Routes 169 and 171, tel: (203) 974-2240. $$$. Skilled regional offerings.

The Inn at Woodstock Hill, 94 Plaine Hill Rd, tel: 203) 928-0528. $$$$. The setting is formal, the cuisine refined yet robust.

WOODVILLE

Le Bon Coin, Route 202, Woodville, tel: (203) 868-7763. $$–$$$. Worth seeking out for sublime French classics.

MAINE

NB: Like its inns, many of Maine's restaurants are seasonal.

BAR HARBOR

Jordan Pond House, Park Loop Rd, tel: (207) 276-3316. $$. A classic spot for tea (and other meals) amid Acadia National Park.

The New Old Lompoc Cafe, 36 Rodick St, tel: (207) 288-9392. $$. A brew pub with international accompaniments.

Porcupine Grill, 123 Cottage St, tel: (207) 288-3884. $$$. Yacht-club spiffy, and culinarily up-to-date.

BATH

Kristina's, 160 Center St, Route 209, tel: (207) 442-8577. $. A popular cafe housed in a pair of 19th-century homes; don't miss the sticky buns.

BETHEL

Bethel Inn and Country Club, On the Common, tel: (207) 824-2175. $$. Yankee classics; mountain views.

Mother's, Upper Main St, tel: (207) 824-2589. $$. Homemade soups and sandwiches; substantial dinners.

BLUE HILL

Fire Pond, Main St, tel: (207) 374-2135. $$$. Dinner only. Closed winter. Inventive New American cuisine beside a trickling stream.

Jonathan's, Main St, tel: (207) 374-5226. $$–$$$. A contemporary cafe serving robust international dishes.

BOOTHBAY HARBOR

The Black Orchid, 5 Byway, tel: (207) 633-6639. $$–$$$. Mediterranean influences pervade this harborside summer house with roof deck.

Ebb Tide, 67 Commercial St, tel: (207) 633-5692. $–$$. A stylish restored dinner with classic comfort foods.

CAMDEN

The Belmont, 6 Belmont Ave, tel: (207) 236-8053. $$$. New American wizardry, in a peaceful setting.

Cassoulet, 31 Elm St, tel: 207) 236-6304. $$$. Neo-continental, with a bold Mediterranean influence.

The Sea Dog, 43 Mechanic St, tel: (207) 236-6863. $. A brew pub housed in a former wool mill.

CAPE NEDDICK

Cape Neddick Inn, Route 1 and Route 1A, tel: (207) 363-2899. $$$–$$$$. Ambitious seasonal cuisine in a neo-traditional setting.

CARRABASSET VALLEY

The Truffle Hound, Village West at Sugarloaf, tel: (207) 237-2355. $$. Rich, rewarding food at the foot of the ski slopes.

CASTINE

The Castine Inn, Main St, tel: (207) 326-4365. $$. Dinner only. Reservations required. Regional delicacies in a dining room painted to depict the town.

Dennett's Wharf, Sea St, tel: (207) 326-4861. $$. Casual, harborside seafood.

The Pentagoet Inn, Main St, tel: (207) 326-8616. $$$. Dinner only. Reservations required. A *prix fixe* dinner party.

CENTER LOVELL

Westways at Kezar Lake, tel: (207) 928-2663. $$. A baronial 1928 mansion with forward-thinking cuisine.

DEER ISLE

Pilgrim's Inn, Main St, tel: (207) 348-6615. $$$$. An exquisite *prix fixe* menu in a rustic barn.

FREEPORT

Harraseeket Inn, 162 Main St, tel: (207) 865-9377, (800) 342-6423. $$–$$$. Fabulous local produce; famed for its buffets.

FRYEPORT

The Oxford House Inn, 105 Main St, tel: (207) 935-3442. $$. Seafood in native and continental guises.

GARDINER

A-1 Diner, 3 Bridge St, tel: (207) 582-4804. $. A 1946 Worcester diner, serving the standards.

GREENVILLE

Greenville Inn, Norris St, tel: (207) 695-2206. $$$. Bountiful dinners accompanied by giant popovers.

HANCOCK

The Crocker House Country Inn, Hancock Point Rd, tel: (207) 422-6806. $$$. Sophisticated native seafood, and a stellar brunch.

Le Domaine, Route 1, tel: (207) 422-3395. $$$. Artful nouvelle cuisine from a transplanted Cordon Bleu chef.

KENNEBUNK

1810 Eatery, 17 Main St, tel: (207) 985-2858. $. A festive and affordable trattoria.

KENNEBUNKPORT

Cape Arundel Inn, Ocean Ave, tel: (207) 967-2125. $$$. Ocean views and an interesting menu.

Federal Jack's, 8 Western Ave, tel: (207) 967-4322. $$. A brew pub with sea views.

Kennebunkport Inn, Dock Square, tel: (207) 967-2621. $$$–$$$$. Delightful regional cuisine with a La Varenne diploma.

Seascapes, On the Pier, Cape Porpoise, tel: (207) 967-8500. $$$. Regional specialities prepared with international panache.

White Barn Inn, Beach St, tel: (207) 967-2321. $$$$. A beautifully appointed barn serving stellar nouvelle cuisine.

Windows on the Water, Chase Hill, tel: (207) 967-3313. A modern restaurant known for its inventive treatments of lobster, which may appear in half-a-dozen succulent guises.

KINGFIELD

The Herbert, tel: (207) 265-2000. $$. Hearty regional dishes served in an airy Victorian dining room.

Longfellow's, Main St, tel: (207) 265-4394. $. A casual riverside cafe with good dishes and good prices.

One Stanley Avenue, tel: (207) 265-5541. $$–$$$. The indigenous foods of Maine, artfully prepared.

LITTLE DEER ISLE

Eaton's Lobster Pool, Blastow Cove, tel: (207) 348-2383. $$$. Water views and fresh-off-the-boat seafood.

NORTHEAST HARBOR

Asticou Inn, tel: (207) 276-3344. $$$$. Yankee standards as well as welcome interlopers, in a grand old dining room overlooking the sea.

Redfield's, Main St, tel: (207) 276-5283. $$$. A summery cafe serving all three meals, New American-style.

OGUNQUIT

Arrows, Berwick Rd (off Route 1), tel: (207) 361-1100. $$$$. Dinner only. Adventurous (and exquisite) international cuisine in an English-country-style farmhouse.

Barnacle Billy's, Perkins Cove, tel: (207) 646-5575. $$$. Classic seafood, right on the water.

PORTLAND

Alberta's, 21 Pleasant St, tel: (207) 774-5408. $$. A congenial cafe with an ever-playful menu.

The Back Bay Grill, 65 Portland St, tel: (207) 772-8833. $$$. Sophisticated decor, sensuous food.

Cafe Always, 47 Middle St, tel: 774-9399. $$. Endlessly inventive cuisine; intimate.

Seamen's Club Restaurant, 1 Exchange St, tel: (207) 772-7311. $$. Seafood standards, with a view of the harbor.

ROCKPORT

Marcel's, Samoset Resort, 220 Warrenton St, tel: (207) 594-2511, (800) 341-1650. $$$$. Million-dollar views, with eclectic cuisine priced to match.

SEARSPORT

Nickerson Tavern, Route 1, tel: (207) 438-2220. $$$. Dinner only. Superb regional cuisine in a former sea captain's home.

SOUTHWEST HARBOR

Beal's Lobster Pier, Clark Point Rd, tel: (207) 244-7178, $. A classic wharfside lobster shack.

The Claremont, Clark Point Rd, tel: (27) 244-5036. The venerable 1884 inn has an ambitious modernist menu.

STONINGTON

Bay View Restaurant, Seabreeze Ave, tel: (207) 367-2274. $$. At-the-source seafood feasting.

VINALHAVEN

The Haven, Main St, tel: (207) 863-4969. An amazingly cosmopolitan bistro on one of Maine's more reclusive islands.

WALDOBORO

Moody's Diner, Route 1, tel: (207) 832-7468. $. A working-class classic.

WATERFORD

Lake House, Routes 35 and 37, tel: (207) 583-4181. $$. Dinner only. Inspired regional cuisine.

WISCASSET

Le Garage, Water St, tel: (207) 822-5409. $$$. Regional American fare in a picture-perfect town.

The Squire Tarbox Restaurant, tel: (207) 882-7693. $$$. Dinner only. A colonial farmhouse serving home-raised delicacies.

YORK

Chef Mimmo's Restaurant, Route 1A, tel: (207) 363-3807. $$. An unprepossessing cafe with an exuberant Tuscan chef.

One Fish, Two Fish, Route 1, tel: (207) 363-8196. $$. An adventurous world-beat bistro.

The Restaurant at Dockside Guest Quarters, Harris Island, tel: (207) 363-2722. $$$. From seaside standards to modern innovations, all with a water view.

YORK HARBOR

York Harbor Inn, Route 1A, tel: (207) 363-5119. $$$–$$$$. Well-considered continental/regional fare.

MASSACHUSETTS

BARNSTABLE

Mattakeese Wharf, 271 Mill Way, tel: (508) 362-4511. $$$. A classic wharfside seafood haven.

BOSTON

Another Season, 97 Mt Vernon St, tel: (617) 367-0880. $$$. Romantic atmosphere and skilled, international cuisine.

Anthony's Pier 4 Restaurant, 140 Northern Ave, tel: (617) 423-6363. $$$. Big, boisterous, and, frankly, mediocre, but a mecca nonetheless.

Aujourd'hui (Four Seasons Hotel), 200 Boylston St, tel: (617) 451-1392. $$$$. The decor is corporate-opulent, the cuisine invariably artful.

Bay Tower Room, 60 State St, tel: (617) 723-1666. $$$$. The main draw is the sky-scraping views; culinary peaks can't be counted on.

Biba, 272 Boylston St, tel: (617) 426-7878. $$$. There's no place trendier; owner-chef Lydia Shire is Boston's most resplendent culinary diva.

Blue Diner, 215 South St, tel: (617) 338-4639. A newly trendy 1947 diner.

Capital Grill, 399 Newbury St, tel: (617) 262-8900. $$$$. Where the suits go to sup on steaks.

Commonwealth Brewing Co, 138 Portland St, tel: (617) 523-8383. $. The pub grub is hearty, the home brew alluring.

Cornucopia on the Wharf, 100 Atlantic Avenue, tel: (617) 338-4600. $$. Entertaining international cuisine and unbeatable water views.

Cottonwood Cafe, 222 Berkeley St, tel: (617) 427-2225. $$$. Artful Tex-Mex, in a cool desert-like setting.

The Daily Catch, 325 Hanover St, tel: (617) 523-

8567. $$. Superb scungili – and other seafood – in the North End.

Dakota's, 101 Arch St, tel: (617) 737-1777. $$$. Surprising elegance, and a menu with Texan touches, at the epicenter of downtown.

Davio's, 269 Newbury St, tel: (617) 262-4810. $$. Old World charm in a Back Bay townhouse.

Durgin-Park, Faneuil Hall Marketplace, tel: (617) 227-2038. $$. Cheap New England classics (chowder, pot roast baked beans), with good-natured insults thrown in free.

East Ocean City, 25-29 South St, tel: (617) 524-2504. $. Chinatown's tastiest new eatery.

L'Espalier, 30 Gloucester St, tel: (617) 262-3023. $$$$. This ultra-elegant Victorian townhouse stays two steps ahead of the culinary cutting edge.

Grill 23, 161 Berkeley St, tel: (617) 542-2255. $$$$. Prime protein amid studied elegance modeled on an old-fashioned men's club.

Hamersley's Bistro, 539 Tremont St, tel: (617) 267-6068. $$$. Deft and imaginative touches dress up this sophisticated comfort food.

Hampshire House, 84 Beacon St, tel: (617) 227-9600. $$$. Nonpareil jazz brunch with a view of the Public Garden.

Jacob Wirth, 31 Stuart St, tel: (617) 338-8586. $$. German fare in an institution preserved since 1845.

Jasper's, 240 Commercial St, tel: (617) 523-1126. $$$$. Jasper White is such a culinary giants, aficionados are willing to overlook a heavy dose of waiterly attitude.

Julien, Le Meridien Hotel, 250 Franklin St, tel: (617) 451-1900. $$$$. First-class French cuisine, amid the marble grandeur of the former Federal Reserve Building.

Legal Sea Foods, Boston Park Plaza Hotel, 64 Arlington St, tel: (617) 426-4444. $$$. The freshest of fish, served seriatim, the moment it's done.

Loading Zone, 150 Kneeland St, tel: (212) 695-0087. $$. Southern-style cooking in the artsy Leather District.

Locke-Ober, 3 Winter Place, tel: (617) 542-1340. $$$. Brahmin (i.e., somewhat boring) cuisine in an atmospheric 1894 landmark.

Maison Robert, 45 School St, tel: (617) 227-3370. $$$$. Classical French cuisine; high prices.

Marais, 116 Boylston St, tel: (617) 542-7799. $$$. Bold California cuisine and an endless bar that's the place to be seen.

Marketplace Grill and Oar Bar, Faneuil Hall Marketplace, tel: (617) 227-2972. $$. Sunny New American cooking in a handsome brick loft overlooking Quincy Market.

Parker's Restaurant, Omni Parker House, 60 School St, tel: (617) 227-8600. $$$. Home of the Parker House roll, and a peaceful redoubt for business lunches and Brahmin dinners.,

Plaza Dining Room, Copley Plaza Hotel, 138 James Avenue, tel: (617) 267-5300. $$$$. Outstanding French cuisine in a barrel-vaulted altar to British Empire excess.

Rebecca's, 21 Charles St, tel: (617) 742-9747. $$$. Smart New American food wows Beacon Hillers and outsiders alike.

Ristorante Toscano, 41 Charles, tel: (617) 723-4090. $$$. True Tuscan delicacies in a handsome upscale trattoria.

The Ritz Dining Room, Ritz-Carlton Hotel, 15 Arlington St, tel: (617) 536-5700. $$$. The menu choices may be stuffy, but this is still the spot for Brahmin-watching.

Rocco's, 5 Charles St South, tel: (617) 723-6800. $$$. North Italian bounty amid eccentrically modern decor.

Rowes Wharf Restaurant, Boston Harbor Hotel, 70 Rowes Wharf, tel: (617) 439-3995. $$$$. Superb harbor views and the best imaginable regional cuisine.

Sakura-bana, 57 Broad St, tel: (617) 542-4311. $$. Nonpareil sushi in the financial district.

Seasons, Bostonian Hotel, Faneuil Hall Marketplace, tel: (617) 523-3600. $$$$. Boston's hottest chefs have earned their stripes here; expect to be dazzled by next season's star.

Skipjack's, 500 Boylston St, tel: (617) 536-3500. $$$. Native seafood with a modernist bent.

Sonsie, 237 Newbury St, tel: (617) 351-2500. A trendsetter's cafe, with exotic fare.

Trattoria Il Panino, 295 Franklin St, tel: (617) 338-1001. A restaurant/cafe/nightclub complex in the financial district.

29 Newbury St, 29 Newbury St, tel: (617) 536-0290. $$$. A perennially popular bistro, with a strategic sidewalk cafe for assessing the passing fashion parade.

Union Oyster House, 41 Union St, tel: (617) 227-2750. $$$. You can find comparable seafood elsewhere, of course, but not the authentic circa 1826 setting.

West Street Grille, 15 West St, tel: (617) 423-0300. $$$. A former Transcendalist salon, now a trendy bistro.

BREWSTER

Bramble Inn, 2019 Main St, tel: (508) 896-7644. $$$. Intimate rooms with interesting decor, and absolutely fascinating food.

Brewster Fish House, 2208 Main St, tel: (508) 896-7867. "Nonconformist" seafood; snazzy desserts.

Chillingsworth, Main St, tel: (508) 896-3640. $$$$. The seven-course *prix fixe* menu (classical French) is the among the ultimate dining experiences the Cape has to offer.

Cobie's, 3260 Main St, tel: (508) 896-7021. A classic 1948 clam shack, near the Rail Trail.

High Brewster, 964 Satucket Rd, tel: (508) 896-3936. $$$. High-spirited seasonal cuisine in a 1738 homestead.

Old Manse Inn, 1861 Main St, tel: (508) 896-3149. $$$. Mediterranean panache; opt to be seated in the sunporch, surrounded by flowers.

Pranzo, 1097 Main St, tel: (508) 896-9350. A deli/cafe with superlative salads and sandwiches.

BROOKLINE

Providence, 1223 Beacon St, tel: (508) 232-0030. It's worth the slight detour suburb-ward for chef Paul O'Connell's artistry.

CAMBRIDGE

Algiers Cafe, 40 Brattle St, tel: (617) 492-1557. $. Turkish coffee and *tabbouleh* for the intelligentsia.

Anago Bistro, 798 Main St, tel: (617) 876-8444. $$$. Daring menus characterize this hidden gem.

Cafe Marino, 30 Dunster St, tel: (617) 491-0616. $ A stylish farm-fresh Italian buffet/cafe in the heart of Harvard Square.

Casablanca, 40 Brattle St, tel: (617) 876-0999. $$. Moroccan/American menu within reach of student budgets; go just for David Omar White's murals of the movie.

Daddy-O's Bohemian Cafe, 134 Hampshire St; tel: (617) 354-8371. $. From '50s standards to contemporary cuisine.

East Coast Grill, 1271 Cambridge St, tel: (617) 491-6568. Barbecue, blue margaritas, and bourbon bread pudding – the theme is Southern, spicy, and stylish.

Green Street Grill, 280 Green St, tel: (617) 876-1655. $$. A drab bar in a marginal neighborhood serves hyper-spicy Islands food to a lively jazz accompaniment.

Harvest, 44 Brattle, tel: (617) 492-1115. $$$. Harvard Square's most reliably innovative bistro, with a civilized bar.

House of Blues, 96 Winthrop St, tel: (617) 876-8330. $$. Southern to international fare, with musical accompaniment.

John Harvard's Brew House, 33 Dunster St, tel: (617) 868-3585. $$. Surprisingly refined pub grub, and made-on-the-premises beers.

Michela's, Charles Hotel, 1 Bennett St, tel: (617) 864-1200. $$$–$$$$. Restaurateur Michela Larson and chef Jody Adams have earned international accolades for their flavorful Mediterranean cuisine.

Miracle of Science Bar & Grill, 321 Massachusetts Avenue, tel: (617) 828-2866. $. A popular MIT bar and grille where the drinks come in beakers.

Salamander, 1 Athenaeum St, tel: (617) 225 2121. $$$. Chef Stan Frankenthaler is a rising star in Boston's culinary firmament for his bold, sure hand and international inspiration.

CHARLESTOWN

Olives, 10 City Square, tel: (617) 242-1999. $$$. Avid patrons put up with long lines to savor Todd English's Tuscan country cuisine.

Figs, 67 Main St, tel: (6617) 242-2229. $. Olive's pizza-parlor cousin, only slightly less mobbed.

CHATHAM

Christian's Restaurant, 43 Main, tel: (508) 945-3363. $$$$. A lively New American bistro; upstairs, an inviting, library-like piano bar.

The Impudent Oyster, 15 Chatham Bars Ave, tel: (508) 945-3545. $$. International takes on local seafood; popular and packed.

The Main Dining Room, Chatham Bars Inn, Shore Rd, tel: (508) 945-0096, (800) 527-4884. A grand old dining room with French and regional cuisine.

Vining's Bistro, 595 Main St, tel: (508) 945-5033. $$$. A wood grill with a taste for exotic spices.

Eben Ryder House, Wequasset Inn, 173 Route 28, tel: (508) 432-5400. $$$. The superb New American cuisine lives up to the scenic setting.

CHILMARK

The Feast of Chilmark, State Rd, tel: (508) 645-3553. $$$$. New York-sophisticate cuisine in a loft carved out of a plain clapboard house.

CONCORD

Aigo Bistro, 84 Thoreau St, tel: (508) 371-1333. $$. Sophisticated Provencale cuisine.

COTUIT

The Regatta of Cotuit at the Crocker House, 4613 Falmouth Rd (Route 28), tel: (508) 428-5715. $$$$. The Falmouth Regatta's inland cousin; exquisite cuisine in a 1790 stagecoach inn.

DEERFIELD

Deerfield Inn, The Street, tel: (413) 774-557. $$$. The setting is appropriately sedate, the menu surprisingly forward-thinking.

DENNIS

Gina's by the Sea, 134 Taunton Ave, tel: (508) 385-3213. $$$. Hearty classics characterize this lively cafe set amid the Cape's "Little Italy."

The Red Pheasant, 905 Main St, tel: (508) 385-2133. $$$. Bold New American cuisine in an 18th-century ship's chandlery.

Scargo Cafe, 799 Main St, tel: (508) 385-8200. Traditional favorites, plus a few wildcards, in a retrofitted captain's house.

EASTHAM

Eastham Lobster Pool, 4360 Route 6, tel: (508) 255-9706. $$$. Unbeatable fresh fish; no frills.

EDGARTOWN

Among the Flowers Cafe, Mayhew Lane, tel: (508) 627-3233. $. Omelettes, quiches, pasta, and other filling, inexpensive fare.

L'Etoile, Charlotte Inn, 27 S. Summer St, tel: (508) 627.5187. $$$$. Superlative nouvelle cuisine served in a candlelit conservatory.

The Newes from America, 23 Kelley St, tel: (508) 627.7900. $. Pub grub in a recently unearthed 1742 tavern; a vast selection of beers, available in sampler "racks."

Savoir Faire, 14 Church St, tel: (508) 627-9864. $$$$. Skilful cuisine with sunny Mediterranean touches in a small, sophisticated restaurant with patio.

Warriner's, Post Office Square, tel: (508) 627-4488. $$$. A robust New American menu; choose the Library room for peace and atmosphere.

ESSEX

Woodman's, The Causeway, tel: (508) 768-6451. $. Home of the original fried clam, invented in 1915.

FALMOUTH

The Clam Shack, 227 Clinton Ave, tel: (508) 548-2626. $. A literal shack (very picturesque) right on the water.

The Flying Bridge, 220 Scranton Ave, tel: (508) 548-2700. $$. Seafood and sociability, with a view of the yacht-cluttered harbor.

The Regatta of Falmouth-by-the-Sea, 217 Clinton Ave, tel: (508) 548-5400. One of the Cape's most sophisticated restaurants, with elegant appointments and celestial nouvelle cuisine, surrounded by the Sound.

FALMOUTH HEIGHTS

The Wharf Restaurant, 281 Grand Ave South, tel: (508) 548-2772. A turn-of-the-century seafood restaurant with plenty of atmosphere and sweeping views.

GLOUCESTER

Bistro at 2 Main Street, 2 Main St, tel: (508) 768-6451. $$. World-beat cuisine defies the small-town setting.

Evie's Rudder, 73 Rocky Neck, tel: (508) 283-7967. $$. A rollicking tavern in the Rocky Neck artists' colony.

White Rainbow, 65 Main St, tel: (508) 281-0017. $$$. Rich, evolved Continental in a dramatic granite-walled hideaway.

GREAT BARRINGTON

Boiler Room Cafe, 405 Stockbridge Rd (Route 7), tel: (413) 528-4280. $$–$$$. Contemporary American/Mediterranean.

Castle Street Cafe, 10 Castle St, tel: (413) 52-5244. $$–$$$. An American/Continental bistro with big-city flair.

La Tomate Bistro Provencale, 293 Main St, tel: (413) 528-3003. The sunny bounty of southern France.

The Windflower Inn, Egremont Star Route 65, tel: (413) 528-2720. $$$. Succulent home-prepared seasonal fare.

HARWICH PORT

Thompson's Clam Bar, 23 Snow Inn Rd., tel: (508) 432-3595. A wall of windows looking out on the boats; nautical decor and menu.

HULL

Saporito, 11 Rockland Circle, tel: (617) 925-33023. $$. A charming neo-Italian trattoria.

HYANNIS

Alberto's Ristorante, 360 Main St, tel: (508) 778-1770. $$$$. Studied yet hearty Italian; Hyannis's most accomplished cuisine.

Asa Bearse House, 415 Main St, tel: (508) 771-4444: $$. People-watching is the focus of a patio lunch; the bar has live music at night.

Baxter's Boat House Club and Fish-N-Chips, 177 Pleasant St, tel: (508) 775-4490. $$. Perched over the harbor, a '50s clam shack with a lively blues bar.

East End Grill, 247 Main St, tel: (508) 790-2898. $$. Behind the Victorian facade, a young, lively crowd and the stuff they like to munch on.

Fazio's Trattoria, 586 Main St, tel: (508) 771-7445. $$. Wood-oven pizza and other Italian delights.

Mooring on the Waterfront, 230 Ocean St, tel: (508) 774-4656. $$$. Seafood, by the ferry.

The Paddock, West End Rotary, tel: (508) 775-7677. $$$$. Fancy Continental, convenient to the Cape Cod Melody Tent.

Starbuck's, 950 Iyanough Rd, tel: (508) 771-8816. $$. Eccentric decor and Mexican-American fare, by the airport.

Steamers, 235 Ocean St, tel: (508) 778-0818. $$. Mesquite-grilled seafood; live music, and a place-to-be deck.

Tugboats, 21 Arlington St, tel: (508) 21 Arlington St, tel: (508) 775-6433. $$. Fun food and great harbor views, especially at sunset.

Up the Creek, 36 Old Colony Blvd, tel: (508) 771-7866. $$. Boathouse decor; international menu.

LENOX

Albion Restaurant, Village Inn, 16 Church St, Lenox, (413) 637-0009. $$$. New American artistry in a venerable 1771 inn.

Blantyre, Route 20, tel: (413) 637-3556. Summer only. $$$$. Contemporary French cuisine in the formal dining rooms of a Tudor mansion.

Church Street Cafe, 69 Church St, tel: (413) 637-2745. Featuring light fare and whimsical decor.

Wheatleigh, West Hawthorne, tel: (413) 637-0610. $$$$. Exquisite nouvelle cuisine, as befits a neo-Palladian mansion.

MASHPEE

The Flume, Lake Ave (off Route 130), tel: (508) 477-1465. $$$. A Native American-owned restaurant featuring such Cape classics as clam chowder, codfish cakes, and Indian pudding.

MENEMSHA

Beach Plum Inn Restaurant, off North Rd, tel: (508) 645-9454. $$$$. Cordon Bleu classics in a seaview farmhouse surrounded by flowers.

Home Port, North Rd, tel: (508) 645-2679. $$$$. Fresh-off-the-boat seafood in a picturesque harbor.

NANTUCKET

American Seasons, 80 Centre St, tel: (508) 228.7111. $$$$. Adventurous dining amid colorful murals.

The Boarding House, 12 Federal St, tel: (508) 228-9622. $$$$. Bold New American cuisine, and the island's most sophisticated sidewalk cafe.

The Beach Plum Cafe, 11 West Creek Rd, tel: (508) 228-8893. $$. Reasonable (for Nantucket) prices and a skilled chef make up for the remote location.

The Brotherhood of Thieves, 23 Broad St, no phone. $$ Great burgers, live music, and good company in an 1840 whaling bar.

The Chanticleer Inn, 9 New St, Siasconset, tel: (508) 257-6231. Classical French cuisine in an opulent auberge-like setting.

The Club Car, 1 Main St, tel: (508) 228-1101. $$$$ The dining room serves gourmet fare; the bar was borrowed from the narrow-gauge railroad that used to go to Sconset.

Espresso Cafe, 40 Main St, tel: (508) 228-6930. $. Cheap and scrumptious international grazing at a vintage ice cream parlor turned cafe.

Rope Walk, Straight Wharf, tel: (508) 228-8886. $$$$. Seafood with nouvelle splashes, on the harbor.

The Second Story, 1 South Beach St, tel: (508) 228-3471. $$$. Exotic fare in an artistic hideaway.
Straight Wharf Restaurant, Straight Wharf, tel: (508) 228-4499. $$$$. Elegant regional fare in a handsome loft space.
21 Federal, 21 Federal St, tel: (508) 228-2121. $$$$. Sensational regional cuisine in a tastefully spare 1847 Greek Revival house.
The Woodbox Restaurant, 29 Fair St, tel: (508) 228-0587. $$$$. Continental dining in a 1709 Colonial house with keeping room.

NEWBURYPORT
Glenn's Galley, Merrimack St, tel: (508) 465-3811. $$. Creative cuisine in a former shoe factory.

NEW MALBOROUGH
Old Inn on the Green, Gedney Farm, tel: (413) 229-7924, (800) 752-1896. $$$$. French *auberge*-style cuisine in a circa 1760 stagecoach inn.

NEW SEABURY
Popponesset Inn, Mall Way (off Shore Dr), tel: (508) 477-1100. $$$$. Superb New American cuisine in a classic beachside inn-turned-restaurant.

NORTHAMPTON
Curtis & Schwartz, 116 Main St, tel: (413) 586-3278. $. A noshery that caters to all cravings.
Spoleto, 50 Main St, tel: 413) 586-6313. $$$. Italian classics in a lively contemporary cafe.

NORTH TRURO
Adrian's, Route 6, tel: (508) 487-4360. $$. Irresistible neo-Italian treats; spectacular views.

OAK BLUFFS
The Oyster Bar, 162 Circuit Ave, tel: (508) 693-3300. $$$. A glamourous '30s-style bistro with rarefied food.
Papa's Pizza, 158 Circuit Ave, tel: (508) 693-1400. $. An old-fashioned storefront serving traditional pies at long wooden tables.

ORLEANS
The Arbor, 20 South Orleans St, tel: (508) 255-4847. $$$. The decor is an entertaining flea-market jumble, the cuisine rich Continental.
Capt. Cass Rock Harbor Seafood, 117 Rock Harbor Rd, no phone. No-frills '50s seafood shanty.
The Captain Linnell House, 137 Skaket Beach Rd, tel: (508) 255-3400. $$$$. Evolved Continental cuisine in a neoclassic 1854 villa.
Land Ho!, 38 Main St, tel: (508) 255-5165. $$. A pub known mostly to locals, who keep it packed.
Off-the-Bay Cafe, 28 Main St, tel: (508) 255-5505. $$$$. An ambitious bistro menu; jazz brunch.

OSTERVILLE
East Bay Lodge, 199 East Bay Rd., tel: (508) 428-5200, (800) 933-2782. $$$$. Outstanding New American cuisine in a formal setting popular among the local gentry for more than a century.
Joseph's Restaurant, 825 Main St, tel: (508) 420-1742. $$. A restful cafe featuring rustic Italian cuisine.

PLYMOUTH
Cafe Nanina, 14 Union St, tel: (508) 747-4503. $$$. Italian country cuisine; on the deck looks out on the Mayflower II.

PROVINCETOWN
Cafe Blase, 328 Commercial St, tel: (508) 487-9465. $. A sidewalk cafe perfect for people-gazing.
Cafe Edwige, 33 Commercial St, tel: (508) 487-1279. $$$. Natural-foods breakfasts, delicious enough to seem sinful.
Cafe Heaven, 338 Commercial St, tel: (508) 487-9639. $. The best burgers in town; breakfasts, too.
Euro Island Grill & Cafe, 258 Commercial St, tel: (508) 487-2505. $$. A Caribbean *tiki* bar perched above the teeming street.
Front Street Restaurant, 230 Commercial St, tel: (508) 487-9715. The cuisine is cutting-edge, the ambiance intimate and intense.
Franco's by the Sea, 133 Bradford St, tel: (508) 487-3178. $$$. Art Deco decor and Italian comfort food to die for.
Gallerani's Cafe, 133 Commercial St, tel: (508) 487-4433. $$$. An appealing bistro with cozy booths and eclectic cuisine.
The Martin House, 157 Commercial St, tel: (508) 487-1327. $$$. A ca. 1750 shingled house with intimate, rustic dining rooms and skilled regional cuisine.
The Mews and Cafe Mews, 429 Commercial St, tel: (508) 487-1500. $$-$$$. On-the-beach elegance; creative cuisine.
The Moors, 5 Bradford St Extension, tel: (508) 487-0840. $$. A chance to sample Portuguese cuisine in a restaurant made of marine wreckage.
Napi's, 7 Freeman St, tel: (508) 487-1145. $$$. A colorful institution built of architectural salvage; the menu spans the world.
The Red Inn, 15 Commercial St, tel: (508) 487-0050. $$$. Festive cuisine and lovely water views, at the very spot where the Pilgrims landed.
Sal's Place, 99 Commercial St, tel: (508) 487-1279. $$$. Classical Italian, loaded with romance.
Spiritus, 190 Commercial St, tel: (508) 487-2808. A pizza mecca, and magnet for the late-night crowd.

ROCKPORT
The Glass Verandah, Yankee Clipper Inn, 96 Granite St, tel: (508) 546-3407. $$$. Studied and satisfying New American cuisine in a formal setting with ocean views.

SALEM
The Grapevine, 26 Congress St, tel: (508) 745-9355. $$. A popular cafe that ranges the globe for inspiration.

SANDWICH
Dan'l Webster Inn, Main St, tel: (508) 888-3622. $$. Surprisingly sophisticated cuisine for a restaurant on this large a scale.

SOMERVILLE
Dali, 415 Washington St, tel: (617) 661-3254. $$. Robust Spanish specialties, and an atmosphere worthy of Hemingway.

SOUTH DEERFIELD
Sienna, 28 Elm St, tel: (413) 665-0215. $$$. Distinguished regional cuisine.

SPRINGFIELD
Student Prince and Fort Restaurant, 8 Fort St, tel: (413) 734-7375. $$. Stout German cuisine in a convincing beer hall atmosphere, since the '40s.

STURBRIDGE
Whistling Swan, 502 Main St, tel: (508) 347-2321. $$. New American cuisine in a formal dining room; more casual fare in a converted barn.

VINEYARD HAVEN
Black Dog Tavern, Beach St Extension, tel: (508) 693-9223. $$$$. Inventive neo-American fare in a simple wharfside tavern.

WALTHAM
Tuscan Grill, 361 Moody St, tel: (617) 891-5486. $$. Northern Italian delights in an unprepossessing post-Industrial town.

WELLFLEET
Aesop's Tables, Main St, tel: (508) 349-6450. $$$. Festive and celestial regional cuisine; delightful attic bar.

Bayside Lobster Hut, Commercial St, tel: (508) 349-6333. $. Shore dinners in an 1857 oyster shack.

Flying Fish, Briar Lane, tel: (508) 349-3100. $$$. A friendly, fun cafe off the tourist circuit.

Painter's Lunch, Kendrick Ave, no phone. A skilled young culinary artist runs this funky lunchroom, a salon for local writers.

WEST BROOKFIELD
Salem Cross Inn, Route 9, tel: (508) 867-2345. $$$. A 1705 "ordinary" (tavern) offering authentic hearth cookery.

WEST STOCKBRIDGE
La Bruscetta Ristorante, 1 Harris St, tel: (413) 232-7141. $$. Dinner only. Traditional, contemporary, and cutting-edge Italian.

WILLIAMSTOWN
The Orchards, 222 Adams Rd, tel: (413) 458-9611. $$$. Accomplished New American cuisine in a setting of studied elegance.

WOODS HOLE
The Fishmonger Cafe, 56 Water St, tel: (508) 548-9148. $$. A lively wharfside cafe with inventive natural foods and fresh seafood.

Landfall, Water St, tel: (508) 548-1758. $$. Seafood in a loft-like space festooned with nautical salvage.

Shuckers World Famous Raw Bar & Cafe, 91A Water St, tel: (508) 540-3850. $$. The freshest of seafood, to be slurped dockside.

YARMOUTHPORT
Abbici, 43 Main St, tel: (508) 362-3501. $$$$. This 1775 house sports drop-dead modern decor and serves knockout Northern Italian cuisine.

Inaho, 157 Main St, tel: (508) 362-5522. $$$. A superb Japanese restaurant, with the freshest possible sushi.

Jack's Outback, 161 Main St, tel: (508) 362-6690. $. Looking for local color? You'll find it here in spades, along with tasty, affordable old-favorites food.

Le Trajet, 223 Main St, tel: (508) 362-3191. $$$$. The old Yarmouthport Inn (ca. 1696) proffers nouvelle cuisine, accompanied by jazz.

Tartufi's, 134 Main St, tel: (508) 362-1133. $$ A charming little trattoria, suffused with *bel canto* and *paisan* cuisine.

NEW HAMPSHIRE

ASHLAND
The Common Man, Main St, tel: (603) 968-7030. $$. Well-priced and popular American fare.

BEDFORD
Bedford Village Inn, 2 Old Bedford Rd, tel: (603) 472-2001. $$$. Country club atmosphere in an updated 18th-century inn.

BRETTON WOODS
Mount Washington Hotel, Route 302, tel: (603) 278-1000. $$. Old-fashioned fare, but a fascinating glimpse of luxury past.

CANTERBURY
Creamery Restaurant, Canterbury Shaker Village, tel: (603) 783-9511. Reservations required. $$. Authentic Shaker cuisine.

CENTER BARNSTEAD
Crystal Quail, Pitman Rd, tel: (603) 269-4151. $$$$. Superb country cuisine, and a well-kept secret.

CENTER HARBOR
Red Hill Inn, Route 25B, tel: (603) 279-7000. $$–$$$. New American creativity in a red-brick summer estate.

CENTER SANDWICH
Corner House Inn, Main St, tel: (603) 284-6219. $$. Continental fare in a charming 1849 house.

CHOCORUA
Stafford's-in-the-Field, tel: (603) 323-7766. $$. Made-from-scratch regional cuisine.

CONCORD
Thursday's, 6 Pleasant St, tel: (603) 224-2525. $. A '60s-era coffeehouse with delicious cuisine and live music.

DIXVILLE NOTCH
The Balsams Grand Resort Hotel, tel: (800) 255-3400. $$$. Reservations required. Lavish buffet spreads.

ENFIELD
The Shaker Inn, Lower Shaker Village, tel: (603) 632-7800. $$$. Traditionally influenced New American in the Great Stone Dwelling.

FRANCONIA
Franconia Inn, Easton Rd, tel: (603) 823-5542. $$$. Ambitious Continental cuisine in a formal mountainview dining room.

Lovett's Inn by Lafayette Brook, Profile Rd, tel: (603) 823-7761. $$. A mix of traditional favorites and more adventurous fare.

GLEN
The Bernerhof, Route 302, tel: (603) 383-4414. $$$. Alpine delights – including *spaetzle* and Provimi veal – ideal for ski country.

HANOVER
The Ivy Grill in the Hanover Inn, Main St, tel: (603) 643-2345. $$$. A successful New American eating

experiment set in a bastion of traditionalism.

HENNIKER
Colby Hill Inn, tel: (603) 428-3281. $$$. A late 18th-century inn with country views and Continental cuisine.

HOLDERNESS
The Manor on Golden Pond, Route 3, tel: (603) 968-3348. $$$. Rich continental cuisine in a baronial setting.

JACKSON
The Dining Room, Wentworth Resrot Hotel, (603) 383-9700. $$$. Continental cuisine in a fancy French Provincial dining room.

The Inn at Thorn Hill, Thorn Hill Rd, tel: (603) 383-4242. $$$. Country-sophisticate cuisine in a handsome country house.

Thompson House Eatery, Routes 16A and 16, tel: (603) 383-9341. $$. Closed winter. Innovative salads and sandwiches, luscious entrees, in an 1800s barn with flowery patio.

Wildcat Inn and Tavern, Route 16A, tel: (603) 383-4245. $$. Owner/chef Marty Sweeney caters to gourmets and gourmands alike.

LITTLETON
The Beal House Inn, 247 West Main St (Routes 302 and 28), tel: (603) 444-2661. $$–$$$. European cuisine in a handsome carriage house.

Tim-Bir Alley, 18 Main St, tel: (603) 444-6142. $$$. Extraordinary sophistication for a small-scale, small-town restaurant.

LYME
D'Artagnan, 13 Dartmouth College Highway, Route 10, tel: (603) 795-2137. Reservations required. $$$. Classically trained chef Peter Gaylor and his wife, patissiere Rebecca Cunningham, have created a temple of culinary arts in a charming Colonial tavern.

MANCHESTER
Red Arrow Lunch, 61 Lowell Ave, tel: (603) 624-2211. $. A 1903 luncheonette, open 24 hours.

MASON
Parker's Maple Barn, Brookline Rd, tel: (603) 878-2308. A 19th-century barn serving home-made pancakes with home-grown syrup.

NEW LONDON
The New London Inn, Main St, tel: (603) 526-2791. $$–$$$. Inventive regional cuisine.

NORTH CONWAY
The Scottish Lion Inn, Route 16, tel: (603) 356-6381. $$$. Tasty English specialties, such as bubble-and-squeak.

Stonehurst Manor, Route 16, tel: (603) 356-3113. $$$. Continental cuisine, plus stone-hearth pizzas.

PETERBOROUGH
The Boilerhouse, Route 202, tel: (203) 924-9486. $$$. A sophisticated bistro overlooking Noone Falls.

Folkway Restaurant, 85 Grove St, tel: (603) 924-7484. $$. A folk-music coffeehouse with appealing cafe fare.

Latacarta, 6 School St, tel: (603) 924-6878. $$$. Health food with a sense of style.

PINKHAM NOTCH
Appalachian Mountain Club, Pinkham Notch Camp, Route 16, tel: (603) 466-2727. Dinner only. $. Hearty fare for hikers.

PLAINFIELD
Home Hill Inn, River Rd, tel: (603) 675-6165. $$$. Classic French cuisine from a native chef.

PORTSMOUTH
L'Auberge, 96 Bridge St, tel: (603) 436-2377. $$. Casual yet authentic French country cuisine.

Blue Strawbery, 29 Ceres St, tel: (603) 431-6420. Dinner only. $$$$. Exquisite New American cuisine in a converted 1797 chandlery.

Cafe Brioche, 14 Market Sq, tel: (603) 430-9225. Croissants, quiches, and a friendly sidewalk cafe.

The Dolphin Striker, 15 Bow St, tel: (603) 431-5222. $$. A riverfront tavern specializing in New American seafood.

The Grotto, 75 Pleasant St, tel: 96030 436-1373. $–$$. Well-priced Mediterranean cuisine.

Karen's, 105 Daniel St, tel: (603) 431-1948. $$. A tiny cafe, unusually creative – especially the breakfasts.

The Library Restaurant at the Rockingham House, 401 State St, tel: (603) 431-5202. International cuisine amid mahogany paneling and masses of books.

Porto Bello, 67 Bow St, tel: (603) 431-2989. $$–$$$. Nuovo Italian, with a view of the harbor.

The Portsmouth Brewery, 56 Market St, tel: (603) 431-1115. $$. A microbrewery with international munchies.

Strawbery Court, 20 Atkinson St, tel: (603) 431-7722. $$$$. Elegant nouvelle cuisine in a brick 1815 Federal house.

SNOWVILLE
Snowvillage Inn, 92 Stuart Rd, tel: (603) 447-2818. $$. Austrian specialties; unparalleled views.

SUGAR HILL
Polly's Pancake Parlor, Route 117, tel: (603) 823-5575. $. All-you-can-eat, maple-drenched pancakes, since 1938.

SUNAPEE
Seven Hearths, Old Route 11, (603) 763-5657. $$$. New American fare, by candlelight.

WILMOT
La Meridiana, Route 11 and Old Winslow Rd, (603) 526-2033. $$. Homemade North Italian specialities in a rambling farmhouse.

WOLFEBORO
The Bittersweet, Route 18, tel: (603) 569-3636. $$. An artifact-packed barn featuring local specialities.

WOODSTOCK
The Woodstock Inn, Main St, tel: (603) 7435-3951. $–$$$. Continental cuisine in the Victorian parlor; casual fare in the tavern.

338

RHODE ISLAND

LITTLE COMPTON

The Commons Lunch, The Common, tel: (401) 635-4388. $. A downhome diner fit for gentleman (and woman) farmers.

NARRAGANSETT

Spain, 1 Beach St, tel: (401) 783-9770. $$–$$$. Authentic Iberian cuisine; generous portions.

NEWPORT

Le Bistro, Bannister's Wharf, tel: (401) 849-7778. $$$$. A charming French cafe in a loft above the bustling harbor.

The Black Pearl, Bannister's Wharf, tel: (401) 846-5264. $$$. A classic harborside tavern.

The Clarke Cooke House, Bannister's Wharf, tel: (401) 849-2900. $$$$. A 1790 Colonial with formal, waterview dining.

The Mooring, Sayer's Wharf, tel: (401) 849-2260. $$–$$$. The former HQ of the New York Yacht Club; seafood staples.

Le Petite Auberge, 19 Charles St, tel: (401) 849-6669. $$$. Classic French in an historic home.

The Place, 28 Washington Square, tel: (4010 847-0116. A bustling new bistro with cutting-edge New American cuisine.

Puerini's, 24 Memorial Blvd West, tel: (401) 847-5506. $$. Affordable, traditional Italian staples, all made from scratch.

White Horse Tavern, Marlborough and Farewell streets, tel: (401) 849-3600. $$. Reputedly the oldest continually operating tavern in the US (established 1673), this atmospheric tavern serves classics like grilled lobster and Chateaubriand.

PROVIDENCE

Al Forno, 7 Steeple St, tel: (401) 273-9760. $$$$. New England's preeminent temple of *nuova cucina*.

Angels, 125 N Main St, tel: (401) 273-0310. $$$. A blend of New American and Mediterranean, in a handsome, intimate space.

Bluepoint Oyster Bar & Restaurant, 99 North Main St, tel: (401) 272-6145. $$$$. Innovative treatment of delicacies from the sea.

Capital Grille, 1 Cookson Place, tel: (401) 521-5600. $$$. Premium dry-aged beef, in the renovated railroad station.

Hemenway Sea Food, 1 Old Stone Square, tel: (401) 351-8570. $$$. Superb seafood, with views of the Providence River.

Pot au Feu, 44 Custom House St, tel: (401) 273-8953. $$$. From bistro-style to neo-classical French.

WAKEFIELD

South Shore Grille, 210 Salt Point Rd, tel: (401) 782-4780. $$–$$$. Wood grilling brings out the best in seafood.

WATCH HILL

The Olympia Tea Room, Bay St, tel: (401) 348-8211. $$. A classic 1916 luncheonette.

WESTERLY

Shelter Harbor Inn, 10 Wagner Rd, tel: (401) 322-8883. $$$. Well-priced regional specialties.

VERMONT

BENNINGTON

Sonny's Blue Benn Diner, Route 7, tel: (802) 442-8944. $. A classic '40s diner serving unconventional as well as traditional fare.

La Brasserie, 324 County St, tel: (802) 447-7922. $$. French country classics, in a modernist cafe or on a shaded patio.

The Four Chimneys, 21 West Rd, tel: (802) 447-3500. $$$$. Polished continental cuisine in a showpiece mansion.

BRANDON

Brandon Inn, Route 7, tel: (802) 247-5766. Regional artistry in a grand old Victorian hotel.

BRATTLEBORO

Common Ground, 25 Elliot St, tel: (802) 527-0855. $. A hippie holdover, featuring natural foods.

Latchis Grill, 50 Main St, tel: (802) 254-6300. $$. International fare, and brews from the on-site Windham Brewery.

Marina Bar & Grill, Putney Rd (Route 5,), tel: (802) 257-7563. $$. Well-priced casual food; waterside deck.

Peter Havens, 32 Elliot St, tel: (802) 257-3333. The locals' favorite New American bistro.

BRISTOL

Mary's, 11 Main St, tel: (802) 453-2432. $$$. A congenial cafe beloved of loyal *cognoscenti*.

BURLINGTON

Daily Planet, 15 Center St, tel: (802) 862-9647. $$. World-beat cuisine; the pulse center of town.

Deja Vu, 185 Pearl St, tel: (802) 864-7917. $$$. Creative bistro cuisine in a handcrafted setting of neo-Deco woodwork.

The Ice House, 171 Battery St, tel: (802) 864-1800. $$$. Fresh seafood; refreshing views of Lake Champlain.

Mirabelle's, 19 Main St, tel: (802) 658-3074. $. An inviting cafe/patisserie.

Trattoria Delia, 152 St Paul St, tel: (802) 864-5253. $$. Rustic Italian dishes, including wild boar.

COLCHESTER

Marble Island Resort, 250 Marble Island Rd, tel: (802) 864-6800. $$–$$$. Fun food on a lakeside patio bar; more elaborate fare inside.

CRAFTSBURY

The Craftsbury Inn, tel: (802) 586-2848: Intriguing *prix-fixe* dinners prepared by a talented chef-owner.

DORSET

Barrows House, Main St, tel: (802) 867-4455. $$$. New American in an intimate setting; the tavern serves lighter fare.

The Dorset Inn, Route 30, tel: (802) 867-5500. $$$. A choice of formal dining or tavern feasting in a 1796 hostelry.

EAST BURKE

The Old Cutter Inn, tel: (802) 626-5152. $$. Chef-owner Fritz Walther's native Swiss specialities, including irresistible *rosti*.

River Garden Cafe, tel: (802) 626-3514. $$.

Bruschetta and *tiramisu* come to the Northeast Kingdom.

EAST DORSET
Chantecleer, Route 7, tel: (802) 362-1616. $$$. Swiss and French provincial cuisine in an former dairy barn.

ESSEX JUNCTION
Butler's Restaurant, The Inn at Essex, 70 Essex Way, tel: (802) 878-1100. $$$. The New England Culinary Institute's "test" restaurant gets all A's.

FAIR HAVEN
Vermont Marble Inn, 12 West Park Place, tel: (802) 265-8383. $$–$$$. Bold "gourmet American" in a pretty Victorian inn.

GREENSBORO
Highland Lodge, tel: (802) 533-2647. Robust regional cuisine, with a view of Caspian Lake.

JEFFERSONVILLE
Le Cheval d'Or, Main St, tel: (802) 644-3556. $$$. Exquisite classic French cuisine in a charming old inn.

Three Mountain Lodge, Mountain Rd, tel: (802) 644-5736. $$ Bountiful native feasts with international flair, in an historic log ski chalet.

KILLINGTON
Cortina Inn, Route 4, tel: (802) 773-3311. $$$. Chefs from the New England Culinary Institute ensure deft and innovative fare.

Hemingway's, Route 4, tel: (802) 422-3886. $$$$. Inspired regional cuisine, consistently hailed as being among the nation's best;

LOWER WATERFORD
Rabbit Hill Inn, tel: (802) 748-5168. $$$. Dazzling New American cuisine in a rural setting of understated elegance.

LUDLOW
Nikki's, Route 103, tel: (802) 228-7797. $$. The decor is polished Hippie Deco, the New American cuisine delightful.

MANCHESTER
The Equinox, Route 7A, tel: (802) 362-5700. $$$. Spectacular regional cuisine in a formal barrel-vaulted dining room looking out on Mount Equinox; Marsh's Tavern serves more casual, but equally delicious fare.

The Garden Cafe, Southern Vermont Art Center, tel: (802) 362-4220. $. A beautifully site for delectable nibbling.

Village Country Inn, Route 7A, tel: (802) 362-1729. $$$. Continental cuisine in a charming French country-style inn.

MARLBORO
Skyline Restaurant, Route 9, tel: (802) 464-3535. $$. Pancakes, waffles, and good old American food galore, with a 100-mile view.

MARSHFIELD VILLAGE
Rainbow Sweets, Route 2, tel: (802) 426-3531. $. This delightful out-of-the-way cafe serves savouries, too.

MIDDLEBURY
Swift House Inn, 25 Stewart Lane, tel: (802) 388-

9925. $$$. Elegant regional cuisine in a formal, paneled Federal dining room.

Woody's, 5 Bakery Lane, tel: (802) 388-4182. $$$. Unfussy regional American; congenial crowd.

MONTPELIER
Angeleno's, 15 Barre St, (802) 229-5721. $$. A pizza and pasta emporium housed in a Victorian manse.

Elm Street Cafe, tel: (802) 223-3188. $$. Adventurous grazing courtesy of the highly skilled students of the New England Culinary Institute.

Tubbs, 24 Elm St, tel: (802) 229-9202. $$$. This NECI enterprise, in a rehabbed jailhouse, is thoroughly elegant, and culinary eloquent.

NEWFANE
Four Columns Inn, 230 West St, tel: (802) 365-7713. $$$$. Creative European/American cuisine, auberge-style.

PUTNEY
Curtis' All-American Barbecue, Route 5, tel: (802) 387-5474. Closed winter. $. Good ol' barbecue, slow-cooked beside an old blue school bus; funky, but divine.

QUECHEE
Isabelle's at Parker House, 16 Main St, tel: (802) 295-6077. $$$. Tasteful continental cuisine in a brick Victorian mansion with grand views.

The Quechee Inn at Marshland Farm, Clubhouse Rd, tel: (802) 295-3133. $$$. Delightful seasonal specialties in a tastefully restored tavern.

Simon Pearce Restaurant, The Mill, tel: (802) 295-1470. $$$. Fine country cuisine, with some Irish touches, in a modern cafe in an old riverside mill.

SHELBURNE
Shelburne House, Harbor Rd, tel: (802) 985-8498. Reservations required. $$$. Gourmet dining (and breakfasting) in a Queen Anne-style manor overlooking Lake Champlain.

SOUTH BURLINGTON
Pauline's, 1834 Shelburne Rd, tel: (802) 862-1081. $$$. Deft nouvelle American cuisine improbably plunked amid a strip mall.

SOUTH LONDONDERRY
Three Clocks Inn, Middletown Rd, tel: (802) 824-327. $$$. Hearty French classics, including fabulous *pommes frites*.

SOUTH NEWFANE
Inn at South Newfane, tel: (802) 348-7191. $$$. Thoughtful regional cuisine in a peaceful, pondside setting.

SOUTH WOODSTOCK
Kedron Valley Inn, Route 106, tel: (802) 457-1473. $$$. Chef Tom Hopewell is not just an artist, but a magician with regional ingredients.

STOWE
Austrian Tea Room, Trapp Family Lodge, Luce Hill Rd, tel: (802) 253-8511. $$. *Gemutlich* treats with fine valley views.

Blue Moon Cafe, 35 School St, tel: (802) 253-7006. $$. A contemporary bistro with lots of charm, vivid cuisine, and great prices.

Cliff House, Mount Mansfield, tel: (802) 253-3000. $$$. Board the world's fastest gondola for a culinary "peak" experience.

H. H. Bingham's, The Inn at the Mountain, Mountain Rd., tel: (802) 253-3000. Sophisticated all-American cuisine, at the foot of Mount Mansfield.

Miguel's Stowe Away, Mountain Rd, tel: (802) 253-7574. Very convincing Mexican, for ski country.

Restaurant Swisspot, tel: (802) 253-4622. $$. Fondue is the specialty; the mood, timeless and cozy.

Stowehof Inn, Edson Hill Rd., Stowe, (802) 253-9722. Elegant and astute New American cuisine, with a dramatic view.

Ten Acres Lodge, Barrows Rd, tel: (802) 253-7638. $$$–$$$$. Skilled regional cuisine, in handsome old farmhouse set amid a meadow.

Topnotch at Stowe Resort and Spa, Mountain Rd, tel: (802) 253-8585. A formal dining room and casual grill offer skilled contemporary cuisine, some of it calibrated for the health-conscious.

Trattoria La Festa, Mountain Rd, tel: (802) 253-8480. Authentic Italian cuisine in an 1859 farmhouse.

WAITSFIELD

R.S.V.P., Bridge St, tel: (802) 496-7787. $. Trendy flatbread pizza in a funky '50s-style lunchroom.

Tucker Hill Lodge, Route 17, tel: (802) 496-3983. Dinner only. $$$$. This country inn is as well known for its imaginative cuisine.

WARREN

Chez Henri, Sugarbush Village, tel: (802) 583-1600. An authentic French bistro in the middle of a bustling ski resort.

The Common Man, German Flats Rd, tel: (802) 583-2800. Country-sophisticate fare in an atmospheric old barn.

Sam Rupert's, tel: (802) 583-2301. $$$. Superb New American cuisine in a cozy, romantic setting.

WEATHERSFIELD

The Inn at Weathersfield, Route 106, tel: (802) 263-9217. $$$. Fine regional fare in a library illuminated by candlelight, with two grand pianos offering accompaniment.

WEST DOVER

Inn at Sawmill Farm, Country Club Rd, tel: (802) 464-8131. $$$$. Cuisine superb in its seeming simplicity; the setting is elegant rusticity.

WILMINGTON

The Hermitage, Coldbrook Rd, tel: (802) 464-3759. $$$$. Game birds raised right on the grounds, and a legendary cellar.

Le Petit Chef, Route 100, tel: (802) 824-5804. $$$. Classic French cuisine in a refined farmhouse.

WINOOSKI

Waterworks, Champlain Mill Shopping Center, 1 Main St, tel: (802) 655-2044. $$. A former wool mill with solaria, beside the rushing river; well-priced contemporary cuisine.

WOODSTOCK

Bentleys Restaurant, 3 Elm St, (802) 457-3232. $$. Eclectic, antique-ish decor and international dishes; a popular spot.

The Prince & the Pauper, 24 Elm St, tel: (802) 457-1818. $$$$. Known for fine regional, seasonal fare, and fantastic desserts.

Woodstock Inn & Resort, 14 The Green, tel: (802) 457-1100. $$$. Regional and New American cuisine in an ultra-formal setting.

DRINKING NOTES

The legal age for both the purchase and the consumption of alcoholic beverages is 21 throughout New England.

Alcoholic beverages are sold by package in state liquor stores and by the drink or the bottle at licensed establishments in all the six states. On Sundays, however, no package sales are allowed and drinks sold only at specified hours.

Often a restaurant without a liquor license will permit customers to bring their own beer or wine; then again, some communities have elected to remain "dry," and if they do, you must, too.

ATTRACTIONS

A CULTURAL CALENDAR

State tourist boards will gladly provide prospective visitors with detailed lists of seasonal events large and small – from teddy bear picnics to antique car rallies (for phone numbers, see the *Useful Addresses* at the end of the this section). Many of these events are so appealing, it would make sense to plan a trip around them – or at the very least commit to a detour. The ideal year in New England might accommodate some or all of the following activities.

Winter: Virtually wherever you are in New England, you can start the year off with a lively sampling of local arts. The **First Night** phenomenon, fomented by a group of Boston artists in 1977, has spread to at least 16 other New England communities at last count (it has some 70 happy imitators across the country, and is likely to go international). These celebratory, grass-roots gatherings – which typically start with a parade and end in fireworks – offer a moveable feast of community-oriented performances and art works on a varying scale. Boston's First Night, the biggest, pours a $1 million budget into nearly 200 sites and events, experienced by over 1 million delighted participants.

Most rural villages hunker down for the rest of the winter, but not the ski town of Stowe, Vermont, which views the frigid weather as one more excuse to party. The **Stowe Winter Carnival**, in mid-January, is a week-long bash featuring dog-sled races, various human races, ice sculptures, and fireworks. Other ski areas throughout the region sponsor all sorts of special events to spice up the season.

Spring: Spring officially arrives with the **Boston Marathon**, held on Patriot's Day (the third Monday in April): while an international roster of runners vie for the title, modern-day Minutemen stage **Revolutionary War Reenactments** in Boston (at the Paul Revere House), Lexington and Concord. In late April, a colorful **Daffodil Festival** on Nantucket marks the first stirrings of the summer season. Back in Boston, in early May, the **Hidden Gardens of Beacon Hill** admit curious visitors, and children participate in a **Parade of Ducklings**, to celebrate Robert McCloskey's classic tale *Make Way for Ducklings*. Soon it's **Lilac Sunday** (400 varieties in bloom) at the Arnold Arboretum in Jamaica Plain.

Flea-market fever descends on the tiny town of Brimfield, Massachusetts, in mid-May (and again in July and September): each of the three **Brimfield Outdoor Antiques Shows**, as these mega-swap meets are called, attracts over 1,000 dealers and some serious antiquaires. Meanwhile, New England's sheep are busy doffing their winter coats: the **Sheep-Shearing Festival** in North Andover, Massachusetts, sponsored by the Museum of American Textile History, and the **Sheep and Wool Festival** in New Boston, New Hampshire, feature border collie demonstrations, as well as the arts of shearing, spinning, and weaving.

Summer: The hills come alive with the sound of music as soon as summer sets in. In early June, Burlington, Vermont's ultra-hip capital city, gives itself over to the **Discover Jazz Festival**, followed by Boston (the **Boston Globe Jazz Festival** in mid-June) and Portsmouth, New Hampshire (the **Portsmouth Jazz Festival** in late June). From mid-June to late August, the Boston Symphony Orchestra, accompanied by scads of stellar guest artists, presides over the world-famous **Tanglewood Music Festival** in Lenox. (Following roughly the same schedule are two fellow Berkshires institutions: the **Jacob's Pillow Dance Festival** in nearby Becket, and the outstanding **Williamstown Theater Festival** in Williamstown.) While the BSO is off to the country, the Boston Pops take over Symphony Hall and also wow the masses with a free **Fourth of July Concert** (with fireworks) at the Hatch Shell on the Charles River Esplanade.

In mid-July, the gilded mansions of Newport, Rhode Island, scintillate to the classical strains of the **Newport Music Festival**, and tiny Marlboro College, on a bucolic hilltop in Marlboro, Vermont, hosts the month-long, internationally renowned **Marlboro Music Festival**. Meanwhile, the towns surrounding Burlington, Vermont, and even the Lake Champlain ferry, serve as sites for the **Vermont Mozart Festival**. The Lowell National Historical Park, located in Massachusetts' one-time leading mill town, holds the **Lowell Folk Festival** – a melange of traditional music and ethnic foods – in late July. The musical season is capped off by two popular harborview musical events in Newport in mid-August: **Ben & Jerry's Newport Folk Festival** (the long-standing folkie Olympus, now sponsored by the innovative ice cream company) and the JVC **Jazz Festival**.

Summer is also a good time to catch up on the work of local artisans. Five hundred of the very best in the country (including a sizable New England contingent) can be found at the ACC **Crafts Fair**, held in mid-June at the Eastern State Exposition fairgrounds in West Springfield, Massachusetts (in September, site of the "Big E," a huge agricultural fair). A smaller sampling show at the **Old Deerfield Craft Fair**, in one of the region's prettiest historic towns, in mid-June and late September. Also visit-worthy are the **Vermont Quilt Festival**, in Northfield in early July, and, in early August, the **League of New Hampshire Craftsmen's Fair** in Sunapee, the oldest crafts fair in the US.

Maine shows off its distinctive craft, improvised and historic, in late June at the **Great Kennebec Whatever Week** (a river race of homemade rafts) in late June, and during Windjammer Days in Boothbay Harbor. A squadron of Jules Verne conveyances converge on Quechee, Vermont, for the **Hot Air Balloon Festival** in late June, and in Kingstown, Rhode Island, for the **South County Hot Air Balloon Festival** in late July.

Vermont's rural Northeast Kingdom is the source of two extraordinary circuses. Based in Greensboro, Circus **Smirkus** – the world's only international youth circus, with participants recruited from as far afield as Russia and China – raises its one-ring big top in towns through Vermont mid-July to mid-August. Early in August, the quirky **Bread and Puppet Theatre** in West Glover mounts its annual Domestic Resurrection Circus, an illuminating mix of radical agitprop and simple celebration.

Martha's Vineyard winds down its summer season in August with the celebrity-studded **Possible Dream Auction** in Edgartown; **Illumination Night**, when the carpenter's Gothic cottages of Oak Bluffs are lit with lanterns; and the **Martha's Vineyard Agricultural Society Livestock Show and Fair**, an old-fashioned county fair in rural Tisbury.

Fall: Harvest festivals mark the foliage season, from large-scale extravaganzas such as the **Big E** in Springfield, Massachusetts, to homey gatherings like the **Common Ground Country Fair** in Windsor ME. Turning a corner in yet another vividly colored, white-steepled village, one is apt to happen upon a grange fair or pie sale, as the tourist season, subsiding, glides gracefully into yet another cycle.

Signposting in New England is not all it could be, most roads started out as meandering footpaths, so call ahead and get clear directions before starting out. Each attraction has its own peculiar hours (and seasons), so you'll need to plan your time carefully; some also stop welcoming visitors half an hour or so before their official closing time, so inquire if you're running late. Most charge nominal admission, but the commercial ventures can be expensive.

CONNECTICUT

AVON

Farmington Valley Arts Center, 25-27 Arts Center Lane (off Route 44), tel: (203) 678-1867. Artists' studios and gallery in old explosives plant.

BRIDGEPORT

Barnum Museum, 820 Main St (I-95, Exit 27), tel: (203) 331-1104. The life and times of famed circus entrepreneur P.T. Barnum and his "Greatest Show on Earth."

BRISTOL

American Clock & Watch Museum, 100 Maple St (off Route 6), tel: (203) 583-6070. Large display of foreign and American clocks and watches dating from the 17th century.
Lake Compounce, 822 Lake Ave, tel: (203) 583-6000. Oldest continuously operating amusement part in the US.
New England Carousel Museum, 95 Riverside Ave (I-84, Exit 31), tel: (203) 585-5411. Over 300 outstanding specimens.

CANTERBURY

Prudence Crandall House Museum, Canterbury Green (Routes 14 and 169), tel: (203) 546-9916. New England's first academy for African-American girls was established in this 1805 Federal house.

COVENTRY

Nathan Hale Homestead, South St (off Route 44), tel: (203) 742-6917 or (203) 247-8996. Built in 1776; original furnishings and family heirlooms.

EAST GRANBY

Old New-Gate Prison & Copper Mine, 115 Newgate Rd (I-91, Exit 40), tel: (203) 653-3563. America's first chartered copper mine (1707) became the state's first prison in 1773.

EAST HADDAM

Goodspeed Opera House, Goodspeed Landing, Route 82, tel: (203) 873-8668. A restored 1876 building; performances, guided tours.
Nathan Hale Schoolhouse, Main St (Route 149), tel: (203) 873-1672. Summer only. Changing exhibits on local history, costumes, accessories, photographs.

EAST HAVEN

Shore Line Trolley Museum, 17 River St (I-95, Exit 51N/52S), tel: (203) 467-6927. Trolley rides; car-barn tour.

EAST WINDSOR

Connecticut Trolley Museum, 58 North Rd (Route 140), tel: (203) 627-6540, 1-800-252-2373. Over 50 cars ca. 1894-1949.

ESSEX

Connecticut River Museum, Main St, tel: (203) 767-8269. Local boating history presented in an 1878 dockhouse.
Valley Railroad, Railroad Ave, (Route 9, Exit 3), tel: (203) 767-0103. Trips on a vintage steam train from Essex to Chester with optional riverboat cruise.

FARMINGTON

Hill-Stead Museum, 35 Mountain Rd (I-84, Exit 39), tel: (203) 677-4787. Hour-long guided tour of a 1900 mansion containing Impressionist art and antique furniture.
Stanley-Whitman House, 37 High St (I-84, Exit 39), tel: (203) 677-9222. A 1720 Colonial homestead featuring furniture, decorative objects, herb gardens and special exhibitions.

GROTON

USS Nautilus Memorial, US Naval Submarine Base, Rt 12 (I-95, Exit 86), tel: (203) 343-0079. Board the world's first nuclear powered submarine.

GUILFORD

Guilford Handcrafts Center, 411 Church St (Route 77), tel: (203) 453-5947. Gallery featuring the work of local artists and artisans.
Henry Whitfield State Museum, Old Whitfield St (I-95, Exit 58), tel: (203) 453-2457. Connecticut's oldest house (1639), with antiques and herb garden.
Hyland House, 84 Boston St (I-95, Ex. 59), tel: (203) 453-9477. Classic 1660 colonial saltbar with rare period furnishings.
Thomas Griswold House, 171 Boston St (I-95, Ex. 59), tel: (203) 453-3176. This 1774 saltbox serves as a museum of local history.

HADLYME

Gillette Castle State Park, 67 River St, tel: (203) 526-2336. An eccentric 1919 mansion, with extensive gardens.

HARTFORD

Bushnell Memorial Hall, 166 Capitol Ave, tel: (203) 246-6807. Connecticut's premiere performing arts center.
Butler-McCook Homestead, 396 Main St (I-91, Exit 29A), tel: (203) 522-1806. A 1782 home showing the evolution of decorative taste in the 18th and 19th centuries.
Carousel, Bushnell Part at Jewel St, tel: (203) 246-7739. A 1914 merry-go-round with hand-carved, brightly painted horses.
Harriet Beecher Stowe House, 77 Forest St at Farmington Ave (I-84, Exit 46), tel: (203) 525-9317. The Victorian cottage home of the author of Uncle Tom's Cabin.
Mark Twain Memorial, 351 Farmington Ave at Woodland St (I-84, Exit 46), tel: 9203) 247-0998. Sam Clemens' riverboat-like mansion.
Museum of Connecticut History, State Library, 231 Capitol Ave, tel: (203) 566-3056. State history

museum housing the 1662 Royal Charter and a collection of Colt firearms.

Old State House, 800 Main St (I-91, Exit 31; I-84, Exit 52), tel: (203) 522-6766. Oldest state house in the country, designed by Charles Bulfinch; houses Gilbert Stuart's portrait of George Washington. History, art, and crafts exhibits; outdoor concerts and farmers' markets in season.

Wadsworth Atheneum, 600 Main St, tel: (203) 278-2670. Paintings, sculpture, porcelain, silver, glass and furniture.

KENT

Sloane-Stanley Museum, Route 7, tel: (203) 927-3849. Early American tools, log cabin, ruins of the Kent Iron Furnace.

LITCHFIELD

Tapping Reeve House and Law School, South St (Route 63), tel: (203) 567-4501. America's first law school, founded in 1773.

White Memorial Foundation, Route 202, tel: (203) 567-0857. State's largest wildlife sanctuary; 4,000 acres with 35 miles of trails.

MADISON

Hammonasset Beach State Park, (I-95, Exit 62), tel: (203) 245-2785. A popular 2-mile beach with a nature sanctuary.

MANCHESTER

Lutz Children's Museum, 247 South Main St (Route 83), tel: (203) 643-0949. Exhibits on history, science, ethnology, art and nature, and live animal exhibits.

MOODUS

Amasa Day House, On the Green (Route 151), tel: (203) 873-8144. Restored 1816 home with original decorations.

MYSTIC

Denison Homestead, Pequotsepos Rd (I-95, Exit 90), tel: (203) 536-9248. Family heirlooms fill this 18th-century building, encompassing a Colonial kitchen, Revolutionary War bedroom, Federal parlour, Civil War bedroom, and early 20th-century living room.

Mystic Marinelife Aquarium, 55 Coogan Blvd (I-95, Exit 90), tel: (203) 536-9631. Some 6,000 specimens of undersea life; training sessions with dolphins, sea lions and whales.

Mystic Seaport, 50 Greenmanville Ave (I-95, Exit 90), tel: (203) 572-0711. A maritime museum featuring a 19th-century whaling village with carefully preserved buildings and ships. Also, steamboat rides, craft demonstrations, whaling talks and planetarium shows.

NEW BRITAIN

New Britain Museum of American Art, 56 Lexington St (I-84, Exit 35), tel: (203) 229-0257. American works from 1740 to the present.

NEW HAVEN

Beinecke Rare Book Library, 121 Wall St (I-95, Exit 3), tel: (203) 432-2977. Rare books – including a Gutenberg Bible – and manuscripts.

Long Wharf Theatre, 222 Sargent Drive (I-95, Exit 46), tel: (203) 787-4282. A major American regional theater.

Peabody Museum of Natural History, 170 Whitney Avenue (I-91, Exit 3), tel: (203) 432-5050. Ancient cultures; Native American relics, dinosaur fossils, Connecticut birds.

Yale Center for British Art, 1080 Chapel St (I-91, Exit 1), tel: (203) 432-2800. Art work and rare books from the Elizabethan period to the present.

Yale Collection of Musical Instruments, 15 Hillhouse Avenue, tel: (203) 432-0822. Western and non-Western traditions are represented.

Yale Repertory Theatre, Chapel and York sts, tel: (203) 432-1234. A chance to see tomorrow's stars today.

Yale University, Phelps Gateway, 344 College St (I-95, Exit 47), tel: (203) 432-2300. Free guided one-hour walking tours.

Yale University Art Gallery, 1111 Chapel St (I-95, Exit 47), tel: (203) 432-0600. An 1832 art museum with 100,000 objects, from ancient Egyptian to contemporary; outstanding collection of American paintings and decorative arts.

NEW LONDON

Lyman Allyn Museum, 625 Williams St (I-95, Exit 83), tel: (203) 443-2545. American Impressionist paintings, Old Master drawings, antiquities from various cultures.

Monte Cristo Cottage, 325 Pequot Avenue, tel: (203) 443-0051. Childhood home of dramatist Eugene O'Neill.

US Coast Guard Academy, Mohegan Ave (I-95, Exit 83; I-395, Exit 78), tel: (203) 444-8270. Museum, multimedia show on cadet life, and periodic military reviews and concerts.

NORWALK

Lockwood-Mathews Mansion Museum, 295 West Avenue, (I-95, Exit 14N/15S), tel: (203) 838-9799. A 50-room Victorian chateau with octagonal rotunda.

NORWICH

Slater Memorial Museum and Converse Art Gallery, Norwich Free Academy, 108 Crescent St (I-395, Exit 81E), tel: (203) 887-2506. Antiquities from several continents, Native American artifacts, American art and furniture from colonial to contemporary.

OLD LYME

Florence Griswold Museum, 96 Lyme St (I-95, Exit 70), tel: (203) 434-5542. An American Impressionist art colony turned museum.

RIDGEFIELD

Aldrich Museum of Contemporary Art, 258 Main St (Route 7), tel: (203) 438-4519. Changing exhibitions, 2-acre sculpture garden.

RIVERTON

Hitchcock Museum, Route 20, tel: (203) 379-1003. An 1829 Gothic stone church houses displays of the locally produced, painted 19th–century furniture.

ROCKY HILL

Dinosaur State Park, West St (I-91, Exit 23), tel: (203) 529-8423. Jurassic dinosaur tracks; nature trails.

SIMSBURY

Massacoh Plantation, 800 Hopmeadow St (Route 10), tel: (203) 658-2500. Six buildings represent three centuries of local history.

SOUTH NORWALK

The Maritime Center at Norwalk, 10 North Water St (I-93, Exit 14N/15S), tel: (203) 852-0700. Exhibits, aquarium, IMAX theatre.

STAMFORD

Stamford Museum & Nature Center, 39 Scofieldtown Rd, (Route 15, Exit 35), tel: (203) 322-1646. A 19th-century working farm with nature trails; art and natural history galleries; planetarium.

Whitney Museum of American Art at Champion, 1 Champion Plaza, tel: (203) 358-7652. This outpost of the New York museum features contemporary art and gallery talks.

WASHINGTON

Institute for American Indian Studies, Curtis Rd (I-84, Exit 15), tel: (203) 868-0518. Exhibits spanning 10,000 years of Algonquin history; reconstructed village, native plant trails.

WATERBURY

Mattatuck Museum, 144 W. Main St, tel: (203) 753-0381. Exhibits chronicling the industrial history of the "Brass City"; period rooms; 19th- and 20th-century Connecticut art.

WATERFORD

Eugene O'Neill Theatre Center, 305 Great Neck Rd, tel: (203) 443–5378. Summer readings and performances.

Harkness Memorial State Park, Route 213, tel: (203) 443-5725. Villa, gardens, beach; summer music festival.

WEST HARTFORD

Science Museum of Connecticut, 950 Trout Brook Drive (I-84, Exit 43), tel: (203) 236-2961. A hands-on natural-history museum with an aquarium and planetarium.

Museum of American Political Life, Harry Jack Gray Center, University of Hartford, Bloomfield Ave (Rte. 189), tel: (203) 521-5362. Over 65,000 examples of campaign memorabilia.

Noah Webster House, 227 South Main St (I-84, Exit 41), Home of the famous lexicographer; changing exhibits.

WETHERSFIELD

Webb-Deane-Stevens Museum, 211 Main St (I-91, Exit 26), tel: (203) 529-0612. A three-house complex of restored 18th-century homes; original furnishings and memorabilia.

WINDSOR LOCKS

New England Air Museum, Bradley International Airport, Route 75, tel: (203) 623-3305. More than 75 aircraft from 1902 to the present.

WOODSTOCK

Roseland Cottage, Route 169, tel: (203) 928-4074. A gaudy pink Gothic Revival summer home with original furnishings.

MAINE

AUGUSTA

Maine State Museum, Route 201, in State House complex, tel: (207) 289-2301. Exhibits on Maine's environment and history.

BAR HARBOR

Abbe Museum of Maine Indian Artifacts, Loop Road Park, tel: (207) 288-3519. Summer only. Artifacts and dioramas.

Criterion Theatre, Cottage St, tel: (207) 288-3447. First-run and classic films in a 1932 Art Deco theatre.

BATH

Maine Maritime Museum & Shipyard, 243 Washington St, Route 1, tel: (207) 443-1316. Nautical history, from intricate models to a full-scale schooner; working boatyard, river cruises.

Shelter Institute, 38 Center St, tel: (207) 442-7938. A school for visionaries wishing to build their own homes; changing exhibits.

BETHEL

Moses Mason House, On the Common, tel: (207) 824-2908. An 1813 Federal house decorated with a Rufus Porter mural.

BLUE HILL

Parson Fisher House, Routes 15 and 176, tel: (207) 374-2459. Summer only. A house built and furnished by Blue Hill's early resident genius.

BOOTHBAY

Boothbay Railway Village, Route 27, tel: (207) 633-4727. Narrow-gauge railroad rides; displays relating to steam railroading era; general store, firehouse and doll museum; antique cars.

BRUNSWICK

Museum of Art, Bowdoin College, Walker Art Building, tel: (207) 725-3275. 19th- and 20th-century paintings.

Peary-MacMillan Arctic Museum, Bowdoin College, tel: (207) 725-3416. A tribute to two pioneering Arctic explorers.

Pejepscot Historical Society Museums, 159-161 Park Row, tel: (207) 729-6606. Regional history.

CAMDEN

Camden Hills State Park, Route 1, tel: (207) 236-3109. Climb – or drive up – Mt. Battie for a view of the bay.

Center for Creative Imaging, 51 Mechanic St, tel: (207) 256-7400. Gallery and learning center dedicated to cutting-edge photographic technology.

Old Conway House Complex, Conway Rd (off Route 1), tel: (207) 256-2257. A restored 18th-century farmhouse, with blacksmith shop and sugarhouse.

CASTINE

Maine Maritime Academy, Battle Ave, tel: 207) 326-4311. Summer only. Tours of the State of Maine troop ship.

DEER ISLE

Haystack Mountain School of Crafts, Stinson Neck, tel: (207) 348-2306. Summer only. Afternoon tours; evening lectures and concerts.

THE FORKS

Northern Outdoors, Route 201, tel: (207) 663-4466. Summer only. Whitewater rafting expeditions.

FORT KENT

Fort Kent Blockhouse, Block House St, tel: (207) 834-3866. Summer only. An 1839 wooden stockade.

FREEPORT

Desert of Maine, Desert Rd, tel: (207) 865.6962. Closed winter. An ecological object lesson.

GREENVILLE

Folsom's Air Service, Lincoln St, tel: (207) 695-2993. Sightseeing by float plane; fly-and-canoe packages.

Moosehead Marine Museum, tel: (207) 695-2716. Summer only. Town history, from 1836 until the last log drive in 1975.

SS Katahdin, tel: (207) 695-2716. Summer only. Cruise Moosehead Lake aboard a 1914 steamboat.

KENNEBUNKPORT

Brick Store Museum, 117 Main St, tel: (207) 985-4802. An 1825 emporium featuring fine and decorative arts, including Federal furniture.

Seashore Trolley Museum, Log Cabin Rd, Route 1, tel: (207) 967-2712. World's largest collection; unlimited rides.

KINGFIELD

Stanley Museum, School St, tel: (207) 265-2729. A 1903 schoolhouse pays homage to the local inventors of the Stanley Steamer car.

KITTERLY

Kittery Historical and Naval Museum, Routes 1 and 26, tel: (207) 439-3080. Exhibits on the national's oldest shipyard.

LIVERMORE

Norlands Living History Center, Route 10, tel: (207) 897-2236. A 450-acre complex presenting and preserving 19th-century farm life.

LUBEC

Roosevelt Campobello International Park, New Brunswick, (506) 752-2922. Closed winter. Official in Canada, and separated from Lubec by a bridge, FDR's summer home is now a 2,600-acre (1,050-hectare) park.

MACHIAS

Burnham Tavern, Route 192, tel: (207) 255-4432. Summer only. Where the first naval attack of the Revolutionary War was plotted.

MILLINOCKET

Baxter State Park, tel: (207) 723-5140. Over 200,000 acres (80,800 hectares) of wilderness, surrounding Maine's highest peak, Mount Katahdin.

MOUNT DESERT ISLAND

Acadia National Park, tel: (207) 288-3338. Mountains, lakes, forest and ocean; perfect for bicycling, horseback riding, bird watching, hiking, swimming and camping.

NEW SWEDEN

New Sweden Historical Society Museum, Capital Hill, tel: (207) 895-5526. Summer only. Artifacts reflecting the history of Swedish homesteading in Maine, including the Lindststen Stuga, an early settler's cabin.

NEWFIELD

Willowbrook at Newfield, Route 11, tel: (207) 793-2784. A 19th-century village with several dozen buildings housing period furniture, crafts, tools and carriages.

NORTHEAST HARBOR

Asticou Terrace and Thuya Gardens and Lodge, Route 3, (207) 276-5130. Summer only. A dazzling hilltop garden on the estate of landscape architect Joseph H. Curtis.

OGUNQUIT

Museum of Art of Ogunquit, Shore Rd, tel: (207) 646-8827. Summer only. Locally inspired art works.

Ogunquit Summer Playhouse, Route 1, (207) 646-5511: Summer only. A venerable strawhat theatre performing crowd-pleasers.

OLD ORCHARD BEACH

Palace Playland, Old Orchard St, tel: (207) 934-2001. Summer only. A classic seaside amusement part with a boardwalk, beach, and a 1906 carousel; also, waterslides.

OWLS HEAD

Owls Head Transportation Museum, Knox County Airport, Route 73, tel: (207) 594-4418. Vintage air and ground vehicles.

PATTEN

Lumberman's Museum, Route 159, tel: (207) 528-2650. Summer only. The history of northern Maine's lumber trade; an 1860s loggers' cabin.

PEMAQUID

Colonial Pemaquid Restoration, off Route 130, tel: (207) 677-2423. A 1620s settlement, under excavation.

Pemaquid Point Lighthouse and Fishermen's Museum, Route 130, tel: (207) 677-2494. An 1824 lighthouse; exhibits on the Maine fishing industry.

POPHAM BEACH

Popham Beach State Park, Route 209, tel: (207) 389-1335. A 41/2-mile (7-km) beach, the site of a failed 1607 colony.

PORTLAND

Morse-Libby House, 109 Danforth St, tel: (207) 772-4841. A lavish 19th-century Italianate villa.

Payson Gallery of Art, 716 Stevens Avenue, tel: (207) 797-9546. Masterpieces of the past century.

Portland Museum of Art, 7 Congress Square, tel: (207) 775-6148. 19th- and 20th-century paintings, sculpture and furnishings.

Wadsworth-Longfellow House, 481 Congress St, tel: (207) 772-1822. A 1785 homestead with Federal remodeling; childhood home of the celebrated poet.

RANGELEY

Wilhelm Reich Museum, Route 4, tel: (207) 864-3443. "Orgonon," the 200-acre research facility of the controversial 20th-century psychoanalyst.

ROCKLAND

Hurricane Island Outward Bound School, tel: (207) 594-5546, (800) 341-1744. A survival course off the coast of Maine.

Victory Chimes, P.O. Box 1401, tel: (207) 594-0755. A three-masted 1900 schooner turned luxury windjammer.

William A. Farnsworth Library and Art Museum, 19 Elm St, tel: (207) 596-6457. Featuring Wyeths (all three), Homer Nevelson.

ROCKPORT

Maine Photographic Workshops, 2 Central St, tel: (207) 236-8581. Highly regarded photography courses; gallery.

Maine Windjammer Association, tel: (800) 624-6380. Summer only. Authentic 19th-century ships; excursions.

Merryspring, tel: (207) 236-4885. Summer only. A 66-acre (27-hectare) garden specializing in indigenous plants.

Rockport Apprenticeshop, Sea St, tel: (207) 236-6071. A boat-building school; observers welcome.

SEARSPORT

Penobscot Marine Museum, Church St, Route 1, tel: (207) 554-2529. Eight historic houses exhibit marine paintings, shipbuilding tools, navigational instruments and charts, and whaling artifacts.

SOUTHWEST HARBOR

Mount Desert Oceanarium, Clark Point Rd, tel: (207) 244-7330. Closed winter. Appealing hands-on exhibits.

VAN BUREN

Acadian Village, Route 1, (tel) 207-868-2691. Summer only. A complex embodying three centuries of Acadian culture.

WELLS

Wells Auto Museum, Route 1, tel: (207) 646-9064. Display of 70 cars, antique bicycles, motorcycles and license plates. Ride in a 1911 Model T Depot Hack.

WISCASSET

Castle Tucker, Lee and High Sts, tel: (207) 882-7364. A brick home built in 1807, expanded in 1860.

Old Lincoln County Jail and Museum, Federal St, tel: (207) 882-6817. An 1811 jail in use until 1913.

Musical Wonder House, 8 High St, tel: (207) 882-7163. An 1852 mansion showcasing some 400 music boxes.

Nickels-Sortwell House, Main and Federal Sts, tel: (207) 882-6218. A Federal captain's house with period gardens.

YORK

Old York Historical Society, 140 Lindsay Rd, tel: (207) 363-4974. Six historic buildings, including the John Hancock Warehouse and the 1719 Old Gaol.

MASSACHUSETTS

ASHLEY FALLS

Colonel John Ashley House, Cooper Hill Rd, tel: (413) 229-8600. Oldest house in the Berkshires (1735).

BARNSTABLE

The Trayser Museum Complex, 3353 Route 6A, tel: (508) 362-2092. An 1856 Customs House showcasing regional history; outbuildings include a 1700 jail.

BELCHERTOWN

Quabbin Reservoir, 485 Ware Rd, tel: (413) 323-7221. The 412-billion-gallon lake with visitor center, observation tower.

BOSTON

Arnold Arboretum, 125 Arborway, Jamaica Plain, tel: (617) 524-1718. Exhibits of north-temperate woody plants.

Boston Center for the Arts, 539 Tremont St, tel: (617) 426-5000. A 3-acre complex comprising studios, a gallery, experimental theatres, and the Cyclorama, which hosts events and antique shows.

Boston Common. Established in 1634 as pastureland, these 50 acres constitute the nation's oldest public park.

Boston Harbor Islands, Boston Harbor, tel: (617) 727-5290. A half-dozen of these historic outposts can be reached by ferry and water taxi.

Boston Tea Party Ship and Museum, Congress St Bridge (Museum Wharf), tel: (617) 338-1773. A "reenact-it-yourself" presentation aboard a replica the Beaver II.

Children's Museum, 300 Congress St (Museum Wharf,) tel: (617) 426-8855. A former factory with four floors of hands-on exhibits.

Christian Science International Headquarters, Massachusetts Ave and Huntington Ave, tel: (617) 450-2000. Free guided tours of the Mother Church and Mapparium.

Computer Museum, 300 Congress St (Museum Wharf), tel: (617) 426-2800. Interactive exhibits, including a 20-times-scale "walk-through" computer.

Copp's Hill Burying Ground, Mill St, tel: (617) 725-4505. A 1659 graveyard – originally known as "Corpse Hill" – with great views, and headstones pocked by British bullets.

Faneuil Hall Marketplace, tel: (617) 523-3886. This 1742 market building houses shops in its lower level, an historic meeting place on the second floor, and on the third the headquarters of the Ancient and Honorable Artillery Company.

Fenway Park, 4 Yawkey Way, tel: (617) 267-8661. The intimate diamond where Babe Ruth made his 1914 debut.

The Freedom Trail, tel: (617) 242-5642. A 3-mile (5-km) itinerary – accessible on foot or by sightseeing trolley – spanning 13 Colonial and Revolutionary sites.

Globe Corner Bookstore, 3 School St, tel: (617) 523-6658. A 1718 brick Colonial shop, once the nexus of literary Boston, now a bookshop specializing in travel and regional lore.

Harrison Gray Otis House (First), 141 Cambridge St, tel: (617) 227-3956. This 1796 Charles Bulfinch mansion serves as headquarters for the Society for the Preservation of New England Antiquities, which maintains 34 historic properties throughout the region. Guided tours by reservation only.

Institute of Contemporary Art, 955 Boylston St, tel: (617) 266-5152. An 1885 police station converted into cutting-edge gallery.

Isabella Stewart Gardner Museum, 280 The Fenway, tel: (617) 566-1401. An 1902 palazzo stuffed with art treasures by a beloved Boston eccentric, "Mrs Jack." Courtyard concerts; cafe.

John Fitzgerald Kennedy Library and Museum, Columbia Point, Dorchester, tel: (617) 929-4523. The life and times of the late President.

John Hancock Observatory, Copley Square, tel: (617) 242-1976. New England's tallest building – 62 stories – provides a spectacular view.

King's Chapel and Burial Ground, 58 Tremont St, tel: (617) 523-1749. The 1754 Anglican church abuts Boston's first town cemetery, and hosts organ concerts and poetry readings.

Museum of Afro-American History, 46 Joy St, tel: (617) 742-1854. An 1834 schoolhouse, one of fourteen sites along Beacon Hill's Black Heritage Trial.

Museum of Fine Arts, 465 Huntington Avenue, tel: (617) 267-9300. Chinese, Japanese, Indian, Egyptian, Greek, European and American collections, silver, period room and musical instruments; gallery talks, library, lectures and films.

Museum of Transportation, 15 Newton St, Brookline, tel: (617) 522-6140. The history of transportation from the 1600s to the present.

New England Aquarium, Central Wharf, tel: (617) 973-5200. A three-story tank holds sharks, turtles, and other species, including human divers; dolphin and sea lion shows are held on a barge next door.

Nichols House Museum, 55 Mt Vernon St, tel: (617) 720-0786. An 1804 house designed by Charles Bulfinch serves as a repository for several centuries' worth of Brahmin memorabilia.

Old North Church, 193 Salem St, tel: (617) 523-6676. The city's oldest church (1723), where signal lanterns were set on the night of Paul Revere's ride.

Old South Meeting House, 310 Washington St, tel: (617) 482-6439. A 1729 church turned Revolutionary hotbed, it still hosts political debates as well as educational programs.

Old State House, 206 Washington St, tel: (617) 720-3292. The site of the Boston Massacre, and seat of the Colonial government.

Paul Revere House, 19 North Square, tel: (617) 523-1676. The ca. 1677 abode of the silversmith/patriot.

Public Garden. An 1859 botanical garden, where fanciful Swan Boats have plied the willow-lined Lagoon since 1877.

State House, Beacon and Park streets, tel: (617) 727-3676. Built by Charles Bulfinch in 1795–98, with subsequent additions; tours offered.

BREWSTER

Cape Cod Museum of Natural History, Route 6A, tel: (508) 896-3867. Collections of birds and mammals; displays on aquatic life; a natural history library and marked nature trails.

New England Fire & History Museum, 1429 Route 6A, tel: (508) 896-5711. Exhibits on firefighting from ancient Rome to the recent past.

Stony Brook Grist Mill and Museum, 830 Stony Brook Rd, no phone. A ca. 1873 mill, left over from the "Factory Village" which once surrounded this alewife herring run.

CAMBRIDGE

Arthur M. Sackler Museum, 485 Broadway, tel: (617) 495-9400. This annex to the Fogg Museum houses ancient, Asian, and Islamic art, in a bold 1986 building designed by James Sterling.

Fogg Art Museum, 32 Quincy St, tel: (617) 495-9400. Harvard University's outstanding collection of fine and decorative arts from ancient cultures to the present.

Loeb Drama Center, 64 Brattle St, tel: (617) 547-8300. Home to the American Repertory Theatre, Harvard University's world-class company-in-residence.

Museum of Science, Science Park, tel: (617) 723-2500. A broad and changing array of fascinating hands-on exhibits; also houses the Hayden Planetarium and Mugar Omni Theatre.

Museums of Natural History, 24 Oxford St, tel: (617) 495-1910. Harvard University's Botanical Museum, Museum of Comparative Zoology, Mineralogical and Geological Museums, and Peabody Museum of Archaeology.

CHARLESTOWN

Bunker Hill Monument, Monument Square, Charlestown, tel: (617) 242-5641. A 22-foot obelisk – with an observatory on top, a museum at the base – marks the site of the 1775 Revolutionary victory.

Bunker Hill Pavilion, 55 Constitution Rd, Charlestown, tel: (617) 241-7575. Presents "The White of Their Eyes," a multimedia show about the Battle of Bunker Hill.

USS Constitution Museum, Constitution Wharf, Charlestown Navy Yard, tel: (617) 242-5601. Launched in 1797, Old Ironsides remains the oldest commissioned ship in the US Navy. Tours, artifacts, documents.

CHAPPAQUIDDICK

Wasque Reservation and Cape Poge Wildlife Refuge, Wasque Rd, tel: (508) 693-7662. Over 700 acres of unspoiled barrier beach.

CHATHAM

Railroad Museum, 153 Depot Rd, tel: (508) 945-0342. Housed in an 1887 Victorian "Railroad Gothic" station.

Monomoy National Wildlife Refuge, Morris Island Rd, tel: (508) 465-5753. Wilderness area suitable for hiking, birdwatching and fishing. Monomoy Island, accessible by boat, shelters 252 bird species.

CONCORD

Orchard House, 399 Lexington Rd, tel: (508) 369-4118. Louisa May Alcott wrote *Little Women* here.

Ralph Waldo Emerson House, 28 Cambridge

Turnpike, tel: (508) 369-2236. The philosopher's home from 1835 to 1889.

Walden Pond State Reservation, Route 126, tel: (508) 369-3254. The site of Henry David Thoreau's 1845 shack; now a popular swimming spot.

The Wayside, 455 Lexington Rd., tel: (508) 369-6975. The 18th-century home of the Alcotts and Hawthorne.

DALTON

Crane Paper Museum, Housatonic St, tel: (413) 684-2600. The history of American paper-making.

DENNIS

Cape Playhouse, 36 Hope Lane, tel: (508) 383-3911. America's oldest continuously operating professional summer theatre, founded in 1927.

Cape Cinema, 36 Hope Lane, tel: (508)385.4477. A luxuriously appointed art cinema modeled on a Congregational Church.

DUXBURY

Art Complex Museum, 189 Alden St, tel: (617) 934-6634. Oriental, European, and American contemporary art.

King Caesar House, King Caesar Rd, tel: (617) 934-6106. A shipbuilder's 1808 mansion.

EAST BREWSTER

Nickerson State Park, Route 6A and Crosby Lane, tel: (508) 896-3491. A 2,000-acre park with walking and biking trails, 8 ponds, and 420 campsites.

EAST FALMOUTH

Ashumet Wildlife Sanctuary, Ashumet Rd, (4 miles east of Route 28 on Route 151), tel: (508) 563-6390. Forty acres of holly trees and other plants.

EASTHAM

Cape Cod National Seashore Salt Pond Visitor Center, Salt Pond Rd (off Route 6), tel: (508) 255-3421. Exhibits, films, nature walks.

The 1869 Schoolhouse Museum, Nauset Rd (off Route 6), tel: (508) 255-0788. Headquarters of the Eastham Historical Society; Native American, agricultural, and nautical exhibits.

EDGARTOWN

Old Whaling Church, 89 Main St, tel: (508) 627-8017. This magisterial 1843 Greek Revival church doubles as a 500-seat Performing Arts Center.

Vincent House, 103 Main St, tel: (508) 627.8017. This 1672 shingled full Cape is one of the oldest houses on the island; tours by appointment.

The Vineyard Museum, 8 Cooke St, tel: (508) 627-4441. A block-square complex encompassing the 1765 Thomas Cooke House, the Francis Foster Museum (maritime art and artifacts), the 1845 Captain Francis Pease House (prehistoric, pre-Columbian, and Native American artifacts), a Carriage Shed (unusual historic vehicles), and the decommissioned Gay Head Light Tower.

FALMOUTH

Falmouth Historical Society Museums, 55-65 Palmer Ave (at the Village Green), tel: (508) 548-4857. Three historic structures linked by a Colonial garden and full of whaling and other treasures.

GLOUCESTER

Cape Ann Historical Museum, 27 Pleasant St, tel: (508) 462-8661. Paintings, furnishings; regional lore.

Hammond Castle Museum, 80 Hesperus Ave, tel: (508) 283-2080. A Medieval castle recreated by a mechanical genius.

Sleeper-McCann House, 75 Eastern Point Blvd, tel: (508) 283-0800. 26 rooms displaying American, European and Oriental antiques.

HARVARD

Fruitlands Museums, 102 Prospect Hill, tel: (508) 426-9028. Native American artifacts, a Shaker house, and transcendentalist memorabilia.

HINGHAM

Old Ship Meetinghouse, Main St, tel: (617) 749-1679. Built in 1681; the oldest wooden church in continuous use in the US.

World's End Reservation, Martin's Lane, tel: (617) 749-8956. A harborside park landscaped by Frederick Law Olmsted.

HYANNIS

Cape Cod Melody Tent, West Main St, tel: (508) 775-9100. Top names in music and comedy form a stellar summer lineup.

Cape Cod Scenic Railroad, 252 Main St, tel: (508) 771-3788. Daytime and dinner tours to Sandwich, departing from Hyannis.

John F. Kennedy Museum, 397 Main St, tel: (508) 775-2201. Photos and memorabilia for the fondly remembered summer resident.

HOLYOKE

Holyoke Children's Museum, 444 Dwight St, tel: (413) 536-5437. Hands-on activities and exhibits.

Holyoke Heritage State Park, 444 Dwight St, tel: (413) 534-1723. The history of an American industrial boomtown.

Wistariahurst Museum, 238 Cabot St, tel: (413) 534-2216. A Victorian mansion with a small but worthy art collection.

IPSWICH

Castle Hill, Argilla Rd, tel (508) 356-4351. A 1927 mansion; summer concerts.

Crane Memorial Reservation, Argilla Rd, tel: (508) 356-4070. A 4-mile beach open to the public.

John Whipple House, 53 South Main St, tel: (508) 356-2811. A 1640 house furnished in period style.

LEE

Jacob's Pillow Dance Festival, Box 287, tel: (413) 243-0745. International-caliber performances of ballet, modern, and jazz dance.

LENOX

Berkshire Opera, 17 Main St, tel: (413) 243-1343. A summer season of opera sung in English.

The Mount, Plunkett St, tel: (413) 637-1899. The 1902 mansion of novelist Edith Wharton; summer home to Shakespeare and Co.

Tanglewood Music Festival, West St, tel: (413) 637-1940. Summer headquarters of the Boston Symphony Orchestra and visiting artists.

LEXINGTON

Museum of Our National Heritage, 33 Marrett Rd, tel: (617) 861-6559. Changing exhibits which feature American life and historic events; films, lectures and concerts.

LINCOLN

DeCordova Museum and Sculpture Park, Sandy Pond Rd, tel: (617) 259-8355. Changing contemporary are exhibits; summer concerts.

Gropius House, 68 Baker Bridge Rd, tel: (617) 259-8843. A 1938 example of Bauhaus architecture.

LOWELL

Lowell National Historic Park, Market Mills, tel: (508) 459-1000. Exhibits commemorating Lowell's role in the Industrial Revolution.

New England Quilt Museum, Boott Mills, tel: (508) 542-4207. Historic and contemporary examples.

MASHPEE

Old Indian Meetinghouse, Meeting House Rd (at Route 28), tel: (508) 477-0208. Built in 1684 for converts from the Mashpee tribe, and still in use.

NANTASKET

Hull Lifesaving Museum, 1117 Nantasket Ave, tel: (617) 925-5433. Strategies and paraphernalia for rescuing shipwreck victims.

NANTUCKET

Coskata-Coatue Wildlife Refuge, Wauwinet, (508)228-6799. A 1,100-acre preserve.

The Maria Mitchell Science Center, 2 Vestal St, tel: (508) 228-9198. The birthplace of the island's noted 19th-century astronomer; natural history museum, observatory, science library.

Museum of Nantucket History, Straight Wharf, tel: (508) 228-3889. An introduction to island history and ecology; discount passes to the dozen historic properties operated by the Nantucket Historical Association, including the Jethro Coffin House and Hadwen House.

Whaling Museum, Broad St, tel: (508) 228-1894. Displays from the whaling era: scrimshaw, rigged whaleboat, outfitting shops and paintings.

NEW BEDFORD

New Bedford Whaling Museum, 18 Johnny Cake Hill, tel: (508) 997-0046. Museum of whaling history, art and local history.

NEWBURY

Spencer-Pierce-Little Farm, Little's Lane, tel: (508) 462-2634. A ca. 1675–1700 farmstead cultivated for over three centuries.

NEWBURYPORT

Cushing House, 98 High St, tel: (508) 462-2681. A 19th-century home housing the collections of the Historical Society of Old Newbury.

Parker River National Wildlife Refuge, Northern Blvd, Plum Island, tel: (617) 465-5753. A 5,000-acre wildlife habitat favored by migratory birds; beaches and nature trials.

NORTH ANDOVER

Museum of American Textile History, 800 Massachusetts Avenue, tel: (508) 686-0191. Exhibits tracing the evolution of the American textile industry.

NORTHAMPTON

Lyman Plant House, Smith College, tel: (413) 584-2748. A complex of 1890s greenhouses harboring species from around the world.

Smith College Museum of Art, Smith College, tel: (413) 585-2760. An outstanding collection emphasizing European and American art.

OAK BLUFFS

Flying Horses Carousel, 33 Circuit Ave, tel: (508) 693-9481. An 1876 Coney Island carousel, purportedly the oldest in the country still running.

OLD DEERFIELD

Historic Deerfield, Main St, tel: (413) 774-5581. Tours of 13 historical houses and decorative arts collections.

ORLEANS

French Cable Station Museum, 41 S. Orleans Rd, tel: (508) 255-1386. In 1891–1941, the strategic communications link between the US and Europe.

PITTSFIELD

Arrowhead, 780 Holmes Rd, Route 7, tel: (413) 442-1793. Home of author Herman Melville; period furnishings.

Berkshire Museum, 39 South St, Route 7, tel: (413) 443-7171. Early-to-contemporary art, sculpture, silver; biology and history exhibits.

Hancock Shaker Village, Route 2 and 4, tel: (413) 443-0188. A restored 19th-century village with exhibits and demonstrations.

PLYMOUTH

Cranberry World Visitors' Center, 225 Water St, tel: (508) 747-1000. Exhibits on the cranberry and its uses, ancient and modern.

Mayflower II, Water St, tel: (508) 746-1622. A 1957 replica of the Pilgrim ship, with actors impersonating the original voyagers.

Pilgrim Hall, 75 Court St, tel: (508) 746-1620. Pilgrims' possessions, from furniture to armor.

Plimoth Plantation, 133 Warren Ave, tel: (508) 746-1622. A recreation of 17th-century Plymouth, with costumed interpreters playing the parts of actual residents.

Plymouth Wax Museum, 16 Carver St, tel: (508) 746-6468. Pilgrim life depicted in 26 life-size dioramas.

Whale Discovery Center, Howland St, tel: (508) 747-0015. Interactive exhibits on whale behavior and ecology.

PROVINCETOWN

Pilgrim Monument & Provincetown Museum, High Pole Hill Rd (off Winslow St), tel: (508) 487-1310. Observatory tower; local history exhibits.

Provincetown Art Association and Museum, 460 Commercial St, tel: (508) 487-1750. Showing stellar local work since 1914.

Provincetown Heritage Museum, 356 Commercial St, tel: (508) 487-0666. Local history and artwork; a half-scale model of a fishing schooner.

QUINCY

Adams National Historical Site, 135 Adams St, tel: (617) 773-1177. Home to four generations of the distinguished Adams family, which produced two presidents.

ROCKPORT

Halibut Point State Park, Gott Ave, tel: (508) 546-2997. A former granite quarry, overlooking the sea.

SALEM

Essex Institute, 132 Essex St, tel: (508) 744-0036. Essex County records and artifacts; 17th-century houses.

House of the Seven Gables, 54 Turner St, tel: (508) 744-0991. A complex of 17th-century houses.

Peabody Essex Museum, East India Square, tel: (508) 745-9500. Collections cover maritime history, Asia export, and natural history.

Salem Maritime National Historic Site, 174 Derby St, tel: (508) 744-4323. Historic wharves and mercantile buildings.

Salem Witch Museum, 19 1/2 Washington Square North, tel: (508) 744-1692. Rather lurid multimedia presentations depicting the witch trials and hangings.

SANDWICH

Dexter Grist Mill, Town Hall Square, tel: (508) 888-0352. This 1654 mill still grinds corn (offered for sale); summer only.

Heritage Plantation, 130 Grove St, tel: (508) 888-3300. Museum complex with extensive gardens and working windmill; collections include antique cars, firearms, tools, folk art, toys, and carousel figures.

Hoxie House, Water St, tel: (508) 888-0352. A 17th-century saltbox, thought to be Cape Cod's oldest house; summer only.

Sandwich Glass Museum, 129 Main St, tel: (508) 888-0251. Display of Sandwich glass, period manuscripts, photographs and paintings.

SAUGUS

Saugus Iron Works National Historic Site, 244 Central St (I-95, Exit 43), tel: (617) 233-0050. A 17th-century house, furnace, forge, and mill; museum and nature trail.

SOUTH WELLFLEET

Wellfleet Bay Wildlife Sanctuary, West Rd (off Route 6), tel: (508) 349-2615. A 710-acre Audubon Society preserve; hiking trails, workshops, excursions.

SPRINGFIELD

Basketball Hall of Fame, 1150 West Columbus Avenue, tel: (413) 781-6500. Lively exhibits celebrating the birthplace of the sport.

Connecticut Valley Historical Museum, The Quadrangle, tel: (413) 732-3080. Early American decorative arts; regional history.

George Walter Vincent Smith Art Museum, The Quadrangle, tel: (413) 732-6092. Decorative arts, especially Oriental.

Springfield Armory National Historic Site, 1 Armory Square, tel: (413) 734-8551. International firearms, exhibited at the site of the US's first arsenal.

Springfield Library & Museum Association at the Quadrangle, 220 State St, tel: (413) 739-3871.

Four museums – on art, science, and regional history – and a major library.

Springfield Museum of Fine Arts, The Quadrangle, tel: (413) 732-6092. From American folk to modern European.

Springfield Science Museum, The Quadrangle, tel: (413) 733-1194. Exhibits, habitats, aquarium, planetarium.

StageWest, 1 Columbus Center, tel: (413) 7781-4470. Accomplished and often innovative regional theatre.

STOCKBRIDGE

Chesterwood, off Route 183, tel: (413) 298-3579. Once the summer estate of sculptor Daniel Chester French; gardens, galleries.

Mission House, 14 Main St, tel: (413) 298-3239. A 1739 house with period furnishings.

Naumkeag, Prospect Hill Rd, tel: (413) 298-3239. An 1885 Stanford White mansion with elaborate gardens.

Norman Rockwell Museum, Route 183, tel: (413) 298-3822. A 36-acre complex housing a modern $9.2 million museum, and Rockwell's last studio, transplanted.

STURBRIDGE

Old Sturbridge Village, Route 20 (I-90, Exit 9), tel: (508) 347-3362. A reconstructed 1830s New England village; events and workshops year-round.

VINEYARD HAVEN

Jirah Luce House Gallery, Beach Rd, tel: (508) 627-4441. Local artwork displayed in an 1804 Federal home.

Old Schoolhouse Museum, 110 Main St, tel: (508) 627-8017. The Martha's Vineyard Preservation Trust's collection of regional artifacts.

WALTHAM

Gore Place, 52 Gore St, tel: (617) 894-2798. An exemplary Federal home, restored.

Rose Art Museum, Brandeis University, tel: (617) 736-3434. Changing exhibits of contemporary art.

WELLESLEY

Davis Museum and Cultural Center, 106 Central St, tel: (617) 283-2051. Medieval to contemporary collections.

WESTON

Cardinal Spellman Philatelic Museum, 235 Wellesley St, tel: (617) 894-6735. Over 300,000 stamps; one of the world's largest inventories.

WEST SPRINGFIELD

Storrowton Village Museum, 1305 Memorial Ave, tel: (413) 787-0136. Restored New England buildings.

WILLIAMSTOWN

Sterling and Francine Clark Art Institute, South St, tel: (413) 458-9545. A strong collection of 19th- and 20th-century art, with an emphasis on Impressionism.

Williams College Museum of Art, Main St, tel: (413) 597-2429. From the 9th century BC to contemporary; American artists highlighted.

Williamstown Theatre Festival, Main St, tel: (413) 597-3400. Broadway and Hollywood actors' favorite "summer stock."

WOODS HOLE

Marine Biological Laboratory, MBL Street (at Water St), tel: (508) 548-3705, Ext. 423. Pre-registration required. Tours of current research projects;

National Maritime Fisheries Service Aquarium, Albatross St, tel: (508) 548-7684. Exhibits, tours, lectures.

Woods Hole Oceanographic Institute Exhibit Center, 15 School St (off Water St), tel: (508) 548-1400. Films and displays on WHOI's worldwide research.

WORCESTER

American Antiquarian Society, 185 Salisbury St, tel: (508) 755-5221. Founded by free-speech pioneer Isiah Thomas in 1812; research library on American history.

Higgins Armory Museum, 100 Barber Avenue, tel: (508) 853-6015. Medieval suits and Renaissance armor, tapestries and artifacts; weapons dating back to the Stone and Bronze ages.

New England Science Center, 222 Harrington Way, tel: (508) 791-9211. Museum, planetarium, zoo, nature trails.

Worcester Art Museum, 55 Salisbury St, tel: (508) 799-4406. Collections range from ancient to modern.

Salisbury Mansion, 40 Highland St, tel: (508) 753-8278. A 1772 Georgian mansion restored to demonstrate the home life of an 1880s family.

Worcester Historical Museum, 30 Elm St, tel: (508) 753-8278. Museum and library on local history.

YARMOUTH PORT

Captain Bangs Hallet House, 11 Strawberry Lane, tel: (508) 362-3021. An 1840 Greek Revival house full of China Trade finery.

Winslow Crocker House, 250 Route 6A, tel: (508) 362-4385. A ca. 1780 Georgian manse furnished with outstanding antiques.

NEW HAMPSHIRE

BRETTON WOODS

Mount Washington Cog Railway, Route 302, tel: (603) 846-5405, 1-800-922 8825. An 1869 steam-powered locomotive climbs 3 1/2 miles at grades of up to 37.4 percent.

CANTERBURY

Canterbury Shaker Village, 228 Shaker Rd (I-93, Exit 18), tel: (603) 783-9511. Closed winter. A Shaker community consisting of six historic buildings; craft demonstrations and gift shop.

CENTER CONWAY

Saco Bound/Downeast, Route 302, tel: (603) 447-3801. Canoe, kayak, and rafting trips.

CHARLESTOWN

The Fort at No. 4, Route 11 (I-91, Exit 7), tel: (603) 826-5700. Replica of 1746 village with 10 buildings, stockade, great hall and watch tower. Early American crafts demonstrations.

CLAREMONT

Claremont Opera House, City Hall, tel: (603) 542-4433. Restored Italian Renaissance-style opera house dating from 1897, concerts and musicals year-round.

CONCORD

The Christa McAuliffe Planetarium, 3 Institute Drive, tel: (603) 271-STAR. A sophisticated interactive projections system simulates actual space travel.

League of New Hampshire Craftsmen, 205 North Main St, tel: (603) 224-3375. Exhibits of traditional and contemporary crafts.

Museum of New Hampshire History, New Hampshire Historical Society, 30 Park St, tel: (603) 225-3381. Locally produced decorative arts and 19th-century Concord Coaches.

CORNISH

Saint-Gaudens National Historic Site, Route 12A, tel: (603) 675-2174. Home and studio of the noted 19th-century sculptor; period furnishings, examples of his work, some contemporary art.

DERRY

Robert Frost Farm, Route 2, tel: (603) 432-8305. The poet's home (1901–1909) hosts tours and readings.

DUBLIN

The Friendly Farm, Route 101, tel: (603) 563-8444. A petting zoo that will appeal to young children.

EAST SULLIVAN

Apple Hill Centre for Chamber Music, Apple Hill Rd, tel: (603) 847-3371. Concerts, workshops.

FRANCONIA

Cannon Mountain Aerial Tramway, tel: (603) 823-5563. A short ride to the 4,200-foot summit; observation deck, hiking trails.

The Frost Place, Ridge Rd (off Route 16), tel: (603) 823-8038. The weathered farmhouse where the quintessential New England poet lived in 1915–20; memorabilia, readings.

New England Ski Museum, Cannon Mountain, tel: (603) 823-7177. Artifacts, exhibits, films.

GLEN

Story Land, Route 16, tel: (603) 383-4293. A small amusement park geared to young children.

GORHAM

Mount Washington Auto Road, Route 16, tel: (603) 466-3988. Closed winter. A sinuous 6-mile toll road to the 6,280-foot summit, the highest point in New England.

Pinkham Notch Visitors Center, Route 16, tel: (603) 466-2727. The Appalachian Mountain Club offers information on hiking and camping, and workshops year-round.

GRAFTON

Ruggles Mine, Village Green, Route 4, tel: (603) 523-4275. Closed winter. An 1803 pit mine; collecting permitted.

HANCOCK

Harris Center for Conservation Education, King's Highway, tel: (603) 525-3394. Workshops; nature trails over 200 acres.

HANOVER

Hood Museum of Art, Dartmouth College, tel: (603) 646-2802. Ten galleries spanning centuries and continents.

Hopkins Center, Dartmouth College, tel: (603) 646-2422. Film, theatre, music, dance.

HARRISVILLE

Harrisville Designs, tel: (603) 827-3996. National Historic Landmark 18th-century mill town; self-guided walking tour.

HOLDERNESS

Science Center of New Hampshire, Route 113, tel: (603) 968-7194. Nature preserve sheltering injured animals; educational programs.

JACKSON

Wildcat Mountain Gondola Tramway, Route 16, tel: (603) 466-3326. A round-trip gondola ride to the summit.

KEENE

Colony House Museum, 104 West St, tel: (603) 357-0889. A Federal house containing Colonial glassware and locally produced pottery.

LACONIA

White Mountain National Forest Headquarters, 719 Main St, tel: (603) 528-8721. Information on hiking, camping.

Belknap Mill, Mill Plaza, tel: (603) 524-13. Oldest brick textile mill in US; now hosts arts and crafts exhibits, cultural events.

MANCHESTER

Association Canado-Americaine, 52 Concord St tel: (603) 625-8577. A 4,000-volume library; archives.

The Currier Gallery of Art, 192 Orange St, tel: (603) 669-6144. Medieval to contemporary art and furnishings; concerts, films, lectures. Tours of the Frank Lloyd Wright-designed Zimmerman House, by reservation.

Manchester Historical Association, 129 Amherst St, tel: (603) 622-7531. Local artifacts and history.

Manchester Institute of Arts & Sciences, 14 Concord St, tel: (603) 623-0313. Arts and crafts exhibits, demonstrations.

MERRIMACK

Anheuser-Busch Brewery, Webster Highway (Route 3, Exit 11), tel: (603) 595-1201. Exhibits and samples.

MILFORD

American Stage Festival, Route 13, tel: (603) 673-7515. New Hampshire's largest professional theatre.

MILTON

New Hampshire Farm Museum, Plummer's Ridge, Route 16, tel: (603) 652-7840. Closed winter. Demonstrations of 18th-century farming methods, tools and artifacts.

MOULTONBORO

Castle-in-the-Clouds, Route 171, tel: (603) 476-2352, (800) 729-2468. Mansion tours; 75 miles of hiking/riding trails.

MOUNT WASHINGTON

Mount Washington Observatory Museum, Sherman Adams Summit Building, tel: (603) 466-3988. Exhibits on the unusual mountaintop ecology, and those who've braved the elements to study it.

NASHUA

Arts & Sciences Center, 15 Court St, tel: (603) 883-1506. Classes and performances year-round.

NEW IPSWICH

Barrett House, Main St, tel: (603) 878-2517. An 1800 house with original furnishings.

NORTH CONWAY

Conway Scenic Railroad, Village Park, Route 16, tel: (603) 356-5251. An antique train ride through the Saco River Valley.

NORTH HAMPTON

Fuller Gardens, 10 Willow Avenue, Route 1A, tel: (603) 964-5414. Closed winter. Formal plantings; rose garden.

NORTH SALEM

America's Stonehenge, Mystery Hill, Haverhill Rd (off Route 111), tel: (603) 893-8300. Closed winter. A primitive astronomical observatory thought to date back 4,000 years.

NORTH WOODSTOCK

Lost River, Kinsman Notch, Route 112, tel: (603) 745-8031. Boardwalks through a natural glacial gorge.

PORTSMOUTH

Strawbery Banke Museum, Marcy St (I-95, Exit 7), tel: (603) 433-1100. Closed winter. Centuries-old waterfront neighborhood with buildings, exhibit rooms and craft shops.

Isles of Shoals Steamship Company, Market Street Dock, tel: (603) 431-5500, (800) 441-4620. Excursions to the islands made famous by pirates and impressionist painters.

The Moffatt-Ladd House, 154 Market St, tel: (603) 436-8221. A 1763 Georgian house with period furnishings and gardens.

Port of Portsmouth Maritime Museum & Albacore Park, Market St, tel: (603) 446-1331. Exhibits; tours of the USS Albacore, a 1952 submarine.

Wentworth-Gardner House, 50 Mechanic St, tel: (603) 436-4406. A fine 1760 Georgian house.

RINDGE

Cathedral of the Pines, Cathedral Rd (off Route 119), tel: (603) 899-3300. Closed winter. Built in 1945 to commemorate the American war dead.

SALEM

Canobie Lake Park, tel: (603) 893-3506. Summer only. A classic 1902 amusement park, updated.

SHARON

Sharon Arts Center, Route 123, tel: (603) 924-7256. Features demonstrations, exhibits on arts and crafts, workshops.

SUGAR HILL

Sugar Hill Historical Museum, tel: (603) 823-8142. The history of a hilltop town centered on summerers and sap.

SUNAPEE

M/V Mount Sunapee II, Sunapee Harbor (off Route 11), tel: (603) 763-4030. A 1½-hour narrated lake cruise covering local history.

WAKEFIELD

Museum of Childhood, Mt Laurel Rd, tel: (603) 522-8073. More than 2,000 dolls; 1890s schoolroom.

WARNER

Mount Kearsarge Indian Museum, Kearsarge Mountain Rd, tel: (603) 436-2600. Artifacts of the Northeast, Plans, and Southwestern Native Americans.

WEBSTER

Old Webster Meeting House, Corser Hill, tel: (603) 796-2211. Daniel Webster's residence as a Dartmouth undergraduate now houses the Historical Society.

WEIRS BEACH

M/S Mount Washington, tel: (603) 366-4837. Cruises around New Hampshire's largest lake.
Surf Coaster, Route 11B, tel: (603) 366-4991. Wave pool and waterslides.

WOLFEBORO

Wolfeboro Historical Society Museum, South Main St, tel: (603) 569-4997. An 18th-century home, 1820 schoolhouse, and mid-19th-century firehouse.

RHODE ISLAND

JAMESTOWN

Beavertail Lighthouse, Beavertail Point, tel: (401) 423-9941. An 1856 granite tower; spectacular sound views from the grounds.

LITTLE COMPTON

Sakonnet Vineyards, 162 W Main St, tel: (401) 635-8486. Tastings and tours.

NARRAGANSETT

South County Museum, Canonchet Farm, tel: (401) 783-5400. Closed winter. The arts, crafts, and artifacts of 19th-century rural Rhode Island life.

NEWPORT

The Astors' Beechwood Mansion, 580 Bellevue Ave, tel: (401) 846-3774. Actors recreate an 1891 party in the 1856 home of "the" Mrs. Astor.
Hunter House, 54 Washington St, tel: (401) 847-1000. A 1748 house showcasing Newport's famed Townsend-Goddard furniture.
International Tennis Hall of Fame, 194 Bellevue Avenue, tel: (401) 849-3790. The 1880 Newport Casino harbors 13 grass courts, open to the public; also, tournaments, memorabilia.
The Museum of Newport History, Brick Market, Thames and Touro Sts, tel: (401) 846-0813. Interactive exhibits spanning the community's 350-year history.
The Museum of Yachting, Fort Adams State Park, tel: (401) 847-1018. Artifacts and memorabilia celebrating the sport of millionaires.
Naval War College Museum, Coasters Harbor Island, tel: (401) 841-4052. This 19th-century poorhouse, site of the worlds first Naval War College (1884), features exhibits on the history of naval warfare and on the naval heritage of Narragansett Bay.
Newport Art Museum, 76 Bellevue Avenue, tel: (401) 847-0719. Permanent and changing exhibits, in an 1862 Richard Morris Hunt mansion.

Old Colony House, Washington Sq, tel: (401) 846-2980. The nation's second oldest capitol building.
Preservation Society of Newport County, 118 Mill St, tel: (401) 847-1000. Tours of Newport mansions.
Redwood Library and Atheneum, 50 Bellevue Ave, tel: (401) 847-0292. The nation's oldest library in continuous use, modeled on a Roman temple.
Touro Synagogue, 85 Touro St, tel: (401) 847-4794. The oldest synagogue in the US, founded 1763.
Trinity Church, Queen Anne Sq, tel: (401) 846-0660. George Washington worshipped in this 1726 church.

PAWTUCKET

Slater Mill Historic Site, Roosevelt Ave, tel: (401) 725-8638. Museum of history and technology featuring working textile machinery and handcrafts demonstrations.

PORTSMOUTH

Green Animals Topiary Gardens, Cory's Lane, tel: (401) 847-1000. Closed winter. A Victorian estate with elaborate gardens; toy museum.

PROVIDENCE

Arcade, 65 Weybosset St, tel: (401) 863-2429. A Greek Revival indoor mall, built in 1828.
First Baptist Meeting House, 75 N Main St, tel: 401) 751-2266. The first Baptist church in America, built in 1775.
John Brown House, 52 Power St, tel: (401) 331-8575. A 1786 mansion; antiques and China Trade artifacts.
Museum of Art, Rhode Island School of Design, 224 Benefit St, tel: (401) 331-3511. Classical to contemporary art.
Providence Atheneum, 251 Benefit St, tel: 401-421-6970. Rare books, prints, and paintings.
Providence Preservation Society, 24 Meeting Place, tel: (401) 831-7440. Guided walking tours of the "Mile of History."
Roger Williams Park, Museum, and Zoo, 950 Elmwood Avenue, tel: (401) 785-9450. This 430-acre (164-hectare) Victorian park features exotic animals in simulated habitats.
State Capitol, 82 Smith St, tel: (401) 227-2357. Tours highlighting local history.

VERMONT

ARLINGTON

Norman Rockwell Exhibition, Route 7A, tel: (802) 375-6423. Hundreds of examples of the illustrator's work.

BELLOWS FALLS

The Green Mt. Flyer Scenic Train Ride, tel: (802) 463-3069. Excursions in restored coaches.

BENNINGTON

Bennington Battle Monument, 15 Monument Circle, tel: (802) 447-0550. An 1891 monolith commemorating the Revolutionary War Battle; an elevator zooms to the 306-foot (93-meter) observation deck.

Bennington Museum & Grandma Moses Gallery,
Route 9, tel: (802) 447-1571. Regional artifacts;
primitive paintings by Grandma Moses.

BRATTLEBORO

Brattleboro Museum & Art Center, Main and
Vernon streets, tel: (802) 257-0124. Exhibits on
regional history and arts.

BROWNINGTON

Old Stone House Museum, tel: (802) 754-2022. A
stone academy housing the collections of the Orleans
County Historical Society.

BURLINGTON

Ethan Allen Homestead, off Route 127, tel: (802)
865-4556. The revolutionary's restored 1787 farmhouse.

Fleming Museum, University of Vermont, tel: (802)
656-0750. Arts and anthropology.

Flynn Theatre for the Performing Arts, 153 Main
St, tel: (802) 86-FLYNN. Plays, concerts, films.

CABOT

Cabot Creamery Cooperative, Main St, tel: (802)
563-2231. Tours and tastings.

CHARLOTTE

The Vermont Wildflower Farm, Route 7, tel: (802)
425-3500. Nature walk; exhibits.

DANVILLE

American Society of Dowsers, Village Green, tel:
(802) 684-3417. Displays on the ancient art of
divining.

DORSET

Dorset Playhouse, Cheney Rd, tel: (802) 867-5777.
Vermont's oldest barn summer theatre.

GLOVER

Bread and Puppet Museum, Route 122, tel: (802)
525-3031. Fantastic masks and puppets from decades of productions.

GRAFTON

Historic Grafton Village, Routes 121 and 35, tel:
(802) 843-2255. Self-guided walking tours of a
meticulously restored 19th-century town.

GRANITEVILLE

Rock of Ages Quarry, Route 14, tel: (802) 476-
3115. Working granite quarries: tours, demonstrations, samples.

ISLE LA MOTTE

St Anne's Shrine, tel: (802) 928-3362. The site of
Fort Anne, Vermont's oldest settlement.

JACKSONVILLE

North River Winery, Route 112 (off Route 100), tel:
(802) 368-7557. Tastings and tours of an 1850s
farmstead.

JAY

Jay Peak Aerial Tramway, Route 242, tel: (802)
988-2611, (800) 451-4449. The summit view spans
three states and Canada.

JOHNSON

Vermont Studio Center, Box 613, tel: (802) 635-
2727. Exhibits and readings.

LUDLOW

Black River Academy Historical Museum, High St,
tel: (802) 228-5050. Regional artifacts and furnishings; includes a library and 1900 schoolroom.

MANCHESTER

American Museum of Fly Fishing, Route 7A and
Seminary Ave, tel: (802) 362-3300. A tribute to the
most meditative of sports.

Hildene, Route 7A, tel: (802) 362-1788. Estate of
Robert Todd Lincoln; original furnishings, family
memorabilia.

Southern Vermont Art Center, West Rd, tel: (802)
362-1405. Exhibits, sculpture garden, botany trail.

MIDDLEBURY

UVM Morgan Horse Farm, Route 125, tel: (802)
338-2011. Breeding, training and showing center
for horses; park and picnic area.

Vermont State Craft Center at Frog Hollow, Frog
Hollow Lane, tel: (802) 338-3177. Contemporary
crafts; demonstrations, workshops.

MONTPELIER

Vermont Historical Society Museum, 109 State St,
tel: (802) 828-2291. Regional memorabilia.

NEWFANE

Newfane Flea Market, Route 30, Newfane, tel: (802)
565-7771. A giant swap meet; occasional concerts.

NORTH BENNINGTON

Park-McCullough House, Park and West streets, tel:
(802) 442-5441. A Victorian mansion with garden.

PITTSFORD

New England Maple Museum, Route 7, tel: (802)
483-9414. Sugaring artifacts; slide show.

PLYMOUTH

Coolidge Birthplace and Homestead, Route 100A,
tel: (802) 828-3226. The house where the laconic
president was raised.

PROCTOR

Vermont Marble Exhibit, Main St, tel: (802) 459-
3311. Factory tour, exhibits, demonstrations.

PUTNEY

Green Mountain Spinnery, tel: (802) 387-4528,
(800) 321-WOOL. Demonstrations, tours.

QUEECHEE

Simon Pearce Glass Factory, Main St, tel: (802)
295-1470. Glass-blowing demonstrations.

RIPTON

Homer Nobel Farm, Route 125, tel: (802) 388-
4362. Robert Frost's summer home from 1939 until
1963; walking trails.

RUTLAND

Norman Rockwell Museum, Route 4, tel: (802) 773-
6095. A large collection of the artist's works.

Wilson's Castle, West Proctor Rd, tel: (802) 773-
3284. Closed winter. A 32-room 19th-century
mansion; tours.

SAINT JOHNSBURY

Fairbanks Museum and Planetarium, Main and
Prospect streets, tel: (802) 748-2372. Natural
history, botany; Native American artifacts.

St Johnsbury Athenaeum/Art Gallery, 30 Main St,
tel: (802) 748-8291. Library, exhibits.

SHELBURNE

Shelburne Farms, tel: (802) 985-9585. A model ecological farm on an 1,000-acre estate designed by landscape architect Frederick Law Olmstead; tours. **Shelburne Museum**, Route 7, tel: (802) 985-3344. Folk art, toys, textiles, and more, housed in 37 historic buildings; also, a side-wheel steamboat and vintage train.

STOWE

Stowe Gondola, Alpine Slide, and In-Line Skate Park. Mount Mansfield and Spruce Peak, tel: (802) 253-3000. A lift to Vermont's tallest peak; a ride down its smaller neighbor; and the world's first in-line skate park, complete with slalom course.

SUNDERLAND

Equinox Sky Line Drive, Route 7A, about 4 miles south of Manchester. A sightseeing drive to the summit of Mount Equinox.

VERGENNES

Lake Champlain Maritime Museum, Basin Harbor Rd, tel: (802) 475-2517. A 19th-century stone schoolhouse showcases the lake's role in war and peace.

WAITSFIELD

Vermont Icelandic Horse Farm, tel: (802) 496-6707. From half-day excursions to weekend tours.

WARREN

Warren-Sugarbush Airport, tel: (802) 496-2290. Lessons, rentals, sightseeing rides.

WATERBURY

Ben & Jerry's Ice Cream Factory, Route 100, tel: (803) 244-5641. An entertaining tour, culminating in samples. **Cold Hollow Cider Mill**, Route 100, tel: (802) 244-8771, (800) 3-APPLES. Cider-making demonstrations; samples of regional foods.

WHITE RIVER JUNCTION

Catamount Brewing Co., 58 S Main St, tel: (802) 296-2248. English-style ales; tours and tastings.

WINDSOR

American Precision Museum, S. Main St, tel: (802) 674-5781. Evidence of the ingenuity that inspired "Precision Valley."

WINOOSKI

Saint Michael's Playhouse, Route 25, tel: (802) 654-2535. An Equity summer stock company.

WOODSTOCK

Billings Farm and Museum, River Rd, tel: (802) 457-2355. An model 1890s dairy farm preserved in pristine condition. **Vermont Institute of Natural Science**, Church Hill Rd, tel: (802) 457-3779. Site of the Vermont Raptor Center. **Dana House**, 26 Elm St, tel: (802) 457-1822. An 1807 house maintained as a museum by the Woodstock Historical Society.

CHILDREN'S ACTIVITIES

New England is a veritable paradise for children. They can entertain themselves endlessly with amusements as simple as observing a tide pool, or take in a bit of readily absorbed history at such "hands-on" living museums as Plimoth Plantation or Old Sturbridge Village. Staff members at these sites are skilled at engaging children's interests; it's best to save the stuffy historical houses and local history museums for a more mature age.

Boston's Children's Museum is one of the most appealing in the country, and smaller facilities with similar agendas are scattered through the countryside. Other Boston attractions are sure to thrill little ones include the Computer Museum (next-door to the Children's Museum, on Museum Wharf), the nearby New England Aquarium, the Swan Boats in the Public Garden, and the view from the 62-story John Hancock Observatory. Bernice Chesler's excellent book, *In and Out of Boston with (or without) Children* can provide leads on lesser-known but equally rewarding attractions.

Cape Cod might as well be a giant sandbox, and the calm, shallow, and somewhat waters on the bay side offer optimal swimming and splashing for those still getting their sea legs. Children's reaction to the many whalewatch excursions offered on the Cape and along the coast up into Maine is invariably "Awesome!"

A number of destination resorts – most notably Smuggler's Notch in northern Vermont – have made a specialty of catering to kids and the parents they hold in thrall. In summer, this ski area basically becomes a camp for all ages, with waterslides, special outdoors events, and a real sense of camaraderie. Some of New England's family-oriented resorts, such as The Balsams, in remote northern New Hampshire, date back a century or more, and are attracting a fifth generation for mannered meals and unstructured enjoyment of the great outdoors.

Regrettably, many of New England's fussier B&Bs shun the company of children (though such discrimination is arguably illegal). If you're blessed with particularly well behaved youngsters, you might try pushing the envelope, but then again, it's no fun to go where you're not welcome. Fortunately, there are plenty of inns where their presence is not only tolerated but actively courted. If in doubt, call ahead or check the detailed listings in *Best Places to Stay in New England*, by Christina Tree and Kimberly Grant.

The fancier restaurants may also exercise their own unpublished strictures regarding children – claiming, for instance, that the place is booked solid when you can see it's half-empty. Here, the best antidote is a reservation. But again, depending on your child, you may enjoy just as pleasant and educational a repast at a ramshackle lobster pound or a nostalgic diner.

NIGHTLIFE

New England offers a wide range of entertainment; there's something for everyone. The rural areas tend to be more slow-paced and relaxed during the evening, while Boston, among the New England cities, supports a varied, exciting nightlife.

Boston outgrew its staid image long ago. At night, the city sparkles with lively and sophisticated activity. The Boston Symphony Orchestra has earned an international reputation; its less formal offshoot, the Boston Pops, also commands a great following. Music permeates the region, ranging from rural chamber groups to big-city rock and jazz. Comedy clubs are also increasingly popular.

Theatre thrives not only in Boston and New Haven (both time-honored proving grounds for Broadway) but in myriad regional repertory companies and "straw-hat" summer theaters. Professional modern dance and ballet can be seen in bucolic settings, as well as in the metropolitan areas.

The larger cities have dance clubs where it's easy to meet and mingle. For more specific information about after-dark entertainment, check the listings in local papers – especially the alternative papers, such as the *Phoenix* (various editions cover Boston, Providence, and Worcester) and the *Advocate* (Pioneer Valley), and the *Vanguard* (Burlington, Vermont).

THE GAY SCENE

Boston has a very active and proactive gay presence, as do, to a lesser extent, other large cities and even rural towns. Northampton, for instance, has in the past few decades emerged as a lively enclave for lesbians, and Provincetown, of course, has long been a preferred gay summer vacation spot; it even has a gay counterpart to the Chamber of Commerce, the Provincetown Business Guild (508-487-2313, or 800-637-8696). Information concerning gay-oriented activities and businesses (including gay-owned and operated inns throughout the region) can be found in the Boston-based newspaper *Bay Windows*, and in *One in Ten*, a supplement produced by the alternative weekly, the *Boston Phoenix*. A good in-town networking source, for those visiting Boston, is the Glad Day Bookshop, at 673 Boyston Street (617-267-3010).

SHOPPING

New England provides as great range of shopping options as can be found anywhere in the country – large department stores, local country auctions, antique shows, craft stores and bargain factory outlets.

Antique stores abound throughout New England, and antiquing in these shops can be both fun and, depending on the level of the stock, relatively inexpensive. Nonetheless, it is always a good idea to keep certain guidelines in mind. If considering value, it is important to make sure that the entire piece is in its original condition and to get a written bill of sale which guarantees the authenticity of the item. Reputable shops should also be willing to offer a buy-back guarantee, since an antique, if rare and desirable, can only grow more so.

American handicrafts are experiencing a renaissance throughout the country and especially in New England. There are probably more quality craft items being produced now than at any time since the Industrial Revolution. Crafts, whether pottery, weaving, scrimshaw or woodworking, will usually be less expensive and perhaps of higher quality when bought directly from the artisans, either at their studios or at a juried crafts fair.

Discount and so-called "factory outlet" stores are an increasingly popular and widespread phenomenon. The world-famous Filene's Basement in Boston (with dozens of branch stores turning up throughout the country) initiated off-price retailing in 1908, and the original store, at the corner of Winter and Summer streets, is still a wild and potentially lucrative place to shop: you might find a designer original reduced to an infinitesimal fraction of its original price. Many companies have since come to recognize the sales potential of offering their own products in bulk at discounted prices. Some outlets, such as the famous L.L. Bean in Freeport, Maine, which specializes in outdoor wear and gear, operate a mail-order business in addition to their outlets, and offer the same high-quality products through both channels. Some outlets, however, specialize in "seconds" (slightly imperfect goods), so check the merchandise carefully. Whether you're shopping for bargains, irreplaceable antiques, or one-of-a-kind works of art, New England has plenty to offer.

SPORTS

New England hosts an abundance of both spectator and recreational sports. There are a variety of professional teams in all the major sports including baseball, basketball, football, hockey and tennis.

Generally, the New England states are represented by Boston's teams – the Boston Celtics in basketball (Boston Garden, September to May), the Boston Red Sox in baseball (Fenway Park, April to October) and the Boston Bruins in hockey (Boston Garden, October to March). The major exception to this rule is football (August to December); the major team is the New England Patriots who originate from suburban Foxboro, Massachusetts (Sullivan Stadium). For up-to-date information on schedules and locations of games, refer to the sports section of any local daily.

Many New Englanders, however, prefer their sports participatory. Depending on the season, one can indulge in almost any recreational sport. From skiing in Vermont to sailing on the Charles River in

Boston, New England is a haven for the outdoor sports enthusiast, regardless of ability or experience. Throughout New England, you can swim, play tennis, go horseback riding or white-water river rafting, hike or rock climb, hunt, fish, play golf, mountain-bike, kayak, windsurf, or rollerblade, to name just a few of the many possibilities. Check with the state tourist boards to find out what activities are favored in the area you intend to visit.

Health clubs are common throughout New England; most resorts, and even some of the smaller inns, have more than adequate and sometimes quite elaborate facilities. The spa craze has also struck New England: notable facilities include the Norwich Inn and Spa in Norwich, Connecticut; Canyon Ranch in Lenox, Massachusetts; and The Equinox and Topnotch Spa in, respectively, Manchester and Stowe, Vermont.

FURTHER READING

ARCHITECTURE

Cityscapes of Boston: An American City through Time by Robert Campbell and Peter Vanderwarker. Boston, 1992.
Preserving New England by Jane Holtz Kay and Pauline Chase-Harrell. New York, 1986.

GEOGRAPHY

These Fragile Outposts: A Geological Look at Cape Cod, Martha's Vineyard and Nantucket by Barbara B. Chamberlain. New York, 1964.
A Guide to New England's Landscape by Neil Jorgensen. Barre, Vt, 1971.

HISTORY

The Flowering of New England by Van Wyck Brooks. New York, 1936.
New England: Indian Summer, 1865–1915 by Van Wyck Brooks. New York, 1940.
The Spread of New England Settlement and Institutions to the Mississippee River, 1620–1865 by Lois Kimball Mathews Rosenberry. New York, 1962.
New England Frontier: Puritans and Indians by Alden T. Vaughan. Boston , 1965.
The Hill Country of Northern New England by Harold Fisher Wilson. New York, 1967.

INTELLECTUAL

The New England Mind: From Colony to Province by Perry Miller. Cambridge, 1953.

LITERARY

Contemporary New England Stories by Michael C. Curtis, ed. Old Saybrook, CT, 1992.
String Too Short to Be Saved: Recollections of Summers on a New England Farm by Donald Hall. Boston, 1979.
Imagining Boston: A Literary Landscape by Shaun O'Connell. Boston, 1990.

ARCHIVAL

Battles of the United States, by Sea and Land by Henry B. Dawson. New York, 1858.
Nooks and Corners of the New England Coast by Samuel Adams Drake. New York, 1875.
A Description of New England by Captain John Smith. Boston, 1865.

OTHER INSIGHT GUIDES

More than 185 *Insight Guides* cover every continent. In addition, a companion series of more than 100 *Insight Pocket Guides* provides selected, carefully-timed itineraries for the traveler with little time to spare.

Titles which highlight destinations in this region include:

ART/PHOTO CREDITS

INDEX

C

N

Q

R

Y–Z